ATLAS HUGGED

ATLAS HUGGED

The Autobiography of
John Galt III

A Novel by

DAVID SLOAN WILSON

Published by Redwood Publishing, LLC
www.redwooddigitalpublishing.com
info@redwooddigitalpublishing.com

Paperback ISBN: 978-1-952106-53-8
eBook ISBN: 978-1-952106-54-5
Library of Congress Control Number: 2020912913

Cover Design: Jennifer Campbell-Smith, Ph.D.
Interior Design: Ghislain Viau
Globe lineart: ShutterStock/AtthameeNi

Printed in the United States of America

10 9 8 7 6 5 4 3 2 1

To my father, the novelist, and my mother, the nurturer.

Contents

*Art is the indispensable medium
for the communication of a moral ideal.*
—*Ayn Rand*

Preface

Ayn Rand's *Atlas Shrugged* is one of the most iconic novels of the 20th century, selling over seven million copies since its publication in 1957. Rand is widely credited for providing a moral foundation to the "greed is good" ideology that now dominates modern life. Alan Greenspan, who served as chair of the United States Federal Reserve between 1987-2006, was a devotee, and one still hears about politicians assigning *Atlas Shrugged* to their staff as a kind of indoctrination. The Atlas Society has chapters on college campuses around the world and the Atlas Group is one of the most effective conglomerates of libertarian think tanks. As Internet memes, the names Ayn Rand and her fictional hero John Galt are mentioned as often as Adam Smith and Friedrich Hayek.

Rand promoted her philosophy, which she called Objectivism, in many ways, but *Atlas Shrugged* was unquestionably her most effective vehicle. She understood that fiction can be more effective than dry philosophical discourse when she wrote, "Art is the indispensable medium for the communication of a moral ideal."

I have written *Atlas Hugged* in the same spirit and as an antidote to the "greed is good" worldview that Rand championed. Like Rand, I am not primarily a novelist. In fact this is my first, although I come by the craft easily since my father, Sloan Wilson, wrote two other iconic novels of the 20th century: *The Man in the Grey Flannel Suit* (1955), which described the corporate army that formed after World War II, and *A Summer Place* (1958), which described changing sexual mores during the same period. I became a scientist rather than a novelist, which enables me to critique the "greed is good" worldview on intellectual grounds. I have done this in many academic works and three nonfiction books for the general public, most recently *This View of Life: Completing the Darwinian Revolution*. Conveying the same themes in fictional form for me is a kind of homecoming.

The idea of critiquing Rand's worldview with a sequel to her novel (in the form of satirical academic critique) is delicious. I wish I could claim credit for it, but it was suggested by someone else during a workshop on economics that I had organized. Since Rand had been so successful at promulgating her ideas through fiction, shouldn't someone be doing the same for the ideas that we were developing? Within minutes, the title *Atlas Hugged* flashed into my mind, along with the beginning of a plot line. The protagonist would be an entirely new character – the grandson of John Galt – whose father is a libertarian media giant like Rush Limbaugh. Ayn Rand was not a character in her own novel, but – since anything goes in fiction – I could transport her into mine in the form of Ayn Rant. It was too delicious not to indulge!

That was seven years ago and I worked on it between my other projects ever since. I was amazed by how the story stayed alive and developed in my mind, even when I didn't have a chance to write anything for months. Every now and then a new plot development would bubble up into my consciousness and I would think: "Of course! *That's* how it must be!" We truly evolved as storytelling animals and creating my own story at such length has been a delight.

When I began to think about sharing my story, the typical publication route was cluttered with obstacles. Whatever my reputation as a scientist and nonfiction author, I was still just a guy peddling his first novel. Also, literary critics hated *Atlas Shrugged* – and rightly so! Judged purely as a story, it is a terrible novel. The same can be said for B.F. Skinner's utopian novel *Walden Two*, which was rejected by two publishers and only accepted by a third under the condition that Skinner write a textbook for them! Nevertheless, both novels had a huge impact and continue to be read because the *stories*, despite their flaws, were good enough to serve as a vehicle for the *ideas*. I would like to think that my story is much better than either of those, but there is no getting around the need for a bit of speechifying to communicate the ideas.

In the end, I decided that the anti-Rand thing to do was to market my story online and let the reader decide how much to pay (including nothing for the e-book), with all proceeds going to support my nonprofit organization, Prosocial World. Such things are easy to do in the age of electronic publishing. If readers hate it, then no harm is done and maybe I'll even learn from the feedback and write *Atlas Hugged 2.0*. After all, writing novels is not my main line of work and there is nothing to be gained from keeping it to myself.

Like *Atlas Shrugged* and *Walden Two*, *Atlas Hugged* is a novel of ideas and a vision for the future. I would never have written it just to tell a story. Exchanging "Shrugged" with "Hugged" also communicates a very different moral ideal. If you want the nonfiction version, read *This View of Life* and my other works. Or, you can learn about it through John Galt III, Eve, and the other characters that I have grown to know and love so well. And don't worry, reading *Atlas Shrugged* first is not necessary. Enjoy!

Who is John Galt?

Call me anything but John Galt. That is my name, but it is also the name of my father and grandfather. I am not like them and the world they created is not the one I desire. The III after my name does not sufficiently set me apart.

Not everyone remembers my grandfather, although nearly everyone has been touched by him. The first John Galt was a brilliant engineer with an unshakeable faith in himself and the folly of those who opposed him. He believed that the advances of civilization were due to a special class of men that he called the doers. Everyone else was dependent upon the doers but didn't understand the source of their welfare. Instead of being grateful and giving the doers free reign, they placed unceasing demands on the doers. My grandfather had a rich vocabulary for describing the mass of humanity as looters, moochers, and parasites, robbing and sucking the blood out of the very people who supported them. If only the doers could liberate themselves from the moochers, the ideal society could be achieved.

My grandfather's brilliance as an engineer caused him to advance professionally, despite his eccentric views. For every ten people that he alienated by treating them as moochers, he gained the allegiance of one person who was admitted into his elite club of doers. There was also his extraordinary claim that static electricity could be converted into usable power, providing an inexhaustible source of clean energy. Most experts scoffed at this possibility, but one automotive company in Michigan decided to take the gamble. The CEO had fallen under the spell of my grandfather's doer philosophy and felt that the dawn of a new era was at hand. If my grandfather had critics, it must be because he was the doer and they were the moochers. He persuaded his reluctant board to fund the project, which would be top secret and under the total control of my grandfather.

Given the secrecy surrounding the project, it is difficult to know exactly what happened. My grandfather issued optimistic but vague reports that always ended with a request for more money. The board became increasingly skeptical but was reluctant to pull the plug on their own investment. The people involved in the project were afraid to oppose my grandfather, knowing that they might easily be banished from the sunlit world of the doers into the dark abyss of the moochers. He also assigned them to different parts of the project so only he knew how the parts fit together. Investment reports began to make fun of the company and its stock value began to plummet. My grandfather attacked the company's pension plan and employees' union as the root of its problem. Then, during a tumultuous meeting of all personnel, my grandfather strode to the microphone, shouted, "I will stop the motor of the world!" and stormed out of the room. When he failed to report to work for several days, security men broke into his office and discovered that he had removed the top secret documents associated with the project, leaving only a large and undecipherable piece of electronic equipment that had been smashed with a sledgehammer. John Galt had become a fugitive.

My grandfather's outlaw status made him an instant celebrity. Before, he was known only to a small group of engineers and investment analysts. After, he was the hero of every self-styled doer who felt besieged by moochers. "Who is John Galt?" the *New York Times* asked rhetorically, and the question went viral as an ironic comment on social dysfunction. Interviews with the people who worked under John Galt revealed what he meant by "I will stop the motor of the world!" He thought that if enough doers stopped doing, society would collapse and the moochers would be brought to their senses. It would be like

Atlas shrugging Earth from his shoulders. By disappearing with the plans for his static electricity engine, my grandfather wanted to start a revolution of doers going on strike.

In the months and years that followed his disappearance, fantastic rumors spread about my grandfather's whereabouts. Some said that he had founded a utopian society of doers in a secret valley out west, powered by his static electricity machine and protected by a force field. Others said that he remained at large like a master spy, persuading other doers to join his cause. Every copycat disappearance, often accompanied by a note that read "Who is John Galt?" was attributed to his influence.

There was a grain of truth to both of these rumors. As it turned out, my grandfather did found a utopian society in a remote tract of land in Colorado owned by a wealthy banker named Midas Mulligan, who had fallen under the spell of the doer philosophy. At first Midas offered his hunting cabin to my grandfather as a hideout, but as they talked together in the rustic surroundings, sipping bourbons under the night sky, they developed a plan to create a self-contained society composed entirely of doers. It would have its own economy, even its own currency, with coins minted in gold and silver.

In addition to their faith in themselves, Midas and my grandfather also had an unshakeable faith in capitalism and the power of unfettered markets. Anything of value could be represented as a dollar value and therefore could be compared to anything else of value by their relative prices. Making money was the surest way to provide value to people, because the best way to make money was to provide what people are most willing to pay for. The system worked so well that no other form of care toward others was required. No empathy. No charity. No loyalty. No forgiveness. Old fashioned virtues had been rendered obsolete by the market. Thanks to the market, individuals could concentrate entirely on making money for themselves and the whole society would prosper as well. No society was bold enough to put this proposition to the test by removing all restrictions on trade. The utopian society that Midas and my grandfather planned to create on the remote tract of land in Colorado would be the first.

To begin, Midas and my grandfather needed to recruit some doers to join the cause. They compiled a list of likely candidates that my grandfather visited on a clandestine basis. This was not as risky as it might sound. It's not as if he was public enemy #1. His legal offense was to abscond with documents owned by his company, which might earn a few years jail time at most. The FBI had better things to do than search for John Galt. Nevertheless, given his celebrity status, imagine what it must have been like for a doer to be approached by someone from the shadows who identified himself as John Galt with an invitation to join a secret society! Some resisted, but others abandoned family and career to follow the siren's call, leaving only the enigmatic note, "Who is John Galt?"

Everyone knows about the existence of cults and their disturbing ability to steal minds. Otherwise normal people give away everything to wait for the second coming of Jesus or aliens from outer space. Midas and my grandfather would scoff at those irrational beliefs, but the society that they founded had all the earmarks of a cult. The first structure that they erected was a giant gold-plated dollar sign atop a granite column. They also invented an oath that members were required to recite at frequent intervals: I SWEAR BY MY LIFE AND LOVE OF IT THAT I WILL NEVER LIVE FOR THE SAKE OF ANOTHER MAN, NOR ASK ANOTHER MAN TO LIVE FOR MINE. The word "give" was banned from their vocabulary. Every human transaction was paid for with the gold and silver coins minted on site. Obviously, this was only possible thanks to the vast wealth of Midas Mulligan, who provided a bank account for each new member based on how much had been "stolen" from them in the form of taxes in the outside world. While the members of other cults waited for Jesus or aliens from outer space, the Galtians waited for society to collapse while working to build a microcosm of the perfect society for themselves.

Most of the Galtians were men, but a woman named Ayn Rant was to become their most important member. Rant was born in Russia and experienced the worst of communist collectivism before immigrating to the United States. This gave her a zeal for free enterprise that bordered on fanaticism. She regarded any form of government oversight as evil and a slippery slope toward the kind of ham-fisted control that made the Soviet economy such a disaster. A self-made intellectual, she earned a reputation writing articles extolling capitalism and heroic profiles of businessmen. She was also quick to slip into bed with the men that she admired. If they were married, this seldom stood in her way because the nobility and passion of the doers trumped a dowdy conventional virtue such as faithfulness in marriage. As a champion of capitalism, it was natural for her to be invited to join the Galtians. As a sexually liberated woman ahead of her time, it was only right for her to realize her ultimate conquest – John Galt himself. My father was their love child. He was presented to the community in a moonlight ceremony at the foot of the golden dollar sign, as if the King and Queen had given birth to the heir of the New Order.

In the heady atmosphere of the newly founded cult, inflamed by the passion of a union with the cult leader who stood for everything she admired, Rant set about creating an entire cosmology for capitalism and the sanctity of the individual. She called it a stylized universe because it was better than real. People who entered her world would have the sensation of flying through the air over the real world, which would appear unendurably dull by comparison. She called it Objectivism and said that it was based on rationality, not selfishness, as if it could be fully validated by logic and science.

Yet, the people who inhabited her stylized universe were nothing like real people. The true Objectivist was a paragon of moral virtue, even if the new morality differed from the old. If two Objectivists were competing for the same job, for example, they would both accurately assess each other's abilities and the inferior person would voluntarily withdraw. As for business, so also for love. If two Objectivists were in love with the same woman, the inferior one would express his love by departing, knowing that his beloved would be happier with the superior man. In this fashion, Rant declared that in her stylized universe, "There are no conflicts of interest among rational men." And while Objectivist men and women reveled in their carnal desires, it was always an expression of their higher ideals and never just the satisfaction of mere lust. Until they found their doer soul mates, they had a stoic's ability to avoid the temptations of the flesh.

The peak of my grandfather's notoriety was based on a stunt that was inspired by H. G. Wells's radio production of *The War of the Worlds*, which described an invasion by aliens from outer space as a breaking news story. Legions of listeners confused it for the real thing and panicked. Impressed by the power of fiction presented as fact, Midas used his enormous wealth to purchase prime airtime from one of the nation's largest radio broadcasting companies. As far as millions of listeners were concerned, their normal programming was suddenly interrupted by the voice of John Galt, as if he had used his technical prowess to take over the airwaves. In what became known around the world as "The Speech," my grandfather spoke for an hour in a thundering voice about the impending collapse of society and the rise of the New Order. By the time his takeover of the airwaves was revealed as a hoax, the desired impact had been achieved. The Speech was the talk of the world. Who cared if it was a hoax? It was *better* than real!

Most cults fall apart when their extravagant expectations are not met, and the Galtians were no exception. They were flesh and blood people, not the paragons of moral virtue that Ayn Rant wanted them to be. They tired of the hard work of building their own society – the house construction, the farming, the boring planning meetings. They disagreed on what to do or who was best qualified. The men fought over women and status. They began to accuse each other of being moochers and having faulty premises.

The first person to leave the cult was my grandfather. He simply disappeared, just as he had disappeared from his engineering job. This time he didn't even leave a note or a boastful proclamation. My father, John Galt II, was two years old and grew up knowing only the legend of John Galt I. Then other members started to drift away. Finally Midas Mulligan reached his breaking point and withdrew his financial support, observing wryly that the Galtians were more heavily subsidized than any socialist society. Like fleas shaken from the back of a dog, the Galtians were forced to make their way back to the society that they'd mocked and seek the forgiveness of family, friends, and former business associates.

The Galtian movement was a failure in every way but one. It had not resulted in a widespread strike of doers. The static electricity engine was a folly. The microcosm of the perfect doer society went the way of so many other utopian visions. But Ayn Rant's better-than-real cosmology was a survivor that had been propagated around the world by The Speech. Everyone who fell under its spell became convinced, as fervently as any religious believer, that the path to salvation was to concentrate exclusively on making money for oneself.

2

The Evil Empire

Most of the Galtians wanted to lay low after returning to society, but for Ayn Rant it was a step up. She had been gone for three years and The Speech had created a sensation a year previously. She wired her former agent that she was returning, and when she stepped off the train in Grand Central Station on June 8, 1955, a crowd of reporters was waiting.

She looked fabulous. Her lean body was tan and muscular from working outdoors. She wore a man's shirt and pants with a scarf providing a splash of color around her neck. Her shirt was unbuttoned just enough to reveal the swell of her breasts. Her black hair was cut thoughtlessly above her shoulders and tousled in a way that hair stylists would imitate after her image appeared in the papers. Her young son perched on her slim hip completed the image. Here was a half man, half woman who exuded sexuality, competence, and intellect. She looked able to rock the cradle and rule the world.

Passing her son to her agent, she strode to the cluster of microphones in front of clicking cameras and popping flash bulbs. A grainy newsreel recorded the event for posterity.

"I bring you greetings from John Galt, whose vision for the future was broadcast around the world last year. That vision has shaken the very roots of conventional society, making it too dangerous for him to operate in public. He has therefore gone into hiding and will be communicating through me to carry on his movement."

Don't even try to trace John Galt through her, Ayn Rant continued with a superior smile, because no one could crack the secret code that they had devised. None of this was true, but Ayn Rant's talent for presenting fiction as fact knew no bounds. The other Galtians were in no mood to disagree and some even preferred the heroic story over the more embarrassing truth. Offers of writing assignments and speaking appearances poured in. New people who had fallen under the spell of the doer philosophy, now elaborated and refined by The Speech, clambered to become part of her inner circle. Ayn Rant had become the leader of her own cult.

Later, she would tell a different story to her most trusted acolytes, swearing them to secrecy. She was devastated by John Galt's abandonment. One moment, they were the king and queen of a new social order. The next moment, he was simply gone, leaving her with a baby and a movement that was falling apart. She had idolized him as the embodiment of her Objectivist philosophy. His departure was not just a personal betrayal but seemed to make a mockery of her ideas. Over time, her disappointment hardened like a diamond into rage. She would *never* forgive John Galt. Forgiveness was not an Objectivist virtue. Objectivists expected to judge and be judged, and John Galt would be judged harshly. If he wanted to abandon her and their movement, then she would use his name as she saw fit. She now *owned* John Galt. His soul belonged to her.

My father was raised at the epicenter of Ayn Rant's stylized universe. They lived in a posh apartment on 5th Avenue that also served as an intellectual salon. As soon as Ayn Rant had money to spend, she indulged her taste in fine fashion and art. The apartment was decorated in 1950s chic: chrome and glass, white shag rugs, and modern art on the walls. Plate glass windows provided a spectacular view of the teeming city below. The centerpiece of the apartment was a large room with plush couches lining all four walls and an expensive leather swivel chair in the center. Almost every night, devotees of Ayn Rant would sit on the couches while she held court in the center, swiveling dramatically to face whoever she wished to address. She dressed flamboyantly to be the visual center of attention, including a black cape that became her trademark. She was seldom without a cigarette in a long holder that she waved to great effect. She regarded the glowing end of a cigarette as a symbol of modernity and man's conquest of nature that began with the harnessing of fire.

The apartment was kept spotlessly clean by a colored maid named Betty, whose husband Chester served as cook and chauffeur. They arrived early in the morning to prepare my father for school and left late after cleaning up the night's events. When I was small and visiting my grandmother's apartment, I loved Betty and Chester and spent as much time as I could with them. The bright yellow kitchen and playful conversation was an oasis of warmth in what seemed to me an otherwise frigid desert. When I grew a little older, I was shocked to discover that they had children of their own, whom they seldom saw due to their service to my grandmother.

My father's upbringing was like traveling along a single road paved in gold, with nothing of much interest on either side. He typically woke to the sound of Betty and Chester letting themselves in and the clank of utensils as they prepared his breakfast. Then Chester would drive him to an elite private school where the boys dressed like CEOs and the girls dressed like debutantes. His mother slept late, so he typically didn't see her until returning from school. She would be in conversation with members of her inner circle or writing in her office at her desk positioned in front of one of the big windows overlooking the city below. She would greet him with a kiss on the cheek and a stiff hug before returning to her work. She was such a captive of her own philosophy that motherhood made her feel uncomfortable. After all, motherhood is about unconditional love for one's child, about giving without expectation of return. The very word "give" had been purged from the Objectivist vocabulary. My grandmother loved her son, but she wanted to be the perfect *Objectivist* mother and this meant subordinating her motherly instincts to the dictates of her creed.

If John Galt II's mother was detached, his father was even more so. John Galt I was constantly being discussed as the God of Objectivism who spoke through the oracle of his mother. He communicated to her through a secret code that couldn't be cracked, but he never communicated to his own son. When my father finally summoned the courage to ask his mother if his father ever spoke about him, she seemed shocked and caught off guard. She had been so busy inventing John Galt for her movement that she had forgotten to invent a relationship with their own son! Soon my father started to receive messages from his father channeled through his mother, urging him to follow Objectivist principles in preparation for the day that they could be together.

This might seem like a barren growth environment for a child, but in fact it was richly rewarding – as long as he traveled along that single golden paved road. After all, he was the anointed prince of the Objectivist movement. He was adored by the people who came every night to receive the Word from his mother. Their eyes misted at the thought that this little boy was deprived of his father by the evil moocher society. From the earliest age, he was allowed to join the nightly discussions. He would enter the room in his pajamas to moans of delight from the women, who outstretched their arms to cuddle him. Dozens of laps served as his pillow and dozens of hands stroked his head as he fell asleep to the sound of his mother's urgent cadence. Unknown arms carried him to his bed, where he awoke to the sound of Betty and Chester letting themselves in the next morning.

Nothing could compete with the adoration that my father received as heir of the Objectivist movement. His schoolmates had little appeal. He could have found warmth in the company of Betty and Chester, as I did, but he soon learned to treat them like the help. His room could have served as a boyhood oasis for using his bed as a trampoline and strewing his toys on the floor, but he soon gravitated toward keeping it as clean as the rest of the apartment and choosing such intellectual toys that his room looked more like a laboratory than a child's bedroom. It even became a tourist attraction for the nightly visitors. They would poke their heads in to watch the prince add chemicals to a test tube or solder wires to a circuit board, a true heir to his father's genius. After a reverential look, they tiptoed away to join the discussion in the central room.

Down in the Bible Belt, some children of preachers soak up so much of their culture that they can play it back at an early age. There they are on the stage at the age of six or so, microphone in hand, praising the lord and casting out devils with all the verve of their fathers. That's how my father became for the Objectivist movement. Falling asleep night after night to his mother's voice, he became able to play it back with uncanny authenticity, as if he was a true savant. Nothing delighted his mother more than to turn a question over to her little son to deliver the answer to the stunned audience. Here was a true genius, exactly what should be expected from the spawn of John Galt I and Ayn Rant.

As my father grew from a boy to a man, he became a full partner with his mother in directing the Objectivist movement. On his thirteenth birthday, she disclosed that she had no contact with John Galt I, who could be dead as far as she knew. She maintained the fiction for the sake of the movement. She hoped he would understand – and he did. John Galt II had observed his mother long enough to know that she had no scruples about constructing her stylized universe. Truth had no value for her. She only cared about effect.

Once this awareness dawned upon him, he watched with admiration as his mother plied her craft. She was like a mosaic artist using truth as her tiles. If a particular fact fit, she would use it intact. Otherwise she would clip it until its shape was just right. Remaining gaps were filled with wholesale fictions presented as fact. The completed work of art acted like a magic spell to convince people of the reasonableness of the Objectivist creed. The biggest deception of all was to call the movement Objectivism, as if it could be fully validated by rationality and science!

Since my father's single golden paved road was to expand the Objectivist empire, he became my grandmother's eager apprentice. In front of others, they maintained the pretense that John Galt I was in constant communication and that Objectivism was based on rationality and science. When alone, they talked like back-room political strategists about how to achieve maximum effect. Their private conversations would have shocked and dismayed their loyal following. He began to pay more attention to his classmates in school, or at least the ones that provided useful social connections. By the time he entered Yale University, he was already a smooth operator, capable of inserting himself into high society. He didn't need to find a business because his business was proselytizing the Objectivist creed. It was an easy sell because nothing sounds better to a powerful person than to be told that their ambitions are morally pure and good for everyone else.

Ayn Rant was a genius at communicating in her own way, but it was my father who exploited the new technologies that arose during the second half of the 20th Century, like successive waves lapping the shore – television, talk radio, cable, the Internet. Ayn Rant was an incurable elitist but my father cultivated a common touch that appealed to the average good old boy in addition to the rich and powerful. As his media empire grew, he became politically powerful. He started to craft the campaigns of politicians who promised to dismantle government and the legislation for them to pass after they were elected. Political cartoons started to portray my father as a corpulent puppeteer with beady eyes, manipulating politicians with his fat fingers.

The bodies of both mother and son were indeed a disturbing reflection of their creed. Their daily routine was to spend almost all of their time indoors – talking, writing, and eating the best food that money could buy. Ayn Rant maintained her slim figure but her skin became bleached and she lost her muscle tone. As she aged, she began to apply thick makeup to remain the visual center of attention, which made her seem grotesque to non-believers. Her constant smoking had given her a chronic cough that punctuated her speech like the sound of an assault rifle.

My father's halfhearted attempts to frequent health clubs were no match for his otherwise sedentary lifestyle. His body began to swell as a teenager and kept on going, until as a man he struggled to keep his weight below 300 pounds. Those political cartoons weren't far off. His eyes did become beady and piggish as they receded into his fleshy face. His fat fingers swelled around his expensive rings, making them impossible to remove. In a strange way, John Galt II didn't mind his bulk because it made him imposing, especially when wrapped in the finest tailor-made clothes.

Overconsumption also seeped into my father's brain. Ayn Rant worshipped modernity and treated every medical advance as a blessing. Her son became an early user of some of the pharmaceuticals that were being developed during the 1960s and '70s to cure mental discomforts and enhance performance. Only later would scientists discover that pumping chemicals into one's brain like that was like trying to enhance the performance of a race car with a sledge hammer. Then there was the alcohol that accompanied nearly every meal and the recreational drugs that were so easy to obtain and use without risk. John Galt II was disciplined about expanding the Objectivist empire, so he kept his drug use within bounds most of the time, but some of his rants against the evils of moocher society had a deranged quality to them.

These disturbing manifestations were only just starting when my father met my mother, Elena Lane, in 1974. Looking at photographs of my mother as a young woman, I think it would be impossible not to love her. Her face had the beauty of a Hollywood starlet but also had a spiritual quality that inspired reverence along with desire. Her body was strong and sensual but not on display. You had to imagine it through her sensible clothes. She wore no makeup and didn't need to. Her skin was naturally smooth and blemish free and her cheeks were naturally tinged with red. In the photograph that I remember best, which was taken for her high school yearbook, her blond hair is tied back to reveal the perfect lines of her face. Her clear blue eyes are looking directly at the photographer as if to say, "Isn't this silly? Please finish up as quickly as you can."

My mother grew up in the tiny town of Coon Rapids, Iowa, and excelled at everything she attempted. She loved reading and could be seen carrying stacks of books in and out of the town library every week. Her parents were teachers at the high school, so the school became an extension of her home. She joined every club and advanced study program. In her senior year, she was class valedictorian, played the star role in the school play, helped her school debate team win the state championship, and narrowly missed winning the state track championship in the 800 meter run. In her valedictory address at graduation, she talked about the limitless opportunity awaiting anyone willing to take life by the horns.

My mother's favorite author at this time was Ayn Rant. Along with legions of other idealistic young people, my mother found Ayn Rant's stylized universe impossible to resist. The God-like portrayal of doers and their limitless horizons spoke directly to her own aspirations. She was so bewitched that she read Ayn Rant's works again and again and even committed The Speech to memory like a catechism. When she learned that her debating team would be visiting New York City for the national championship, she realized that she might actually be able to meet her idol in the flesh. She wrote a letter and was ecstatic to receive a hand-written reply in spidery script. Yes, my mother would be welcome to attend one of the nightly soirees during her visit to New York City.

Imagine my mother's excitement as a small town girl with big ambitions visiting The Big Apple for the first time. She entered the ritzy apartment building on 5th Avenue and was taken by the elevator operator to the thirty-second floor. Ringing the bell of the apartment seemed like the dawn of a new life. A colored man took her coat and directed her down the hall, which led to a large room with couches lining the walls and a leather chair like a throne in the center. There was Ayn Rant, small in stature but giant in presence, talking with a few people who had arrived previously. By her side was John Galt II, who she had also read about. All eyes turned to my mother as she entered the room and the conversation abruptly stopped. They stared at her for so long that she blushed. Later, my father told her that they were rendered speechless by her beauty.

Once they recovered, they surrounded her and peppered her with questions. Her humble origins and courage in making the pilgrimage were inflated to mythic proportions. For the rest of the evening, my mother sat in rapt attention on one of the couches as the others posed questions to Ayn Rant, who swiveled to face them and answer with absolute certainty, embellishing her points with waves of her cigarette holder. Her son roamed the room with relaxed confidence, weaving in his own comments. Midway through the evening, my mother felt that she could say something that wasn't completely stupid. Summoning her courage, she asked a question and watched at full alert as the great Ayn Rant swiveled in her chair to face her.

"That's very perceptive of you, Elena," she began, and delivered a commentary on the point my mother had raised. Then her son also praised her point and added some comments of his own. It was the high point of my mother's young life.

The romance that ensued between my father and mother was inevitable. She was impossible not to love and he represented everything she aspired to. Merely meeting Ayn Rant seemed too good to be true. Becoming John Galt II's Princess was better than any fairy tale she could imagine. He was larger and older than she imagined for a lover, but in every other respect he made a fine Prince Charming – funny, urbane, attentive, and on his way to becoming an important man of the world. He had received his MBA from Harvard after graduating from Yale and was already building his media empire. She had just graduated from high school and had a full scholarship at the University of Iowa, but her fateful trip to New York City changed all that. Ayn Rant held universities in low regard as bastions of liberalism and was especially scornful of state-supported education. Elena could receive no better education than Objectivism, with John and her as her teachers. In short order, my mother turned down the scholarship and moved to New York City, where she stayed as a houseguest in Ayn Rant's apartment. Her family and friends were shocked, as if she had been stolen away by a religious cult. My father had his own apartment in addition to his room in his mother's apartment, where he occasionally slept over when the evening discussions went late. My mother stayed in this room and in no time they were sleeping together. When Objectivists find their soul mates, they defy social conventions and have sex like wild animals in full rut. Ayn Rant beamed with approval and treated my mother as one of her most important disciples. I was conceived within weeks and my parents were married when my mother was three months pregnant. Strictly speaking, objectivists don't believe in marriage, but John's emerging media empire required some concessions.

Alas, my mother's fairytale world began to fall apart almost immediately. Long before she arrived, most of the idealism had departed from Ayn Rant and her son. Building a media empire was too much work to believe in the façade that you were constructing for others. Their backroom manipulations were not visible to my mother at first, but they became impossible to conceal after a while. Several months were required to figure out that John Galt I didn't exist, but other blatant truth-clipping took place on a daily basis. The nightly soirees that thrilled her so at the beginning became especially repugnant upon repetition. The whole point of Objectivism was to subject all aspects of one's life to rational examination, to be constantly checking one's premises. "Check your premises" was an Objectivist mantra that was used repeatedly during the nightly soirees. The more my mother observed the proceedings, the more she realized that the true meaning of "Check your premises" was "Conform or else." No meaningful dialogue ever took place during the nightly soirees. Mother and son were always right and anyone who disagreed was guilty of having faulty premises. All would be forgiven if they quickly repented, but if they persisted, mother and son would freeze up and the others would act as if the sinner had a disease. They would sit farther away from the person with the faulty premise, avoid eye contact and conversation. My mother watched in dismay as the most interesting people who showed up at the soirees, the ones that she most enjoyed talking with, soon stopped coming, leaving only sycophants masquerading as discerning rationalists.

At one point, my mother became so disgusted that she decided to challenge the system. She made a point that she knew would rub mother and son the wrong way. Ayn Rant swiveled in her chair and explained why this was a faulty premise. Before she could swivel away, my mother pressed the matter. Ayn Rant acted surprised and her answer became more imperious, as if elaboration shouldn't be necessary. My mother pressed the matter still further and the entire charade came to a halt. Mother, son, and the entire congregation stared at her as if to say, "What are you – *stupid*? Don't you know the *rules*?" My mother stopped regularly attending the nightly soirees after this evening. She had already moved into my father's apartment and found it easy to stay at home with me, her newborn son.

I think my father genuinely loved my mother at the beginning and hoped that their fairytale romance would work. He didn't realize how difficult it would be to conceal the inside story from my mother or the depth of her disappointment at the fraud that the Objectivist movement had become. Once he experienced her disapproval, he was faced with a difficult choice. Either he must redeem himself in her eyes, or he must stop caring about what she thought of him. It was a hard choice, but it was also no contest. As much as he wanted my mother's love, it was no match for the empire that he was building with his mother on his path down that golden paved road.

By the time I was born, they were already living largely separate lives. Their apartment became our domain and my father spent most of his time traveling or strategizing with his mother in her apartment. My earliest memories are of glorious closeness with my mother and my father nowhere in sight. Her wonderful face will forever hover above me in my mind, as it did when I played on her lap. Later she told me that I was the only thing worth living for during that period of her life.

I also remember my trips to my grandmother's apartment, which my mother could not entirely avoid. My earliest memory of my grandmother was when she caught me jumping on the couches and shouted "STOP!" as if I had committed a mortal offense. Her ambitions and Objectivist philosophy had bled all the human warmth out of her. Her cape and aging face, with bright red lipstick and dark rings of mascara around her eyes, made her look like a ghoul to me. Her voice was harsh and insistent and to have it punctuated by uncontrollable hacking was more than one could bear. I avoided her as much as possible and sought refuge in the bright yellow kitchen with Betty and Chester.

My earliest memories of my father sadden me to this day. His relationship with me was inextricably linked to his relationship with my mother. I would see him mostly in my grandmother's apartment, where I would be handed to him for a few minutes before being handed back. I think that he wanted to hold me, but there was no way of becoming close to me without becoming close to my mother, which was impossible. Occasionally we would spend a day together that he would try to make special. Going to the circus. Skating at Rockefeller Center. A shopping spree at F.A.O. Schwarz, the world's largest toy store of its day. Alas, these outings were so laden with unspoken expectations that we were both relieved when they were over. I knew my father scarcely better than he knew his father.

As I grew from a toddler to a young boy, my mother's desperation went into free fall. Her personal life was in shambles. Her youthful idealism had been crushed by her inside knowledge of the Objectivist movement. She had given up a college education. She disrespected her husband and was repulsed by his expanding body. She had no friends and despised the sycophants that infested the movement.

My mother's personal desperation was great, but it was small compared to what she thought she was witnessing on a worldwide scale. The Objectivist movement was nothing less than a cancer unleashed upon society. A cancer is a cell that has mutated and now promotes its own growth rather than participating in the economy of the body. It grows into a tumor and then spreads to other parts of the body — metastasis. When the cancer cells interfere with the economy of the body too much, the body and the cancer die. Cancer is the ultimate short-sighted recipe for success.

If cancer cells could talk, they would say to the rest of the body: "Look how fast we are growing! Follow our example and *everyone* can grow this fast!" That's an absurd idea for real cancer and real bodies, but it was precisely the message that Ayn Rant's Objectivist creed conveyed to the body politic, and for a period of decades it was taken seriously. People who fell under the spell of her stylized universe felt entitled to enrich themselves without limit. The idea that their personal wealth was also profiting the economy created the illusion that everyone could follow their example — that everyone could be a cancer cell. As more and more people followed the creed, the body politic started to fall apart. Nobody understood the reasons, least of all the true believers. If society wasn't working well, it was because they weren't applying their principles strongly enough!

Her repulsive husband and freakish mother-in-law were actually succeeding at spreading their cancerous gospel around the globe. The rich and powerful were the first to convert because it enabled them to take more and more without guilt. Indeed, they could feel downright self-righteous about it. They were joined by legions of idealistic young people, like herself, because it appealed so much to their sense of possibility at the dawn of their adult lives. This cancer had been spreading ever since The Speech and the media empire being assembled by John Galt II would dwarf his mother's impact. Without ever proving itself good for anything, the stylized universe was worming its way into the heads of world leaders and the captains of industry. If John Galt II had his way, he would not only get his Objectivist zombies elected, but he would craft the legislation for them to pass. The legislation would divert the flow of the economy into their pockets, just as cancer cells grow at the expense of the body. John Galt II and his ilk would grow richer and richer. His eyes would recess deeper and deeper into his fleshy face. His fat fingers would swell more and more around his expensive rings. He would buy one mansion, then five, then ten, and airplanes, yachts, and fleets of cars to travel between mansions. He would pay more for a single suit of clothes than a month's salary for Betty or Chester. And when the vital organs of society began to fail, John Galt II would bellow through his media empire, "You're just not following our Objectivist principles *hard* enough!" In her darker moments, my mother thought that she was witnessing the destruction of the world.

Then there was me, the only joy in her life. What would become of me? If she sought a divorce, her husband could hire the best lawyers in the world to win a custody battle. After all, I had not been abused in any way and she had none of the grievances that typically justify a divorce. I would enter his domain and would be set upon that single golden-paved road. Even if she was allowed to keep and raise me as a single mom, what would prevent me from being seduced by Ayn Rant's stylized universe, just as she had been? This was the most terrible thought of all.

Then, from the depth of her despair, my mother conceived a plan to save herself, me, and just possibly the world. I was seven years old and still remember the change in her mood, as if she had finally acquired a purpose in life. Over the course of the next year, she compiled so much damning evidence about the inside story of Objectivism as to cause deep embarrassment, if not to shut down the movement altogether. The non-existence of John Galt I was just the tip of the iceberg. Then she drew up the conditions for remaining silent. First, John Galt II would agree to an amicable divorce. Second, he would grant full custody of me to my mother. He wouldn't even have visitation rights without her permission. Third, he would provide child support that would cover my education and living expenses to the age of twenty-one. Fourth, he would establish a trust fund in my name that would be calibrated to exactly ten percent of his own wealth, which I would take control of when I turned twenty-one. My mother asked nothing for herself.

When I was older, my mother told me how she brokered the agreement with my father in three meetings. For the first meeting, she summoned my father to their apartment and handed him a thick manila envelope summarizing the damning evidence that she was prepared to release to the world. His face turned white as he scanned the first page.

"I need to study this," was all that he said before leaving.

The second meeting outlined the terms of the divorce. My mother handed him a second manila envelope and watched his face again turn white when he read about the trust fund. "I'll need to study this," was all he said before leaving.

For the third meeting, my father was accompanied by a team of six lawyers. They must have had a three-martini lunch together beforehand because they barged into the apartment full of swagger and noisy conversation. Suddenly they stopped short at the sight of my mother sitting at the dining room table with a thin man in an old suit, a hawk-like beak of a nose, and white wavy hair atop a high forehead.

"*You!* What are *you* doing here?" my father gasped.

"Good afternoon, Mr. Galt. Good afternoon, gentlemen." the thin man said in a pleasant voice. His name was Abraham Baryov and he was an accountant of such legendary stature that my father and team of lawyers knew him by sight. A rarity among accountants, he regarded his profession as a noble calling and had become a watchdog against unscrupulous accounting practices, whether legal or illegal. He had the expertise to follow wealthy individuals and corporations through the maze of loopholes that they constructed to avoid being taxed. He also had the courage and integrity to call them out in public. His opinion was so widely respected that when he criticized a company its stock value invariably plummeted, which had become known as "the Baryov effect." Some people even called him the soul of the accounting profession.

My father and his team of lawyers had entered the room expecting to bully my mother and whatever two-bit lawyer she had hired to establish the terms of the divorce. Sitting across the table from Abraham

Baryov wasn't part of their game plan, but they bravely proceeded to explain that the laws for setting up trust funds would make it illegal to provide ten percent of my father's wealth to me. After they finished, it was time for Abraham Baryov to speak.

"Mr. Galt. I have made an initial inquiry into your financial dealings. Your lawyers and accountants have been exceptionally creative at processing your earnings through foreign banks to avoid paying taxes. Everything you have done has been legal, thanks in part to laws that you have been influential in pushing through Congress. Are you saying that you and your team lack the creativity to ensure that ten percent of your wealth flows to your own son? If so, then I and my firm would be happy to lend you a hand."

My father and his team of lawyers glowered at my mother and Abraham Baryov from across the table. They were Masters of the Universe and unaccustomed to being opposed in this way. Their faces turned red and their arms started to flex as if searching for something to strangle.

"Why are you becoming involved in this?" my father asked stupidly. "You're not even holding us accountable. You're saying that you'll help us exploit loopholes on behalf of my son."

"I'm offering my services to your wife on a pro bono basis," Abraham Baryov replied with an amused smile. "Let's just say that I regard it as a good cause."

My mother said nothing during the entire proceeding, merely staring across the table with her arms folded and a contemptuous expression on her face. She had approached Abraham Baryov after watching a profile of him on television. She reasoned that he was a good man who might be willing to help her and was surprised when he not only offered advice but also volunteered his personal services.

In the end, my father and his lawyers made a cold, hard calculation that ten percent of his wealth would be considerably less than the loss of revenue if the information compiled by my mother was released to the world. Another consideration that might have softened the blow for my father was that the money would go to his own son. He didn't know why my mother wanted to provide for me in this way, but perhaps he wasn't entirely opposed. Maybe it would even bring me closer to him when I matured and escaped the influence of my mother.

My mother revealed the trust fund to me on my thirteenth birthday. To celebrate, she had taken me to a fancy restaurant that served one of my favorite desserts – lemon meringue pie. I could sense that she was working up the courage to tell me something important, but I couldn't remotely guess what it might be.

"Johnny," she began after a big slice had been placed in front of me, "in the old days, thirteen years was considered the age when a boy turned into a man, so I have chosen today to tell you more about my divorce from your father."

As if to deflect the gravity of her words, I concentrated on my slice of pie, pushing my fork through the white foamy meringue, through the bright yellow lemon custard, through the flaky pie crust, and up to my lips, savoring its complex tastes and textures for as long as I could before the reply that was required of me.

"OK …"

"It must be confusing why I have shielded you from him and his world so completely. It is not that I think he is evil, or that he doesn't love you. But something about the world that he has constructed with his mother *is* evil. That is why I had to leave and protect you from it by preventing him from having any contact with you."

I felt as if a chasm was opening up in front of me. My mother was so alienated from my father while they were married and my own relationship with him was so attenuated that the divorce was not a traumatic event in my life. I even relished having my mother even more to myself and for her to be so much happier on her own. To be told that we had escaped something evil, which still existed at a distance, was completely new to me. It was too big for me to even begin to process, so I pushed my fork through my pie even more slowly than before, studying the brown peaks and white valleys of the meringue as if they were a miniature mountain range. When it became clear that I couldn't even summon an "OK …" to hold up my end of the conversation, my mother continued.

"Johnny, there is something else that I felt I had to do as part of the divorce settlement. It wasn't enough for me to protect just us from the evil of your father's empire. I had to do something to combat the evil itself. So …"

My mother was struggling so hard on her end of the conversation that now she lapsed into silence. I was so immobilized that I just bent my head and stared at my plate. The noises around me – the conversations and clatters of the plates as the waiters cleared the tables – seemed louder than before, as if someone had turned up their volume. Finally my mother found the courage to continue.

"… I made it happen that ten percent of his wealth would come to you on your twenty-first birthday."

Those words jolted me out of my catatonic state.

"To *me*?"

You'd think that the prospect of inheriting a fortune would be received as good news, but that's not how I took it at all. My mother's intention was clear. This fortune was not to be used for my pleasure, but to combat something evil that she associated with my father and grandmother. For me to combat their evil empire, I would need to know what was good. I didn't know what was good. I didn't even know for myself that my father's empire was evil.

My mother had no reply to my two-word question. Her single decisive action was to steal some of my father's fortune for me. Now she was beginning to realize how many questions she couldn't answer.

"Why *me*?"

My mother's expression softened as she prepared at last to answer my question.

Her face was older than the first photographs that I have seen of her. There were lines that reflected the ordeal that she had weathered to bring us to this point. But her face still had the beauty of those photographs and its spiritual quality had even deepened.

"Because I have faith in you, my son."

3

The Village School

At the time of my parents' divorce, I was like a tiny plant that had sprouted and grown to the limits of the nourishment provided by the seed, waiting patiently for an additional influx of water, nutrients, and sunlight. A mother's love can only go so far on its own. I was tall for my age but skinny, all arms and legs. City life afforded little scope for exercise or time outdoors, so my skin and muscle tone looked and felt like cooked pasta.

I was shy – painfully shy – especially around children my own age. Outside of school, I was entirely in the company of adults. The private school that I attended was so bent on boosting my IQ that I don't remember having any fun and can scarcely recollect anything at all. Placed next to my father, no one would guess that I was his son. Not only were our bodies comically different, but so were our personalities. He filled the room, not only with his bulk but with his self-confidence. His first impulse was to take charge. My first impulse was to hang back and observe. Only when I had thoroughly taken stock of the situation was I prepared to speak or move.

And another thing. I appeared to have inherited a double dose of my mother's empathic nature. I responded to the joys and sorrows of others in the same way that the strings of an unplayed violin vibrate when placed next to a violin that is being played. Given my mother's desperate situation and my closeness to her, mostly I resonated to her sorrow, as if everything was my fault. I don't remember it myself, but according to her I had a habit of following her around saying, "I'm sorry! I'm sorry!" No wonder she was so desperate for the two of us to escape!

After she became liberated from my father, my mother had lost all interest in college or any career that would bring her into contact with an Objectivist. She found a job as a librarian at a tiny arts college in Connecticut. A cottage by a brook at the back of the picturesque campus was being used for storage and my mother asked if she might use it for lodging. Within weeks, she turned it into a storybook cottage bedecked with flowers and impeccably chosen furniture purchased from garage sales and Goodwill stores. This was like a shaft of sunlight falling upon the little plant. I can recall playing outside by the brook amidst flowers like a Kodacolor photo in a family album.

My mother wanted nothing from my father for herself, but for me the divorce settlement provided the best education that money could buy. She researched the options carefully before choosing a boarding school that would hurl me as far away from Objectivism as possible. It was called the Village School and was located deep in the Adirondack Mountains of northern New York State. In stark contrast to the elite schooling my father received and the Objectivists' worship of modernity, the Village School was built to resemble a colonial village, complete with a working farm and houses surrounding a central green. My father probably snorted in disbelief when he learned how I was to be raised.

Students were conveyed to the school in the fall by buses that left from various gathering points. Ours was the parking lot of a Howard Johnson's restaurant just off the Interstate. We arrived early to have a last meal together before parting. My mother watched with amusement as I washed down two hot dogs and an order of fried clams with a strawberry milkshake. How could such a skinny kid eat so much? When it was time for me to board the bus, we fell into each other's arms for a long embrace. It's hard for any eight-year old boy to part from his mother, but for us it was like cleaving a single organism into two. I took a seat by the window and watched her weeping as I rolled out of sight, through tears streaming from my own eyes.

My shyness at full throttle, I kept to myself as the other students boisterously horsed around, my thin arms wrapped around my knobby knees. One of the adults on the bus must have sensed my insecurity and sat next to me.

"Hello there, little man! My name is Alan. What's your name?"

I was so overwhelmed by everything new around me that I couldn't even utter a reply. I just looked at him with big eyes, fighting back the urge to cry.

"Would you like me to sit next to you?"

Yes, I nodded, beseeching with my eyes that I would do anything to have him sit next to me so that one of those boisterous people my own age wouldn't. He seemed to accept my need to remain silent to attend to the inner maelstrom of my thoughts. I stared out the window, as much to avoid conversation as to watch the scenery.

After several hours we left the Interstate and the scenery commanded more of my attention. The roads became smaller and the mountains taller. Water tumbled down streams into lakes whose still surfaces dotted with reeds and lily pads appeared more black than blue. I felt puny amidst the giant boulders by the roadside that had crashed down from the heights, careless of what lay in their path. The mountains cast deep shadows over our route, even though it was only midday. At last we entered a small sunny valley and turned onto a dirt road that ran past a big barn of weathered wood, a fenced pasture with horses and cows, and a field dotted with bright orange pumpkins. We crossed a little brook, turned a corner, and a cluster of buildings surrounding a central green came into view.

We had arrived at the Village School. The returning students seemed delighted to be back, spilling out of the bus, rushing around to find their friends, and disappearing to visit their old haunts. I was shown to one of the buildings and introduced to my dorm parents, a young couple named Matthew and Sarah, who taught by day and became surrogate parents by night.

The Village School was founded by an iconoclast named Walter Gold, who traveled widely during World War II and was struck by the vitality and resilience of village life. From the Eskimos of Greenland to the South Sea Islanders, villages seemed to run themselves without the need for any outside assistance. Unlike the utopian societies like the Galtians, which almost invariably fell apart within a lifetime, villages stretched back to time immemorial.

Gold was not so naïve to think that the villagers he encountered were noble savages. He saw that they were much like him and the people who lived in so-called modern society. They had weaknesses and ambitions that set them against each other. They warred at a small scale, much as the so-called developed nations were warring at a large scale, but something about life at the scale of a village kept conflicts among the villagers from getting out of hand. If there was a secret to peace on Earth, perhaps it could be found by unlocking the secret of peace within a village.

Walter Gold also observed that the villages he visited had no schools or anything else that resembled formal education. The children were left to their own devices for the most part. The oldest wanted to become adults, the younger kids wanted to be like the older kids, and everything seemed to be learned as a form of spontaneous practice and play. Adults offered help when needed, and various rituals and secret societies taught esoteric knowledge, but this was not until the children had become young adults.

Despite the absence of anything resembling school, Gold realized that the knowledge being passed down the generations was anything but simple. Gold was the son of intellectual parents and had been attending Harvard University when he interrupted his studies to enlist in the Navy. Far from feeling superior, he was in awe of the knowledge possessed by native people, especially in the frozen north where he served for two years on the Greenland Patrol. The knowledge required to survive in that hostile climate would have occupied an entire library of how-to books, but somehow it was learned and transmitted without any books at all.

Walter Gold was so moved by this experience that when he returned to Harvard after the war, he threw himself into studying human societies around the world and the history of the European nations. He had always planned to become an educator but now it seemed that modern education and much of modern life had gone terribly wrong. He therefore decided to conduct a bold experiment in education by starting a school that emulated a village. He was a quiet man that no one had regarded as a leader before, but his conviction made him charismatic. He assembled a group of teachers and they borrowed money from wherever they could to buy a tract of land in the Adirondacks. They constructed the buildings themselves and the first class consisted of only a dozen students, whose parents had also become converts to Gold's new educational philosophy. Some of them were wealthy, and when they saw how their children thrived, they spread the word and provided financial support. When I arrived, the school was in its third decade and had acquired a devoted following. Walter Gold and his wife Leonora were in their sixties, and still lean and strong from the life that they'd created for themselves and others. When I first saw him as an eight-year old boy, I knew that I was in the presence of greatness, even though he was doing nothing whatsoever to advertise the fact.

After a few weeks of homesickness and acclimation, I, too, grew to love the Village School. There were roughly a hundred students, the youngest a little younger than me and the oldest seventeen. The teachers ranged from their twenties to their sixties and some of them had children, so the whole school really was like a village. The maxim of learning by doing meant that classroom studies were kept to a minimum and students took part in all aspects of village life. On any given day, I might be sweeping the floors, waiting the tables, or loading dishes into the big metal dishwasher. Then there were the barn chores. Feeding the chickens and collecting their eggs. Milking the cows. Standing on a giant mound of compost at the end of the barn and waiting to receive the daily load of manure mixed with straw in a metal contraption called the honey cart.

Chores and classes occupied about six hours a day. The rest was glorious free time to do what we wanted. Well, not quite. There were strict rules against such things as contraband substances and harming others, but within those limits, every student could follow his or her bliss. On any given day, some kids might be found curled up in the common room reading a book, or playing board games, or in the shop learning how to work with wood. The teachers were around to help if asked but mostly left us to our own devices. We learned at least as much from the older kids as from the teachers, and teaching the younger kids was educational for us as well. Kids live for summer, when they can get up in the morning with the entire day stretching before them. Every day was like that at the Village School.

Much as I grew to like the adults, my fellow students, and social activities, my bliss became the outdoors. Perhaps my early childhood spent in a Manhattan apartment gave me a special hunger, but something pulled me out of the buildings of the Village School to explore the countryside by myself. I became a passionate fisher of the brook trout that inhabited the little stream. In the fall, when the goldenrod were in bloom, I would first catch a grasshopper to thread onto my hook and then creep, Indian-like, to the bank of the stream, where I would let the grasshopper drift with the current. The trout darted out from under the bank in a flash of color to take the bait. I waited breathlessly to give them time to swallow and then pulled their dancing bodies onto the bank. Nothing can match the beauty of the speckled sides and milky white belly of a brook trout. They were only ten or so inches long, but the thrill of the hunt was all that I needed.

Outdoor activities abounded. The school had its own ski hill that had to be cleared of vegetation during the fall. I remember cutting down saplings side by side with Walter Gold as the first snowflakes fell. He was dressed as a workman and had more stamina than anyone else. During the skiing season, we were pulled up the hill by a long loop of rope powered by an old automobile engine at the top. Wearing thick leather mittens, you picked up the rope with one hand in front of you and the other behind your back, and slowly tightened your grip to be conveyed to the top. Then you let glorious gravity take you down, leaping over moguls on the steep open slope or taking the gentle meandering path through the woods. Numb fingers and toes and icy eyelashes only seemed to add to the pleasure.

On weekends during the spring and fall we went on overnight hikes to climb some of the Adirondack high peaks. They weren't tall by world standards but they were plenty majestic for a small boy. I remember the smell of the campfire, the sound of wind through the pines and water tumbling over stones, and brilliant night skies undimmed by city lights. One trek involved climbing a slope where all of the pines had been blown down by a hurricane years earlier. We had to make our way through the maze of their bleached trunks as if they were giant pickup sticks.

The barn animals had to be cared for no matter what the weather, in driving rain or temperature so cold that it froze the hairs inside your nose. One of my favorite chores was to feed the chickens and collect their eggs, which were delightfully warm to the touch. I also loved to feed the pigs, pouring the slop and kitchen scraps into the trough and watching them crowd around, oinking with unadulterated joy. Now and then I would jump onto one of their backs and hang onto its hard bristly body for as long as I could before being thrown to the ground, laughing without anyone around to listen. Milking cows was another delight, first squeezing the top of the teat between thumb and forefinger, and then the rest of the teat with my other fingers, to send a stream of milk hissing into the bucket, or the mouth of one of the barn cats.

When spring approached, we made maple syrup. This involved drilling holes in the trunks and inserting metal spigots. Pails with metal roofs were hung on the spigots to collect the sap. Every day we walked in the melting snow alongside a tractor pulling a large tank for the sap. On a good day, the pails would be full of the crystalline fragrant liquid. Then to the sugar house, where the sap was boiled in flat pans heated by a wood fire. The smell of the fire and steam rising from the pans was intoxicating. Forty gallons of sap were required to make a single gallon of the golden syrup that we poured on our pancakes for breakfast and gave as gifts to our parents as a token of our unique education.

Almost as much fun as being outdoors was working with my hands. The entire ground floor of one of the buildings was devoted to crafts, including a woodworking shop, a ceramic studio, and a leatherworking area. There was no division between boys' and girls' crafts; the boys were told that the sailors of old made excellent seamsters and knitters. I made a leather knapsack by cutting out the pieces, piercing holes along the edges with an awl, and sewing them together with strong waxed thread. It was my constant companion until I outgrew it and still hangs in my closet.

Village School students went home for three-week vacations at Christmas and Easter and ten-week vacations during the summer. Parents visited the school for Thanksgiving and at graduation. The first time my mother visited, I rushed into her arms and immediately began towing her around to see my favorite things and people. I had never seen her more happy than to share in my own delight. It was hard for us to be apart, but nothing gratifies a mother more than to see her child thriving. When she met Walter Gold for the first time, she took his hand in both of hers as if to say, "Thank you! Thank you! Thank you!"

Vacations with my mother were another matter. It was wonderful to be with her and taste the delights of civilization, but my shyness returned as soon as I left the familiarity of the Village School and the outside world was increasingly appearing as a foreign land to me. The Village School ran a camp during the summer and that was where I belonged. It had truly become my home.

One of the things that Walter Gold learned about villages around the world is that all adults take part in their governance. The more important the decision, the more mandatory their involvement. This was true even for societies with chiefs and big men, who might seem able to push others around but in reality were firmly beholden to their so-called followers. In some cultures, the ritual for becoming a chief was to heap abuse on him, as if to say, "Use your power wisely! We can take it away as easily as we bestowed it!"

The great danger of village life was to be pushed around and taken advantage of. Over immense spans of time, villages that succumbed to infighting fell apart and those that avoided infighting survived. The villages that Walter Gold observed and studied were like polished stones that had been perfected by this process. Someone who tried to get their way in a village was like a disease trying to invade an organism with a well-developed immune system. The defenses weren't perfect, especially against the most artful self-serving strategies, but they were pretty darned good and kept people operating in solid citizen mode most of the time.

Many people today look upon the social control of village life as an unwanted restriction on their freedom, but it is difficult for us to fathom the degree to which members of villages depended upon each other in the past. Back then, you might need to rely upon your neighbor to watch your back in battle, to share food during a famine, or to take care of your children if you died. If your neighbor misbehaved, there were no police to intervene on your behalf. Village life revolved around trust, and social control is liberating, not restrictive, when it is understood as a guarantor of trust.

Besides, the hair trigger sensitivity against bullying created an odd kind of personal freedom within villages. The cardinal rule was not to act superior and boss others around, so people tended to mind their own business on matters that didn't impact the welfare of others. Communal values and stubborn independence coexisted like a Yin and Yang that kept village life on an even keel.

Something that Walter Gold discovered to his surprise when he returned to Harvard after the war and began to study villages as a scholar was that American democracy was founded upon village life. The first Englishmen to colonize North America thought that they would rule over the Native Americans, like the Spanish conquistadores in Central and South America. When that didn't work, they tried to recreate a feudal society by importing British laborers, who were housed in barracks and forbidden to leave upon pain of death. But the laborers had other options. They could slip away to become pioneers or join other groups that gave them more say. In just a few decades, Jamestown and the other colonies were forced to become more egalitarian to survive. They became like the villages of the Native Americans and tribal people around the world, even though that's not how they started out. When they grew and combined into a federation, they retained the Yin and Yang of communal values and stubborn independence.

At the Village School, Walter Gold took equality one step further. Not only did the adult staff function as a society of equals, but the students were admitted into the society when they turned thirteen, which marked the onset of adulthood in many traditional societies but had become part of an extended childhood in modern life. All decisions were made by groups that included student representatives with an equal vote. Simple decisions were quickly made, in part because group leaders could be trusted to make the right choice on behalf of the school. More difficult decisions were settled by a process in which every group member was required to state their view. If a consensus could not be achieved, then the decision-making circle was widened. The most important decisions were made by the whole school, and even the younger students were swept into the conversation. In some ways this process seemed inefficient. Weeks might be required for a consensus to emerge. Viewed another way, however, it concentrated the mental resources of the group on the most important concerns and provided a more intense education on civics and moral values than any book-learning experience. One might not agree with a given decision, but one couldn't complain about the fairness of the decision-making process.

When I turned thirteen, my new adult status at the Village School was compounded by my new knowledge of the fortune that I was to inherit from my father to combat his evil empire. In my own mind, this set me apart from everyone else and not in a good way. I didn't feel superior, or lucky, or entitled. I felt confused and afraid. Something great was expected from me and I felt inadequate to the task. It was a new situation, unlike any I had encountered before, and given my pensive nature, my response was to withdraw. This one would have me brooding for a long, long time.

I had no one to talk to about it. My mother evidently thought that while I needed to be told on my thirteenth birthday, nothing more needed to be discussed until I became older. Also, she was moving on with her own life. When I was twelve she met a doctor specializing in cancer treatment named Sean Gaston, and was preparing to marry him when I turned thirteen. Comparing Sean with my father, she used to joke that he cured cancer rather than being one. Bald and always impeccably dressed, he combined compassion with a no-nonsense attitude required for his profession. The only thing that could anger him was a job poorly done. I quickly learned to love him, along with their two children, Jessica and David, who were born in short order. But my mother's engagement with Sean made me feel even more alone in the quest that she had set me upon.

To make matters worse, it quickly dawned upon me that what I had just learned had probably long been known by my teachers and perhaps even some of my fellow students. The facts were too juicy to be kept secret. The terms of the divorce settlement had made the newspapers. The rest of the world quickly forgot but the local grapevine would keep the gossip alive. Walter Gold undoubtedly knew most of all. I sometimes caught him looking at me with a strange expression, as if watching the figure of a tragic play. Maybe the distance that I felt from some of my peers was not due to my shyness but the fact that they knew my fate would be completely different from theirs. I had my entire past life at the Village School to reinterpret!

To make matters still worse, I was starting to grow from a tall, scrawny funny-looking kid into a tall, lean good-looking man. It might sound absurd to describe my adult form as a liability, but for me it added to an unshakable impression that I was a fraud. If my outside was like my inside, I would be a thin spectacled scholar, not the captain of the football team or a lady killer. All eyes turned to me as if I must be a decisive leader, when at decisive moments it was a struggle for me to even utter a sentence! As for the girls at the Village School, I fell in love with every pretty shape and face and they seemed to look longingly at me, but the idea of stealing a kiss from one of them filled me with terror.

More than ever, I sought solace from being outdoors. Nature didn't judge me. It was outdoors where I could forget my future and dwell in the moment. Also, it was outdoors where I felt capable, befitting my outward form. I might be socially awkward and only a B student, but I could ride a horse, scale a rock wall, navigate off trail, and ski like the wind.

When I was fourteen, Walter Gold approached me with the offer of working at the Village School during the summer rather than attending camp. Since I had become physically strong and demonstrated such a passion for the school, I would work alongside the adult staff. My room and board would be paid, along with a modest salary. I immediately accepted and proudly told my mother that I had become self-sufficient and did not require support from my endowment. I spent a glorious summer clearing land, helping to build a new house, and working the farm. I will always remember the euphoria of hard work drenched in sweat on a hot day, splitting wood or throwing hay bales onto the bed of a truck.

The adults began to treat me less as a student and more as a peer during that summer and the ones that followed. They were an odd lot. Some were college educated, while others were from local stock who could build, fix, or grow anything but seldom opened a book with their calloused hands. Their differences made for spicy conversation as we worked together. The locals ribbed the scholars for their lack of real-world knowledge. The scholars ribbed the locals for their lack of book knowledge. The underlying message conveyed through humor, in classic village style, was "You're not superior to me!" Everyone admired Walter Gold, who was as skilled at swinging a hammer or scythe as discoursing on Plato or John Dewey.

This "You're not superior to me!" attitude also helped me to feel at ease. I didn't know if they knew I was to become a multi-millionaire, but if they did know it wouldn't make any difference to them. They would hold me to the same standards as everyone else.

One thing that united everyone was our mutual love of the outdoors. The locals came from families that had been hunting, fishing, trapping, and wayfaring for generations. Most of the scholars had come to work at the Village School in part to indulge their passion for outdoor recreational sports such as skiing and rock climbing. They invited me to join them on adventures during their free time, which went far beyond what was offered to the students at the Village School. Starting that summer and for the rest of my time there, I became an accomplished hunter and tracker. If you and I were to play hide and seek in the woods, I would find you immediately because every one of your steps would leave traces clear to my eyes. I learned how to orient off trail and endure cold and hunger. I became an expert climber and skied the mountains in winter, leaving tracks like ribbons in the virgin snow. I learned how to fix cars and farm equipment, and became as comfortable hanging out with the locals in their dark taverns after our adventures as in the classroom discussing book knowledge.

Another common denominator among the young men at the Village School was wrestling. One of the locals won the state championship in high school and one of the scholars belonged to a Division I team in college. They would square off during breaks from work and teach others their moves. I was never able to beat them but I learned to handle myself pretty well and lost my fear of physical confrontation when it couldn't be avoided, such as the occasional bar fight.

My physical growth continued and by the time I graduated from the Village School I reached my final height of six feet and four inches, a full head above most of the adults. Along the way, my friends bestowed upon me the affectionate nickname of Abe, for Abe Lincoln. The resemblance wasn't that great. I did have his tall lean frame and my rustic life at the Village School did resemble his rail splitting youth in Illinois, but I didn't have his face. Abe was regarded as ugly and an embarrassment to the office of president in his day. Once, when accused of being two-faced, he quipped, "If I had two faces, do you think I'd be wearing this one?" We love Abe's face today because of what it stands for. If you could separate a person's face from what it stands for, mine would be called more handsome than Abe's. At the time, I would have given a lot to be uglier. Like my stature, my good looks made me feel like a fraud. What people took me for bore no resemblance to the way I felt on the inside. Later in life, I realized that beautiful women often have the same problem. Their looks make them strangers to everyone around them.

I suspect that the main reason for my nickname was my serious demeanor. There was something serious about Abe Lincoln. Even though he had a great sense of humor, there was a lot on his mind. Abe didn't get blasted on weekends or carry on with his secretary. The world was pressing down upon him too much for that. Looking back, I think it was the weight I felt pressing down upon my shoulders that reminded people of Abe.

In my senior year at the Village School, I took the tests required to apply to colleges and applied to Harvard, Yale, and Princeton, thinking that this was how I must prepare to combat my father's evil empire. When I informed Walter Gold of my plans, he gently suggested that I should aim a little lower, just in case, and pick a college where I knew I would be happy. Somewhere in close proximity to mountains, perhaps? I therefore added the University of Wyoming to my list. Sure enough, my test scores were mediocre and the Ivy League schools were unimpressed with my skill set. The Village School had taught me many things but grooming me for the elite colleges was not among them. I would be attending the University of Wyoming.

My last summer at the Village School was bittersweet. It was the perfect life for me and I wanted nothing more than to stay. I had become family. I could join the staff and bestow my fortune upon the Village School. Yet all of us knew that something else awaited me. When it was time to leave, everyone crowded around me for an embrace. I felt awkward with my height, bending down as if they were children. Walter Gold was the last to embrace me and then held me at arm's length, looking deep into my eyes with his own, as if to communicate something that was beyond words.

From the Village School I paid a brief visit to my mother and Sean before heading west. It was great to drop in for a few days. My mother said that she always felt complete when I came home, as if happily-ever-after had already arrived. She seemed to think that her role in combating my father's evil empire was finished when she set my own quest in motion. As far as she was concerned, I had grown into a fine young man and had been inculcated with values at the Village School that would enable me to combat my father's evil empire with the fortune that was compounding itself by the day. What I would have given for even a small piece of her peace of mind!

The only advice that my mother gave me as I left for college was delivered with a laugh as she wrapped herself around my waist.

"Whatever you do, *don't join a cult!*"

4

Howard Head's Cult

I don't know if it's what my mother intended, but the Village School made me a stranger in my own land. Leaving it was like entering a carnival, with blaring music, bright lights, crowds of people, and barkers everywhere, shouting to sell you their useless activities and wares. At first it was dazzling but quickly became bludgeoning. Up to now, I could always escape back to the Village School. Now the carnival had become my permanent home.

Not only had the Village School become a part of my past, but everything that I loved to do there seemed like something I should put behind me. I took the path that my mother set me upon seriously. She had evidently encountered a great evil in the form of the Objectivist movement, started by Ayn Rant in the name of my grandfather, and then turned into a world-conquering empire by my father. She had escaped from the movement at great cost to herself to protect me, her precious son. She had also stolen a portion of the empire's treasure, not for our comfort, but to bring about its downfall. And I was the person who was supposed to lead the charge.

The only weapon that she equipped me with was the upbringing of the Village School. True, that upbringing had turned me into a strapping young man who stood literally head and shoulders above most other men. Wherever I went, heads turned in my direction.

Women couldn't take their eyes off me. Some tried their best with furtive glances. Others just stared with undisguised sexual interest. Men also couldn't take their eyes off me, but for a different mix of reasons. Who was I? A rival? A celebrity? Someone to follow into battle? Every moment that I spent in the company of others conveyed the message that some kind of greatness was expected of me.

In the days of old, leading might have been as simple as grabbing a sword and galloping off on a horse. Now something else was required for me to become a leader and I didn't have the slightest idea what it might be. My father had also been born with a path to follow and had become a victorious emperor. No doubt it required talent and hard work, but my father's path was easier to follow than my path for a simple reason. His path was paved with gold. Every step along the way was greeted with applause, which ceased whenever he stepped off the path. His path was one of least resistance. I had no such encouragement. No mother to teach me a catechism. No adoring group of disciples. No powerful people eager to be told that their desires for themselves are morally pure and will also improve the common good. Just me, a young man who experienced a joyous boyhood, inside a body that looked like it could hoist the world upon its shoulders.

While my father was greeted with applause at every step along his path, I was greeted with applause at every step *off* mine. Even before acquiring a fortune at the age of twenty-one, I could start tasting the pleasures of modern life right now. Someone with my body and face but a different mind could have their pick of women and could become a big fish among men in some small pond. With the money I would inherit, I could have a mansion on every continent and a yacht to sail between them without working a day of my life. I had to forsake these temptations to follow my path.

It wasn't even correct to say that I was on a path with temptations on both sides. Imagine being dropped by a helicopter into a pathless wilderness. There is no pre-existing path to follow. You must blaze your own path. The Village School had equipped me with those skills. Drop me in an actual wilderness of mountains and forests and I could find my way out with a full belly. Now I needed to find my way out of the wilderness that modern life had become, so that others could follow the path that I blazed. But my wilderness skills seemed useless for modern life. I needed to acquire a new set of comparable skills, which presumably could be learned at college. My mother chose the Village School, but it was up to me to choose a college. I chose what I thought were the best – Harvard, Princeton, and Yale, my father's alma mater – but they didn't choose me. So now I was boarding a plane to attend the University of Wyoming, a run of the mill state university, chosen at the suggestion of Walter Gold because it was close to mountains and actual wilderness.

This did not seem like an auspicious beginning. I was not attending college to hone my existing wilderness skills, but to learn some new ones. I resolved to resist the temptations of the mountains surrounding Laramie, Wyoming, just as I was resisting the temptations of the flesh. I was going to college to study.

My trip to Wyoming was the first time I had traveled by air. This was such a common part of modern life that my mother just dropped me off at the airport, assuming I would know what to do, but every step of the check-in procedure was filled with uncertainty. I felt like an idiot as the attendants told me what everyone else in line clearly already knew. Their body language conveyed mild discomfort that someone in their midst didn't know the right moves. Something was wrong with me. I absurdly toyed with the idea of speaking in a thick accent to explain myself to these strangers, who I would never see again. I'm not simple-minded, I wanted them to know, I just come from a country where they don't have airplanes!

When I finally boarded the plane, I discovered that my seat next to the window was impossibly small. It was small for a normal person, but I could barely fit into it and I had to tuck my knees under my chin. Thankfully, I didn't get motion sickness and I quickly acclimated to the concept of hurling through the air far above Earth's surface. It seemed as if I could watch the cloud formations and land below forever, even though no one else gave them a glance. Even I tired and dozed as we traversed the flat Midwest, but when the mountainous terrain of the west began to appear, I was all eyes. These mountains were much taller and more majestic than the Adirondacks. The Adirondacks were thrust up from Earth's crust earlier than the Rockies and millions of years of erosion had worn their once sharp peaks into the stooped shoulders of an old person, the tallest a mere mile high. The Rockies were still young and strapping. Their tops were bare rock with sharp ridges, already capped with snow in September, and their alpine zones had an open meadow-like quality unlike anything I had experienced in the Adirondacks. How I would love to lose myself in those mountains, hunting elk much larger than whitetail deer, catching trout much larger than brookies, climbing their rock faces, skiing down their slopes of virgin powder snow, and gazing over their vistas from peaks that loomed above the plane as it descended to the Laramie airport. But I did not come here to lose myself in the mountains. I came to study new things.

The University of Wyoming wore its cowboy heritage proudly. Its logo was a rodeo cowboy riding a bucking bronco, one hand on the reins and the other holding his hat up high. It was founded in 1886, when Wyoming was still a territory, and the first building was constructed in a monumental style out of white granite from a nearby quarry. It was built with pride that the sons and daughters of Wyoming need not return east to become educated. The first building was still the centerpiece of the campus and will be standing a century from now, if American civilization lasts that long. The same could not be said for the newer buildings, which looked ephemeral by comparison. The good citizens of Wyoming held tight to their money and gave little in taxes. Their credo was that the best government is no government. Hence, the newer buildings were thrown up to provide dorm, classroom, and laboratory space as cheaply as possible. Durability and aesthetic appeal were luxuries that could not be afforded. When I arrived, it boasted 7,000 students and had a decent reputation among state universities, whose legislatures were similarly begrudging for the most part. About half of the students were Wyoming residents, the grandchildren of ranchers, miners, and adventurers who settled the west. Many who came from elsewhere were drawn less by the University's academic reputation than the glorious outdoors. As I explored the campus upon my arrival, some of the students were dressed in a western style but others had purchased their clothes from the outlets that can be found clogging the arteries of any US city, or indeed any city in the world.

Banners directed me to the Union, where the many clubs and other organizations on campus had tables set up to attract new members. Outdoor clubs, team sports, fraternities and sororities, the debate club, Campus Crusaders for Christ – an entire bazaar of distractions that I would need to avoid to concentrate on my studies. Still, it was fun to window shop and it afforded an opportunity to talk with some of the girls staffing the tables. One table had the enigmatic name "The Secret of Life Club."

"What's that?" I asked a girl staffing the Campus Crusade for Christ table nearby.

"Oh, that," she laughed. "That's a bit of a cult. Howard Head and the Secret of Life." The last sentence was uttered in a zombie-like voice with arms outstretched in front, to giggles from the other Crusaders.

"Really!" I smiled back. "My mother warned me not to join any cults."

"Well, stay away from that one. They think they can explain *e-ver-y-thing*." The last word was sarcastically drawn out, syllable by syllable, while she made spiral motions with her fingers in front of her face to indicate pinwheels for eyes, to more giggles from the other Crusaders.

I politely accepted brochures for their club and edged closer to the Secret of Life table. It was staffed by two boys and two girls who appeared to be more interested in having fun with each other than recruiting new members. Their main display was a poster with the words "Discover the Secret of Life!" like a movie marquee above a circle of images – a strand of DNA, an amoeba, a frog, a bird, a photograph of an alpine meadow, a man and woman locked in a sexy embrace, a Roman phalanx of soldiers, the Manhattan skyline, and the planet Earth. In the center was a photograph of a face with a comical expression and a halo of fine white hair that made him look a bit like Einstein. To accentuate the halo effect, someone had photo-shopped rays of light, as if his head was discharging electricity. Below the face was a caption that read "Howard Head." The bottom of the poster provided contact information for the club.

What the hell was that supposed to mean?

I gave the table a wide berth and was preparing to exit the Union when Howard Head himself brushed past me. It was hard to mistake him, having just seen his photo. He was medium height and looked to be in his early sixties. He did indeed have a halo of fine white hair that refused to lie down on his head. His frame was thin and he walked with a determined stride, weaving between knots of people on his way out of the building. He was dressed sensibly in khaki-colored pants and a red flannel shirt. Curious, I followed behind him. As he made his way across campus, his hair caught the afternoon sun and lit up, as if his head really was discharging electricity. No wonder they photo-shopped his image that way!

Despite my longer legs, I had to walk briskly to keep up with him. His gait was extraordinary. Every now and then he would punctuate his determined stride with a little dance; a hop here or a sideways movement there. For the most part he kept his gaze in front of him, but twice he recognized someone and his arm shot out with a friendly wave. Then, to my astonishment, he approached an outdoor staircase and actually slid down the central handrail rather than taking the steps, sticking his arms out for balance, as if he was a ten-year-old boy. The students nearby laughed at the sight but Howard Head paid no notice. I stopped at the top of the stairs and watched him disappear out of sight.

Howard Head was certainly an odd duck but I had no time for the Secret of Life Club or any other extracurricular activity. I had enrolled in a demanding list of introductory courses to begin my new training. Philosophy, World History, Psychology, and Economics. Like my mother, I took pride in relying upon my father's money as little as possible, but I did allow myself the luxury of a single dorm room, since I did not want the distraction of a roommate. It was tiny and my feet dangled off the end of the bed, but I still took pleasure in lining the bookshelf with my thick textbooks and neatly stocking my desk drawers with office supplies purchased from the University Bookstore. My new life was about to begin.

My first semester at the University of Wyoming was like falling down a bottomless pit, and fifteen weeks is a long time to fall. It soon became sickeningly clear that the Village School had not prepared me for college. Learning at the Village School was like assembling a jigsaw puzzle, piece by piece. The search for each piece was guided by what had already been assembled. Finding the right piece and snapping it into place was accompanied by a jolt of satisfaction and a desire to repeat the experience. The Village School was remarkably good at helping each student assemble their own puzzle.

College was like being asked to memorize thousands of jigsaw puzzle pieces without assembling the puzzle. I couldn't do that, any more than I could memorize the names from a telephone book. I didn't see how *anyone* could do that or why anyone would *want* to do it. Moreover, there was no awareness of the need for each individual to assemble their own puzzle. For the introductory courses taken by the freshmen, hundreds of us were herded into large lecture halls to hear the same lectures and receive the same textbook assignments.

Even worse, my first four courses – World history, Philosophy, Psychology, and Economics – seemed to bear no relationship to each other. They were like four separate boxes of puzzle pieces. The pieces within each box might conceivably fit together, but the ones from separate boxes might *never* fit together. My economics and psychology courses never mentioned history. My philosophy course taught bodies of thought that originated in Europe centuries ago, or in Greece millennia ago, but otherwise didn't mention history either, as if the bodies of thought had some sort of eternal celestial status and had merely been discovered, like stars, during those periods.

Of all my courses, economics mystified me the most. This was deeply troubling because it was also the subject that I assumed I most needed to master to combat my father's evil empire. Our economics professor was the only one who dressed in business attire, as if he was attending a board meeting. On the first day of class, he explained that economics is different than all other branches of the social sciences (he meant superior) because it alone is based on a mathematical theory. In this theory, individual people are like atoms and the economy is a product of their interactions. Just as physicists require very precise assumptions about the properties of atoms to build their equations, economists need very precise assumptions about people. He then proceeded to list the assumptions made by economists about people, under the heading *"Homo economicus,"* as if this was a description of a biological species.

Homo economicus was "entirely self-regarding," my professor explained. This was not exactly the same thing as being selfish in the conventional sense of the word, but it did mean having a set of preferences that remains constant and is not influenced by the preferences of others. A person's self-regarding preferences determine what they strive for. In economic jargon, people attempt to "maximize a utility." To a first approximation, this could be assumed to be monetary gain. It took a long time for my professor to get there, but the bottom line seemed to be that according to this mathematical theory that makes economics superior to all other branches of the social sciences, people only care about making as much money for themselves as possible.

In addition, *Homo economicus* is incredibly smart about achieving its goals. As my textbook put it, "*Homo economicus* can think like Albert Einstein, store as much memory as IBM's Big Blue, and exercise the willpower of Mahatma Gandhi." All of these assumptions enabled economists to write graphs and equations that said something about the economy. My professor wrote one of the most important results on the board in large block letters.

THE FIRST FUNDAMENTAL THEOREM
OF WELFARE ECONOMICS:
LAISSEZ FAIRE LEADS TO THE COMMON GOOD.

These ideas filled me with confusion and anxiety. My economics professor was saying that society works best when people are allowed to make as much money as possible for themselves, unfettered by rules and regulations. That was the creed of my grandmother and father, but they weren't mentioned by my professor or my economics textbook. The ideal Objectivist portrayed by Ayn Rant was nothing like a flesh and blood person. Neither was *Homo economicus*, but the two fictions were also different from each other! My grandmother and father claimed that Objectivist principles were fully supported by science, but they never used a single equation or graph. Economists seemed to use nothing but equations and graphs, and their first fundamental theorem made it sound as if "laissez faire leads to the common good" had the same certainty as Newton's Laws of Motion. How on earth could I stand up to such certainty, when I couldn't even understand the graphs and equations that were filling the blackboard during the first week of Econ 101?

As if my academic problems weren't bad enough, on the third week of the semester, the following item went viral on Facebook.

HOTTEST MAN ON CAMPUS

Ladies! We know you can't stop drooling over John Galt, the freshman hunk who towers over everyone else, but did you know that he's also rich and famous? His father is *the* John Galt, the radio talk show host and political pundit. Rumor has it that a nasty divorce separated our John from his father at an early age but that he gets a sizable chunk of Daddy's fortune when he turns 21. Tall, strong, handsome, and soon to be rich – what's not to like?

Suddenly I was the epicenter of attention. Fraternities invited me to their social events in hope that I would rush them. A sorority tried to organize an event like the television show *The Bachelor*, where contestants would compete for the prize of a hot date with me. One girl sent me pornographic photographs of herself. Since my father was a political lightning rod, both the conservative and liberal political clubs wanted to know where I stood. The basketball and football coaches encouraged me to try out for their teams. Surely someone with my physique must be a natural.

Never had I felt like a fraud in so many different ways! I was failing my own expectations as a student. I would surely fail the expectations of a sports coach, since throwing hay bales is hardly a substitute for throwing a basketball or a football. I was unprepared to argue either for or against any political position or to either critique or support my own famous father. The idea of attending a beer blast at a frat house was foreign to my Abe Lincoln demeanor. And much as I craved sex, the idea of a casual hookup filled me with terror. Even if I could alter my personality and somehow go through with it, she would probably expect me to perform like a porn star, and I had yet to even kiss a girl!

To escape all this unwanted attention, I took refuge in the top floor of the main library, where tables for studying were interspersed among rows upon rows of books. So much information was available electronically that students seldom visited the library any more, which was fine with me. To make extra sure that I wouldn't be bothered, I arranged piles of books around me like a fortress so that no one else could sit close to me, as if I was engaged in an incredibly important research project. More fraudulence. I was merely trying to do my homework. Why was it so difficult, when so many other students seemed to take it in stride?

Whenever I stepped outdoors, the mountains ringing Laramie in the distance beckoned to me. How I wanted to wander their slopes and fish their streams! But to do so seemed like retreating into the past rather than heading into the future. I stoically refused to visit the mountains or to seek any other relief from my studies, but the harder I worked the more I fell behind. No amount of willpower could make up for my shortcomings.

Whenever I encountered Howard Head's name or saw him striding across campus, my thoughts returned to the Secret of Life club. The poster had his face at the center of the wheel of images, as if something emanating from his head could explain everything from DNA molecules to the Manhattan skyline – or *e-ver-y-thing*, as the girl manning the Campus Crusade for Christ table sarcastically put it. Most cults claimed to explain *e-ver-y-thing*. The Objectivists certainly did. The Campus Crusaders wanted me to know that *e-ver-y-thing* could be explained through Jesus. Christianity was not regarded as a cult, but it was when it started and the main difference between then and now was the number of people who believed in it. What exactly *is* a cult, I found myself wondering. Is it possible to explain *e-ver-y-thing* and *not* be a cult?

During an idle moment when I couldn't force myself to study, I looked up Howard Head on the Internet. He was a biologist by training and evidently one of the better known professors on campus. The list of publications on his website was divided into two sections labeled "Biology" and "Humans." Judging from the publications in the biology section, he seemed to study a menagerie of plants and animals. One of his articles was titled "Personality Differences in Trout." What on earth did that mean? The articles listed in the humans section were published in journals that reflected a menagerie of disciplines, such as anthropology, psychology, philosophy, economics, and history. He even seemed capable of holding forth on religion. Maybe he really could explain *e-ver-y-thing*!

The Secret of Life was listed on his website not as a club or cult but a course for non-majors taught during the spring semester. The course description said that the secret of life was evolution, which could be used to understand the length and breadth of humanity in addition to the biological world. The course would provide a broad overview and no pre-requisites were required.

Since Howard Head had published articles in history journals, I plucked up the courage to approach my history professor after class and ask what he knew about him.

"Oh, yes!" laughed my history professor. "I know Howard. He thinks that he can explain *e-ver-y-thing*!"

Now I was thoroughly confused. It was one thing for the Campus Crusaders for Christ to regard Howard as a cult leader. It was quite another for my history professor to agree. Since when was the leader of a cult allowed to hold a faculty position at a state college? If he was a cult leader, how did his articles survive the review process of academic journals, which is designed to weed out bad science and scholarship?

Whatever. I was fighting for my own survival and had more to worry about than Howard Head.

When the fall semester was over, my highest grade was a C+ in World History and I flunked Econ 101. I hadn't made a single friend or done anything to alleviate the stress of studying. I couldn't bear to go home for the Christmas break and the spring semester was bearing down upon me like an oncoming train.

Something had to give. Walter Gold had gently suggested that I select a college close to mountains. In his wisdom, he must have anticipated that college might not start well for me. It was time to act upon his wisdom. On the first day of winter break, after most of the students had left campus, I ambled into Cross Country Connection, one of Laramie's finest outdoor stores. At the Village School we prided ourselves on not buying the fanciest gear, but the high-tech clothing and gear at the Cross Country Connection made me feel like a kid in a candy shop. I had spent almost nothing of my father's allowance and could afford whatever I wanted. The sales staff was highly knowledgeable. They clearly lived what they sold. I peppered a young woman with questions about the wicking properties of the clothing, the backpack frames, and the merits of snowshoes made from tubular metal and synthetic fabrics, compared to warped wood and rawhide. She answered with a perplexed smile, as if wondering how I could be so knowledgeable in some respects and so ignorant in others. Where had I been for the last twenty years of sports technology?

The next morning, I lashed my snowshoes to my backpack and walked, ski poles in hand, to Rt. 130, where I hitched a ride west. A food distribution truck pulled over.

"I'm not supposed to pick up hitchhikers, but get in!" a man with a big belly smiled.

It felt great riding in the cab of the truck, listening to country music and talking about matters that had nothing to do with college or my father's evil empire. I helped him unload his deliveries to the convenience stores along his route and listened to him talk about his time in Iraq and his wife and children, whose photographs graced the dashboard of the cab. He liked his job. He said that he had all the excitement that anyone could want during the first Gulf War and regarded it as a privilege to drive through the spectacular countryside, which he described in poetic terms.

As we approached the Medicine Bow mountain range, my pulse began to quicken. The snow became thicker as we climbed in elevation and the prairie vegetation turned to fir forest. When we crossed a bridge over a mountain stream, I asked him to pull over. My friend was beaming with vicarious pleasure for me.

"It's great to be young!" were his parting words.

I scrambled over the ridge of snow along the road thrown up by the snowplows and to the layer of fallen snow on the other side. It came up above my knees and would be much deeper higher up. I unlashed the snowshoes from my backpack and strapped them to my feet. I shouldered the backpack, slipped my hands through the straps of the ski poles, and followed the stream uphill. I had to admit that the high-tech snowshoes were fantastically light and a big improvement over the wood and rawhide variety. I broke into a run, high-stepping to avoid digging the front of the shoes into the snow and planting my ski poles in front of me to keep balance, laughing with glee. Within minutes I was winded. How had I let myself become physically inactive for so long?

I was also sweltering from my heat-trapping high-tech clothing. I stripped down to a single long-sleeved shirt and continued to make my way along the stream at a slower pace. The water was gin clear and my fisherman's eye picked out the locations where a well-placed fly would likely raise a trout in spring. The air smelled of pine and the track of a rabbit weaved among the trunks. The slope became steeper and a rocky escarpment came into view above and to the north. Thin wisps of clouds raced over the top of the escarpment, even though the air was still where I stood. I left the stream and made my way toward the base of the escarpment. By the time I arrived it was mid-afternoon. The sun had already disappeared to the west over the escarpment, which cast its long shadow over me, but there would still be several more hours of daylight.

I found a spot that offered a good view looking east and prepared to make camp. Using one of my snowshoes as a shovel, I scooped out a shallow cave in the deep snow and lined the floor with pine boughs. I gathered enough dry wood to kindle a small fire at the cave entrance and settled in for the night. I kindled the fire and melted some snow in an aluminum cup to drink. My dinner was a small bag of nuts and dried fruits. I was accustomed to enduring hunger during my outdoor adventures at the Village School and wanted to feel it again. I let the fire die out. I knew that after a period of chill my body would stoke its internal fire.

The sky turned cobalt blue and then black. The stars and moon were even brighter than I remembered from my winter camping trips in the Adirondacks. It must be the higher altitude. It was easy to imagine Earth as a mere speck in a universe that extends beyond end. By the time the sun rose in the east, I had decided two things. First, never again would I deprive my body and soul of the nourishment of the outdoors. Second, I would take Howard Head's Secret of Life course during the spring semester.

The Secret of Life

On January 27, 2011, I filed into a lecture hall with nearly 200 other students to hear Howard Head explain the secret of life. I had no plan for improving my grades during the spring semester but I was in a better frame of mind. After my night on the mountain, I spent the rest of the winter break in glorious outdoor pursuits. To get around, I purchased a beat up Dodge Ram four-wheel drive pickup truck with a cap to store my gear. It was my first vehicle and I developed a great fondness for it.

It was easy to join up with like-minded people for snowshoeing, backcountry skiing, and ice climbing expeditions. They were happy to have an experienced person join them and I was more than happy for the company. They were an eclectic mix of university types, environmentalists, and drifters who were willing to work any job to support their outdoor habit. Everyone got along well on the basis of our common denominator, our love of the outdoors. I might not be making progress defeating my father's evil empire, but at least I was feeding my own soul and doing something that I was good at. I comforted myself with the thought that as a worst-case scenario, I could forget about my father's evil empire and use my millions to support environmental causes.

Howard Head was pacing in front of the lecture hall as the students found their seats. The ceiling lights caught his hair and gave him the radiant glow that he was evidently famous for. He had a funny absent-minded way about him. He was dressed in rumpled trousers, a cotton shirt, and a baggy sweater. One moment he was chatting with a young man who he was about to introduce as his graduate teaching assistant. The next moment he was staring at the floor in front of his shoes, as if lost in thought. Then he was scanning the seats, as if trying to discern who he would be teaching this semester. His eyes drifted to me – unsurprising, since I was the largest person in the room and always looked comical stuffing my oversized frame into those seats, like a normal size adult trying to sit in a chair for an elementary school student. Our eyes met and he acknowledged me with a hint of a smile and a peculiar gesture, touching his index finger to his forehead and then pointing it at me, as if transmitting something from his head to mine.

A final glance at the clock and he called the class to order.

"OK, everyone! Time to get started!" When that didn't work as fast as he wanted, he cranked up the volume on his lapel microphone and theatrically cleared his throat. Now the class was at attention.

"Welcome to … the … *secret of life*!" The last three words were spoken melodramatically with a smile. The students smiled back with quizzical looks on their faces. Who was this guy? A professor or a standup comic?

"I will begin by asking you some questions. How many of you are Freshmen? Sophomores? Juniors? Seniors?" Some students raised their hands in response to each question. Even though this was a 100-level course for non-majors, it was evidently worth the attention of older students, not just freshmen like me.

"How many of you are Biology majors? Psychology? Anthropology? History? Economics, Political Science, or Sociology? One of the humanities departments? School of Management? School of Engineering? A department that I didn't mention?" Once again, at least some students raised their hands in response to each question. That poster with Howard Head's head in the center of a circle of diverse images evidently had some substance to it.

"How many of you regard yourself as political liberals? Conservatives? Libertarian? Hate politics? How many of you regard yourselves as religious believers? Agnostics? Atheists? How many of you accept Darwin's theory of evolution?" Hands went up and down. Their numbers meant little, since many students were unwilling to divulge their various beliefs to a roomful of strangers, but the point was made, to me at least. Whatever Howard Head intended to teach us this semester was meant for everyone, no matter what their backgrounds, interests, or beliefs. As if in answer to my own thoughts, Howard Head brought his list of questions to a theatrical conclusion.

"To all, I say … *Welcome!*"

The next few minutes were spent outlining the mechanics of the class. The graduate assistant was Rick O'Conner, who was one of Howard's graduate students and spoke in an affable Irish brogue. Rick was in charge of a team of eight undergraduate student assistants, who had previously taken the course and were introduced in turn. Six would lead discussion sections and two would help with the analysis of experiments that would take place during the course.

"That's right!" Howard exulted. In this course, we don't just *learn* about science, we *do* it, and *you* will play the role of the guinea pigs in addition to the role of the mad scientist." Howard Head gave a lame caricature of a mad scientist, hunching his back, rubbing his hands together, and uttering a menacing "Moooah ha ha!" The students around me were simultaneously amused and uneasy. What did it mean that they were to become guinea pigs? Would they be forced to do things without their consent?

"Something else about this class is that I don't use a text book," Howard continued. "I use articles from the best popular science magazines, such as *Scientific American*, and from the primary scientific literature – which means articles written by scientists for scientists. This is like teaching you how to swim by pushing you into the deep end of the pool, but don't worry! Every year, most students learn to dog paddle, some become quite graceful, and only a few lie lifeless at the bottom of the pool."

Howard Head laughed at his own joke, while the sense of unease spread among the students. Were they in the right place? This was a 100-level course for non-majors, without any prerequisites. Some of the students were majoring in subjects such as English Literature and were terrified of science. Even the science majors took it for granted that years of training were required to become a scientist. How did

Howard Head propose to treat his students like scientists from the very beginning? It seemed too good to be true. Surely he was promising more than he – or they – could deliver.

"Since you'll be reading material that's over your head," he went on, "I can't expect you to master it, so the tests will be limited to basic concepts appropriate for your skill level." The class heaved a collective sigh of relief.

"In addition, you are required to write a short commentary on every reading assignment, which is due before the reading is discussed in class." Some students groaned. That sounded like hard work.

"Poor wittle things!" Howard Head replied in mock sympathy, to the laughter of some of the other students. "Think of it this way. The essays are useful for consolidating your thoughts and are graded for your good faith effort to understand and discuss the material to the best of your ability. They account for a good chunk of your grade. I have designed this course to give you an intellectual workout in a way that nearly anyone who is conscientious can earn a good grade." The sense of relief in the classroom was palpable. That sounded like a fair deal.

After describing a few more mechanical details, Howard Head declared that it was time to get down to business.

"The secret of life is evolution, but I realize that I have some 'splainin to do to make this sensible to you." Few students caught the reference, but I did and it made me laugh out loud. He was alluding to the old television show *I Love Lucy*, which I used to love watching with my mother. Whenever Lucy had a mishap, which was often, her husband Ricky would look at her reproachfully and say in his thick Cuban accent "Lucy – you have some 'splainin to do!" Howard Head was growing on me. He seemed to have a talent for combining the serious with the playful. The secret of life leavened with *I Love Lucy*.

"Consider life, in all its diversity and complexity. Millions of species, some still present ..." The screen displayed a collage of familiar animals and plants. An elephant. A grasshopper. A redwood tree. A dandelion.

"... and others long gone." The screen displayed a collage of extinct animals and plants. A dinosaur. A trilobite. A fern the size of a tree.

"Every species exists in some parts of the world and not others, such as this salamander species found only on the west side of the Sierra

Nevada mountains in California." The screen displayed an image of a salamander, with its moist skin and bulbous eyes, and a map of California with a colored area representing the only place on Earth where it existed.

"Every species more exquisitely designed than any watch or other human-made device." Howard Head flashed through a series of amazing photographs of animals and plants in action. A peregrine falcon with its wings in a tucked-in posture, hurling itself downward at a speed of over 150 miles per hour and about to hit an unsuspecting duck. A chameleon with its tongue extending longer than its body length to catch an insect. A dandelion seed head with the seeds becoming airborne. A Venus fly trap catching an insect.

"Molecular, physiological and developmental processes so complex that the more we study them, the more miraculous they seem." Another series of photographs displayed a human embryo, a complicated diagram of a chemical pathway called the Krebs cycle, and an artist's rendering of DNA being transcribed into RNA. These images were flashed before our eyes in less than two minutes, but they effectively conveyed a sense of grandeur and wonder, at least to me. I felt a bit as I did staring at the night sky during my night on the mountain.

"Everything known about life prior to Charles Darwin was like so many disconnected puzzle pieces, or hopelessly misinterpreted by religious worldviews. Darwin's theory of evolution provided a key for assembling the puzzle into one coherent picture. I and virtually all other biologists today are busy assembling the puzzle pieces using Darwin's key. You might think that a theory this comprehensive must be complicated, but Darwin's theory is so amazingly simple that it can be summarized in four words." A click of Howard Head's remote device brought the following words onto the screen in huge block letters.

VARIATION
FITNESS CONSEQUENCES
HERITABILITY

"Variation means that for just about anything that can be measured, individuals of a given species tend to differ from each other. Fitness consequences mean that individual differences tend to *make* a difference for survival and reproduction. If you're bigger than me, you might be able to take my stuff. If I'm smaller than you, I might be more likely to survive the winter. Heritability means that offspring tend to resemble their parents. Darwin didn't know *how* they did mechanistically, but *that* they did was a very well-established fact."

Howard Head was taking giant strides over his subject matter. The diversity and complexity of life was covered in a few minutes and now the basic ingredients of evolution were covered in four words, elaborated with a few sentences. In a sense he hadn't said anything new. I had learned this much in my biology classes at the Village School. But Howard Head was claiming an import for the theory of evolution – nothing less than the secret of life – that was new for me. I wanted him to slow down so I wouldn't miss it, but he barreled onward.

"These three ingredients of Darwin's theory are so obvious that they must be true, but they have a momentous consequence. To pick a simple example, imagine a species of moth that varies in its coloration. Some are more difficult to see against their backgrounds than others." The screen displayed a schematic of light and dark moths against dark background, which made the light moths more conspicuous. It also displayed a graph with a bell-shaped curve representing individual differences in coloration.

"Now suppose that predators remove the most conspicuous moths." An animated bird flew across the screen, several of the light moths disappeared, and a second curve appeared that reflected fewer light moths.

"Then the survivors reproduce. If offspring resemble parents, then the average moth in the offspring generation will be *more cryptic* than the average moth that started the parental generation …" A third curve appeared on the screen to make this point. "… and over the course of many generations, the moths will become extremely difficult for predators to detect."

The next image showed a photograph of real tree bark. "How many of you can see the moth in this photograph?" Howard Head asked. The students stared hard, but only a few falteringly raised their hands.

"That's because there *is* no moth in this photograph. It's just a picture of tree bark." Howard Head cracked a big grin while the class laughed at the joke that he had played upon them. "But these next photographs *do* show cryptic species against their backgrounds."

We then watched, riveted, at a real moth against tree bark, a flounder against a sandy sea bottom, an insect that exactly resembled a leaf, the babies of a ground nesting bird species that exactly resembled their pebbly background, and a bright yellow spider that was nearly invisible against the background of a flower. Several seconds were required to pick them out and it was easy to imagine them being missed by a passing predator. It was amazing to contemplate that their coloration had been brought about by the culling action of the predators themselves.

"Notice that these are very different creatures. Insects, fish, birds, and spiders have different genes and physical exteriors. There is a sense in which the physical make-up of the species doesn't matter. As long as the physical makeup results in heritable variation, then it becomes a kind of malleable clay that can be molded by the forces of natural selection. This gives us a kind of instant intelligence for predicting the properties of organisms, knowing only a little about them in relation to their environments."

Once again, Howard Head was taking giant strides over the subject matter and I was struggling to keep up. I sensed that something momentous was at stake. It sounded simple coming from him but I hadn't internalized it and wouldn't be able to describe it in my own words.

"To show you what I mean, I'm going to ask *you* to think like evolutionists, even though I have given you only an ounce of training." His tone had turned serious and I had never seen a classroom of college students at fuller alert. He had a way of looking over his audience as if he was locking eyes with each and every one of us.

"Instead of coloration, let's think about something else – like infanticide. Adults killing babies." A single atmosphere had enveloped the class and there was a small jolt of moral revulsion. What a horrible thing to consider!

"Since the name of the evolutionary game is having babies, it might seem pathological to kill them, but there are a number of environmental contexts that favor infanticide as an adaptation, just like cryptic coloration. With a little bit of thinking, I'll bet that you can come up with them."

Usually students are reluctant to answer questions, especially in a large lecture hall, but a dozen hands shot up almost immediately.

"Like, when there isn't enough food?" ventured one student.

"That's right!" replied Howard Head, with a theatrical bow from the waist and sweep of one arm to the student. "Absence of resources. Natural selection favors parents who maximize their number of offspring over the course of their lifetimes. When times are hard, it is sometimes necessary to cut your losses. What are some other environmental contexts that favor infanticide?"

"Like, when it's born with a defect?" Howard gave another low bow.

"It might sound cruel, but from an evolutionary perspective, the only reason to have offspring is for them to have offspring. If an offspring is unlikely to itself survive and reproduce, then it represents a poor investment of parental resources." I felt another small jolt of moral revulsion from the class. Infanticide for any reason was a heinous crime in our culture, although what was abortion but a form of infanticide? Abortion was legal, but I knew that many of the more conservative and religious students in the class regarded it as a form of murder. Howard Head was talking about killing babies in cold, hard, calculating terms.

"There's one more major environmental context favoring infanticide," Howard said. After a couple of suggestions that he rejected, saying that he would explain why later in the course, a student got it.

"Like, when it's someone else's baby?" Howard made a third low bow.

"That's right! For the most part, evolution is about having and raising your own children, not someone else's. I know that some of you are thinking about adoption as an exception to that rule. We'll get to that – and did you know that adoption occurs in some species besides our own? But in many other species, natural selection has favored adults who kill the babies of others so that they can have their own."

Howard Head concluded the exercise by stretching his arms out wide, as if to embrace the entire class. "Congratulations! I knew you could do it!" he beamed, and the words "Lack of Resources," "Poor Offspring Quality," and "Lack of Genetic Relatedness" appeared on the screen. Then he paused and let the silence linger. I had never seen a lecture with so many mood changes, but the silence indicated that some kind of climax was about to take place.

"Now here's what I want to know: *What ... made ... you ... so ... smart?*" Each word was separated by a pause, as if to let it sink into our heads before the arrival of the next word. "You haven't read anything about infanticide and I certainly hope that you haven't experienced it for yourselves. I have provided only an ounce of evolutionary training, but, like a heat-seeking missile, it enabled you to make very intelligent guesses about the properties of organisms that you otherwise know nothing about. And, as for cryptic coloration and infanticide, so also for an infinitude of other questions that we can ask about life on Earth, or any other planet inhabited by living creatures.

"Why are males much bigger than females in some species, and females much bigger than males in others? Why are some species social and others solitary? Why do individuals of some species age much faster than others?" Each of these questions was illustrated with an image on the screen, as if the parade could go on forever.

"And what about *us*?" Howard Head concluded with an image of a family taken during the early days of photography, all dressed up in their best clothes and staring awkwardly at the camera. "We are also a product of evolution, albeit a very special one. This class will be as much about us as the rest of life, but that's enough for one lecture."

With that, the first lecture of Howard Head's Secret of Life class came abruptly to an end. The students blinked and looked around at each other as if released from a spell. This was different from what most of them expected. The average college lecture is completely impersonal. You struggle to maintain your concentration and even when you become interested in the material, it seldom relates to your everyday life or innermost thoughts. Howard Head barged across that line. Although he didn't say it outright, the subtext of his lecture was "This is important! This can change the way you see everything in the world around you! Not just the birds and the bees, but everything about you and the entire human condition!"

His lecture style was also disturbing. One moment he was making you chuckle with a lame joke or comical gesture, and the next moment he was locking eyes with you and speaking with the intensity of an evangelical preacher, as if your salvation depended upon it. It made you wonder if he was a little bit crazy.

Most disturbing, for me at least, was that Howard Head's first lecture made so much sense. The contrast with the first lecture of my

Economics class during the fall semester was telling. My Econ professor also boasted about a special body of knowledge, but what he said in words about *Homo economicus* seemed like a complete fiction, not to speak of the mystifying graphs and equations. Howard Head used no graphs or equations and his four-word summary of Darwin's theory – variation, fitness consequences, and heritability – was undeniably true. When he talked about instant intelligence he wasn't just boasting. He pulled it out of the mouths of the students on the very first day of class! Since I couldn't deny the truth of those four words, the only question was where they would lead, should I have the courage to follow.

These thoughts must have occupied me more strongly than the other students, because I remained in my chair as they filed out and even as the students for the next class started to file in. I was so absorbed that I didn't even notice Howard Head until a few moments before he left the lecture hall. He had been disconnecting his laptop, gathering his papers, and putting on his coat. He seemed weary and fragile, as if his lecture required a great effort that left him weak. As he made his way up the steps of the lecture hall, he noticed that I was still there and repeated his peculiar gesture with a tired smile, touching his index figure to his forehead and then at me – from his head to mine.

6

Eve

Howard Head's Secret of Life course was the start of my college education. Before, I was like a person lost in a wilderness without any clues for orientation. Attending his first lecture was like stumbling upon a footpath. I didn't know where it would lead, but I still felt saved.

It never occurred to me that my quest to defeat my father's evil empire might begin with the study of nature, where I felt so at home. His whole world was so disconnected from nature that I assumed I must leave my world to enter his. The idea that studying nature might arm me to enter his world was a revelation. After all, Darwin's theory of evolution had tremendous authority in the biological sciences. If that authority somehow extended into the human realm, then I would have a powerful weapon indeed – a veritable Thor's hammer. Without a moment's hesitation, I dropped two courses that I was planning to take and added the two introductory courses required to become a biology major. The only non-biology course that I retained was an introduction to World Religions, just because it seemed interesting.

The lectures for the Secret of Life course were on Tuesdays and Thursdays and my weekly discussion section was on a Wednesday afternoon. Discussion sections of college courses are typically humdrum affairs. Their purpose is to clarify and elaborate on the material presented in lecture. Truth be told, most students and most courses fall far short of the romantic ideal of higher education, as I learned during my first semester. The courses offer disconnected puzzle pieces and the students mostly want to know what will be on the tests. Discussing ideas for their own sake is a rarity and any attempt to get such a conversation going during a discussion section must contend with most of the students glancing at their watches, disappearing into their mobile devices, or walking out.

The atmosphere at the beginning of the discussion section following Howard Head's first lecture was different. His lecture signaled that his course would be unlike the others. Important issues were at stake that had nothing to do with exams or even careers. His whole demeanor suggested that he was offering something of enormous value, like a treasure behind a door. He had only opened the door a crack during his first lecture but that was enough to make the students curious, which was palpable as they found their seats and waited for the teaching assistant to appear. Some of them gave a little start when they saw me, the future multimillionaire and hottest man on campus, who could barely fit into his chair and who nobody could figure out. I had grown accustomed to this reaction as my lot in life.

A woman who looked no older than the rest of us entered the room. She was small in stature, perhaps 5'2," which made her very small in comparison to me. Judging by her clothes, I guessed that she might be a Wyoming native rather than an import such as myself. It was hard to decide whether she was pretty because she made little effort to be. Her straight black hair was tied into an old fashioned ponytail that fell almost to her waist. Her skin was bronze in tone, whether from the sun or from her ancestry I didn't know. She wore no makeup – her only jewelry was a delicate turquoise necklace around her neck. Blue jeans and a pale yellow long sleeved shirt in a floral design clothed her slim body. She moved easily, like an athlete or a dancer.

"Hello, everyone! My name is Eve Eden and I'm your TA for the semester." She responded to the inevitable smiles about her name with a practiced "I know, Mr. and Mrs. Eden couldn't resist naming their daughter Eve."

Eve Eden explained that she was a sophomore who took the Secret of Life course the previous year. It was Professor Head's custom to invite students from past classes to join a team to help teach the current class under the supervision of Rick O'Conner, the graduate student TA, and himself. She loved taking the course and now looked forward to meeting with us once a week. In addition to discussing the material, we would participate in a number of studies that involve taking surveys and playing games that reveal aspects of our personalities and social behaviors. After serving as the guinea pigs for these studies, we would help to analyze them and compare the results with the published scientific literature. In preparation, we were asked to create a code name consisting of the first letter of our mother's first name, the first letter of our father's first name, and the last four digits of our social security number. We should use our code name rather than our real name in all of the studies to ensure anonymity.

"All scientific research on animals and people at this and other universities is carefully regulated and must be approved by a review board," Eve Eden explained. "You are not required to participate and if you elect to opt out you will be given an extra reading assignment. All of our studies have been approved and most of them are enjoyable to take. How many of you like to take surveys in magazines that are supposed to tell you about yourselves?"

Most of the women and a few of the men smiled and raised their hands.

"That's what our surveys and games are like, except that they really do tell you something about yourself."

There was that jab again, implying that Howard Head and his merry band of students were somehow going to give us a glimpse of our own souls.

Next, Eve Eden handed out a survey that measured our knowledge of evolution coming into the course. My parents were so divorced in my own mind that it felt wrong to put the first letters of their first names together as part of my code name on the top line. The survey required about ten minutes to complete and asked questions about my religious and political beliefs in addition to questions about evolution, such as the age of the Earth, whether people coexisted with dinosaurs, and whether people were descended from apes. I had scarcely seen the inside of a church and had no problem answering those questions correctly, but

I had to mark "Almost Nothing" for a question that asked how much I knew about evolution in relation to human behavior and culture.

"Let's share some stories about what we know about evolution and introduce ourselves to each other at the same time," Eve Eden suggested after collecting the surveys. An awkward silence ensued. We were accustomed to stating our names in discussion sections and giving impersonal information such as our majors, but now we were being asked to disclose more personal information such as our religious beliefs. No one wanted to go first. A look of fear flickered across Eve Eden's face and I realized that beneath a veneer of confidence she must be feeling nervous about being thrust into the role of teacher at such a young age.

"OK, I'll go first," I volunteered and Eve Eden flashed me a grateful smile. "My name is John Galt and I'm from back east. My parents aren't religious so nobody told me that evolution doesn't occur, but I don't remember it being discussed at home at all. Everything I know was learned in biology classes at school, but please don't quiz me because I might not remember!"

Laughter ensued. Now that I had broken the ice, the other students felt comfortable sharing their stories and the conversation took on a party atmosphere. A large fraction of students did have a religious upbringing and were taught by their parents and churches to disbelieve evolution. Others, like me, had been taught about evolution in biology classes but not in a way that made much of an impression. One student said that he had learned about Social Darwinism in his social studies class as an ideology that justified cruel survival-of-the-fittest policies such as withholding welfare from the poor and the holocaust during World War II.

After the last student finished, I spoke again.

"Ms Eden …"

"Call me Eve."

"Eve … What about you?"

All eyes were on Eve as she smiled and gathered her thoughts. "Well, in the spirit of full disclosure, my parents are *very* religious, as you might guess from my name. I was taught that Darwin's theory of evolution was the devil's work and everyone in my family and church accepted this as the gospel truth. But I was rebellious and started to question a lot of things in high school. I didn't know what to believe and nothing made sense to me. Then I took Howard's course and ..."

Eve's voice broke and her lower lip trembled. Some of the students cast their eyes downward as she struggled to compose herself. My attention was riveted upon her. What body of information could have such potency? And what kind of intimacy prompted her to call Howard Head by his first name in her emotional state, when she had referred to him as Professor Head earlier?

"... a lot of things came together for me."

Our hour was up and I was surprised when Eve approached me as the other students filed out of the room. The difference in our size was comical. She had to tilt her head back just to talk to me.

"Thanks for breaking the ice."

"No problem. Thanks for sharing your story. You got a little intense toward the end."

"Yeah, well, that's how I get sometimes."

Then our eyes locked. Her lower lip began to tremble again. I found myself studying her in minute detail. Her delicate nose. Her brown eyes. Those trembling lips. Her high cheekbones. The wisps of hair that had escaped being gathered up in her ponytail. Her ear lobes and the line of her jaw. The veined blue turquoise pebbles around her smooth neck and the points of her collar bones. Her breasts and lean body beneath the yellow fabric of her shirt. I felt drawn to her like a meteor hurling toward Earth. My waist started to bend to bring my face closer to hers. The faint smell of her body was delicious. Her eyelids lowered. Her lips parted to reveal the edge of her white teeth. She began to raise herself up on her toes. Then we snapped out of it at the same instant and backed away, flustered, averting our eyes to compose ourselves.

"Yeah, well, your intensity appears to be contagious!" I joked in a brave attempt to return our conversation to normalcy.

"I guess! Well ... see you in class tomorrow." We went our separate ways.

Far from distracting me from my studies, my encounter with Eve redoubled my interest in Howard Head's Secret of Life class. Her testimony strengthened my own sense that I had found a path worth following. That the same path might free me from my lonely existence was completely unexpected. Eve's features had become etched into my brain. For the first time in my life, everything that I longed for appeared attainable by following the same path. No one had a greater incentive to study than me.

I returned to the top floor of the library, where I had spent so many unhappy hours during my first semester. As before, it was nearly deserted. So much information was available in digital form that most students acted as if libraries were obsolete. If they entered at all, it was to use the kiosks of computers located on the ground floor. The table that I had used on the top floor was at the end of a corridor of bookshelves facing a blank wall to avoid distractions. Now I chose a different table facing a floor-to-ceiling window with a view of the campus below and mountains in the distance. I pulled the table a few feet back so that I could stand in front of the window when I wanted to stretch my body. As before, I assembled a wall of books on the table surrounding my workspace to deter other people from sitting next to me. I also wrote "Please Leave" on a piece of paper so that the custodial staff wouldn't dismantle my wall to replace the books on the shelves. I wanted them to think that the books were being used for some incredibly ambitious research project.

The daily routine that I developed involved waking in time to eat and make my first class at 10:05. After my last class in the late afternoon I ran errands and ate a second meal. Then I went to the library for a glorious stretch of uninterrupted time from early evening to the wee hours of the morning. I got to watch the rotation of the sun, moon, and stars over the distant mountains and the bustle of campus life through my window. I alternated sitting with pacing the long corridors of books, so narrow that they could barely accommodate my shoulders, or leaning against the window, my hands high above my head, to stretch my body. On weekends I climbed into my truck and disappeared into the mountains to refresh my body and soul with an outdoor adventure, either by myself or with the other outdoor addicts that I had met.

Little did I know that by removing myself from campus life I was contributing to the legend of John Galt that was forming on campus. The burst of interest in me at the beginning of the school year had subsided but my story was too juicy to be forgotten entirely. If you asked the famous question "Who is John Galt?" on the UW campus, most students could tell you that I was the son of *the* John Galt; that I was estranged from my father for obscure reasons; that my father's empire would nevertheless make me unimaginably wealthy at the age of twenty-one; that I was a chick magnet but had not had a single hookup; that I showed no sign of being gay either; and that I had rejected every offer to become involved in team sports or fraternal organizations. Some might know that I was a skilled outdoorsman. Nobody knew my abysmal academic performance and the terror that I experienced during my first semester, feeling like a fraud in every way. To them, I seemed like some god-like personage who couldn't be bothered with the petty affairs of earthlings. That impression was reinforced when I adopted the top floor of the library as my headquarters. The few who ventured onto the floor would encounter me stalking the aisles or at my seat with my back to them surrounded by my wall of books. The sign "Please Leave" was interpreted as an order for them to leave rather than a request for the custodians to leave my wall of books. And every time I stretched my body at night in front of the window, feeling very much alone, my giant frame was silhouetted against the light for all the campus to see, like Batman above Gotham City!

One group of people who couldn't leave the top floor of the library was the custodians. At first they were deferential but when they found me easy to approach we would enter into conversation, which I found a refreshing break from my studies. I enjoyed listening to their stories and they were amazed that I paid them any attention at all, since most college students act as if custodians are beneath their notice. Soon they began bringing their friends during their work breaks, who told their friends that they were pals with the legendary John Galt. Before long, I was greeted by hearty handshakes and shouts of "Hey, John! How are ya!" from the custodial staff on campus, which added to my legendary status among the students. John Galt. Hero of the common man. Pondering the secret of life with his titanic intellect from his fortress of solitude above the UW campus.

Actually, if you took away "hero of the common man" and replaced "titanic intellect" with "titanic desire," that description wasn't far from the truth. I had created a fortress of solitude on the top floor of the library and I was pondering the secret of life as if my own life depended upon it.

My first breakthrough came like a thunderbolt as I was doing my homework surrounded by my wall of books. To construct my wall, I had chosen single books from all over the library because I didn't want to leave any conspicuous gaps on the shelves. I amused myself by reading their titles and flipping through their pages during study breaks. "Ritual and Belief in Morocco." "The Irrational Augustine." "Himalayan Polyandry." Who would spend years writing books on such esoteric subjects and who would read them? A glance inside the front covers confirmed that almost no one had checked them out. Some of them seemed absurdly specialized, such as "A Small Town in Medieval England: Godmanchester 1278-1400," "The International Legal Status of Austria 1938-1955," or the hilariously titled "The Many Panics of 1837." Given that these were more or less a random sample of the tens of thousands of books lining the shelves of the library, it seemed as if scholarly book writing might just be the most wasteful activity on Earth.

Then it hit me that all of these books had one thing in common: A deep commitment on the part of the authors to tell the truth about the particular corner of the world that they were writing upon. And not just the authors. The readers of each book might be small in number, but they, too, were passionate about getting all the details right. Before each book could be published, it was checked from stem to stern by other experts on the same subject. Only with their blessing could the book be published to be read by their tiny audiences.

This truth-seeking process, which took place for each of the tens of thousands of scholarly books on the library shelves, stood in stark contrast to the mosaic artistry of my grandmother and father. For them, a truthful detail was just a tile to be used, clipped, or exchanged for a bald-faced lie in the construction of their stylized universe. If there were no scholars and everyone practiced mosaic artistry, then the truthful details of the past and present would be irretrievably lost.

Alarmingly, my grandmother and father were by no means alone in their craft. Religions were also stylized universes, as I was learning from my "Religions of the World" class. The most striking aspect of a religion to a nonbeliever is its flagrant departures from factual reality, something that the believers are somehow willing to overlook. Truth be told, every human being is a mosaic artist in one way or another, selectively remembering and clipping the truthful details of the world, consciously or unconsciously, for their own purposes. No one is a natural born truth-seeker and anyone who tried would most likely fail because an entire culture of scholarship is required to establish norms of truth-seeking and hold everyone accountable. It takes a village to be a truth seeker.

These thoughts, which came crashing upon me all at once as I was sitting in my chair, gave the authors of my wall of books a nobility and even a holiness that few people attribute to scholars, least of all the scholars themselves. If factual knowledge about the world is sacred, then scholars are the monks, their books are the sacred texts, and I wanted to join the order. Whatever I did to combat my father's evil empire would adhere to the factual details of the world. I would not become a mosaic artist. To make good on this pledge, I could not act on my own. I must become part of the Cult of Scholars, as I now began to regard it, feeling compelled to capitalize the words to reflect my newfound reverence. My mother had warned me against joining any cults, but this was one that I was willing to join and even – in my eighteen-year-old imagination – to defend with my life. I began to picture myself as Luke Skywalker from *Star Wars*, dressed in a monk's robes and armed with the light saber of factual knowledge.

As fanciful as this might seem, treating factual knowledge as sacred did arm me with a weapon that I could use against the Objectivist empire, if evil it proved to be. Its biggest falsehood, like the energy source pulsating at the center of the Death Star in *Star Wars*, was to adopt the name of Objectivism, as if everything about it could be justified by rationality and science. Since my grandmother didn't invoke any gods and scorned conventional religions, the only other basis of authority that she could claim was rationality and science. Yet, this was only a stage prop. She worshiped modernity but knew nothing about science. Her idea of rationality was the constructions that she would spin from her swiveling chair, leading to utterances such as, "There are no conflicts of interest among rational men." She made no efforts to engage with scientists or scholars, who in turn had few reasons to pay attention to her, especially when her movement was small. As my father expanded the empire, he moved away from the atheism and philosophical pretentions of his mother and adopted his good old boy style of appealing to the masses, including Evangelical Christians, by triggering their emotions. He seldom used the words rationality, science, or even Objectivism. But that was the name of the movement and that was the authority that he would need to fall back upon if his stylized universe came under attack. For my part, if I joined the Cult of Scholars, I could claim to be the rightful heir of Objectivism because everything I said *would* be based on rationality and science, to the best of our current knowledge.

These thoughts were so powerful that I spent the entire night in the library working them out while pacing the narrow aisles between the bookshelves, passing the thousands upon thousands of scholarly books, each a vessel of sacred knowledge. Soon I realized that my breakthrough, powerful as it was, would need to be followed by other breakthroughs. There is a reason why all of us are more naturally inclined toward mosaic artistry than to truth-seeking. Mosaic artistry, by its very nature, is *oriented toward a purpose* – to construct a set of beliefs that will *animate action*. When we fall under the spell of a powerful stylized universe, we arise each morning brimming with purpose, firm in our belief that our efforts will contribute to a higher good. Every important falsehood contributes to that impression. This means that mosaic artistry, the process of constructing a stylized universe, is not inherently good or evil. What makes a stylized universe good or evil *depends upon what it motivates us to do*. This insight, which came crashing down upon me along with so many others that night, went a long way toward explaining the crazy mix of good and evil actions motivated by religions, as I was learning in my "Religions of the World" class or by listening to the daily news, for that matter.

When I judged my father's empire by its actions, I could see grounds for agreeing with my mother that it was evil. Its artful blend of fact and fiction deluded people into thinking that the single-minded pursuit of their own welfare was also best for society as a whole. That's why someone as morally pure as my mother as a young woman, along with legions of other optimistic young people, could be seduced by it. My mother wasn't selfish when she encountered the Objectivist movement. She saw herself as a pilgrim helping to establish a new and benign world order. For that matter, even my grandmother, who set the whole thing in motion, couldn't necessarily be accused of selfishness. As a product of Soviet Russia's ham-fisted style of social engineering, she might well have believed to the depth of her soul that she was working toward the betterment of society. The problem was that her stylized universe, so artfully constructed and presented to the world through The Speech, was immune to disconfirmation. True believers typically benefitted themselves by their actions over the short term, which they regarded as a confirmation of their worldview. Harmful effects on others and unforeseen consequences that might come looping back to afflict even the True Believers over the long term went unnoticed. These cancerous effects of Objectivism were already starting to manifest themselves when I was pacing the library having these thoughts. More and more wealth was being concentrated in the hands of fewer and fewer people. Governments were being successfully branded as evil and the word "regulation" had become a dirty word. Every failure of society caused by the toxic effects of Objectivism was blamed on not applying its principles thoroughly enough. My mother was right to fear that she might be witnessing the destruction of the world. Objectivism was *systemically* evil, judged by the actions that it motivated, regardless of the individual motives of the True Believers.

If I were to succeed at vanquishing my father's evil empire, I would need to replace it with some other guide for *how to behave*. Moreover, my guide would need to be *highly motivating*, capable of getting people out of bed every morning brimming with purpose. Finally, it would need to be *easy for anyone to grasp*. On all of these counts, the Cult of Scholars that I had decided to join was a dismal failure. The tens of thousands of scholarly books that I passed on the library shelves were silent on how I or anyone else should behave in our daily lives. Reading them was anything but motivating and required an advanced education. And the scholars themselves, who I was newly regarding as monks of a Holy Order, would be shocked at the thought of becoming warriors in a battle to overthrow the evil Objectivist Empire!

That was why I knew my first breakthrough would need to be followed by others and why I looked to Howard Head for the next breakthrough. His lectures were easy to understand. Something about them churned the emotions in addition to the intellect. I couldn't yet see how they provided a guide for daily living, but they seem to have that promise.

Then there was Eve. She came from a devout Christian background. Christianity was one of the greatest masterpieces of mosaic art in the history of the world. Yet, she had left that stylized universe and after a period of feeling lost had found something in Howard Head's worldview that she regarded as even better. Assuming that Professor Head had not himself succumbed to the temptations of mosaic art, then Eve was proof that the Cult of Scholars could defeat the stylized universes of the world on their own terms.

I now had two reasons to gaze at Eve during Howard Head's lectures and to engage her in conversation during our discussion sections: As someone who had been saved by evolution and as someone who might bring my self-imposed solitary existence to an end. Although a skilled hunter, pursuing a woman as my quarry was new. I needed to be discreet. Not only must I avoid the impression of ogling her, but there were rules about students having affairs with their teachers. These rules were very strictly enforced for professors and also might apply to Teaching Assistants for all that I knew. Out of the corner of my eye I ogled her at every opportunity. It is typical for students to select a seat at the beginning of a course and stay loyal to it for the whole semester. Eve sat in the front row next to the left aisle so she could get up and help distribute handouts. I chose a seat three rows from the front so I could have a clear view of her profile.

I especially delighted in watching Eve on the move. She seemed especially attentive to what needed to be done and was usually the first of the undergraduate TAs to approach the table in front of the class to pick up a stack of handouts. Then she would race to the top of the aisle, as light as a dancer, and work her way down the steps distributing the pages. I'll never know if it was Eve or the fact that she was the first woman I felt I could draw near to, but I fell in love with her just by watching her move.

I continued to serve as the icebreaker during discussion sections. Soon animated conversation became the norm and even extended past the hour, something almost unheard of. Whenever possible, I attempted to detain her for a few minutes as the other students filed out, always keeping a distance so that I wouldn't fall into her orbit like the first time.

"Eve, you look like you spend time outdoors. What kinds of activities to you enjoy?"

Eve's face expressed surprise, quickly followed by pleasure at being asked a personal question.

"My family owns one of the oldest ranches in Wyoming. I've loved the outdoors since I can remember and my mother calls me her wild child. Horses, hiking, fishing, hunting, skiing – you name it. I have three older brothers, which makes it easy to be a tomboy. I'm even the long-distance snowshoe racing champion of the county, including the men."

"No way! You beat the men at snowshoe racing?"

"Yes," she grinned. "On snowshoes it helps to be small and light."

The fact that Eve shared my passion for the outdoors seemed almost too good to be true.

"I'm a wild child, too! I could challenge you to a snowshoe race!"

"You? Didn't you say that you came from back east?"

"Hey! Not everyone from back east is a city slicker!"

"By the way, I've been wanting to thank you for speaking up so much in class and during this discussion section. I teach another discussion section and getting them to talk is like pulling teeth. Our section is the envy of all the TAs."

"My pleasure. This course is more important for me than you might know."

Then it happened again. Our eyes locked and our faces took on expressions of serious intent that could not find words. This course was important for both of us, even life-saving, which set us apart from most of the other students. Our mutual need created a powerful attraction, on top of the physical attraction that drew me to Eve and perhaps drew her to me. Several seconds elapsed before I again broke the spell.

"What do you know about the Secret of Life Club?"

"Oh, that!" Eve laughed, grateful to be back on safe ground. "It's a club for students who graduate from the course and want to learn more. We get to hang out with Howard and his graduate students ... assist in their research ... do research of our own ... that sort of thing."

"Are you a member?"

"Of course! I wouldn't miss it for the world, especially the potluck dinners at Howard's house every week."

"Do you think that I could join?"

Eve's eyebrows arched in surprise. "Of course! Why not? I didn't think of it before because most students only join after completing the class, but you seem to be a natural. Why don't you come to the next potluck this Friday and I'll introduce you to the others. I'll email you the information."

I left that conversation floating on air.

Eve was not the only object of my attention during the lectures. It was Howard Head who held the key to the Secret of Life. Here is what I started to learn from him, which paved the way for my second breakthrough.

Back in the old days, before Charles Darwin and Alfred Russell Wallace made the scene, the study of nature was a scholarly pursuit, similar to the study of human history and other human-centered topics. It was called natural history and it abided by the same truth-telling norms as the scholarly books that made up my wall in the library. One of the main challenges of natural historians was simply to describe and catalog the many thousands of plant and animal species around the world. Carl Linnaeus (1707-1778), a Swedish natural historian, invented a way of cataloging species that is still in use today. In many ways it is similar to the system for cataloging books invented in America by Melvil Dewey in 1876, which is also still in use today. In the case of the Dewey Decimal System, books are first given a number that assigns them to the broad categories of Philosophy (100), Religion (200), Social Sciences (300), Language (400), Natural Sciences and Mathematics (500), Technology (600), Arts & Recreation (700), Literature (800), and History and Geography (900). Then they are assigned numbers that subdivide each category into progressively finer categories. For example, mathematics, part of the Natural Sciences and Mathematics Category (500), is assigned the number of 510. Geometry, a branch of mathematics, is assigned a number of 516. Analytic geometry, a branch of geometry, is assigned a number of 516.3. Metric differential geometry, a branch of analytic geometry, is assigned a number of 516.37. In this fashion, every book receives a unique number that allows it to be quickly found on a library shelf.

The system invented by Carl Linnaeus assigned each species a place in a nested series of categories: Kingdom, Phylum, Class, Order, Genus, and Species, based on their anatomical similarity to each other. Today we know that species are anatomically similar because they are descended from common ancestors, but Linnaeus had no glimmering of this fact. He and almost everyone else at the time assumed that each species was a special creation of God. Why God had chosen to make species anatomically similar to each other, including the similarity between humans and the great apes – a fact that Linnaeus duly noted by placing them together in the family Hominidae – was not for him to question. A few bold thinkers speculated that species give rise to other species, including Darwin's own grandfather, but they did not unlock the secret of how it actually happens, which is why Darwin's and Wallace's theory of natural selection was so singularly important.

Carl Linnaeus was celebrated during his time as one of the world's great scholars. Jean-Jacques Rousseau said that he knew "no greater man on Earth" and Johann Wolfgang von Goethe wrote, "With the exception of Shakespeare and Spinoza, I know of no one among the no longer living who has influenced me more strongly." The fact that great thinkers about the human condition such as Rousseau and Goethe held a natural historian in such high regard shows that the partitioning of knowledge that we take for granted today did not exist back then.

Great as it was, however, the classification system invented by Linnaeus did little to organize the burgeoning information about all those species of plants and animals that natural historians were accumulating from all over the globe. The same can be said for the Dewey Decimal System. Yes, it can be used to find a book on a library shelf and conveniently locate other books on the same topic, but it is useless for explaining meaningful connections between books that have been placed in different categories. That's why the theory of natural selection, derived independently by Darwin and Wallace and explained so easily by Howard Head during his first lecture, was so singularly important. In a single stroke, Darwin and Wallace had provided a way to *organize* all of the natural history information that had been accumulating around the world. Wherever they turned their gaze – the fossil record, the geographical distribution of species, their anatomical similarities and differences, their development, and their wonderful contrivances that adapted them to their environments – the patterns of information could be explained by the three simple ingredients of variation, fitness differences, and heredity. Never had so much been explained on so simple a basis.

During the same period, scholars of all sorts were refining their abilities to determine the truthful facts of the matter. Instruments were perfected to see ever smaller (microscopes) and more distant (telescopes) objects. Other instruments were developed to measure forces such as electricity that are invisible to our five senses. Procedures were developed to make comparisons that differed in only a few carefully controlled factors (experimental design). A branch of mathematics known as statistics refined the ability to know whether a particular difference could have occurred by chance. In short, all of the instruments and practices that we associate with science began to emerge during roughly the same period as Darwin's and Wallace's theory of evolution. There is one thing that everyone needs to keep in mind, Howard Head thundered during one of his early lectures, with all the melodramatic theatrical techniques that he could muster: *Science is nothing more or less than a highly refined form of scholarship.* The nuclear physicist in her laboratory and the author of "The Many Panics of 1837" in his book-lined office are brethren. They both belong to the Cult of Scholars (my words), honor-bound to tell the truth about the particular corner of the universe that has attracted their attention.

Fast forwarding to the present, the study of life has been transformed several times over by evolutionary theory, providing a way to organize knowledge that goes far, far beyond the classification system invented by Linnaeus. Yet, for complex reasons that Howard Head promised to reveal, the organization of knowledge about humanity had not progressed much beyond the Dewey Decimal System. It was when making this point that Howard Head's theatrics went over the top, his voice at top volume, his arms flailing around him, his eyes peering into our souls, and always that light refracting through his hair as if discharging from his head. *When it comes to knowledge of humanity, the Darwinian Revolution has yet to arrive!*

Other students shook their heads at such moments or laughed to discharge the tension. No wonder that everyone who knew Howard Head joked that he claimed to explain *e-ver-y-thing* and, by this joke, discounted the possibility that he actually could. After watching Howard Head, lecture after lecture, I felt that I was beginning to understand what made him tick. At some point in his career, the realization that what *had* taken place for biology *had yet* to take place for the study of humanity came crashing down upon him, in the same way that the theory of natural selection came crashing down on Darwin and Wallace and my first breakthrough about the Cult of Scholars, I suppose, came crashing down on me. None of these people – certainly not me – were towering geniuses. Attributing a great discovery to the greatness of the discoverer is facile to the extreme. What Darwin, Wallace, Head, and (dare I say it?) I did share was the courage and openness to accept what came crashing down upon us and to work out its consequences wherever they might lead. When Howard Head became maniacal in front of his perplexed students, he wasn't being theatrical. He was actually confessing the intensity of his own thoughts. Realizing this, I could not help but love him for it.

On March 2, 2012, a third of the way through my second semester at the University of Wyoming, I stood at the front door of Professor Howard Head's house with a bag of potato chips in my hand. Eve had emailed me the address and told me to bring something to share for the potluck dinner. I couldn't help but recall the story my mother told me about her first visit to the apartment of Ayn Rant and how the opening of that door seemed like the gateway to a new life. The door opened and

I was greeting by Nancy, Howard Head's wife, who invited me in. She was a plain but friendly-looking woman with short white hair and thick glasses. I would have type-casted her as a librarian, which is exactly what she was. It was a modest home with a combined dining and living room. The dining room table held a stack of plates, forks, knives, and spoons inserted into ceramic mugs, and the potluck offerings. A plastic cooler on the floor held bottles of beer and soda embedded in crushed ice. I could see that this was an arrangement that could be thrown together, week after week, without requiring too much work for anyone.

A couple dozen people were in conversation in the living room area, beers in hand. I picked out Howard Head and Eve immediately, along with Rick O'Conner, the graduate assistant for the course, and several of the other undergraduate TAs. The others were mostly young, an equal proportion of men and women, and an interesting ethnic mix as well, especially for the University of Wyoming, which was not very ethnically diverse. The conversation stopped when I entered the room, as it always did with my huge frame and mysterious reputation. Eve was the person who broke the ice.

"Hey, everyone! I want to introduce you to John Galt, who some of you already know as the most talkative student in Howard's Secret of Life class this semester. John's interest is so exceptional that I invited him to join our group even before completing the class."

Everyone shouted a hello and Howard Head raised his beer bottle with the words "It's the big guy! Welcome!" Then there was a quick round of introductions. When it came to me, I said:

"Well, I'm John and I come from back east but please don't confuse me for a city slicker (laughter). I love the outdoors and I've even challenged Eve to a snowshoe race (more laughter and appreciation that I was already becoming part of their group). I want to thank Professor Head for saving my life, in a way (silence and a bit of surprise that my little speech was taking a serious turn). During my first semester here, I tried as hard as I could to get good grades and ended up pulling a C- average (laughter, a bit of surprise that I would disclose such a thing, but appreciation for my honesty). Everything was so disconnected. That's why I appreciate the main message of Professor Head's course, which is that a single simple theory can explain *e-ver-y-thing*."

Boisterous laughter greeted the end of my speech, by Howard Head most of all. All of them had heard the long drawn out *e-ver-y-thing* many times as a humorous way to dismiss the import of what Howard Head and his Secret of Life class stood for. My repetition of the word instantly made me an insider. Eve was beaming with pleasure.

The rest of the evening was nothing like the soirees at Ayn Rant's apartment that my mother described to me. Instead, it had the easy familiarity of my days at the Village School. Howard Head, like Walter Gold, made no effort to be the center of attention. He did not dominate the conversation and spent much of the evening sitting on the floor, his back against the wall and his legs straight out in front of him, shoes off, absent-mindedly peeling the label from his beer bottle, lost in his own thoughts. His authority was gifted to him by the others. He had no need to take it.

Several of the young men and women were also romantic partners. After the potluck dinner, as we settled down over tea and coffee to continue the conversation, the couples would sit next to each other and hold hands or one would affectionately stroke the hair of the other. These gestures passed without comment as part of a general atmosphere of contentment. Good food, good company, and good conversation about things that matter. What more could anyone want? If only Eve and I could be like those other couples, my life would be complete.

7

The Conquest

"Have you heard of the Lodge?"

"No."

"It's a big old mountain lodge that was bequeathed by its owner to the University. Now it's a biological station. Lots of the biology profs and grad students spend summers there doing research. There are also summer classes for undergraduates. I'm paid to check on it once a month during the winter to make sure that the pipes aren't frozen, that bears haven't broken in, and that sort of thing. Would you like to come with me? My family's ranch is on the way and we can pick up my snowshoes so that we can have that race you keep talking about."

I had heard about hearts skipping beats but this was the first time it happened to me.

"You're on! When do we go?"

"How about this Saturday?"

"Done! Let's take my truck because all of my gear is already in the back."

Eve and I had settled into a warm friendship by the middle of the spring semester. We clearly enjoyed each other's company, had much to talk about, and had the opportunity during the weekly potlucks in addition to the moments after our weekly discussion section. But our relationship fell far short of the closeness that I craved in every way – emotional, intellectual, physical, sexual. It struck me that since leaving the Village School and my brief visit to my mother, I had not touched or been touched by a single human being. A huge deficit had accumulated and whenever I accidently brushed Eve's arm or our fingers met when passing a dish, the sensation was out of all proportion to the significance of the event. Eve's invitation signified that our relationship might be on its way to a new plateau. I would meet her family! We would be alone together outdoors and in a rustic mountain lodge! Sexual fantasies flooded my mind.

Or maybe not. Maybe she was just being nice and had no interest in anything other than a platonic friendship. This business of hunting a woman was driving me crazy! I had no experience to go on and obsessing over every detail was exhausting.

Despite my fears, the joy of riding in my truck with Eve in the passenger seat was something that I could treasure all by itself. She was in a great mood and everything we said was tinged with laughter, from commenting on the country music songs on the radio to our upcoming snowshoe race. It was great to leave the university behind – even the gravitas of The Secret of Life, for that matter – and watch the countryside go by. As we drew near to her family's ranch, she began to prep me for the meeting that was about to take place.

"OK, so here's the score. My family is extremely religious and close knit. All three of my brothers operate the ranch with my father. All of them are involved in their church and I'm certain that my mother will ask you about your religious affiliation within five minutes. *Do not use the E-word*. I can grab my gear and we can be out of there within five minutes."

We turned off the highway and travelled along a dirt road that had been recently plowed with about three feet of snow on each side. I had visited enough farms during my Village School days to know that their state of repair said a lot about their owners. So much effort is required to maintain a farm that any misfortune – an injury, a divorce, an alcohol problem, financial trouble – results in physical disorder. As a farmhouse and cluster of corrals and outbuildings came into view, I could see at a glance that there was something to admire about Eve's family. All of the buildings were well maintained and every tool was in its place.

Four men were standing around a backhoe, presumably Eve's father and her three brothers. They stood about a head shorter than me, well built, with the sons a few inches taller than the father. All four wore Cargill insulated jackets and pants and steel-toed boots, the uniform of a rancher on a winter day. I pulled my truck alongside the backhoe and we climbed out.

"Men, I'd like you to meet my new friend, John. This is my father, Joe, and my three brothers, Mark, Matt, and Luke."

Joseph – the husband of the virgin Mary – and three of the Gospel writers in the order that they appear in the New Testament. A fourth son would have undoubtedly been named John.

"Well, I see that I fit right in!" I observed and all four of the men cracked wide smiles, getting the allusion. Eve stood by my truck and looked at me with an intrigued smile. I approached the backhoe and entered their circle.

"What seems to be the problem?" The four men looked first at each other, then at Eve, who shrugged her shoulders, and then at me. Since when did one of Eve's friends from the university know about backhoes?

"Something about a leaky fuel pump that we're having difficulty figuring out," Joseph replied.

Soon we were in conversation about leaky fuel pumps. I told them that I grew up on a farm and missed the work. Maybe they could use a hand on the weekends?

"Sure, John! We can always use a hand and a strong back!"

Eve's mother came out of the house to say hello.

"Mary! Come meet John, Eve's new friend!" Joe called heartily to his wife.

"John! That's what we would have named a fourth son. How are you?"

"Fine, Mrs. Eden, just fine!" I smiled and took her hand. "What a lovely place you have!"

"Won't you come in for a piece of pie? Eve! Don't just stand there by the truck. Come and help me feed this big boy. He looks hungry!"

Eve laughed and followed us into the house, where she immediately opened cupboards and shelves to set a place for me. Her way of sensing and attending to what needed to be done was one of her most endearing qualities to me.

"Tell me, John, do you belong to a church?"

"Mother! How many times do I have to tell you not to try to convert my boyfriends!"

"Now, Eve, it never hurts to ask."

"The answer is no, Mrs. Eden, but I would love to visit your church."

"See?" Mary Eden said triumphantly to her daughter.

Eve stood between me and her mother while transferring the slice of warmed pie to my plate so we could exchange looks. "What on earth are you doing?" her look seemed to say.

I had plenty to chew on as I ate my slice of pie and drank my glass of milk. Eve said that she had left her church and rebelled in high school but her relations with her family appeared warm and even her scolding of her mother was good-natured. I wasn't putting on an act. Just setting foot on her family's ranch made me homesick for farm life and the joy of physical work. Much as I was nurtured by my mother and the Village School, I often felt that there was a hole in me where a family should have been. Seeing what for all appearances seemed like a strong and loving family made me ache to join it. I even wanted to go to church – not because I was in the least bit tempted to convert, but just to see what it was like, to experience what I was only reading about in my "Religions of the World" class.

Nor did it escape my attention that Eve had called me her boyfriend! My thrill at the label was quickly followed by despair that I was evidently the latest in a long parade of them. Or maybe she had just used the word thoughtlessly. This obsessing over every word and gesture of Eve's was driving me mad!

Eve left the kitchen and returned with a day pack, snowshoes, and ski poles. As we returned to my truck, she told the men that we were going to have a race up to the lodge.

Mark, the eldest brother, replied, "Go easy on him, Eve, he's probably unused to being beaten by a girl. Come back any time, John!"

As soon as we were alone and heading back to the main road, Eve turned to me with an amazed smile. "Do you realize that you won the hearts of my entire family in five minutes?"

"Let's hope that I can sustain it!" I laughed. "Now for the main event – beating you in a snowshoe race."

"Not a chance!" We both smiled broadly at each other. How I wanted to place my hand on hers, but my cursed inexperience and fear of spooking my quarry kept it on the steering wheel.

As we drove toward the lodge, the elevation increased and the snow became deeper – a good four or five feet on the ground and towering over the truck where the plows had piled it on each side of the road. Eve instructed me to turn onto a side road and park at a trail head.

"The lodge is about a mile up this trail, so this can be our race course," she said as she bounced out of the cab with her gear. I fetched my gear from the back. Morning was approaching noon, the air was still, and the temperature was about twenty degrees Fahrenheit, but we still stripped down to our t-shirts in anticipation of the exercise, stuffing warmer clothes into our day packs. We strapped our snowshoes onto our boots and slipped our hands through our ski poles with big baskets and were ready to start.

If you have ever tried to run on snowshoes, you know that it is one of the most demanding of all physical activities. It isn't a recognized sport and is only played by true backcountry people. I never raced at the Village School but I had plenty of experience running on snowshoes just for the fun of it. What makes it demanding is that you have to high-step to keep the front of the snowshoe from digging into the snow. Yet, if you high-step too much, your weight when you land on each foot will cause your snowshoes to sink more deeply into the snow than you want them to. Also, snow is not uniform in its consistency, so you can never predict to what degree it will support your weight. Every step can throw you off balance, which you must be prepared to correct with the placement of your ski poles. The poles have big baskets – the rings with webbing close to their ends – so that they don't sink too deeply into the snow. Someone who can run gracefully for a mile uphill on snowshoes is a true athlete, even if hardly anyone recognizes the fact.

"Ready! Set! Go!"

I sprung forward in a burst of speed, as much to impress Eve as to win a race. I easily outdistanced her at the beginning with my long legs. It felt great to be charging uphill, sucking the brisk cold air into my lungs, my sweat beginning to dampen my t-shirt despite the cool weather. Soon I realized that I would need to slow down to last a mile.

After a few minutes at a more sustainable pace I heard swishing sounds coming from behind and Eve pulled up alongside me.

"Very good! I'm impressed! You really know how to use those things!"

Damn! Not only had she caught up but she actually had enough wind to talk to me! I was breathing too hard for that and I had to concentrate on my balance too much to even look over at her.

"See you at the finish line!" she laughed, accelerating with the ease of a sports car shifting into a higher gear. Now that she was in front of me, I could watch her without losing my balance. Of course, she was only a little more than half my weight, which meant that her snowshoes kept her on top of the snow much more than mine. Smaller and lighter is truly better when you are on snowshoes. In addition, her stride and balance were impeccable, without a single wasted motion. It seemed as if she was levitating uphill. I stopped just so I could watch her disappear around the bend.

After ten more minutes of slogging, I came upon Eve's snowshoes under a huge pine tree with its branches hanging low under their heavy load of snow. Before I could think about where she might be, she called, "I'm up here!" and I looked up to see an enormous wad of snow, shaken from one of the upper limbs, descending onto my face with a splat. Peals of laughter followed as I cleared my eyes to see Eve jump back onto the ground in front of me, as light as a cat. The force of her descent caused her to sink into the snow up to her knees so that her head only came up to my waist. From that position, she lay down in the snow and flapped her arms and knees back and forth, like a little girl, to make a snow angel. Then she closed her eyes and said with a satisfied smile: "I win!"

What happened next was beyond my control. Some beast within me reached down, placed my hands under her arms, plucked her from the snow, and enveloped her in a bear hug as I mashed my face into hers in what had to be the most awkward kiss in the history of the universe. Then the beast departed and left me, John Galt, staring into Eve's face with a terror-stricken look on my own. What had I done? Everything was ruined!

Eve looked at me in astonishment, whether at my action or my contorted face I'll never know. Then she reached her hands behind my head, grabbed my hair in both fists, and pulled me into a kiss of her own. Her legs, which had been dangling vertically, wrapped themselves around my waist.

"What took you so long?" she said when she finished her kiss.

Eve leapt off me and back onto her snowshoes. "To the Lodge!" she shouted, and levitated up the trail. Following her, I emerged from the forest onto as pretty a mountain lake as I have ever seen, with a rocky peak looming above it on the other side. The broad expanse of the lake was frozen with a thick blanket of snow but I could imagine its turquoise water reflecting the mountain and clouds during the summer. Pine trees laden with snow and the bare canopies of aspen trees ringed its edge. To my left, Eve's tracks led to an enormous lodge, a veritable log mansion, and a cluster of other buildings.

The lodge was a magnificent example of the rustic palaces that the timber, mining, cattle and railroad barons built for themselves during the Gilded Age of the late 19th and early 20th centuries. With unlimited money, cheap labor, and stone and lumber already on site, the sky was the limit for what they could create. This one had a huge stone patio in front of the lake that could easily accommodate a gathering of 100 people. Removing my snowshoes and following Eve's footprints, I entered into a central room with cathedral ceilings and animal heads, mounted fish, firearms, and Indian artifacts lining the walls. A wall of windows afforded a view of the patio and vista from the inside. On the opposite wall was the biggest fireplace I had ever seen, built of local stone running up to the ceiling and a mantelpiece from a single great log squared with hand tools, as I could see from the cut marks on the wood. Open doorways on each side wall led to the rest of the mansion.

The sole occupants of this magnificent lodge, one of the most romantic settings on Earth, were two teenagers on fire to make love. Eve had put on additional layers of clothing from her daypack to protect herself from the chill, now that the race was over. I did the same.

"You build a fire while I check for burst pipes and bears," she commanded before disappearing outside. Fortunately, there was every-thing needed to build a fire: logs, kindling, newspaper, and matches.

I built several towers of kindling next to each other with plenty of air space to lay the logs upon. The abundance of air and dry wood created a blaze in no time. A little smoke escaped the fireplace until a draft was established but then it funneled up the chimney. I crouched and warmed myself in the spreading heat, obsessed with images of what was about to take place but also with a gnawing fear.

Eve came charging back into the room and looked at the fire. "Nice! No bear break-ins and no burst pipes. Let's move this couch closer to the fire to trap the heat."

We moved a big overstuffed couch in front of the fireplace, leaving a space of about ten feet to trap the heat. Then Eve disappeared down one of the hallways and returned carrying such a big armful of pillows and blankets that I could barely see her behind her load. She dumped them on the floor between the couch and the fire and we spread them around. Enough heat from the fire was being trapped by the couch to make a cozy nest. We removed our outdoor boots and stepped off the cold wood floor onto the bedding. It was time to make out.

I sat with my back against the couch and Eve straddled my lap to give me a long, delicious kiss. The time had come. I could postpone it no longer.

"Eve …"

"What?"

"There is something that I need to tell you."

Eve sat back with a puzzled look on her face. There was a mood breaker for you.

"What?"

"This …"

"*What?*"

"This …"

"*Come out with it!*"

"This is my first time."

I had heard about a person's jaw falling open in surprise as a figure of speech but this was the first time that I saw it happen. Her eyes bugged out and her jaw dropped open as she looked at me for a few seconds that felt like an eternity.

"Are you gay?"

"No, no, no." A few more eternal seconds elapsed.

"How did you fight the girls off?"

"It's a long story," I laughed weakly.

More eternal seconds elapsed as Eve processed my news. Then a mischievous smile crept upon her lips.

"Well," she said, bringing her face only a few inches from my own and staring directly into my eyes, "it looks as if I am going to be your *teaching assistant!*"

That was funny. And arousing.

Eve stood up and instructed me to do the same.

"Strip."

"What?"

"You heard me. Strip."

Off came my clothes. Windbreaker. Fleece sweater. T-shirt. Pants. Socks. Underpants last. Standing naked in front of her caused me to lose my erection. Eve gazed at me for more eternal seconds. Her face was flushed and her eyes had a smoldering look. Then off came her clothes. Windbreaker. Fleece sweater. T-shirt. Bra. Pants. Underpants. Socks last. My eyes devoured her as we stood facing each other without touching.

"Lie down," she commanded. I did as I was told.

"Prop your head up with a pillow." I did as I was told. The fire crackled and played its light across her skin, bronze where it had been exposed to sunlight and amber where it had been protected by clothing. She reached both hands behind her head and removed the band that held her hair in a ponytail. She shook her head and her long black hair cascaded down her back, shoulders, and golden breasts.

Eve straddled my body on her knees about halfway up my chest. She took my right hand with her two hands and inserted my forefinger into her mouth, where she played with it with her lips, tongue, and teeth. The sensation spread through my whole body. My erection was back in force but standing alone and neglected behind her body. Then Eve took my moistened finger and ran it gently down her neck, across her collar bone, and to her left breast.

"This ... is a nipple," she said softly in a lecturing tone, with a smile at the humor of it but also with the earnestness of someone who is sexually aroused. Her brown nipple was already hard and protruding as she circled it with my finger. "It is one of a woman's erogenous zones. It likes to be touched, kissed, licked, and sucked. No need to be too gentle. After all, babies chew on it." She illustrated by increasing the pressure of my finger on her nipple. Then she returned my finger to her mouth and made a moist trail to her other breast.

"This ... is the other nipple. The same rules apply, but remember that nipples get jealous when you pay too much attention to only one of them." She returned my finger to her mouth for another moistening.

"Now to the lower parts, but there's no need to hurry. Take your time, there's lots to explore. The whole body can be an erogenous zone ..." Guided by Eve's two hands, my finger made a journey down the front of her body, briefly visiting both of her breasts again and then down the center of her flat stomach to the top of her triangle of fur, detouring to the right to travel down her leg, then up the inner part of her thigh almost to the top and crossing over to the other leg, down its outside and up its inside to at last reach its destination. Eve's grip tightened as she applied pressure to move my finger slowly back and forth between her legs. The journey of my finger had already made her wet with anticipation. As for myself, even though my tactile input had been confined to my one finger, I had never experienced so much sexual longing.

Eve continued her lecture. "The vagina is the canal where the penis is inserted and babies are born," she said as she circled its opening with my finger, "but it is not the most erogenous zone down there. Some men don't know that. The most erogenous zone is the clitoris, which is actually like a tiny penis. Just as female breasts have their counterparts in male nipples, the male penis has its counterpart in the female clitoris. It is this and its surrounding area, the labia majora and minora, that make women go wild." Eve illustrated by massaging her engorged clitoris with my finger. The pressure that she applied became more insistent. This lecture was not just for my benefit.

Eve moved her grip from my finger to my forearm and continued to rub herself back and forth against the inside of my wrist with my hand facing upward.

"The buttocks are another erogenous zone for both men and women. Spread your fingers so that they brush against my buttocks and see what happens."

I did as I was told and Eve's desire shifted into a higher gear as she moved my wrist back and forth against her clitoris and my fingers brushed gently up and down the insides of her firm buttocks. Her arms, pressed against the sides of her breasts, moved them rhythmically toward and away from each other as part of the same motion. Her face took on a look of fierce concentration until suddenly she stopped, panting, to collect herself before resuming her lecture.

Eve dismounted and repositioned herself so that she was sitting cross-legged by my waist.

"Now for the male anatomy. The penis is an amazing organ capable of existing in a flaccid or erect state. Yours is very, very erect." She ran her forefinger down the length of my penis and lightning bolts of pleasure surged through me. My entire body had been waiting for this.

"The bulbous tip of the penis is called the glans." Eve moistened her finger with her mouth and ran it around my glans. "Scientists speculate that it is shaped the way it is, not only to deliver sperm up a woman's vagina, but also to displace the sperm of other men who may have also mated with her recently." A troubling thought of Eve having done this with other men during the last few days briefly intruded, but then I returned to the moment.

"The testicles are where the sperm is produced." Eve's hands moved down to my testicles. "They are contained in a skin sack called the scrotum, which seems like a bizarre arrangement, since you'd think that something as important as your reproductive organs would be protected by being located inside your body. The reason is because sperm needs to be stored at a lower temperature than the temperature of your body. The scrotum regulates the temperature by expanding or contracting, so that the testicles can either hang low to cool or tightly against the body to be warmed."

"Now here is how you give a man pleasure." Eve cradled my testicles in one hand and formed the fingers of her other hand into a ring, which she ran gently up and down the length of my penis. It was too much pleasure to bear. Luckily, she sensed my tremors and stopped before I would have erupted.

"Absurdly easy," she concluded.

Eve got up and straddled my body again, this time lower down.

"Sexual reproduction occurs when the penis of the man is inserted into the vagina of the woman." She ran the tip of my penis around the rim of her vagina and started to insert it.

"Careful now, big boy. This is going to be a tight fit."

"Am I too big?" I asked stupidly. It was the first time I had spoken during her entire lecture.

"Don't be silly," she replied. "Babies come out of here."

An incredible moist tightness enveloped my penis. I instinctively started to gyrate in synchrony with her motions.

"Now the breasts again." Eve grabbed my hands and placed one on each breast, moving them with her hands in a circular motion. Then all of her motions accelerated, like a sports car showing what it can do on the open road. She released my hands and flung herself against my chest just as I erupted, pouring myself into her. I threw my arms around her in a massive hug and we both made grunting noises in a final paroxysm of movement, as if some beast within us that long predated language had been authorized to speak.

Eve remained clinging to my chest for a few moments before raising her head and looking at me with the biggest smile I had ever seen, her black hair in glorious disarray.

"Hot *Damn*, that was good!"

Such an incredible day and it was only mid-afternoon. We found our clothes scattered among the bedding and put them back on. Eve visited the bathroom and showed me its location as she went into the kitchen to look for something to eat. By the time I entered she had found a cabinet with canned goods, including some soups that would do well enough. Hunger is the best sauce, the saying goes. While I heated the soup, Eve explored some other locations. I heard a whoop and she came back holding a bottle of red wine. Perfect! We ate our soup and sipped our wine on the great stone patio facing the lake and rocky peak, despite the chill and a moderate wind that had sprung up. She pointed out the other buildings that had been constructed to turn the Lodge and property into a biological station after it had been donated to the University in the 1960s.

"I spent last summer here and it was *fantastic*. I assisted the research of Professor McDougall, who works on crows and ravens. Next to Howard, she's my favorite professor. The students stay in that row of little cabins over there. Each has a wood stove for the chilly nights. That building has a dining hall on the top floor and classrooms and laboratories on the bottom floor. The boathouse was part of the original estate. There are several motorboats for aquatic research but no other motorboats are allowed on the lake. There is a collection of kayaks and canoes for recreation, along with one sailboat owned by the director. The university owns the entire watershed around the lake and there is no trespassing to prevent hikers from disrupting the field experiments and equipment, so the students, scientists, and staff have it to themselves. The lodge and patio are used by the University for workshops and fundraisers, but we get to enjoy them between these events."

"Are you coming again next summer?"

"Are you kidding? Wouldn't anyone? I even come up early to help Anne – that's Professor McDougall – band the crows and ravens. I'm their main tree climber." Now I understood how Eve was able to climb that pine tree so fast and dump a load of snow on my face. "You can enroll in some summer courses and probably assist some of the grad students in their research, now that you have joined the Secret of Life club."

Oh my God, I thought, as I contemplated such a summer, living on the wilderness estate of a robber baron in the company of my lover while being inducted into the Cult of Scholars for the natural world. Had I died and gone to heaven?

"Are the cabins co-ed?" I asked with a smile.

"Not as they are assigned," Eve smiled back, "but the students have their ways."

We returned inside to warm ourselves by the fire and finish our bottle of wine. We hadn't planned to spend the night but no one was expecting us back, so hours and hours stretched before us. Our nest by the fire was toasty and the rest of the great hall was also starting to warm. Eve added more logs, positioning them to provide enough air. I could see that she was no stranger to building a fire. Then she lay down on the couch with her upper back against the side rest. She motioned me to sit beside her, threw her legs over my lap, and contentedly cradled her wine in her two hands. This was precisely the intimacy that I longed for, almost as much as sex, like the couples at the potlucks who affectionately draped themselves over each other.

"Now for that long story about how you managed to remain a virgin until now."

"Me second. I want to hear your story first."

"Well, one thing you should know is that I am adopted, but I still know some things about my ancestors."

Of course! That explained why she looked different from the rest of her family.

"My European ancestors were among the first to travel west. My great, great grandmother was kidnapped as a little girl in the 1830s by Comanches, who killed the rest of her family, in what is now the state of Texas. Back then it was Comanche territory and the European settlers were invaders."

"Really!"

"Honest Injun. She was raised as one of them and became the wife of a war chief, bearing him two children, a daughter and a son. By the time she was discovered by other settlers she had forgotten how to speak English, other than her name, and looked so much like an Indian that the only thing that gave her away was her blue eyes. She had no desire to return to white society, but the settlers were so convinced that she was being held against her will that they massacred her entire village, except for her and her two children. She led a miserable and lonely existence until she died in her forties.

"Her daughter assimilated back into white society but as you might imagine, there weren't many opportunities for her half-breed son except to become an outlaw. He was my great-grandfather."

"Amazing!"

"Colorful, at the very least. Most law-abiding citizens think that outlaws are mean to each other just because they are mean to them, but that's not how it goes. Most outlaws lived in tight-knit groups and were loyal to each other. They had families and took care of each other's women and children when one of them was killed. They kept track of their genealogies and were proud of their ancestors. I've read that the same is true of pirates, who would do unspeakable things to their victims but were models of democratic fairness toward each other.

"Another thing about outlaws and pirates is that they were relatively colorblind. It didn't matter whether you were black, white, red, brown, yellow, or any mix in between. The only things that mattered were that you were tougher than nails and could be trusted. My great grandparents, grandparents, and parents were so color blind that I'll bet I have every color running through my veins."

I had no way of knowing how much of this was truth or fable passed down to Eve, but her beautiful honey-colored skin didn't lie. It was an alloy of pale-skinned Europeans and ancestors who had spent many generations in sunnier climes.

"As the west was tamed, my grandparents' and parents' generation became the underbelly of society. The type of person who might be a war chief or an outlaw was the same type of person who might slug a foreman for being an asshole. They couldn't stay in school or keep jobs and became drifters. They easily succumbed to alcohol and drugs. They were colorblind but to the respectable world they were non-white. My mom was sixteen when she got pregnant and gave me up for adoption. Joseph and Mary Eden were the ones who adopted me."

"How did all of this knowledge about your ancestors reach you?"

"My birth mother was proud of her ancestry, especially her Indian and outlaw heritage. It made her feel important rather than a nobody. She wrote it down and gave it to the adoption agency, who in turn gave it to my parents. My parents shared it with me on my thirteenth birthday. It made me proud also."

"Do you know why your parents decided to adopt you?"

"Well, they're devout Christians, in case you didn't notice, and helping the poor is the Christian thing to do," Eve smiled as she sipped her glass of wine. "Also, they had three strapping sons and thought it would be good to adopt a daughter rather than gamble on another child of their own. My mom really wanted a daughter to raise. On a ranch, having kids isn't a big drain. They start helping out at an early age and my mom wanted someone to teach and to help with the womanly arts – cooking, sewing, housekeeping – that sort of thing."

"I notice that you do that well. You seem to know what needs to be done and do it before anyone else."

"Thanks!" she replied, pleased that I had noticed such a thing. "I loved my family, my church, and everything about my upbringing. Everyone doted on me, including my father and brothers. Luke and I are especially close. It helped that I was crazy about ranching and the outdoors in addition to the womanly arts, so the men had as much to teach me as my mom. They started to call me their wild child when I stayed outdoors in all weather. As soon as I could ride a pony I was off on my own or tagging after the men on their horses. Ranchers aren't as protective of their children as city folks and suburbanites. They figure that kids learn how to stay out of trouble by getting into it."

"It sounds so idyllic! Like my own upbringing but in a different way. But you said during the first day of discussion section that you became rebellious."

"Right. That began when I lost my virginity to my Pastor."

"*What?*"

"You heard me." Eve smiled to herself as she stared into her wine. "He was a new pastor assigned to our congregation who came from down south. Different from us and a real smooth talker with that accent. He was young, handsome, and had a great singing voice. A little bit like a pious Elvis Presley. All of the women had a crush on him. He was married but his wife wasn't happy here and kept going back to her hometown for long periods. I was the perfect little church girl, the pet of my congregation just like the pet of my family. There were lots of opportunities for us to be alone together. At first I was flattered that he was paying attention to me. I suppose that I was also a little flirty. After all, I was fifteen and beginning to wake up sexually."

"*Fifteen*?? That was statutory rape!"

"I guess so. Anyhow, he told me that Jesus wanted me to relieve an enormous pressure on him. Would I do it for Jesus? I found it very confusing. I knew it was wrong, but I was also attracted to him and even the fact that it was wrong excited me a little. So I allowed it to happen. Only later did I decide that it was really wrong and should never happen again."

"Did you think of telling your parents?"

"Absolutely not. My father and brothers would have killed him. Ranchers out here practice rough justice when they want to. They would have lured him into the mountains, pushed him off a cliff, and he never would have been heard from again."

"They would have killed their own *pastor*?"

"Sure. You don't understand. Congregations don't stand in awe of their Pastors. They are more pragmatic than that. The congregation is the enduring unit, governed by its Elders and Deacons who are elected internally. They have the real power. Pastors are assigned by the Diocese and are supposed to provide leadership, but if they fail, the discontent of the congregation makes itself felt and the pastor is reassigned. In fact, that pastor didn't last long with our congregation. Maybe he was messing around with other women. He was replaced by another pastor who looked like an Old Testament prophet. Nobody would want to have sex with him! Anyhow, if my men learned that their pastor had done something truly evil in their eyes, like having sex with their fifteen-year old daughter, they wouldn't have gone through channels to have him removed. They would have killed him. I thought what he did was wrong, but I didn't want him dead. Besides, I couldn't deny that I led him on a bit at the beginning and could have escaped if I wanted to."

"What happened next?"

"I thought I would let it pass but then he wanted to continue the relationship. That's when I started to get angry, not only at him but at the whole Church. I mean, it's not just that he wanted to continue having sex, but he was telling me that *Jesus* wanted me to continue having sex! If he was using Jesus as a tool in that way, how *else* was he using Jesus as a tool?

"The more I thought about it, the more I saw my religion as a monstrous charade. Think of all the malarkey that you're expected to believe. Stuff that's totally loony to a nonbeliever we were supposed to take as Gospel Truth – and we did, adults and children alike. The Bible can't even get its story about Jesus straight! Mark, Matthew, Luke, and John all tell different stories that contradict each other at every turn.

Doesn't it seem strange to you that a group of people might regard Jesus as by far the most important person in their lives and *not care* that the four accounts of him don't match up?

"I wasn't just angry that our Pastor was using Jesus as a tool to make me do wrong. I also became angry that Jesus and everything I was taught in church was being used as a tool to make me do right. Why couldn't right and wrong just be discussed in straightforward terms, instead of through this elaborate tissue of lies?"

Eve was becoming agitated as she relived this period of her life. The knuckles of her hands gripping the empty wine glass had turned white.

"Yet more that angered me was that my church couldn't change its mind about what was wrong or right – not easily, anyway. I loved both the womanly and manly arts that I learned from my mother and the men, but soon enough I realized that my church was pushing me in the direction of the womanly arts and would have ever less tolerance for the manly arts. Even my own parents, who love me dearly, are stuck that way. Did you know that they refused to pay my way through college?"

"*What?*" I was stunned. This struck me as inconceivable. Eve had lost her composure. Her lower lip was trembling with emotion, she was breathing heavily, and for a moment it seemed as if she might start to cry.

"They expect me to follow the womanly path and only indulged me as a child! The days of forcing me to do what they want are gone, but they can still draw the line at paying for my college education! They think that they're doing right by me and they have the backing of the whole church. That's a church for you, to turn love into an instrument of coercion!"

Now Eve did break into tears and a spasm of self-loathing to have lost control of herself in front of me. Tough people aren't supposed to cry. After a few moments she regained her composure enough to continue.

"I got so angry that I ran away from home. Mom and the men were beside themselves with worry. They didn't know what was going on and I had no way of telling them. One of my friends at school had a single mom who offered to take me in. My parents reluctantly agreed because it was better than having me live on the streets or leave town altogether.

"Leaving my church didn't make things better. It made them worse. People who don't grow up in a strong church can't understand how dependent it makes you. I didn't want to see right and wrong through a tissue of lies, but when I took away the tissue it wasn't as if I could see right and wrong all by myself. My friend's life had no structure. Her dad was gone and her mom worked long hours. On weekends, her mom would either bring boyfriends home or spend the night at their houses. To my amazement, neither one of them knew how to cook. We ate at fast food restaurants, out of cereal boxes, and frozen foods heated up in the microwave.

"As you might imagine, we were faced with all sorts of temptations. Boys wanted to have sex with us and plied us with alcohol and weed. We could provide her house as a place to hang out and her mom didn't seem to mind. After all, that's how she grew up so we were following in her footsteps. The boys would assert their manliness and independence around town by writing graffiti and destroying property. We played a game of hide and seek with the cops.

"At first it was kind of fun to be naughty but I could see it was going nowhere. I entered that world about halfway, but for the other half I remained the perfect little girl and teacher's pet. It was important to keep my grades up to get a scholarship to UW. Otherwise I knew that my life would be done. I couldn't stay in the groove laid down for me by my church and my only independence would be to work in service jobs like my friend's mom. So I studied real hard and got a full scholarship. Now all I had to do was earn my living expenses."

I listened to all of this with rapt attention. My love and admiration for Eve was growing by the minute. What a fighter!

"My first semester at UW was a bit like the way that you described your first semester when you introduced yourself at the potluck. High school didn't prepare me for my college classes. They weren't difficult so much as *senseless*, like being asked to memorize the names in a telephone book. The so-called 'good' students were like dairy cattle content to chew their cud, day after day. Once, during a lecture that seemed terminally boring, I raised my hand and asked 'Why do we need to know this?' The teacher and everyone else just stared at me as if I had farted. Between being bored out of my skull and waitressing long hours to earn my living expenses, I flunked my first semester and was put on probation for my scholarship. Luckily, during my second semester I was saved by Howard."

I couldn't help but laugh. I was so accustomed to having the words "saved by" followed by the word "Jesus" that having it followed by the word "Howard" was hilarious.

"It's true!" Eve protested. "He saved me several times over! To begin, his Secret of Life class made great sense. I enjoyed the lectures and gobbled up the readings. I knew that I was going to earn an A, when I couldn't even pass my courses during the previous semester. Amazingly, not only was I doing well in Howard's class, but that class was helping me do better in my *other* classes. Thanks to Howard, I might just keep my scholarship. If that's not being saved, what would be?"

I had to admit that Eve was right and that Howard's class was also helping me make sense of my other classes. Not only my introductory biology classes, but even my "Religions of the World" class.

"Then there was the fact that Howard opened up career paths that I never even knew existed. I wasn't just learning about all those awesome plants and animals with their adaptations to their environments. *I could be the person who studied them*. I could be a field researcher and get paid spending my time outdoors! That would be even better than becoming a rancher! Moreover, I didn't need to wait to get started. By joining the Secret of Life club, I could begin assisting graduate students and dabbling in my own research right away!"

Eve's voice had the cadence of a preacher reaching the crescendo of his sermon. Fair enough, I thought. She had been doubly saved by Howard.

"Then there was the fact that Howard started finding paying jobs for me after he learned about my situation, like checking up on the Lodge every month during the winter and being a climber for Anne – Professor McDougall. Thanks to him, I don't have to waitress anymore." Eve had been triply saved.

"Then there is the company I get to keep. How many friends did you make here during your first semester and who were they?"

"None. Zero."

"OK, that makes you weird," Eve teased. "Your story comes next. I made some friends but they had little in common with each other.

My roommate and dorm mates. People I would meet in bars. Sports or other clubs that I might join. These friendships were fun as far as they went but they didn't add up to anything. The Secret of Life club offered something a little more like my church. We meet every week to eat, drink, and enjoy each other's company, but also to discuss matters of importance to us and the world. I can't say a lot more about this. Remember that I only took the Secret of Life class a year ago, so I'm not much further along on my learning curve than you are, but I get the strong feeling that Howard can provide what I left my church to find – a way to tell right from wrong without having to peer through a tissue of lies."

Wow. That blew me away. Eve had described the essence of what drew me to Howard and his Secret of Life club. The only difference was that Eve's tissue of lies was her Christian church and my tissue of lies was the cult of Objectivism. Our eyes locked, as they had several times before. Silence communicated better than words that what drew us together went beyond sexual attraction and shared interests. We were both searching for meaning in life that did not require peering through a tissue of lies. It was as important to us as any quest recorded in the annals of history or fiction. It was our Holy Grail. We couldn't speak about it that way to others or even to ourselves, but we could by staring into each other's eyes.

This time it was Eve who broke the spell.

"There is one other way that Howard saved me. The fact that my skin isn't white didn't matter very much when I was growing up. I was still the darling of my family and church. People think that conservative Christian churches are racist, but look at their congregations and you'll see that they are more of a rainbow than the progressive Protestant churches, which tend to be lily white no matter how much they blab about diversity. In my high school there was a clique of kids who cared about being white. There was no way that I was going to break into that club, but I didn't care because I had other opportunities.

"It wasn't until I got to college that I began to feel dirty for not having white skin. That would shock the college administrators. They do everything possible to celebrate diversity, including their current advertising campaign that plays on the word 'U-Diversity.'"

It was true. The campus was plastered with posters that featured "U-Diversity" in large letters and images of smiling people of color. The majority of the faculty and student population was white, however, and the lower down you went on the salary scale of the staff, the darker their skin became. Mostly Hispanic and Native American, because the African-American population in Wyoming was very small and few blacks from out of state had any incentive to attend the University of Wyoming.

"It was like high school, except that the clique of students who cared about being white was now the majority and everyone else was a minority. It usually wasn't overt. A lot of the white students would be as shocked to know about their skin color bias as the university administrators. It's the unconscious bias that gets to you – the turning away when you approach, the friendliness that's clearly put on, the sitting together that causes you to sit elsewhere. Just do a study of who sits next to who in a lecture hall and you'll see segregation staring you in the face."

It was true and so obvious, once pointed out, that a study scarcely needed to be done.

"In refreshing contrast, Howard's Secret of Life club is pretty color blind. You'll notice that the grad students are really diverse, including international students that come to work with Howard and the other professors – Japanese, Chinese, Indian. But the undergrads who join the Secret of Life club are also diverse, including Omar, one of the very few black students on campus. He's one of Howard's grad students now but he came here as an undergraduate."

I had noticed the international grad students and Omar at the potlucks. It was hard to avoid noticing Omar. He had the body of an elite athlete and looked so handsome that women melted when he went by.

"The reason that the Secret of Life Club is relatively color blind," Eve continued, "is because there is a strong common interest that makes skin color irrelevant, a bit like my church, the outlaw gangs of my ancestors, and sports teams – another kind of group that is relatively color blind. In the Secret of Life club, you are liked to the degree that you exhibit an interest in the subject, help out in shared activities, or have something interesting to say. Skin color recedes into the background real fast. Since your skin color is white, you'll never know how refreshing it is, after receiving subliminal cold shoulders all week long, to attend a gathering where you are known for who you are and your skin color truly doesn't matter."

"I think that your skin is the most beautiful color that I have ever seen," I volunteered, stroking her bare forearm.

"That's because you want to get laid!" Eve laughed and slapped my hand. "There is one more thing I want to tell you about Howard before I end my story. He made me think of race in a completely different way than I did before."

"You're kidding. How?"

"It's a bit of a long story that begins with a toad."

"Oh, come on!" I laughed. "Here we are in the world's most romantic setting and you're going to tell me about what Howard Head said about a toad?"

"No, really!" Eve laughed in return. "You haven't heard this lecture yet but it will blow you away. The Australians introduced a species of toad from South America to control insect pests in their sugar cane fields. It's the biggest, baddest toad you ever saw and it's poisonous, which means that it can eat everything and nothing can eat it. Soon enough, the Aussies realized that they had unleashed a monster on their continent. The cane toad population started to spread beyond its point of introduction, eating everything in its path."

"This is horrible!" I exclaimed.

"Now think about this. Cane toads vary in their propensity to move. Which toads will you find at the edge of the invasion front?"

"The ones who move the most."

"Right. They mate and have babies, who also vary in their propensity to move. Which toads will you find at the edge of the invasion front during the next generation?"

"The ones who move the most."

"Right. Now think about Howard's three ingredients of natural selection – variation, fitness differences, and heredity."

It took me a few seconds, but then the answer came to me in a flash.

"Holy cow! By definition, the invasion front is selecting for move-ment! Every generation, the toads that move least will become part of the interior and toads that move most will become part of the edge. After enough generations, toads at the edge will become different creatures than those at the center. They will be born to move!"

"That's right!" Eve exclaimed triumphantly. "And that's what the scientists found. At first, the toad population was expanding at the rate of about ten kilometers every year. After five generations it was expanding at the rate of fifty kilometers a year. It was easy for the scientists to compare toads from the interior and edge to confirm that they were genetically different. The toads at the invasion front had evolved longer legs. Their lust for movement was so great that they would injure their bones, like athletes that over-train. They even evolved to move along roadways so as not to be impeded by barriers. They had become veritable road warriors!"

"Incredible!" Eve had succeeded in getting me more interested in the Australian cane toad than the world's most romantic setting. "But what does this have to do with human races?"

"Don't you see? Our species is like the Australian cane toad!"

Eve's voice had risen to the maniacal heights of Howard Head during his most impassioned moments. Then she calmed down just enough to explain.

"Our ancestors started to spread out of Africa to colonize the rest of the world about 100,000 years ago. Who do you think was at the edge of that invasion front?"

"The movers!"

"Who do you think crossed the Bering Strait into the North American continent about 20,000 years ago to become the Native American population?"

"The movers!"

"Which Spaniards and Portuguese colonized South and Central America in the 1500s and eventually worked their way into western North America?"

"The movers!"

"Which Europeans colonized North America in the 1600s and eventually migrated west?"

"The movers!"

"Which African slaves were bold enough to escape bondage and move out west?"

"The movers!"

"And who has a concentration of all those mover genes winnowed from all of those so-called races?"

"YOU DO!!!" I was so giddy with excitement that I scooped Eve into my arms and smothered her with hugs and kisses, our empty wine glasses spilling onto the bedding at our feet. She beat her fists against my chest in play combat and pulled herself free, straddling my legs on her knees, hands on my shoulders, her face inches from my own.

"That's right. If there is anything that my genes tell about me, it has nothing to do with skin color. My genetic essence is that I'm a mover. An adventuress."

Eve's face and arched back had the look of a proud Amazon queen. I wanted to have sex with her again right then and there but beat back the impulse. I was only starting to climb my "Secret of Life" learning curve and knew almost nothing about genes and environment, nature and nurture, but the idea that Eve was "born to move" – genetically predisposed to an adventurous life – made great sense of her biography. No wonder her adopted parents called her their wild child!

"Eve," I said after we had settled down, "there is one final part of your story that I must know. How did you get back together with your family?"

"Well, as soon as I regained my balance thanks to Howard, I was no longer threatened by my church. Its tissue of lies no longer governed my behavior, so I could enjoy the good company that it offered and let the rest roll off my back. Likewise, my family was overjoyed that I had regained my balance and wanted to spend time with them again. They didn't ask how or why and they certainly didn't grill me on my religious beliefs. I don't try to force them down my path either. As we ranchers like to say, if it ain't broke, don't fix it. That goes for our happiness as much as a piece of farm equipment. I bet they would even back down and support my college expenses if I asked them, but I don't now as a point of honor."

Eve's story was so powerful for me and cathartic for her that we needed to clear our minds before I could begin my story. We decided to take a tour of the biological station. Night had fallen and the brilliant moon and stars that filled the sky, except for the outline of the great peak, provided enough light for us to walk on our snowshoes past the row of cabins, each with snow up to its windows and a stovepipe rising out of its tin roof, to the main building. We entered through a door that Eve had dug out earlier in the day to check for burst pipes. A humming furnace was maintaining the temperature at about fifty degrees, cold but still a lot warmer than the outside. We were not dressed for the night-time temperature but could warm back up at the lodge soon enough. The classrooms and laboratories on the lower floor were stocked with equipment: Insect nets, aquatic nets and traps, binoculars, microscopes, desktop computers and electronic equipment whose purpose I could only guess at. I was accustomed to going outdoors in summer with rod, gun, or rock climbing gear. Now, in only a few short months, I would be going outdoors with a new set of tools for adding to the vast storehouse of factual knowledge, mined and guarded by the Cult of Scholars. I looked upon the equipment with a reverence that would have been impossible to explain to anyone, with the possible exception of Eve. This was not a time to wax poetic about insect nets and binoculars, however. We were shivering and it was time to return to the Lodge.

After another meal of soup and hot tea mugs in our hands instead of wine glasses, it was my turn to lay on the big couch with my back against the side rest and my legs draped over Eve's lap. It was time for my story.

"Well, unlike your colorful ancestors, mine were a boring mix of northern Europeans. To be honest, I never had much interest in learning about them. My story begins mostly with my grandfather. How much do you know about the first John Galt?"

"Nothing," Eve replied. Her voice had a tiny edge on it, as if irritated that she was supposed to know about him. Who did I think I was – some kind of royalty?

"How about Ayn Rant?"

"I've heard the name. I think I remember a newspaper story recently about a senator who swore by her and insisted that his staff read her books."

"That's the one. Now how about my father, John Galt II?"

"Sure. Everyone knows about him. He's the big fat blabbermouth on radio and television. He's your father?"

I paused, confused. In my isolated bubble, I assumed that everyone on campus knew that piece of information. How deceived was I?

"Just kidding," Eve laughed. "Yes, I know that John Galt II is your daddy and that you are going to become a multi-millionaire when you turn twenty-one. Why else do you think that I lured you up here to seduce you?"

Eve laughed again at the startled look on my face. She was having lots of fun keeping me off balance.

"Hey, are you going to let me tell my story or not?" I protested.

"OK," she replied and gave me a kiss to reassure me that she was not out for my money. Having been put firmly in my place, I resumed.

"My grandmother and father started something called the Objectivist movement. I suppose you could say that my grandfather started it, but he left it at the very beginning. He just disappeared without a trace and no one has heard from him since. So my grandmother was the real originator, maintaining the fiction that my father was in hiding and in communication with her."

"Why was he hiding?"

"He wasn't hiding, except maybe from her. He was just gone. But my grandmother said he was hiding because it was too dangerous for him to be out in the open."

"How very melodramatic."

"Everything about her was melodramatic. She was all theater. Anyhow, according to Objectivism, the world is divided into doers and moochers. The doers are responsible for everything that is good and the moochers just weigh them down. Only when the doers rise up and shrug off the moochers can the ideal society be achieved."

"Sounds simplistic."

"No more so than a battle between God and the Devil, I suppose. There is no God for Objectivism, except maybe the Market. The way that Objectivists are supposed to act is by trying to make as much money as they can for themselves. The Market ensures that this will deliver the highest value for society as a whole. So, all of the conventional virtues that you were taught in your Church are turned upside down and become vices."

"How convenient."

"Right. To pull this off, my grandmother couldn't say that it is OK to lie, steal, and rape. So she divided selfishness into two types: A type that's good for everyone and a type that's bad for everyone. Objectivists can tell the difference by checking their premises. Once their premises are correct, then they are entitled to pursue the good form of selfishness no matter what the opposition, secure in the belief that everyone will benefit in the long run. As my grandmother liked to say, 'There are no conflicts of interest among rational men.'"

"Sounds appealing, if you don't worry about whether it's true."

"Exactly. A bit like your church, but also completely different from your church. Two kinds of people were drawn to Objectivism: Wealthy and powerful people, who liked to believe that their ambitions were morally pure; and young and idealistic people, who wanted to change the world. My grandfather tried to create a utopian society with wealthy and powerful people and it was a disaster. It imploded within a few years. But through a clever hoax, they managed to broadcast a speech on the radio that went viral around the world. Ever since, it has been called 'The Speech.' I won't be surprised if you haven't heard of it, because all of this took place in the 1950s."

"You're right, I haven't."

"Anyhow, The Speech caused the Objectivist movement to spread, despite its abject failure on the ground. The one big thing in its favor was that it was *infective*. It made people feel noble for enriching themselves and robbed their opponents of any moral force. First my grandmother and then my father were geniuses at spreading the creed, until now it is influencing economic and political decisions around the world."

Eve looked genuinely alarmed. From what I knew about her, she didn't pay much attention to current events, preferring to ignore them rather than getting upset about them, since they were beyond her control in any case. Now she was confronting them and was duly upset.

"My mother was one of the legions of idealistic young people who were attracted to the creed. You'll love her – I can't wait to introduce you. She was raised in the Midwest but came to New York City to meet the great Ayn Rant and in no time became my father's lover and pregnant with me."

"That was fast!"

"Right. Almost as fast, she saw Objectivism for what it was – a tissue of lies, as you put it for your church, to influence the perception of right and wrong. There she was, pregnant and married to a man who had lost her respect and witness to a movement that was spreading like a cancer through the body politic."

"Good heavens! What was that like for you?"

"I think I was sheltered from it at first. What does a small child know? I seldom saw my father, but that's not unusual for families with a strong division of labor between the breadwinner and the housewife. As someone who never knew a warm relationship between my parents, a frigid relationship didn't appear unusual. There were no noisy arguments and certainly no physical violence. I had all the material comforts I could want, but other than my close relationship with my mother, I frankly don't remember much about that period of my life."

Eve's eyes were growing wider with sympathy with every installment of my story.

"My mother became deeply depressed but then came up with a rescue plan. She gathered a dossier of damaging evidence about the Objectivist movement and threatened to make it public unless my father granted her a divorce with full custody of me. She also forced him to provide for my education and to create a trust fund containing exactly ten percent of his wealth that would become available to me on my twenty-first birthday. She couldn't have done this without a legendary accountant named Abraham Baryov, who took an interest in her predicament and offered his services for free. He's the one who's keeping my father honest, or rather keeping him honest setting ten percent of his dishonest earnings aside for me."

"How much is ten percent of his fortune?"

"I don't have the slightest idea. My mother took nothing for herself and I have been frugal with my expense account as a point of honor, a bit like you. I could be driving a Lexus and living in a condo right now if I wanted to, but it doesn't seem right."

Eve's eyes flashed with admiration. As I was talking, I began to realize how melodramatic my story really was. A battle between a father and son with the fate of the world at stake. A virtuous damsel in distress. Even an old and powerful wizard in the form of Abraham Baryov, who appears at just the right moment to save the day. But it wasn't a melodrama. It was my life and it didn't require embellishment.

"The divorce took place when I was eight years old. My mother sent me to a boarding school named the Village School in the Adirondack Mountains of New York. That's why I'm not a city slicker. The Village School was like your ranch and church put together. I don't mean that it was religious – it wasn't at all – but it was a warm and close community set in a beautiful natural environment, complete with a working farm. Apart from my wonderful mother, my life began with the Village School. Only starting then do I have something approaching a continuous memory of my past.

"I thrived at the Village School in every way. I especially gravitated toward the outdoors and became a wild child, like you. Yet, something seemed to set me apart from everyone else. You talked about all the subliminal ways that you are made aware of your skin color. Likewise, I was subliminally reminded of being different. I would catch them looking at me out of the corner of my eye. I didn't feel different in a bad way – in fact maybe in a good way, as if I was a prince among commoners. I didn't dwell on this too much, but it was always there in the background.

"When I was thirteen – the same age that you learned of your ancestry – my mother told me about the trust fund. When I asked her why I was getting all this money, she just said that she wanted to capture some of the money that was being used for evil to be used for good. That was all she said by way of explanation."

Just as Eve had been transported back to her childhood when she recalled the anger that caused her to leave her church and family at the age of fifteen, I too was transported back to the time when I learned my destiny from my mother. The young man in front of Eve, who was nearly twice her size, had become a thirteen-year-old boy.

"It took a long time for me to process this information from my mother. In fact, I'm still processing it. Sometimes it seems that it's all

I do. In some moods I would swell with pride. Boys like to play at being future kings, and for me it wasn't made up. Now I understood why everyone was always looking at me and acting as if I was set apart. But in other moods I worried over how I was going to bring about the greatness that was expected of me. The fact that my father was evil and that I was supposed to oppose his empire also confused me. At first it was something that I had to take on faith from my mother. Later, when I became aware of him as a public figure, it seemed that some people hated him while others loved him. What was I supposed to know? How could I fight evil when I didn't even know if it was evil?

"These thoughts weren't too intrusive while I was at the Village School. I figured that my mother had sent me there for a reason so I was content to learn its joyous lessons, even if I didn't have the slightest idea how they would prepare me for my quest. My first rude shock was when I applied for the elite colleges that my father attended, thinking that was my next step, and wasn't accepted. UW was my 'safety' college and I chose it because the head of the Village School, a wonderful man named Walter Gold who I'm sure you would love, advised me to choose a college close to mountains. Mountains??? How was that supposed to be my next step?!

"My first semester here was the most humiliating time of my life. Everyone was taking notice of me and I was flunking all my courses. I felt like a fraud in every way. That's why I made no friends, much less girlfriends, to answer your question about why I remained a virgin until today. The idea that I could do something as light-hearted as hook up with a girl isn't possible for me, even though I'm attracted to them all and they all seem attracted to me.

"So that's how I was when I began my second semester by taking Howard's course. I laughed when you said you were saved by Howard, but I was saved by him, too. Like you, I'm just at the beginning of my learning curve, but I feel like I'm on a path that just might enable me to succeed on this crazy quest that my mother set me upon. When you said that you wanted a way to tell right from wrong without peering through a tissue of lies, that nailed it for me. That's what I want, too, and when I find it, I might have the weapons to fight my father's evil empire, if evil it proves to be.

"But there's one final thing to complete my story. I wasn't just saved by Howard. I was saved by you. You're the first human being I have ever shared this with …"

Eve could sit still no longer. She freed herself from under my legs and pounced on top of me, straddling my waist with her knees and grabbing my fleece jacket with her fists.

"Do you know who the villain of your story is? *Your mother!* What kind of mother burdens her son with the weight of the world like that? All I want is to know right from wrong without peering through a tissue of lies for myself. Your mother expects you to do that and then *convert the whole world?* She's a monster!"

At first I felt a spike of resentment. Eve could say anything she wanted about my father but my mother was sacred to me. Then I realized that I had aroused Eve's own maternal instincts and she was protecting me as she would her son. I buried my head against her breasts and wept.

"Come on, Atlas," she said tenderly, "Let me take the world from your shoulders."

8

The Second Breakthrough

The next morning, Eve and I put the Lodge in order and trekked back around the edge of the lake with the looming rocky peak reflecting the morning light, past the snow angel and tangle of tracks that marked our first kiss, along the prints of our snowshoe race, and to my truck. Those tracks were only a day old but they seemed – and were – part of a previous life.

We were famished and stopped at the first diner on our return home to wolf down pancakes, eggs, hash brown potatoes, corned beef hash, orange juice and coffee. The waitress, a thin woman in her forties who kept up a playful banter with the regulars, had a misty look when she took our order, as if remembering when she was young and freshly in love. After she cleared the table, we lingered over a final cup of coffee to discuss our future together. We were seated in a booth that provided a bit of privacy. Our hands reached across the table and entwined.

"We'll need to be discreet until the end of the semester," Eve said. "I don't think that teaching assistants are supposed to fuck their students."

"Let's check the ethics guidelines to make double sure."

We decided to keep our weekday schedules exactly as they were and to reserve the weekends for each other off-campus. There was a reason for this arrangement, in addition to the need for discretion. Eve and I were so moved by each other's stories that our work – our separate quests to find meaning in life without peering through a tissue of lies – took on a sacred quality. We longed to be with each other, but never in a way that would compromise our work. The best way to ensure this, at least at this point in our lives, was to refrain from making demands on each other during the weekdays. Also, if something work-related came up on a weekend that prevented us from being together, then it would take priority and was not to be questioned by the other. None of this required any discussion. We both just sensed that the way to make our relationship strong was by subordinating it to each other's work. You might even say that it was a way of worshiping each other.

"I'm not kidding that I'd like to spend time with your family on some of the weekends and even attend a church service or two – as long as we can work in some sex one way or another."

"I think that can be arranged," Eve smiled mischievously. The wild child liked the prospect of figuring out how to mix wholesome family and church life with some raunchy sex. "Also, Anne's field season starts up in just a few weeks. Unlike Howard, who studies *e-ver-y-thing*, Anne studies only crows and ravens – or big black birds, as she likes to call them. She's a world authority and has been studying them up at the lake for over twenty years. They're marked as individuals so she can follow their lives in minute detail. The best way to capture and mark them is before they fledge, which requires locating and climbing up to their nests. That's where I come in. I'm her chief climber. No one can climb a tree faster or higher than me."

"I get it," I replied. "Small and light wins the race, just like on snowshoes."

Eve beamed with pride. "I'd be even faster if she let me free climb, but she makes me use ropes for insurance purposes. At first it was a paying job that Howard found for me. Now I still get paid but I've also become part of Anne's research team. I want to be a professor exactly like her – not necessarily studying big black birds, but that kind of field research. Her group starts visiting the lake on weekends in April to begin locating the nests. I'm sure that you'll be welcome to join us, especially if you're as good at orienteering as you say you are. There's a lot of acreage to cover and those nests can be pretty hard to find. We'll find ways to have sex on those weekends also."

Life kept getting better and better. Thanks to my first breakthrough in the library, I already regarded esoteric knowledge, like the many panics of 1837, as glamorous, even holy. Now I was soon to become involved in gathering esoteric knowledge of the natural world. A silly thought of adding a book to my wall in the library titled "Everything you could possibly want to know about big black birds" by Professor Anne McDougall flitted through my brain. And after helping to gather esoteric knowledge about big black birds – sex!

So it went. My weekdays were spent in a blaze of work. Never was it easier to concentrate during lectures, assimilate the homework, and go beyond the homework to investigate my own ideas. I began to keep a notebook and pen with me to jot down thoughts, keeping them in a small leather belt pouch that I had made at the Village School. I discovered that searching the scientific and scholarly literature online was insanely easy. Using Google Scholar was as easy as using Google, the difference being that Google Scholar retrieved information that had been vetted by the Cult of Scholars and was therefore vastly more trustworthy than the rest of the Internet, although not entirely without bias. Search engines such as Web of Science, which were available only to faculty and students of colleges that had purchased licensing agreements, were even more powerful. For example, after learning about the Australian cane toads from Eve during our night at the Lodge, I typed "Australian cane toad" into the search box of Web of Science and in seconds had a listing of every book and academic journal article on the subject. Each journal article began with a short abstract that could be read in a minute and most of the full articles could also be downloaded in seconds, depending upon the licensing agreements that colleges had with the publishers of academic journals. In a matter of a few hours perusing the abstracts and reading the full articles that appeared most interesting, I had a solid overview of the best of our current scientific knowledge about rapid evolution for movement in Australian cane toads. I could do the same for any other topic that interested me in the vast world of factual knowledge presided over by the Cult of Scholars. No wonder that few people felt the need to enter a library anymore!

Eve and I pretended to be just friends during the discussion sections and the Friday potlucks. I struck up relationships with the others at the potluck and got along especially well with Omar. I learned that he grew up in inner city Chicago and came to UW on a track scholarship. He would never have been admitted on the basis of his high school grades and his coaches expected him to take the softball courses that are created for athletes like him. As he told the story, he always loved nature and there was a surprising amount of it in the Chicago area if you knew where to look. On a whim, he walked into the Department of Biology Office, asked to speak to someone, and was sent to Howard.

"Do you think I could become a Biology major?" Omar asked.

"Sure, why not?" Howard replied without even glancing at Omar's academic record, "but be sure to begin with my Secret of Life class."

That was all the encouragement that Omar needed and the rest was history. Not only did he break school records in track, but he pulled A's in his classes and began to demonstrate graduate student potential, to the amazement of his coaches. Another soul saved by Howard. Now he was Howard's graduate student and already had a number of publications under his belt. Howard claimed that Omar's street smarts were actually an asset to him as a graduate student.

Our first two weekends were spent with Eve's family, including a Sunday church service. Everyone was surprised by how fast I seemed to become part of the family and congregation. Part of it was my joy at doing farm work and my ability to pitch right in without needing to learn. Part of it was my joy at partaking in family life, such as dinner around the table and watching football games together around the big wide screen monitor that was the centerpiece of the living room; simple pleasures that I had never known. Part of it was seeing that Eve was so happy. True to the adage "If it ain't broke, don't fix it," nobody probed Eve or me on religious doctrine and we didn't try to push evolution onto them. True, I did notice them watching me during the church service, hoping that I might have a born-again experience, but when that didn't happen nothing was said. On my part, I loved watching Eve practicing the womanly arts at home and church. Baking bread with her mother. Chatting amiably with people who had known her since girlhood. Always with her uncanny ability to sense and do what needed to be done in the daily commerce of life.

The remaining weekends of the semester were spent up at the Lodge with Anne McDougall and her team of three grad students: Jenn, Rebecca, and Doug; and three undergraduate students in addition to Eve: Sheila, Conner, and Kim. Eve and I would arrive in my truck and the others arrived in a van owned by the biology department for field research. By then the entrance to the biological station had been plowed so we could drive right to the Lodge without needing to trek up from below. There was still a thick blanket of snow but it was beginning to turn heavy and granular with daytime temperatures above freezing. The maple sap would be running at the Village School about now.

Anne McDougall was a small woman, perhaps an inch taller than Eve, with a face weathered by a lifetime spent outdoors and an abundant head of salt and pepper hair. I guessed that she was in her fifties and could well imagine her ancestors living a hard scrabbled life on the Scottish highlands. Her active lifestyle as a field biologist had kept her body as trim as a woman of any age could wish for. Despite her small size, I could see at a glance that she commanded the same kind of respect among her students as a person such as Howard and Walter Gold – freely given without being asked for. For over twenty years, she had been chronicling the lives of the crows and ravens that inhabited the watershed surrounding the lake. Like some kind of family doctor, she had given nearly every crow that was born and survived to the late nestling stage an examination, measuring its proportions, drawing a sample of its blood, placing a durable metal band with a unique number around its leg, and attaching a square of durable plastic fabric to each wing that allowed identification from a distance through binoculars or a spotting scope. The color of the fabric indicated the year and the letter-number combination indicated the individual. Instead of being given names such as Mark, Matthew, and Luke, the big black birds were given names such as H6, LY, or 7G. In this fashion, Anne McDougall had not only brought the current generation of big black birds into the world, but also their parents and grandparents.

All of this required finding the nests that the big black birds started to build during late winter and early spring, which was our mission. Each of the grad students, who had already gained some experience during previous years, went off with an undergrad to a different section of the forest. I tagged along with Anne and Eve to learn the ropes. They pointed out old nests, which were large stick structures but often surprisingly difficult to see among the branches of the tall pine trees from the ground. Then Anne started to speculate about where new nests were likely to be built, based on esoteric knowledge that only she and her experienced students possessed. AP had lost his mate to a Great Horned Owl and wouldn't be building a nest until he found another. 6Q had joined up with a male and attempted to breed last year but it hadn't worked and she might be spending this year back home with her parents. The ZH clan had grown so large that it might annex the territories of the neighboring clans. These dramas sounded so human, but Anne's big black birds were more closely related to dinosaurs than to us!

"Eve tells me that you're good at orienteering. Is that right?"

"That's true, Professor." I still couldn't bring myself to call her Anne, but one thing I was self-confident about was wayfinding.

"Well, there's one area that we seldom get to because it's far away and the terrain is rugged – the area just underneath the peak. Do you think you could check that out?"

I responded with a huge smile. I had wanted to check out the peak ever since first laying eyes upon it. Leaving Eve with Anne, I trotted across the lake on my snowshoes in its direction and penetrated the woods on the other side. It was impossible to get lost with such a huge landmark and soon I was at its base. It was true that the terrain became more rugged, but the rock debris that had rained down from the heights during past ages and accumulated at its base was still covered with a thick blanket of snow that made travel easy at this time of year. When I got to the base, I examined the sheer face of the peak. It would certainly be a popular rock climbing destination if there was public access. It started out easy and became more difficult toward the top. Free climbing was safe for at least the first two hundred feet. I removed my snowshoes and began my ascent. Within ten minutes I was well above the tree canopy with a fabulous view of the lake and forest below. I found a spacious ledge where I could sit. Opening my daypack, I removed a pair of binoculars that Anne had provided and a detailed topographic map of the area that I had purchased and brought with me.

Big black birds were flying above the forest, often accompanied by raucous calls. Some were about twice as large as the others and had distinctively different calls – ravens and crows. I could see that most of them had wing tags that Anne and her group had placed upon them, although they were too far away for me to identify their letters and numbers. At first their movements made little sense to me, but gradually I began to see that they were centered around certain trees and some of the big black birds were even carrying sticks. The topographic map was sufficiently detailed that I could mark the location of these trees with fair accuracy. I spent the entire day on my perch before climbing down and rejoining the group at about the time that they were packing up their gear to return back to Laramie.

"There you are!" Anne called to me. "We thought that perhaps you had become lost!"

"Not likely with a landmark like that!" I replied. "I climbed up a little way and watched your big black birds from above. Here are some probable nest locations."

I handed the map to Anne and her eyes bugged out a little. Some of the locations were nests that she already knew about but others were new for her.

"My, my, my. You are now an official member of the Anne McDougall big black bird group!" Everyone broke into smiles, Eve's and mine the largest of all. From then on, they implemented canopy watches as part of their routine.

The blaze of work on the weekdays and engaging weekend activities did not prevent me from also thinking about my continuing sex education. Eve's idea of being my teaching assistant continued to excite us with its humorous erotic potential. We decided that she would pick the location every week and I would pay for it if money was required. As someone who pinched every one of her own pennies and understood my desire to be frugal as a matter of principle, there would be no stays at luxury hotels. For one of our trysts, it seemed that Eve had gone out of her way to find the seediest motel in Laramie. But mostly she was able to find locations that were cost-free.

Every week, Eve had five days to reflect upon her lesson plan and I had five days to fantasize about it. By the time the moment arrived, both of us were already quivering with anticipation. Lesson two – after her introductory lesson at the lodge – was held in the loft apartment of a friend from Eve's waitressing days who was gone for the weekend. It was titled "Removing the clothes." We teasingly removed each other's clothes and redressed three times before flinging ourselves at each other for the final climax, the buttons popping from our shirts. Lesson three, at the seedy motel, was titled "Orgasm without penetration." We practiced driving each other wild with hand and mouth. Lesson four, back at the Lodge after Anne and her group had departed, was titled "Penetration without orgasm." We practiced how I could enter Eve early in the lovemaking process without losing control. Lesson five, also back at the Lodge, was titled "Who's on top?" We practiced how I could be on top without squashing her like a bug.

Every week we tried to extend our lovemaking as long as possible, knowing it would be another week before our next chance. Often this meant separating and staring at each other, panting, until we had calmed down enough to continue. When we could resist no longer and it was over, we talked long into the night, fleshing out each other's stories in ever more detail, face to face, front to front, our arms gently stroking our hair and backs.

"Are you curious to know about my experiences with other boys?"

"I figured you'd tell me as much as you wanted, when you wanted to."

Eve planted a gentle kiss on my lips. "That makes you the sweetest man on Earth. Even though I knew that what I did with my Pastor was wrong, it still felt mighty good except for some pain at the end. I can't speak for other girls, but I have a strong sex urge. Maybe it's part of being a mover and adventuress. I already told you that I had lots of opportunities after moving in with my friend and her mom during my final year of high school, with lots of alcohol and weed to break down inhibitions. I was too confused to put up any resistance so I just went with the flow, although I did insist that they wear condoms. The fact that I only half entered that world, and that the other half of me firmly intended to go to college, gave me a kind of detachment. I wasn't going to be entrapped so I could have fun. And have fun I did.

"But one thing I discovered is that there is really no such thing as casual sex. Take the biggest bad-ass boy, who you'd think would be the 'slam, bam, thank you ma'am!' type, and get him talking to you after having sex, as we are now, and you'll discover the most amazing vulnerabilities. Horrible family lives. Fathers who leave and are replaced by boyfriends who abuse them and their mothers. The need to act tough when you don't feel tough at all. Knowing that all that's in front of you is the military, a construction job with an asshole foreman, or something even worse. When they confess those things to you after having sex, their attitude toward you changes entirely. They might have thought that you were a one-night stand, but now they want to go steady. They crave the opportunity to open up to a sympathetic person even more than they crave sex. And when they discover that *you* wanted it to be a one-night stand – that you never had the slightest intention of going steady with them – they are crushed! They withdraw into their tough guy shell even more! You realize that you did more harm than good by offering them a glimpse of heaven – one night of sympathetic understanding – and then taking it away forever!"

Eve had become distraught reliving these experiences. Tears were forming at the corners of her eyes.

"After a few experiences like that, I stopped having so-called casual sex until I got to college. Then I got caught up in it again because it was the trendy thing to do. You know – speed dating, friends with benefits, and all that."

I didn't know but let her continue.

"Chastity was for our parents' generation. The new norm was for sex to come early in the process of getting to know your peers. Girls having sex with other girls in addition to boys, although boys having sex with other boys was still out of bounds unless you put yourself in the separate category of being gay. That's bound to change, too – mark my words. These trends are farther along on the East and West coasts but they've made their appearance at UW and, adventuress that I am, I gave it a whirl.

"What I discovered wasn't much different than in high school. When someone opens up to you after having sex, more often than not they confess vulnerabilities and fears that they haven't been able to share with anyone for a long time – maybe never. They're confused and don't really know what they want to do with their lives. It might seem that a college student has more opportunities than a high school dropout, but I know that a kid whose grooming himself to become a dentist or a lawyer can be as uncertain about the meaning of life as a kid facing a lifetime delivering pizzas or flipping burgers.

"So, I left the speed dating scene during my first year of college. My experience taught me that sex is a form of searching and that I need a sexual partner who can help me in my own search for meaning, rather than wasting sex on people who I can't help and who can't help me. That made me about as lonely as you were, even though your loneliness took the form of celibacy and mine took the form of promiscuity. Isn't that ironic? In any case, you don't need to worry about me being faithful to you. You're the only one."

It was at moments such as this that Eve and I made love in a different way, like the second time we made love during our first night at the Lodge. Less athletic. More tender. Craving full body contact. Wanting to merge our two bodies into a single organism as soon as we possibly could.

The end of the spring semester brought a whirlwind of activity. Our blaze of work on the weekdays caused both of us to ace all of our courses. Our last weekend tryst was titled "Final exam," in which I got to initiate all the moves. Afterwards, she presented me with a diploma that she had lovingly drawn in her own hand stating that I had graduated from the Eve Eden Sex School "Magna Cum Loudly." After the grades for the Secret of Life course had been entered, we no longer needed to conceal our relationship. When we walked into the next potluck holding hands, everyone in the room burst into applause. Now at last we could sit together affectionately, draping our arms around each other like the other couples.

All talk revolved around summer research at the lake. Howard used to be a regular but had stopped coming years ago, except for occasional visits, when his interests shifted to humans. The big black bird group was estimating the right day to climb to each nest. Too early and the nestlings would be too small to band. Too late and they would catapult out of their nest at the approach of the climber. Omar would be there and asked if I would like to be his research assistant. I leapt at the opportunity and decided to take some plant and insect identification courses as well.

Of all the communities that I have known or read about, including the Village School and the Eden family's church congregation, none came closer to a utopia than the Lodge Biological Station when it was in session during the summer. It began with the spectacular location. The robber baron who built the lodge might have been willing to plunder the rest of Wyoming but he kept one of its finest jewels pristine for himself – over nine thousand acres, the entire basin that fed water into the crystalline lake. The forest had never been lumbered other than to build the lodge and boathouse. The trout had seldom seen a hook and the rabbits and deer had more to fear from bobcats and cougar than hunters, other than the robber baron and his friends when they were in residence. The peak rose over 600 feet above the basin like a cathedral spire, its appearance changing throughout the day as the rising and setting sun struck its fissures at different angles, perfectly mirrored along with the clouds on the lake's surface when the wind was still. When the wind was up, it caused the leaves of the aspen trees ringing the shore to shimmer and the waves to sing a lullaby as they lapped the stony shore.

Now, this wilderness paradise and rustic palace had been given over to a community of people with a singular purpose – to mine it for factual knowledge. It was a monastery for the Cult of Scholars. The professors and students who converged every summer were almost as diverse and eccentric as at Hogwarts, the imagined school attended by Harry Potter. The most elderly professors were the ones who taught plant and animal identification, passing on the classification system started by Carl Linnaeus over 300 years before. My entomology professor, a kindly old gentleman who everyone called Shep, was in his seventies and had suffered a mild stroke that affected his gait but not his mind. His feet could be heard slapping against the floor long before he appeared with a toothy smile, wisps of hair sprouting from his bald head, carrying his insect net and magnifier around his neck.

My botany professor was an imposing woman named Pat Black who was known to be a tough grader. When she wrote her name on the blackboard during the first day, she capitalized the A's and made them larger than the other letters.

"Who says there are no A's in this class?" she told the trembling students, looking more like a drill sergeant than a professor. Yet, she was loved by the students who managed to meet her tough standards.

The younger professors were a new breed of wizard employing techniques for mining factual knowledge that had only been developed during the last few decades. They could receive the blood that had been withdrawn from the veins of a crow by Anne McDougall and extract its DNA, the very code of life. Reading it letter by letter, they could divine the crow's pedigree, as if from an ancient book. They could take a core of mud from the bottom of the lake, cut it into tiny slices, and reconstruct the history of the forest from the pollen that had been deposited and preserved, like buried treasure. They could even bring previous generations of zooplankton back to life by hatching resting eggs that had been deposited into the mud and were still viable, to compare them with their own descendants!

The students who arrived at the lake every summer were almost as strange a menagerie as the students at Hogwarts. Discovering a love of nature was like discovering that you have wizard blood in you. It could happen to anyone – even a black kid like Omar growing up in inner city Chicago. When you looked around the dining hall, you saw the cool kids and the nerds, the plain Janes and the prom queens, the straights and the gays, all colors. Unlike so much of the rest of life, they did not segregate into their own kinds. They were all called to study nature and that common denominator pushed their differences into the background. That was one of the biggest reasons why the community was closer to a utopia than almost any other community I had experienced or read about.

The daily round of life was a delight from beginning to end. I usually began the day by rising early and taking a long swim around the margin of the lake. It was bracingly cold and a sensory treat with the water flowing over my body and the light playing on the rocky lake bottom below. Then a hearty breakfast with coffee to fortify me for a day spent adding to my plant and insect collections or helping Omar on his research. In the late afternoon I'd go trail running with Omar or kayaking with Eve if she was available. Then dinner and a beer or two as we watched the sun set. Whenever we felt like it, Eve and I slipped into the forest with our sleeping bags to make love and talk through the night under the starry sky.

Learning how to identify plants and insects was a revelation for me. Despite my lifetime spent outdoors, I had always concentrated my attention on what I could catch and eat or what was aesthetically pleasing. The new game of collecting and identifying as many plant and insect species as possible made me realize that I had not been seeing nature at all. Every species, from the tallest pine to the tiniest insect feeding on a single needle of that pine, had a story to tell that stretched back thousands of generations, indeed back to the origin of life in an unbroken chain. Each one had been sculpted by natural selection to survive and reproduce in its challenging environment, which is why it still remained on Earth. This gave each one a value for me that had nothing to do with its utility, something to revere and learn from rather than to consume or trample. Most of the professors and students felt this reverence, even if they did not express it in spiritual terms.

Merely identifying a species did not tell much about its evolutionary story. That was when scientists such as Anne and Omar came in with their detailed studies of single species, with Eve and me serving as their apprentices. While my main assignment was to help Omar, I also joined Anne's group now and then, especially to watch Eve climb to reach the nests, which could be at the tops of the tallest pine trees. The first challenge was to reach the lowest branches. Depending on the tree, this might be accomplished with a ladder or by ascending a rope that had been slung over the lowest branch. Small, light, and strong, her head protected by a hard hat and carabiners attached to her waist, Eve ascended the rope to the lowest branches with ease. Then she made her way up the trunk, weaving between the branches, as the rest of us watched admiringly from below. A belayer sitting on the ground fed her rope that she would periodically tie to the tree with the carabiners so that if she lost her footing she would only fall a few meters. This was a concession to Anne for insurance purposes. If it was up to Eve, she would be free climbing as she did when she was a wild child on her ranch. I loved to watch Eve through my binoculars as she was climbing a tree, as graceful as a monkey, a look of uncomplicated joy as she concentrated on her task.

Once she reached the nest, she sent down a line that we attached to a plastic bucket, which she hauled back up. She placed the nestlings in the bucket and lowered it carefully back down to avoid spilling its precious cargo. The nestling crows were on their way to becoming sleek flying machines, but at their current stage of development they looked like Goth teenagers with half-grown feathers sprouting out of their pink skin. Some became catatonic as Anne gave them her examination and decorated them with leg bands and wing tags, while others fought back. Animals have different personalities, much like humans, as I had already read about in the Secret of Life class and on my own. Now I was seeing it in the flesh.

Anne's big black birds were among the most challenging species to capture and observe. By contrast, Omar had chosen one of the easiest – the common water strider, or *Aquarius remigis* to use the Latin nomenclature of Carl Linnaeus. It was already familiar to me from the brook that ran by the Village School and was one of the first that I had added to my insect collection. When most terrestrial insects fall onto the surface of a stream, they become trapped by the surface film and unable to make their way quickly back to shore. All of their adaptations to terrestrial life work against them on the water. That's why they become prey to the common water strider, which calls the water surface home. The body of the water strider is shaped like a rowing scull, held above the water by the front and back pairs of legs and the middle pair of legs acting like oars. The tips of the legs of the front and back pairs are covered with waxy hairs that are so water repellent that sixteen water striders could be stacked on top of each other without the bottom one breaking through. Some of the highest tech water repellent clothing copies the microstructure of water strider feet.

Amazingly, the legs also serve as an organ of perception. A struggling terrestrial insect creates ripples that spread over the surface of the water. When the ripples reach a water strider, they cause its legs to bob up and down. The flexing joints trigger nerve signals to the brain, which then instructs the leg muscles to move in just the right way to skate over to the prey and suck out its juices with its mouth shaped like a hypodermic needle. If a trout were to attempt to capture a strider from below, like Bruce the shark captured the woman in the opening scene of the movie *Jaws*, then it would create a bulge on the surface of the water. This causes the leg joints of the strider to flex in a different way, which results in the strider leaping out of the way like a trampoline artist. In this fashion, every event relevant to the survival and reproduction of the strider that results in a disturbance of the water surface is perceived by the legs and interpreted by the brain to prompt the right behavioral response. It will take a long time before human technologies of robotics and miniaturization can match what natural selection has accomplished with the water strider.

This much I knew from reading the literature prior to working with Omar. By choosing this species to study, Omar was joining a sizable order of the Cult of Scholars that already existed. Omar's challenge was to add to their store of knowledge. On my first day working with him, we headed to one of the streams that fed into the lake. There were plenty of water striders and most of them sported dots of enamel paint on their backs that identified them as individuals, just like the leg bands and wing tags on Anne's big black birds. The striders, however, were ever so much easier to capture, measure, and mark.

"Look for striders that don't have paint on them."

"There's one!"

With a flick of the wrist, Omar caught the unmarked strider in his aquatic insect net. Not much skill was required and that was a *good* thing. When it comes to field research, the easier the better, unless you're a glutton for punishment like Anne and her group.

Omar removed the strider from the net with practiced movements and placed it in a contraption that he took from his shirt pocket. The contraption held the strider in place under a piece of glass. Omar placed his smart phone against the glass and took an image. Then he took a small box of enamel paints, the kind that I used to paint model airplanes as a kid, and dabbed a color combination on its back.

"I can get all the measurements that I need from the image – sweet!" Omar remarked, feeling smug about how difficult it was to get the same information on the big black birds. Omar was always on the lookout for shortcuts. As we moved up the stream, he noted the locations of all the marked striders and we captured, photographed, and marked all of the unmarked striders. When we got to the end of the section of stream that he was monitoring, we returned to the laboratory building, where he downloaded the images onto a laptop computer. As he was waiting for the files to download, he plugged an MP3 player into the audio jack.

"Do you know about Twista?"

"No," I smiled.

"He's a Chicago rapper who held the Guinness Book of Records for the fastest rapper in the world when I was growing up. 598 syllables in fifty-five seconds. That's in*sane!*"

When Omar called something in*sane*, with a strong emphasis on the last syllable, it was his highest compliment. The words of Twista emerged from the computer, at a much lower volume than Omar would have liked, in deference to everyone else in the building who would have been in earshot.

Girl, I see you in them apple bottom jeans, chinchilla on your back I wanna know your name,/Girl, I'm Twista, I can throw your brain, put you in the chameleon 04 range/ Still sexy when you smoke that flame, jerkin' like a chicken when you throw that thing,/ She got me hotter than an oven the way that she talk, switchin' and freaky, so I'm lovin' the way that she walks ...

As Twista rapped, Omar brought up each image on the screen, renamed it, and used the mouse to move the cursor over the image of the strider. With every click of the mouse, a dot appeared where the computer had captured the x,y coordinate of the image. In less than a minute, the entire body of the strider was outlined in dots along with a dot at each joint and tip of each of the legs. A few key strokes brought up the next image to repeat the procedure. In less than an hour, Omar had completed measurements that would have taken Anne and her team hours and hours with their calipers. Sweet!

I couldn't get enough of Omar. In addition to his killer good looks and sculpted body of an elite short distance runner, he was always in good humor. He wasn't a rapper, but he kept up a constant patter of conversation, telling stories about himself or making observations about life that reflected a perspective very different than my own.

"My father is in*sane*! Once on a cross-country trip when I was about ten, we ate at roadhouses without paying a cent. The first time I didn't know what was going on. He said that he was going to the bathroom in a loud voice and gave me a big wink. The next thing I knew, he was outside motioning for me to join him through the window. Another time, we were walking our dog in a park and passed some people who my dad thought looked at him the wrong way. When we got back to the parking lot, he figured out which was their car and instructed me how to slash their tires. He's in*sane*!"

Omar was so mirthful when he told stories like this that it was hard for me to know what to think or even what Omar really thought, other than life is one insane and funny thing after another. Omar did not come from a broken home. He had a loving father who schooled him in the art of surviving in inner city Chicago. Later, I was to read what the Cult of Scholars had to say about the city of Chicago. It is divided into neighborhoods that vary greatly in their quality of life. Average life expectancy in the best neighborhoods is *twenty-five years longer* than in the worst neighborhoods (late seventies vs. early fifties). Omar grew up in one of the worst neighborhoods, requiring a unique set of survival skills. Money is scarce. Don't trust strangers and game the system whenever you can. Don't let anyone push you around or else you'll be a nobody. If you get some cash, spend it immediately. Women won't give you a second look if you're not rich and can't protect your reputation. Keep a posse around you. Nobody can push you around if you have a posse.

Omar told me that he learned his love of nature from his father in addition to his survival skills. They had a pit bull and would take walks in the park together. Also, a woman in their neighborhood came from the Caribbean and had turned a vacant lot into an oasis of flowers and vegetables. Everyone came there to hang out.

Thanks to his athletic prowess, Omar was able to escape his neighborhood and come to Wyoming. It was an odd choice but proved to be inspired. At a college with lots of black athletes, he would have been one among many. As one of the only black athletes at UW and by far the best short distant runner, his race played in his favor. The white athletes lined up to be part of his posse and the white girls lined up, too. Omar was on top of the world at UW. Yet, while remaining half in that world, he also heeded the call of nature, so to speak, and became a biology major and now a successful graduate student. It seemed completely incongruous, but there he was, amidst the menagerie of other students at the station, saying things like "Ooooh! Look at this – the red milkweed beetle, *Tetraopes tetrophthalmus*. Sweet!"

Nobody could resist Omar's charm, exotic (to them) personality, and eternal high spirits. Eve was especially amused at our friendship.

"So, you're a jock now?" she teased when she encountered us returning from a trail run, sweat dripping from our bodies.

"That's right, but don't worry. You can still be my woman until the next one comes along."

Omar let out another one of his good natured laughs. "That's in*sane*!"

The more I hung out with Omar and assisted him with his research, the more I understood why Howard thought that his inner city upbringing was an asset. No matter how tranquil the stream appeared to me, for the water striders it was a ghetto.

"Whoa! Look at that! That male *nailed* that female!" Omar was calling my attention to an event that had just taken place on the surface of one of the placid pools. Sensing the ripples emanating from a female, a male had approached to within a few centimeters, sprung into the air like a trampoline artist, and landed on her back. She struggled to dislodge him as he struggled to insert his penis into her opening. He won the contest and she seemed to accept her fate, rowing herself around the pool with her middle pair of legs, as she had before, with the male on her back.

"She's stuck with him now. Have you read about the water strider penis yet?"

Actually, I had read about the water strider penis as part of my review of the literature. There is no limit to the level of detail that scholars are willing to add to their storehouse of knowledge. Not only is there a small army of them studying water striders, but some of them are studying water strider penises.

"Right. Its tip is shaped like a combination of a shoehorn and a stiletto. The male forces his way into the female and then inflates another part of his penis into a spiny balloon so that she can't get rid of him without ripping her reproductive organs apart."

"Right!" Omar laughed good naturedly. "Isn't that in*sane*?"

"The females only need to mate once and can store all of the sperm that they need. It's only to the advantage of the males to mate. Other than their first mating, the females want nothing to do with males. The water strider population would be better off, too. The females would have more time to feed and they would have more babies. The males and their penis-weapons aren't good for anything other than themselves."

"Right!" said Omar with another good-natured laugh.

For Omar, this kind of conflict and strife was life as he also knew it, but I couldn't laugh it off so lightly. The big black birds studied by Anne and her group were also riven by conflict and strife. In addition to the hardships imposed by other species – predators, diseases, and the like – they imposed hardships on each other. It wasn't as if their lives were entirely nasty, brutish, and short. There was a nurturing and cooperative side to big black bird nature, and even to water strider nature, just as there is for human nature. But the wolves of conflict and strife always seemed to be at the gate.

As for water striders and the big black birds, so also for all of the insect species that I was pinning and plant species that I was pressing in my identification courses – indeed, for almost every species on the face of the Earth. I didn't need to speculate. I merely needed to type a species name into Google Scholar or Web of Science and, like saying a magic word, I would be transported to the storehouse of knowledge about that species, mined and guarded by that particular order of the Cult of Scholars.

The conclusion was inescapable. What the Buddha called the First Noble Truth – that life contains inevitable, unavoidable suffering – applied not just to human life but to all of life. The other Noble Truths were that suffering is caused by greed, will end only when greed is ended, and that a path exists that can bring this about. I was still a humble apprentice learning the Secret of Life from Howard Head, but it seemed that the first three Noble Truths could be understood not only as the teaching of one of the wisest sages that the world has ever known, which nevertheless must be taken on faith, but also could be understood in terms of the three ingredients of natural selection – variation, fitness differences, and heredity – which did not need to be taken on faith. If so, then I had taken a giant step toward finding the Holy Grail that Eve and I were looking for – a way to tell right and wrong that could be justified entirely by factual knowledge.

These thoughts came crashing down upon me in the same way as my first breakthrough in the library, when I swore allegiance to the Cult of Scholars. They crowded out everything else in my mind. I stopped attending classes or assisting Omar. I spent hours pacing the trails and the edge of the lake, scribbling thoughts in my notebook. My scribbles alternated between appearing profound and obvious. Of course, understanding the first three Noble Truths from a purely scientific perspective was not enough. It was the Fourth Truth – finding a path that could alleviate suffering – that mattered.

Then a solution to that problem seemed to come crashing down upon me so hard that I stood frozen in place. The solution was right in front of my face. In fact, I could look anywhere except up at the sky and the solution would still be in front of my face. I feverishly scribbled these words in my notebook:

To find a world free of suffering, look inside any healthy organism.

My mind raced back to one of the introductory biology courses that I had taken during the spring semester, along with the Secret of Life and Religions of the World course. It was the cell and molecular biology course and I found it difficult until I got the hang of it. It was describing life as it takes place inside organisms and especially inside single cells. It required a lot of physics and chemistry that the Village School did not prepare me for very well. What made it easier was when I started to think of it like a car mechanic. Cars are also complicated machines but their many parts make sense when understood in the context of the whole. Once I started to think about the molecular processes taking place within the cell that way and caught up on the basics of physics and chemistry, I was able to ace the course and became fascinated by the incredibly complicated machinery of the cell that kept everything in working order.

That was just the point that was hitting me now. The parts of a cell don't impose suffering on each other. They work harmoniously together for the common good of the cell. An evolutionary path existed, had been followed, and had been achieved, at least at the scale of the cell. The same could be said for multi-cellular organisms, where literally billions of cells interacted in a symphony of cooperation, at least in the absence of cancers and infectious diseases. An evolutionary path existed, had been followed, and had been achieved at *that* scale. That's why the solution was in front of my face everywhere I looked except up at the sky.

Now something that I learned in Howard's Secret of Life class came crashing in. All of the pieces of my second breakthrough had been there all along. The crashing was the sound of the puzzle pieces fitting together. By great good fortune, another graduate student working at the station held the newest piece in his hand. I ran back to the station to track him down. Thankfully, dinner was still in progress and he was in the dining hall. I tried my best to compose myself.

"Sudhindra, we've only talked a few times, but would you mind if I tagged along to learn a little more about your research?"

"Certainly, John! I would enjoy that. We can start after breakfast tomorrow. You can join my other undergrads who are helping me out.

It was poetic justice that Sudhindra was a Buddhist from India, speaking in that precise clipped accent, slim, reserved, and strikingly good-looking with coffee-colored skin and jet black hair tied back into a short ponytail.

"What's the matter with you? You're pacing like a tiger!" Eve observed as we hung out after dinner. I sat down and brought my face close to hers so that our conversation could be private.

"It's hard to explain. My mind is on fire. I feel like I'm on the verge of some big breakthrough, but I'm not at all sure. One of my biggest problems is that it seems so arrogant to think that I could be the vessel for such a thing. I worry that I might be having some sort of manic episode with delusions of grandeur or voices speaking to me. Not really, but it crosses my mind."

"John! Do you want me to be with you tonight?"

"No, but I love you for asking. I'm not really worried about my sanity. We both take our work so seriously – no one knows that better than you. I just need to calm down and collect myself. It will be great when I can tell you more about it, even if it's not as momentous as it seems to me now."

Eve squeezed my hand and allowed me to return to the inner maelstrom of my thoughts.

The next morning I met up with Sudhindra and his students at the appointed time. I had come to a resolution during the night that my reasoning was sound. I wasn't deluding myself and needed to get used to it as the new normal rather than running around like a chicken with its head cut off. I even got a few hours of sleep, so there was nothing in my demeanor to suggest that I was anything more than an undergraduate student eager to learn more about honeybees.

Sudhindra explained that he was not a graduate student from UW but rather from Indiana University in Bloomington. He was studying how honeybee colonies make foraging decisions and came to the station for its deep forest.

"The beauty of studying honeybees is that there is a whole industry that trucks beehives around to pollinate agricultural crops. That makes it easy to truck one up here and put it into the deep forest where there are almost no flowers. Then I can provide my own artificial nectar sources and study the comings and goings of the worker bees in minute detail."

"Sweet!" Omar would have said if he had been with us.

A twenty-minute walk brought us to the beehive, a modified version of a standard commercial beehive with a clear glass panel for observing the bees on the surface of the comb. Sudhindra's students split into two groups that manned artificial feeding stations located 100 meters away east and west of the hive. I was free to drop in on each of the groups or stay with Sudhindra, who assured me that the bees would not be disturbed by my movements.

"We're going to begin by making the artificial nectar twice as sweet at the east feeding station," Sudhindra informed me. I walked over to that station, which consisted of a small dish containing the artificial nectar, sitting at the center of a colored disk of paper on a wooden platform. Evidently, this was sufficient to be interpreted as a flower by the bees.

"Here's the first scout!" commented Martha, one of Sudhindra's undergrad assistants, a heavyset girl with a broad friendly face. Sure enough, a honeybee alighted on the rim of the dish and began to drink the nectar. Fred, an awkward-looking kid with uncombed hair and thick glasses, marked the scout with a dot of red enamel paint on its thorax, just as Omar did with his water striders. Where would field biologists be without their enamel paint? After the scout bee had drunk its fill, it departed in the direction of the hive.

"That scout is going to perform a dance on the surface of the comb to recruit other bees," Martha remarked. I had read about the famous bee dance, which was discovered in the 1930s and described in every biology textbook. By now an enormous amount of information had been mined by the Cult of Scholars, to which Sudhindra was adding with his research. It was one thing to read about it and another to see it, however. I headed over to the other station.

"Have you been visited by any scout bees yet?" I asked.

"We've had two," replied Hilde, a pale slender blonde who looked like she came from Norwegian stock.

"Of course, which station is found at the beginning is a matter of chance," added Kim, whose parents came from South Korea. They had dabbed the two scouts with green enamel paint.

I trotted back to Sudhindra, who was observing the surface of the comb through the glass panel. Sure enough, one worker with a red dot and two workers with a green dot were performing a dance, each surrounded by a circle of onlookers. Sudhindra pointed out the elements of the dance that indicated the direction and distance of the food source. A wave of awe swept over me. This was one of the great miracles of nature.

Over the course of the morning, more and more bees visited the two nectar sources, but here was the truly amazing thing. The better nectar source was visited by twice as many bees as the other one! Somehow, the bees had made a decision about which source was best and directed more of its workforce there. At noon, Sud reversed things so that the west station had the sweetest nectar, and the bees shifted their attention to that station over the course of the afternoon.

"Incredible!" I exulted. "How do they do it?"

"That's what I'm figuring out. I already know, actually, but I'm building up my sample size. Very few bees visit both patches so they don't have the information to make an informed decision. Instead, the information is contained in the duration of the dance. The better the nectar, the longer the dance."

"So the bees on the surface of the comb observe different dancers and use the information of the one that dances the longest?"

"No. That was one of my hypotheses, but it proved to be false. A bee that is being recruited watches only one dance and uses the information of that dancer."

"Then how does a decision get made, if no one is making a choice?"

"Think about it and see if you can guess," Sudhindra said with a smile.

It took me a minute but then it came to me. "Oh my God! No individual bee needs to make a decision! The fact that bees from the best food source dance longer introduces a statistical bias! That's why more bees end up going there! It's brilliant!"

"Very good!" Sudhindra smiled. His pearly white teeth shone brightly against his coffee-colored skin and raven-black hair. He was bursting with pride at what he had discovered, adding to the mountain of information that had already accumulated on the honeybee dance language. His work would surely be included in future textbooks and he would be offered a plum job at some college or university.

"So there is no conflict of interest anywhere in the process, right?"

"No. Everything is done for the good of the colony, just like the cells in our bodies."

"The bees don't impose suffering on each other?"

"That's a strange way of putting it, but no. Actually, there are ways that bees can cheat but these are pretty effectively punished."

"Honeybees punish each other for cheating?"

Another brilliant smile shone from Sudhindra's face.

"It sounds funny to put it that way in human terms, but it's true and how honeybee biologists talk about it to each other. Honeybees that couldn't police each other are not among the ancestors of today's honeybees."

"Sudhindra, this work is magnificent and you've confirmed every-thing I wanted to know. Thanks so much!"

Sudhindra sounded startled. "Certainly, John. You are most welcome!"

It was only after I departed to return to the station that I realized why Sudhindra had sounded startled. The way I phrased my compliment sounded as if I was a peer or even a professor rather than a student who had only just completed his freshman year.

Everyone who attended the potlucks at Howard Head's house traded their cell phone numbers to coordinate activities and that included Howard. Only during the 21st century was it possible for me to call him as I was walking along the trail on my way back to the station.

"Hello?"

"Howard – Professor Head – this is John Galt. The Big Guy."

"John! How are you? Are you up at the lake?"

"Yes. I've been thinking hard and I'm eager to talk with you. Do you have plans to come up here?"

There was a pause. "No, but I wouldn't mind coming up. It's been quite a while since I have been up there."

Suddenly I realized how arrogant I must have sounded, as I had with Sudhindra, summoning Howard up to the lake to talk with me when I should have offered to travel to him.

"Of course, I'd be happy to meet down there."

Another pause. "No, let me come to you. It will be good to get away. How about tomorrow at 3pm on the patio?"

"Thank you! And thank you for meeting with me so soon!"

"Certainly, John. I'll see you tomorrow." Howard must have sensed my urgency to have offered to come up the very next day.

Howard was already sitting on the patio when I arrived at three the next day. He was talking with Shep and had a beer waiting for me in addition to one for himself.

"How did you manage to drag Howie up here, John?" Shep asked jovially. "I haven't seen him up here in years!"

"I used to be a regular during my fish days," Howard reminisced.

"Was that when you were studying personality differences in trout?" I asked.

"Yes," Howard said wistfully. "I miss those days. I have to admit that it was more fun than what I am doing now."

Shep sensed that Howard and I wanted to begin our conversation and made a graceful exit. I sat across a small table from Howard and thanked him for the beer. The other people on the patio disappeared from my consciousness. I didn't have time to explain all the background and had to get quickly to the point.

"I greatly appreciate the opportunity to talk with you, Howard. By chance, I happened to take a Religions of the World class at the same time as your Secret of Life class."

"Excellent."

"Not that I have become an expert on either subject, but based on your course and what I have learned up here, what Buddhists say about suffering seems to apply to all species, not just us humans."

"That's right. Evolution does not make everything nice. Quite the contrary."

"It's not as if life is only about suffering. There is goodness also, but it is always locked in a battle against what would be called evil in human terms."

"Correct."

"Then I realized that there is an important exception to this rule. Goodness has decisively triumphed over evil within every healthy organism."

Howard's eyebrows went up and his hand went to his chin. "That's an interesting way to put it," he eventually said.

"Then I remembered what you taught us in your Secret of Life class, that the concept of organism is not as simple as it might seem."

"Correct."

"That an organism need not be bounded by a membrane."

"Correct."

"That it is a matter of cooperation and coordination, not physical boundedness."

"Correct."

"That a honeybee colony qualifies as an organism, for example, even though its workers are dispersed over an area of several square kilometers."

"Correct."

"Then you said that our species is the primate equivalent of honeybees."

"Right."

"Which makes a small human group an organism of sorts."

"When it is structured in the right way."

"And that holds for small groups today."

"Yes."

"Such as a religious congregation."

"That's how they describe it to themselves – the body of the church united by the head of Christ."

"But that religion isn't required."

"Correct. There are other ways to create a group organism."

"Such as a village, for example."

"Yes, as long as it is appropriately structured."

"The community right here might qualify?"

"Yes. Do you see suffering here?"

"No. Only joy. Except, perhaps, for the suffering that people bring with them."

"There is your proof."

"Then you said that human cultural change qualifies as an evolutionary process, different in its details but similar in its fundamentals to genetic evolution."

"Correct."

"And that some larger societies, which are products of cultural evolution, also qualify as organisms."

"Only when they are appropriately structured. It is a matter of degree, not all or none."

"Which means that the whole Earth could become a single organism – that this is possible in principle, no matter how difficult to achieve in practice."

There was a long pause while our eyes locked, in the same way that my eyes locked with Eve.

"Yes, it is theoretically possible."

"In which case suffering would be eliminated from Earth."

"At least the suffering that we inflict upon each other."

"And that we can make this statement without appealing to religion or any other system of beliefs that depart from factual reality. That this statement can be justified entirely by science."

"Yes. Entirely by science."

Another long pause ensued as we took each other's measure through our eyes.

"Are we the only two people who understand this and take it to heart?"

"Just about."

"Will you guide my education for the next three years?"

"Of course. I will be happy for your company."

Our conversation was over and we both rose from our chairs. Something was called for to reach closure. I extended my hand but then we fell into an embrace. Not a short one, but one that lasted for a good five seconds. I understood why I was clinging to Howard and thought that I understood why he was clinging to me. Nothing I said had been new to him. He had arrived at this place long before and with far more knowledge than I currently possessed. How long ago? Probably about the time that he stopped coming to the lake. In all those years, despite all of the times that he taught the Secret of Life course and all the souls that he saved, I was the first to perceive organisms as a triumph of good over evil and the prospect of eliminating self-imposed suffering from the world by transforming it into a single organism. In that regard, he had been utterly alone. No wonder he was happy for my company and clung to me as much as I clung to him.

After we separated from our embrace, we walked together to the edge of the lake. The sun was setting and casting its glow on the great rock face, almost perfectly reflected on the calm surface of the water.

"Take a good long look and enjoy the rest of your summer here to the hilt," Howard said. "Come back and replenish your soul whenever you can. Where we're going isn't nearly as much fun, but it's necessary to reach our destination."

After Howard departed, I wrote these words in my notebook.

False Objectivism: The Sanctity of the Individual.
True Objectivism: The Sanctity of the Earth as an Individual.

What a difference three additional words could make. I had found my Holy Grail, my moral compass, my sense of right and wrong that did not require peering through a tissue of lies. I was eighteen years old. Now all I had to do was bring it about.

9

Enough

Abraham Baryov was a name that I had heard many times from my mother as a wizard who came to her rescue during her darkest hour. An accounting wizard, not one with a tall hat and staff, but like Gandalf the Gray in the *Lord of the Rings*, he was a powerful force for good who showed up in the nick of time. Thanks to him, my mother was able to steal exactly ten percent of my father's ill-begotten fortune to be used for good rather than evil. Like the virtuous Queen of a folk tale, she kept nothing for herself but guarded it with the help of her wizard for her boy prince until he reached symbolic manhood on his twenty-first birthday.

In other words, today. That's why I had flown back east and was meeting with my mother and her wizard in his Manhattan office. I had flown on the red eye and came directly from the LaGuardia airport. I hadn't seen my mother in over a year and for Abraham Baryov it was my first time. They were talking amiably with each other, having developed a warm friendship over the years, when I was shown into the room by his secretary. In his sixties when he came to my mother's rescue, he was now in his early eighties and looking somewhat frail, with thin white hair combed back from a tall forehead, a big beak of a nose, and translucent skin. His suit was threadbare and his office humble, despite serving as an accountant for some of the largest and most powerful corporations in the world.

"Johnny!" my mother exclaimed when I entered the room, rushing over to greet me. I dropped my backpack, bent over so she could throw her arms around my neck, and lifted her off the floor for a couple of twirls.

"So good to see you, Mother!" I always melted at the sight of her. Now in her forties, she retained her striking physical beauty and exuded a spiritual quality even more than ever.

"Fresh from the woods, I see!" Abraham smiled as he stood and offered me his hand. I hadn't thought to wear anything different than my canvas pants and blue cotton shirt, with my leather holster holding my notebook on my belt. I suppose I did look pretty rustic.

"It appears that I owe a great deal to you, Mr. Baryov."

"Please call me Abraham. Having managed your accounts all these years and heard so much about you from your mother, I feel like your uncle. Shall we begin?"

I was motioned to sit across a table facing my mother, Abraham, and a stack of documents.

"I must say, in addition to the pleasure of helping your mother in this worthy cause, the opportunity to watch your father and his team of lawyers and accountants practice their dark craft has been priceless. Their ability to make money without paying taxes is breathtaking, although perhaps not so much when you consider that they helped to create the labyrinth of laws and loopholes in the first place. As a result, your father is one of the richest men in the world with a net worth of 3.2 billion dollars. That places him in the so called top .01 percent."

If Abraham and my mother expected me to be stunned, I wasn't. This figure was easily available on the Internet and I had already absorbed it as best I could.

"So that makes my net worth 320 million dollars, right?"

"Correct." Then we all burst out laughing at the absurdity of it.

"How could anyone possibly sequester and spend all that money for themselves?" I asked Abraham.

"Oh, they can, they can," Abraham replied, "and they can feel self-righteous about it, too. Some of them turn to philanthropy, like Bill Gates, but most of them spend it on themselves and continuing to expand their empires. For them it is about power and ranking more than their absolute wealth. The reason that a .01 percenter throws a million dollar party or pays $20,000 for an outdoor grill is to put the .1 percenter in his place. There's no such thing as enough when everyone is trying to be on top."

"Well put," I said. "No such thing as enough."

"Have you thought about what you will do with your wealth?"

"I have. First, I would like your help continuing to manage it and to pay you for the service. I know from my mother that you have been donating your services up to now. That is very noble of you."

Abraham registered the compliment with a wave of his hand. "Thank you. As you can see from my own clothing and office, I was never tempted by that game. As a result, I can afford to be generous with my money. But I will be glad to continue to help you and to bill you for the services of my firm at the normal rate." My mother observed the conversation with approval. She was sharing the room with two fine men.

"It's interesting that you used the word 'enough,'" I continued, "because I have been thinking a lot about that word myself. Thanks to my mother's example, I've always drawn upon my expense account as little as possible."

"I've noticed," Baryov interjected. "The cost of living must be very low out there in Wyoming. I sometimes worry that you might be living under a bridge."

"I'm not that frugal!" I protested. "In any case, I would like to continue in that vein. To make it easy, I'd like to receive an annual income for myself that is calibrated to be at the lower cut-off point for the top ten percent of Americans. Making that single decision will help me to budget all my other decisions. I've decided that being a ten percenter should be more than enough. If I can't be happy in the top ten percent of the American income bracket, then I should re-examine my values. As far as I can tell on the Internet, that works out to $133,445 for this year."

My mother was swelling with pride at the young man I had become. "Oh, come on!" I laughed, "It's not *that* noble! Think of all the decisions that I won't have to make. Whether to buy the $300 running shoes. Which wristwatch to wear from my collection. Whether my clothes from Versace are still in fashion. Whether to buy a condo in Mexico for when winter in Wyoming gets tiresome."

"You're planning to stay in Wyoming, then?" asked my mother.

"Yes, and that brings me to the second use of my money. I want to create a nonprofit organization that I will run with my mentor and friend, Howard Head. I suppose you could call it a think tank. I envision primarily holding workshops on scientific topics, that sort of thing. The expenses will be a drop in the bucket as far as my wealth is concerned."

"That sounds straightforward," Abraham observed. "I'll be happy to set this up or recommend specialists in creating nonprofits if necessary."

"Perhaps I should explain myself a little more," I said. "The idea that I should be using this money for some kind of good, as opposed to just my own pleasure, is something that I have taken seriously ever since my mother first told me about the trust fund when I was thirteen. *Thanks, Mom!*"

They both laughed. It was the first time that I had hinted about the burden placed upon me and I was glad that I could do it through humor.

"Of course, I could begin using my money for a variety of philanthropic purposes, like a midget version of Bill Gates, but instead I think I can do something that more directly confronts and repairs the damage that my father and grandmother have done with their Objectivist movement. I don't know if that's what you had in mind, Mom, but it's what I am now aiming for."

"I didn't have anything specific in mind!" my mother confessed. "I was only a young woman myself. I stole it without knowing how to use it. I sheltered you from it until you were thirteen but I had to tell you eventually!" She had become distraught at the thought that she had harmed me with her decisions.

"And what damage is that?" Abraham asked.

"Well, not only has the Objectivist movement made it possible for my father to become obscenely wealthy, but it provides a moral justification for the rest of the .01 percent to become obscenely wealthy as well. You know better than I do how much the wealth of the world has become concentrated into their hands. What is it by now? Half of the world's wealth? There are individuals who are wealthier than entire nations!"

Howard's way of getting worked up into a lather had rubbed off on me. I calmed myself down and continued.

"It's probably unknowable whether the Objectivist movement actually caused this obscene concentration of wealth and all its attendant ills. Maybe it would have happened if my grandmother and father had never existed. Either way, Howard and I think that we can destroy the moral foundation that justifies the current state of affairs and replace it with another that is oriented toward the welfare of the whole Earth. We intend to take back the Objectivist movement. We've been preparing for a number of years but the nonprofit organization is needed to continue our preparation. Once we are ready, there will be more uses for my money."

I stated this with such certainty that both of them stared at me without replying. Was I mad? Was I trapped in some kind of Luke Skywalker adolescent fantasy? Who was Howard Head? Was he the leader of another cult who had stolen me away, as my mother had been stolen away by Objectivism? Could such a thing just possibly be true? I reminded myself to be more guarded about disclosing my convictions in the future. Finally, it was my mother who broke the silence.

"That sounds *amazing*, Johnny. I never imagined that you might attempt something so ambitious. I'm dying to learn more about it."

Mother and I returned to her home in New Jersey on the commuter train. After we found our seats, I made a call on my cell phone.

"Mark Shattuck, please ... Mark, this is John Galt ... Fine, thank you. We can go ahead with the purchase now, using the contact information that I gave you earlier. I look forward to closing as soon as it can be arranged. Thanks for your efforts."

"What was that about?"

"Some land, Mom! I've had a lot of time to think about my future. One thing I've learned is that I should always retain a connection to nature, so I've purchased a small plot of land adjacent to the University of Wyoming's biological station. It's remote and only three acres, so I can afford it as a ten percenter, but it gives me access to the most exquisite 9,000 acres of wilderness you ever saw. I plan to build my own homestead and can't wait!"

"John, I've never met anyone your age who is so self-assured. You've really blossomed. How is Eve?"

"She moved down to Ecuador about six months ago. She has a fantastic opportunity to study the primates and help to create an ecological reserve down there. It's so remote that she's living with one of the last Amazonian tribes practicing their indigenous lifestyle. As far as I can tell from her letters, she's never been happier."

"That must be hard for you and your relationship. I'm dying to meet her."

"Strangely, our relationship is designed to not only survive but to thrive on absences such as these. I know you'll love each other when you do meet, but watch out – she can be like a mother bear protecting her cub! The first time I told her my story, she said that you were a monster for putting the weight of the world on my shoulders."

"Oh, Johnny, I feel terrible! How could I know that you would take it so seriously?"

"Don't worry, Mom. Remember what Nietzsche said: That which does not kill us makes us stronger."

"Johnny, stop it!"

I laughed and pulled her close to me in a sideways hug.

"OK, I'll stop kidding you now. Here is the honest truth. Extracting me from my father's world and sending me to the Village School was the best thing that you could have done for me. Aside from a rough patch during my first semester, I have thrived at the University of Wyoming. I have become more purposeful than anyone I know. That's not innate, something I was born with. It was acquired, or rather assembled. I jokingly say that I have joined the Cult of Scholars, but what that means is that I have become dedicated to the pursuit of knowledge, which is the opposite of what most people regard as a cult. I'm deeply in love, have a wise mentor, and I'm filled with zeal for spreading the new factual gospel. All because of you."

Oops! I did it again. When was I going to learn to curb my enthusiasm?

"Well, I'm glad that you didn't join a cult because you would make an excellent cult leader!"

We arrived home just when Jessica and David, now nine and seven years old respectively, had come home from school. The days of climbing me like a tree were over. We exchanged a quick round of hugs and they resumed their own engaging lives. Sean had surgeries to perform and wouldn't be home until seven. My mother went into the kitchen to prepare dinner and I went outside into a garden area with flowers surrounding a swimming pool like an oasis. My mother beautified her surroundings wherever she went.

I sat down at a glass table and withdrew a powder blue sheet of paper from between the leaves of my notebook. It was an old-fashioned airmail letter, the kind that is as light as a feather and folds to become its own envelope. Eve had discovered a stack of them in a cardboard box in a hallway of the biology building, containing the contents of the desk of one of the retired professors. In our peculiar way, we decided to use them to write each other when we were apart, not only because Eve would have only sporadic access to the Internet in Ecuador, but to make our communication more special. This was my most recent letter from Eve. I had already read it many times and looked forward to reading it again. The handwriting was small and neat to fit as many words as possible onto the single page.

My Dearest John,

I cherish your last letter, which I have read again and again. Good luck with your trip back east. Now at last I can start cashing in on my investment in this relationship!

I'm as busy and happy as I can possibly be, setting up my field site and settling into Shuar village life. How I wish you could be with me to share in the glories of the tropics. Fantastic species are everywhere, including no less than 12 primate species in the region that we are trying to establish as an ecological reserve, to be managed by the Shuar. This kind of field work makes the big black birds look easy by comparison, but you know that I like a challenge.

The Shuar are expert hunters, naturalists – and tree climbers! Only the men climb trees and watching them extract honey from a beehive is quite a sight. They hunt with blowguns and poison darts and they can hit a bird the size of a sparrow. Monkeys are one of their main food sources and one of my challenges is figuring out how both the monkey populations and Shuar traditional lifestyle can be maintained in a world that is increasingly intruding upon them.

As you might imagine, my tree climbing ability gives me a lot of cred. You should have seen the expression on their faces the first time I offered to retrieve a monkey that they had shot with their blow guns, which died up in the canopy and had to be retrieved! They're even starting to call me "monkey woman" in their own language and it seems to be more than a nickname. More on that later after I figure it out for myself.

What you say about village life certainly holds true for the Shuar. Everything runs on an even keel in the little Colone where I live. Historically, however, violent conflict between groups was rampant, as you know from my previous letters, including the headhunting expeditions for which the Shuar are so famous. An anthropologist who passed through estimates that before contact, over a third of the men died violent deaths. Whatever one might think about Christianity, we can thank the missionaries for putting an end to tribal warfare for the most part.

Please come visit soon! The young Shuar men are cute with their facial tattoos and they all think that I'm hot. And they're more my size. Just kidding! I love you when you're absent for cheering me on my own path. And I love you when you are present – Oh boy, will I ever …

Yours forever,
Eve

How I missed her! I withdrew another blue sheet from between the leaves of my notebook and began to write.

My Dearest Eve,
Your most recent letter is also becoming tattered with frequent reading. I now have 320 million dollars at my disposal – isn't that surreal? I outlined my plans for remaining a 10 percenter, which they considered noble. I didn't tell them about all the ribbing you have been giving me – about being a rich boy playing at being poor, living a life of self-denial on "only" the top 10 percentile, without having to work for it. I keep telling you that it's not intended to be a statement, just a way to keep myself within bounds!

It's great seeing Mom & Co. and to finally meet Abraham Baryov, but I'm also excited to begin homesteading and working with Howard at a more ambitious scale. It seems that my life for the foreseeable future will consist of three strands, each separate but hopefully combining into a strong braid. Homesteading and remaining close to nature, working with Howard to change the world, and you.

I know how much you think that I shouldn't try to take the world on my shoulders, that it is too big a job for anyone and shouldn't be required for my happiness. But that is my goal and it is important for me to be able to confess it to you. It sounds crazy when I tell it to others and even, sometimes, when I tell it to myself. My gift to you is to cheer you on your way along your path, even when it takes you away from me into the Amazonian jungle. Please cheer me on my way along mine, even if you have reservations and it takes me into cities, governments, and corporate offices, where I know that you – wild child that you are – don't want to go. I need your help imagining that my path is possible.

As for that third thread – you – I'll suggest some dates in my next letter. It all sounds so fantastic – the tropics, getting to hang out with your Shuar friends, and falling back into your arms. You'll need to brace yourself for a tsunami of sexual desire!

OK, back to reality. I live to see the next powder blue envelope in my mailbox.

Forever yours,
John

After a quiet birthday celebration with Mom & Co., I returned out west to weave the three strands of my life together into a braid. A sunlit June morning found me bouncing in my truck up Timber Ridge Trail, a seasonal road whose maintenance during the winter was up to the residents. My new property was at the very end, with one side adjacent to the biological station property that I already knew so well. The cell tower that provided Internet access for the biological station also reached my property. The whole wide world would be only a few keystrokes away from my homestead. My nearest neighbor along Timber Ridge Trail was a quarter mile down the road so I felt utterly alone – exactly as I wanted it.

My three acres included a little brook that reminded me of my Village School days. I was musing about where to locate my house when a truck coming my way made itself heard in a noisy crescendo. Soon it appeared and pulled behind my truck. A man who looked to be in his forties stepped out of the cab and approached.

"Hey, there! I'm ...."

"Wait! Don't tell me ... let me guess ... is your name *Ron*?"

Ron's face opened up into a smile, revealing a mouthful of tobacco-stained teeth, with one missing on the upper right side. The words "Ron's Contracting" were emblazoned on the side of his truck, his baseball cap, and his sweatshirt. His dark hair sprouted from under his cap, his tanned skin explained where the term "redneck" comes from, his chin sported a few day's growth of a beard, and his pants and shoes were splattered with mud from his current contracting jobs.

"And you're John Galt, the new owner of this property."

"Hey – you're smarter than you look!"

More grins and our hands swung out from our sides in an exaggerated arc, meeting in the middle with a big clap of a handshake. I've always been grateful that my Village School education made me as comfortable in the company of the locals as the scholars. I knew lots of people like Ron back in the Adirondacks.

"I knew the previous owner, along with everyone else on this road," Ron explained. "He wanted to build a hunting cabin but didn't have the cash. What are your plans?"

"A year-round homestead."

"Off the grid?"

"As much as possible."

"Build it yourself?"

Actually, I had been planning to build it myself, but Ron's appearance made me realize something that I should have known all along. I wasn't alone out here. I was part of a community of houses living along this road, who knew people on the other roads that fed into the little town of Timber Ridge, with its school, diner, post office, churches, and general store. I was the newest addition to this community and Ron had come to check me out. He already knew my name from the previous owner. Now he wanted to know what kind of community member I was going to be. Was I a rich guy who was going to treat them as if they didn't exist? Was I a tree hugger who was going to condemn them for hunting, fishing, and logging? Was I a bleeding-heart liberal? If I had cash, was I going to share it out or keep it to myself? A lot was riding on this last question – like food on the table for himself and the people he employed.

"Well, I have the skills, but I'm not sure I have the time."

Ron lost no time making his pitch. "You'll need a contractor. You can't build it entirely by yourself and you'll never know who does good work and who can be trusted around here the way that I do."

"Well, I'll have to think about that. I'll need to see your work."

That was exactly the right thing to say. If I was too easy, Ron would have lost respect for me. Now he was eager to rise to the challenge of demonstrating his skills and integrity.

"Hop in my truck and I'll show you my work! I'll bring you back here when we're done."

A few empty Coors Light cans littered the floor of Ron's truck. Fishing gear was stashed behind the seats and an empty gun rack was mounted on the back window. I could tell that Ron was working overtime trying to figure me out. I spoke his language in some ways but in other ways I didn't compute.

"Where are you from?"

"From back east, but don't confuse me for a city slicker. I just graduated from the University of Wyoming and spent a lot of time at the biological station. That's why I purchased this land, so I can still have access to the station property.

"They don't allow access to us locals," Ron said sourly. I could see that this was a bone of contention.

"I'm still working with one of the professors, so that gives me access." All of this was creating a distance between us.

"What's on your hip?"

"What? Oh. That's a notebook."

"What do you do with it?"

"Write down ideas." More distance.

"At first it looked like a gun holster. We don't have open carry laws in Wyoming, but we're hoping." Ron directed my attention to underneath his seat, where the handle of a handgun lay within easy reach.

"They call me the Sheriff of Timber Ridge Trail," he said proudly. "I like to keep my eye on things. Everything is real safe around here. Nobody locks their doors and hardly anything is ever stolen."

"An armed society is a polite society," I observed.

"That's right! Well put!" Ron answered approvingly. I had passed a major test. What he didn't know was that my apt phrasing was something I remembered from a scholarly book on cultures of honor around the world.

"Here's my place!" I had passed it coming up without having any reason to notice. Now that it had my attention, I could see at a glance that Ron would probably be good to work with. It had the same orderly appearance as the Eden ranch, except on a more modest scale. A deck, undoubtedly built by Ron, surrounded a double-wide mobile home, which in turn was surrounded by a big vegetable garden in its early stages of growth. A separate garage had its doors open to reveal shop equipment, and two horses were in a muddy pasture attached to a pole barn. The yard was filled with vehicles, most of them old but otherwise looking in good shape. A tractor, a backhoe, a small dump truck, another pickup truck, a muscle car on blocks, and a half-dozen all-terrain vehicles in a variety of sizes. All were parked neatly in their places, except for the smallest ATV, which was blocking the driveway. Ron jumped out to move it out of the way and then jumped back in to pull up to the garage.

"That's Ronnie's," Ron said with a laugh. "He's ten and doesn't know any better. Tyler is my older son, he's sixteen. My wife Sarah is the horse lover. She works for the insurance agency in town and can give you a good price on insurance. Come into the shop."

Wife and children were away at work and school, so it was just the two of us and a big dog barking to be let out of the house. Ron ignored it as we entered the shop area, which included just about everything one could want. A lifetime of accumulated power and hand tools. I realized that my plan to build my own house wasn't very well thought out. I'd be hard put to duplicate what was already available right here.

"Very nice!" was all I said and he took the compliment in stride. He grabbed a three-ring binder and headed toward the house, where he let out Zeus, his big black dog, who quickly decided that I was his friend when I offered pats and hugs. Ron led me past the living room, with a wood stove, a couch, and a large screen TV, to the kitchen, where he opened a couple of Coors Lights, to the deck with a big grill, a smoker, a picnic table, and a funny-looking wooden bar.

"Look at this!" Ron said, pointing to the bar. "I made it last weekend when I was bored, entirely out of pallets!"

Sure enough, it was made entirely out of the rough wood from pallets, the platforms that are used for shipping. The items to be shipped are stacked on top of the pallets, which are constructed so that the tongs of a forklift can be inserted and the load can be raised and moved. Pallets are often discarded after their cargo has been delivered and can be had for free. Ron had used this free building material to make his bar, fitting the irregular pieces together, sanding them smooth, and coating them with a dark stain and varnish. It looked as good as a bar made out of pallet wood could possibly look.

"Now *there* is a redneck bar!" I exulted. "That one is worth a picture!" I snapped a photo with my iPhone of Ron standing proudly in front of his bar, Coors Light in hand, chest thrust out, and with his large toothy grin.

Ron put the three-ring binder on the bar and showed me photos of his work. Roofs and pole barns, interiors and exteriors. He said that he was known for offering low prices that his competition couldn't beat and I believed him. But there was something that had to be said, which might test our infant relationship.

"Ron, I can see that you do good work at a good price, but the house I would build for myself would be made out of local wood. It wouldn't necessarily be shaped like a box. I want to make it as energy efficient as possible and install solar with the latest battery technology. I'm not filthy rich, you need to know that, but I figure that I can build something really special on my budget. You might even say a work of art, especially if I keep it small and take my time. I don't know if that can fit within a contractor's need to get jobs done quickly and inexpensively – no matter how good the contractor."

Ron wasn't offended, but he certainly wanted me to know that he was the man for the job.

"You want custom? I can do custom! You think I like working with cheap material and having to get the job done fast? Nobody around here has the cash to pay for anything else! If we use local wood then the material costs will be low and your money can be used for labor costs. I know a dozen good men who would cut their labor costs to create a 'work of art,' as you put it!"

Ron and I entered that zone beyond words by locking eyes. I was the one who broke the spell.

"I need to think about it."

Ron returned me to my truck and I headed back to Laramie to keep a 3pm meeting with Howard. What a life, to be bantering with a redneck in the morning and plotting how to change the world with a professor in the afternoon! The two-hour trip down the mountain, across the rangeland, through the suburbs and into the city gave me time to reflect upon my weekly meetings with Howard, which had been taking place for three years. He usually began with his signature greeting, "It's the Big Guy!"

"How was the rest of your summer at the lake?" he asked at the beginning of our first meeting and the start of my sophomore year.

"Fabulous, just fabulous. It's hard to return to campus."

"I'll try to make it worth your while. I've been thinking about how to guide your education, as you put it during our meeting up there."

"Thank you, Howard. That's very generous of you."

"Not so much an act of generosity as a conspiracy, of thieves," Howard said with a mischievous smile. "In its wisdom, the University has something called an Independent Major, which allows exceptionally independent students to form their own curriculum with the guidance of a faculty advisor. This will provide the flexibility that we need. The different departments on campus will mean nothing to you. You'll be taking courses and reading the literature in Anthropology, Art History, Biology, Dance, Economics, Engineering, History, Literature,

Medicine, Music, Philosophy, Political Science, Psychology, Religion, Theater, Sociology. After all, what are all of these topics but different facets of a single species?"

"That makes so much sense when you put it that way, but why did these bodies of knowledge become separated in the first place?"

"Hold that thought. We'll get there. Lecture courses are sometimes the best way to learn this material, but just as often they get in the way. I therefore propose to assign you readings in addition to your coursework, which we can meet once a week to discuss. The progress that we make every week will determine what we cover the next week. Much of the material will be over your head. Have you ever played a game such as tennis with someone who is much better than you?"

"Yes. In my case it was wrestling when I was in high school. I could never beat them but I learned a lot."

"Precisely," said Howard. "I will be your sparring partner for learning the secrets of life."

A sensation ran down my spine. When I talked this way to myself, I worried that I was having a manic episode or some other dysfunction of the brain. When Howard talked this way, it made me feel that it was real, that there really were secrets of life that could be revealed for the benefit of humanity. Then again, Howard talked this way all the time, which made people think of him as a showman and buffoon.

"Howard – since the course that you teach year after year is framed this way, and so many of your students are influenced by it, what is different about the way that it has influenced me, which seems to merit such special attention from you?"

I was beginning to learn that the novelty of what I had to say to Howard could be measured by the amount of time he took to answer. He leaned back in his office chair with his feet on his desk, placed the tips of his fingers together and against his lips, and stared into space as if I wasn't there. Finally he spoke.

"Good question. Part of the answer is that most of the students in that course are nature lovers who have a distaste for the madding crowd of humanity. Once they discover the Secret of Life for the natural world, it is all that they want and need to indulge their love of nature. Eve is a good example of that kind of person. Another part of the answer is that for those students who do take an interest in humanity, it is a scholarly interest that doesn't carry over to their everyday lives. They become evolutionary psychologists, anthropologists, economists, but they keep it inside the Ivory Tower. Three things seem to make you different. First, you are interested in morality, in what counts as right and wrong. Second, you take this interest outside the Ivory Tower. Third – and this is what makes you truly different – you think it is possible to change the world with your efforts."

Howard's thinking was so precise in the way he parsed his answer that I felt as if I had watched a karate master perform a perfect kata. It made me want to elevate him above me in my language, to call him Professor, Master, Senai, Guru, rather than just Howard.

"I feel like I'm an open book to you. Why are you also different in these ways?"

Howard gave me a sharp look and then settled back into his thinking posture, tips of his fingers together and against his lips, staring vacantly into space.

"Another good question. Part of the answer is that my love of nature is secondary. Did you know that I had a religious upbringing of sorts? Two, actually. My father was Irish Catholic and my mother was Jewish. They were both theater people who had left their faiths before they met and married. But no one who grows up in a strong faith can leave it entirely. And theater is also a faith of sorts that asks big questions about the human condition. When I took an interest in nature, I was a seed falling far from the tree. When I realized that the theory I learned as a biologist could also be used to understand the human condition, it was like an unexpected homecoming. I could be a scientific Rabbi, Priest, Playwright. In a heartbeat, I dropped my animal studies and turned my attention to my own species. I never looked back and have no regrets, even though being out in nature is a lot more fun."

Of course! Now I knew where Howard's theatrics came from.

"So, that is why we find ourselves in the same place, but there is one thing that sets you apart even from me. I have a clear sense of what needs to be done, but no sense of how to bring it about. At times it seems that I can do no more than witness a tragic play. You don't yet know how to bring it about, but you are actively searching and won't rest until you find a way."

"That's right!" I exclaimed. "I even put it in front of my own happiness!"

"Let's hope it doesn't come to that!" Howard laughed. "The happiest people in the world are the ones with a strong sense of purpose. And you seem to have found a soul mate in Eve. When you walked into the potluck holding hands, I couldn't have been happier for you both."

What a kind person he was.

"You're right," I corrected myself. "At this moment I am blissfully happy. I was referring to before I met you and Eve – or perhaps what the future might bring."

"Well, the future won't bring anything if we don't come down to Earth and put one foot in front of the other. Let's discuss your course of study."

Thus began a rather monastic existence that continued for the next three years. I found an attic apartment in a quiet neighborhood with gabled windows that looked out upon a canopy of trees. My bed was a futon on the floor covered with a colorful tie-dyed bedspread. An old orange crate served as a table for my lamp and radio. A low table in front of one of the windows served as my desk. I had learned that sitting cross-legged on a cushion was more comfortable and kept me more alert than sitting in a chair. The kitchen was just large enough to include a table for two. Up until the time she left for Ecuador during my senior year, Eve and I continued our arrangement of living and working separately during the week and meeting up on weekends. Thus, my apartment served double duty as monastery and love nest.

Given my high regard for Howard and my own driving ambition, the idea of beginning our weekly meeting with the words "I didn't get much done" was unthinkable. I typically arose with the first light of dawn, washed while the coffee was brewing, and got straight to work reading and scratching ideas in my notebook. Homework for my lecture courses was quickly dispatched, allowing ample time for the material that Howard was feeding me. Much of it was indeed over my head, as he had promised, but I learned to extract what meaning I could, knowing that I could always return to it. By the same token, I learned to extract what I needed from my lecture courses without obsessing about grades. If I pulled a B rather than an A, it was because I had better use of my time and attention. It took about a week to fill a 5"x7" eighty-page notebook with my scratchings. My leather holster typically carried two notebooks; the one I had most recently finished and the one that I was working on, with earlier volumes accumulating on the bookshelf next to my low table.

By late morning I had a solid four or five hours of study under my belt. The rhythm of the neighborhood provided a pleasant backdrop, starting softly with a chorus of birds, rising to a crescendo with kids going to school and adults going to work, and then subsiding to a Largo movement with stay at home parents and elderly residents walking their dogs and tending their gardens. Squirrels and birds enacted their soap operas in the trees above the human soap opera below, but at my eye level.

During the midday I attended lectures, ran errands and often met up with Omar for some physical exercise. As a graduate student, he was no longer eligible to compete in college sports but he still hung out with the undergrad athletes and joined their workouts to stay in shape. He brought me into their circle and I even flirted with the idea of joining the wrestling team before deciding against it. That would be a road not taken. Joining the workouts was enough. Then, physically refreshed, I returned to my monastery for a simple dinner and more work.

I couldn't have sustained this routine without the potlucks and weekends with Eve. The potlucks were indeed like a weekly church service, stripped of ritual but still providing good company over food and an opportunity to talk about matters of importance. These were my brethren, my Cult of Scholars, and I felt a strong bond with them. My weekly meetings with Howard altered their attitude toward me. They started to jokingly call me "Howard's disciple," but beneath the humor was a recognition that something set me apart, even though I was one of the youngest members of the group. No one else rose at dawn to work, had a course of studies on top of their formal courses, and kept a notebook strapped to their hip. No one else had a demeanor that invited comparison with Abe Lincoln. It was the same as I had experienced at the Village School, except back then I felt it was unearned, whereas now I felt that I had grown into it. Even Eve, who was so good at cutting me down to size, sometimes looked at me that way.

After nearly every potluck, Eve accompanied me back to my apartment to begin our weekend together. Our lovemaking on Friday nights – especially my part of it – was animal in its ferocity. Everything impulsive in me had been repressed during the week and now would have its way. Adventuress and wild child that she was, Eve was happy to rise to the occasion and the apartment was often in shambles by the time we were done. Then, as from the very start, our lovemaking acted as a portal to deep conversation as we lay face to face, front to front, half wrapped in the multi-colored tie-dyed bedspread, stroking each other's backs and arms as we continued telling our stories.

Saturday and Sunday mornings were domestic bliss as Eve practiced the womanly arts that she learned from her mother, rustling up a big breakfast while I made the coffee. Then we planned the day, which might range from an outdoor adventure to staying contentedly at home.

My weekly meetings with Howard started at 3pm and typically lasted an hour.

"Howard," I asked at one of our meetings during my sophomore year. "You were going to tell me why knowledge about humanity has become fragmented into so many branches."

"Right!" replied Howard. "For most of human history, almost all knowledge was of the mosaic art variety, as you aptly put it. Beliefs were created, combined, and defended on the basis of what they caused people to do. I call this practical realism. Whether a belief accurately describes something that's out there – what I call factual realism – was always subordinated to practical realism. If the truth (as scholars and scientists define it) is useful, then by all means it should be preserved; otherwise it should be clipped or discarded entirely in favor of falsehoods (again, as scholars and scientists define it) that have greater effect."

"I get that now," I replied. "It's the only thing that makes sense from an evolutionary perspective. Our minds evolved to produce beliefs that help us survive and reproduce, which is not just a matter of apprehending factual reality." Although I now understood this intellectually, it was still unsettling to realize that my father and grandmother were behaving more naturally, in a way, than a scholar or a scientist.

"Exactly. This is an example of how evolutionary theory provides a new foundation for a venerable philosophical topic such as epistemology – the nature of knowledge – at an elementary level. The most profound evolutionary insights are at the elementary level, not the advanced level. That's what made Darwin a genius. He thought at an elementary level. As far back as 1838, when he was a young man not much older than you, twenty years before he published the *Origin of Species*, he scribbled in his private notebook, 'Origin of man now proved … Metaphysics must flourish … he who understands the baboon will do more for philosophy than Locke.' He understood the implications at an elementary level."

I was thrilled by the image of a young Darwin scribbling thoughts into a notebook, just like me. I did not have him in mind when I started to keep a notebook, so I was not copying him in that way. We are so accustomed to putting major historical figures on pedestals that we conclude in our own minds that *we cannot possibly be like them and that to pretend otherwise is an act of hubris*. I wrestled with this problem all the time. A voice within me was always saying *these thoughts cannot be great because you are not great*. It was a constant effort to get this voice to shut up and to remind myself of the banality of attributing great thoughts to great people. Great thoughts are the entering of some new mental territory, and mental wayfarers are the explorers. When I had my breakthroughs, with elementary conclusions crashing down upon me, it must be close to what Darwin experienced when he scribbled, "Metaphysics must flourish …"

"Only now and then in human history," Howard continued, "did cultures arise that placed factual realism above practical realism – Cults of Scholars, as you like to say. You might think that they would never arise at all or that they would go quickly extinct, given what we have already said about practical realism being all that counts from an evolutionary perspective. But a body of knowledge that scrupulously respects the facts of the matter can be immensely useful in a practical sense over the long term, at least under some background cultural conditions. A case in point is Europe during the period that historians call the Enlightenment. There you have an increasing number of people adopting and enforcing the norms of respecting factual realism. First scholarship and then science as a refined form of scholarship were born, or rather reborn, since similar emergences took place at other times and places in history, only to be washed away by a tide of norms that reassert the tyranny of practical realism over factual realism."

"That makes science and scholarship fragile, right? So fragile that they didn't exist at all for broad stretches of human history and might not exist again?"

"Correct," Howard replied grimly, "unless we're vigilant about asserting and enforcing the norms of scholarship and science, we could easily enter another Dark Age."

An image of an army of Orcs standing at the gates of the fortress defended by Frodo and the Fellowship of the Ring flashed into my mind. The battle of practical realism against factual realism could not be dispelled as fiction, however. It was real.

"As factual knowledge accumulated, it had to be organized. The classification system of Linnaeus was a breakthrough of sorts, although it only classified life according to what we now know to be historical similarity, based on identity by descent. It was the French polymath August Comte, during the 19th century, who labeled the branches of academic knowledge that are familiar to us today – Physics, Biology, Psychology, Sociology, and so on. These split into finer branches as still more knowledge accumulated.

"But there is more to the story than the accumulation of knowledge. Scholars and scientists don't churn out facts and memorize them at random. They assemble them into configurations that have meaning for them. In many respects, the Cult of Scholars is playing the same game as the mosaic artists, except with a more stringent set of rules. They are also trying to assemble a meaningful big picture, but no clipping or discarding of facts and no outright falsehoods are allowed. Now let's take a little detour through biology, which provides another example of how evolution adds insight at an elementary level. Let's say that I colonize two islands with the same species of bird, one hundred birds on each island. There is no dispersal between islands. What is likely to happen."

"The populations will diverge over time." This was elementary. Anyone who took an evolution course could answer that question.

"Why?"

"In part just by chance. The mutations that arise on one island don't necessarily arise on the other. The frequencies of the existing genes also change by chance, especially when the populations are small. This is called genetic drift."

"Correct. What if each island has more than one ecological niche – say, mangrove swamps and mountain tops."

"The species on each island are likely to split into different species to occupy the different niches."

"Correct. And all of this is elementary, right?"

"Totally. I even learned it in high school before I got to college."

"Right, although to Darwin and Wallace it was a revelation to discover that the diversity of life could be explained by a combination of isolation and ecological diversification. That was one of the simple truths, elementary in retrospect, that came crashing down on them. *Now* …"

By the way that Howard said the word *Now*, I could tell that the climax of the conversation was at hand, but I still couldn't fathom how it would go.

"Imagine taking 200 scholars, shuffling them like a deck of cards, and dealing them onto two islands isolated from each other, 100 scholars to an island. Then have them do their scholarly thing. What will happen?"

Now I had it in a massively pleasing Aha! moment, similar to what I experienced with Eve's Australian cane toad story.

"The two groups of scholars will *diverge*! Even when they stick to the facts of the matter, they will churn out different facts and assemble them into big pictures that are meaningful for them in different ways!"

"And the counterpart to speciation would be?"

"*Mutual incomprehension*! If they stayed isolated long enough, they wouldn't be able to understand each other even if you put them together again!"

"And more generally?"

"*The diversity of scholarly knowledge is like biological diversity! It can be explained on the basis of isolation and ecological diversification!*"

"And what did Sherlock Holmes say to his dear Dr. Watson?"

"ELEMENTARY!" I was so delighted that I had to stand up and do a victory dance, to Howard's amusement.

"Very good, John. It is a pleasure to be your teacher. But we haven't quite crossed into the end zone yet. Nature lovers tend to regard biological diversity as always a good thing, but some forms of diversity aren't worth wanting. If you're bleeding and ask me how to get to the hospital, only to discover that I speak a different language than you, then you would wish for less linguistic diversity. If academic knowledge is in fact an Ivory Archipelago rather than an Ivory Tower – many islands of thought with a different language spoken on each island – then there must be a common language that can be spoken across islands. The Ivory Archipelago must become the *United* Ivory Archipelago. Evolutionary theory is the common language, but the unification has taken place mostly for knowledge of the natural world. To a remarkable extent, knowledge of humanity remains untouched by evolutionary theory and therefore remains a vast number of mutually incomprehensible islands of thought. This makes our work much like missionary work. You encounter proud people, certain of their own beliefs and reluctant to change their minds. Give me a college freshman to teach rather than a distinguished professor any day! That's why I look back so fondly on my earlier days when I studied personality in fish. Being on a lake is so much more pleasant and the fish don't talk back. So, John, to conclude our meeting, before we reach the Kingdom we have a lot of heathen to convert."

The readings that Howard chose for me were intended to introduce me to a particular "island of thought," such as religion or anthropology, to learn its indigenous language and to translate it into the language of evolutionary theory. We weren't the first to make this attempt. Typically, we were preceded by others stretching back to Darwin's day, but their progress had been so slow, in part because of resistance on the part of the "natives," that the scholarly knowledge surrounding any given topic area remained a separate language.

With practice, I began to see that the same way of parsing information, which Howard often called a "toolkit," could be used to make sense of any subject – any island of thought in the vast Ivory Archipelago.

This was already common practice for the study of the natural world, which had been largely unified by evolutionary theory, but it was new and revolutionary for the study of humanity. Howard liked the practicality and down-to-earth quality of calling evolutionary theory a toolkit. He liked to think of himself as little different than a carpenter or a plumber: arriving at a site, sizing up the job, and reaching for the right tools to get the job done. How interesting, I thought, that Jesus was also a carpenter by trade.

At the start of my Junior year, Howard and I began to explore how my vast wealth could be used to spread the evolutionary gospel when I turned twenty-one.

"Howard, do you know that I will come into a lot of money at the end of my senior year?"

"That's common knowledge around here."

"I would like to use some of it to support our cause."

"That's very generous of you."

"Not generous so much as a conspiracy of thieves."

Howard smiled, remembering that I was repeating his words when I thanked him for his generosity at the beginning of my sophomore year.

"Forgive me if I don't act more surprised at your news. Knowing you as well as I do by now, it is the only way that you would decide to spend your money. Nevertheless, I am tremendously grateful to you and excited about the prospect of expanding our reach with your wealth. I have already given it a lot of thought."

"And?"

"Are you familiar with the concept of catalysis?"

"Sure. From chemistry. A catalyst is a substance that greatly increases the rate of a chemical reaction, even when added in tiny amounts, and is not used up in the process."

"Correct. Do you know how this is accomplished?"

"Well, in crude terms, a catalytic molecule latches onto other molecules and holds them in a position that binds them to each other. Once they are bound, the catalytic molecule is released so that it can repeat the operation. That's why it isn't used up in the process."

"Correct. You really have become well spoken, John. No one would guess that you are just entering your Junior year. Even though the concept of catalysis is easy to understand, it is almost miraculous in what it can do. Imagine a chemical reaction taking place slowly or not at all, and then – poof! – just a sprinkling of the catalytic substance is transformative. If that's not magic, what would be?"

"Right!" I laughed. "As magical as any spell."

"Now let's think about catalysis in the context of cultural change."

Poof! No one could do metaphorical transfer better than Howard. First he rehearsed the familiar, in this case chemical catalysis, and then moved it over to a new context, in this case rates of cultural change. I began to get the connections immediately but let him continue.

"Let's think about the acceptance of Darwin's theory as like a chemical reaction that spread quickly and spontaneously for the study of the natural world – although decades were still required – and much more slowly or not at all for the study of humanity. That's where things stand today, but adding a catalytic agent could change everything."

"And you think that my wealth could be used as a catalytic agent."

"Yes, but only if we go about it the right way. No amount of money will be enough if we go about it the wrong way."

"And the right way is …?"

"It's not as if I know all the answers, but let's think about how we might function as catalytic agents. We'd find people and organizations that we want to connect and bring them together until they bond, releasing us to repeat the operation. In principle, we could accomplish in a matter of years what would otherwise require decades or centuries. It would appear magical, but it would be only the magic of catalysis."

Howard and I had two years to refine these thoughts before my twenty-first birthday. When we met on the same day that I met Ron the contractor, it was merely to set our plans in motion.

After my long day, first with Ron and then with Howard, I returned to my attic apartment for a simple dinner. The ghost of Eve was on the bed, in the kitchen, everywhere. The two strands of my life, homesteading and changing the world, would be nothing without the third strand. Then, to my joy and delight, I spied a powder blue envelope among my mail.

My Dearest John,

So glad that your trip east went well and that you are back to braid the three strands of your life, as you so poetically put it. This letter will have to suffice as the third strand. Life here is getting almost as surreal as your unimaginable wealth. In some ways it seems that I have found one of the last truly remote places on Earth – therefore my heaven. Untouched rainforest. An intact primate fauna. People living as they have since time immemorial. But in other respects that is an illusion. The Shuar are perfectly aware of the outside world and the outside world is perfectly aware of them. The Ecuadorian government knows that its citizenry consists of dozens of indigenous tribes in addition to people of European descent. At least some politicians are trying to do the right thing by including them in representative governance. Type "Ecuadorian parliament" into Google and you'll see the most remarkable images. Tribal representatives in their traditional dress, even holding spears, side by side with people in business suits.

My Shuar friends are torn between old and new. Some – and not just the older ones – want to continue the culture of their ancestors. Others – and not just the younger ones – are tempted by the allures of modern life. Even the traditionalists know that they will need to innovate to stay the same – such as by joining the ecotourism industry. That road is fraught with dangers. What could be more horrible than to turn your culture into a kind of Disney World for rich people?

As if that weren't surreal enough, you can add the oil, mining, and timber interests, squatters wanting to turn the rainforest into homesteads, and rebel groups hiding out in the jungle – thankfully over the border in Peru so far. To think that I was expecting to spend all my time establishing an ecological reserve and studying the primate community! That one damn primate species Homo sapiens ruins everything!

Humph. Now you know what I think of your "humanity," as if you didn't already know. Thankfully, there are a few exceptions, such as my Shuar friends and you. As for my Shuar friends, I will do everything in my power to protect them. As for you – if you

don't get down here soon I'm going to explode with desire. Barring
that, a powder blue envelope will have to do.
  Your devoted curmudgeon, Eve

As I was reading Eve's letter the third time, a text message from
Ron appeared on my iPhone. We had traded our phone numbers.

"U coming up here soon? Have surprise."

I texted back: "Sure thing. My place tomorrow at 11am"

Ron's surprise, as I pulled onto my property, appeared to be a
camper that he had placed on a level spot.

"It's my hunting camper, but I don't need it until hunting season. I
thought that you could use it when you are up here. I decorated it myself."

I entered the camper to discover that it was decorated entirely
in camouflage. Camo curtains. Camo wallpaper. Camo sheets and
bedspread. Camo upholstery. Camo dishware. Even a camo toilet seat
and camo toilet paper.

"Ron," I said after exiting the camper. "You could shoot a deer
from there without even getting off the toilet!"

Ron let a great laugh out of his toothy mouth. Then he gave me
an uncertain look. I realized that he had taken a risk with this gesture.
It appeared that he wanted very badly to have this job, not just for the
money, but for the opportunity to make a "work of art," as I had put
it. His gift of the use of his camper was like a boy bringing a bouquet
of flowers to a girl he was courting. Ron's look of uncertainty reflected
a fear of rejection. I came up close and punched him on the shoulder.

"Ron, you dirty bastard, if you don't help me build the best damn
work of art in the state of Wyoming, you'll have me to answer to!"

Ron let out a whoop and we fell into a manly hug, slapping each
other's backs and shoulders.

"I've already started to research the technology!" he exulted. We
decided to meet at his place later in the afternoon and stay for dinner
so I could meet his family and we could begin to plan the details.

"I'll make ribs! Nobody makes ribs like I do! Meat falling off the
bones!"

After Ron departed, I entered the camper, withdrew a powder blue
piece of paper from among the leaves of my notebook, and started to write.

My dearest, most wonderful Eve,

How can I hate humanity when you are part of it? Our lives are following weirdly parallel tracks. Just as you discovered that there is nothing remote about your jungle, my thought of building my own remote homestead has been shattered by a character named Ron. The best single word to describe him is "redneck," but one with a heart of gold. Since you're a rancher, you'll recognize the type. In any case, it seems that the construction of my homestead will be a community affair.

This might be for the best, given what's happening in Laramie. Now that we've pulled the trigger on our plans to create the Evolution Institute, there's a lot to do, starting with finding an executive director who can keep the administrative burden off our shoulders. I never thought that I would hear myself saying this, but there is no way that I can make it down there in the foreseeable future. My third strand will need to remain these powder blue letters.

Eve, when I entered my apartment yesterday afternoon, your ghost was everywhere. Only you can understand how you can be the most important thing in my life and yet how I can make a decision to postpone seeing you. At least I hope you can understand. If I thought that my absence was weakening our relationship, I would put everything else aside to see you. My braid would be nothing without my third strand.

Everlastingly yours,

John

For the next six months, my life was incongruously split between the creation of a nonprofit institute with Howard and the co-creation of a work of art in the forest with a community of rednecks. Of the two, the first was made easiest by a young woman named Ashley Daily who we hired as an executive director. Ashley was not one of Howard's students but could have been, having caught "the evolution bug" in other ways. In addition to understanding the mission of the Evolution Institute, as we decided to call it, she had the administrative skills to serve as executive director. Once she was in place working with Howard, I was only required to attend weekly meetings and could spend the rest of my time in Ron's camo camper on my three acres.

Ron and I quickly developed a close relationship as we put our heads together to plan the structure. Although I had building experience at the Village School, he knew far more and became my mentor. He also became a father of sorts and I became part of his family. The hole in me where a family should have been, which drew me to Eve's family, also drew me to Ron's. The simplest things that they took for granted, such as watching television after dinner, was novel and refreshing for me, especially given the heaviness of that other strand of my life.

Given Ron's curiosity and penchant for poking around on the Internet, it was inevitable that he would come across my strange story. One thing I knew about rednecks is that they stay out of each other's business. As long as you do well by others, you can do anything else that you damn well please. It was therefore only after we had become close that Ron started to ask me questions about my life.

"How come you don't like your father?" We were driving down to Timber Ridge in my truck to get some supplies. He had no practice with this kind of conversation so he just blurted it out. I looked at him, returned my eyes to the road, and thought a bit before replying.

"I don't know my father as a person. I haven't seen him since I was eight years old. I only know the impact that he is having on the world."

"A lot of folks around here like your father. Listen to him all the time."

"I know! He tells a great story. Pushes all the right buttons. But the end result is highway robbery. My father and his ultra-rich friends are stealing from folks like you."

"A man deserves to keep the money he makes."

"You don't mean that and I can prove it."

"Go ahead and try!" Ron was getting excited by this conversation. He didn't get a chance to cross mental swords like this often.

"Why do they call you the Sheriff of Timber Ridge Trail."

"Because I keep an eye on things."

"And you also put a stop to things, right?"

"Damn right!" Ron said proudly.

"Like what?"

"Trespassing, hunting and fishing out of season, dumping, building without a permit, family abuse ..."

"Family abuse?"

"Sure. One of Tyler's friends had bruises on him all the time. We couldn't let that stand so we called in social services. Then Sarah and I got training to be foster care parents …"

"Really!" I exclaimed in admiration. "That's noble of you!" Ron swelled with pride as I continued. "In the old days before social services, you might have just taken him in for a while, made sure that he stayed with a cousin or grandparent, or something like that. But you wouldn't let the problem just stand."

"No way."

"So there's my point. Rednecks like to say that they do as they please and stay out of each other's business, but that's only true within limits. If someone on Timber Ridge Trail strays beyond those limits, you and others like you will bring them back into line. Right?"

"Right." Ron had no choice but to agree with me.

"So a man doesn't deserve to keep the money he makes, or otherwise have his way, if he strays beyond those limits."

"OK, you have me there."

"What would happen if you were prohibited from acting as Sheriff and, worse, all of us were prohibited from keeping people who truly cared only about themselves in line? What would Timber Ridge Trail be like then?"

"A mess."

"So, Timber Ridge Trail works well only because it has those protections. And the world is a mess because it doesn't have those protections. And my father, whether he knows it or not, plays a large role in undoing the protections. He and his friends became ultra-rich because they could operate in a world without sheriffs. And just by pressing a few psychological buttons, they get rednecks cheering them on. You guys are getting played!"

Ron looked at me admiringly and let his silence indicate that I had won that particular joust. Then he raised another topic.

"The Internet says that you could buy the whole town of Timber Ridge if you wanted."

I gave him another look and returned my eyes to the road for a spell before replying.

"Do you think that I'm playing you when I say that I'm not made out of money?"

Ron's face flushed with indignation. "No! I'm just trying to figure you out!"

"I'm sorry," I replied, chastened. "I shouldn't have said or thought that about you. I don't use that money for my personal gain. I pay myself a yearly salary that's calibrated to be on the lower edge of the top ten percent of Americans. My father is a 0.01 percenter and I'm a ten percenter. That works out to a little over $130,000 per year. I figure that if I can't be happy with that, then I need my head examined, not more money. So that's exactly how much money I'm made out of. The rest of it is for making the rest of the world more like Timber Ridge Trail."

"Well, shit!" Ron concluded. "That makes you the truest redneck there ever was!"

It took us three weeks to imagine the structure that we would build, draw up the plans, and begin to assemble the materials. Now it was time to recruit a crew of workers. Ron put the word out and I awoke from my camo sheets and bedcover one morning to the sound of a small fleet of cars and pickup trucks heading up Timber Ridge Trail. Ron's truck was in the lead as they pulled around the camper and a dozen people stepped out. They ranged in age from their sixties to their twenties, all men except for one young woman with a tool belt strapped to her hip. None of them would be pegged for an artist by the look of them.

"These are the people who really want to work on this project and have the skills," Ron announced. "Suzy over there – she's been doing construction with her father since she could walk. We realize that this is a pretty big crew and that you're not loaded with money. On the other hand, a big crew will get the job done faster. Anyhow, we've talked it over and they're prepared to work for fifteen dollars an hour."

The dirty dozen looked at the ground, folded their arms, and shuffled their feet as they waited for my reply.

"What's the normal hourly wage around here."

"Aaw, John, there's no normal wage around here. In Laramie they'd get thirty-five dollars an hour. Around here we take what we can get."

"Well, I'm just a dumbass kid from back east who went to college in Laramie, so I don't know any better than to pay the Laramie rates. I'm just grateful to you that I don't have to pay the east coast rates."

A cheer arose from the dirty dozen as they learned of their good fortune. Now they were more excited than ever to create something truly special. Work would begin the next morning. After everyone else left, Ron lingered to talk.

"How can you afford to be that generous on your ten percent? I was figuring with your ten percent in mind."

"I'll take out a mortgage, the way other ten percenters do. Wait until the bank officer sees my credit rating."

Ron let out another one of his great toothy laughs and we set about preparing for the coming day.

It required only two months to turn our imagination into a reality, in part because of the number of people involved and in part because the structure itself was quite small. It was in the shape of a hexagon, like a single cell of a honeycomb, only thirty feet in diameter, rising from the highest level ground of my three acres. A local sawmill provided wood that was already cut and dried in exchange for logs from my property, which we marked for cutting to enhance the view. The ground floor was a utility area on a concrete pad, including a bathroom with a composting toilet. A staircase built against the wall led to the first floor, which was a combined kitchen, dining and living area without any partitions. A wood stove would provide ample heat for the relatively small and extremely well-insulated space. Two doors led outside to a deck that wrapped around the entire building, which could also be reached by an external stairway, and windows all around admitted abundant light. Insulated shades would trap the heat during the winter. Solar panels on the south face were wired to batteries on the ground floor.

The stairs from the basement continued to rise along the wall above the first floor to a sleeping loft with a built-in closet and shelves for my clothes. Then the stairs continued to rise to a second loft, positioned at a 120-degree angle to the first, that would serve for my office. From there, the stairs rose still further to a doorway that led outside to the roof of the structure, which looked like the turret of a castle or the crow's nest of a ship, with a fire pit in the center.

The idea of a fire pit was Ron's and only occurred to him when the building was nearly complete. We were leaning against the hexagonal wall of the turret, admiring the view, when he remarked, "Wouldn't it be incredible to be sitting around a fire up here?" Only a few modifications were required to ensure that stray sparks from a fire would not ignite the building.

The dirty dozen worked overtime to complete the structure, like an Amish barn raising. They competed against each other to display their craftsmanship. Their families and friends stopped by to watch the progress, bringing baskets of food for us to eat. I took up the slack, pitching in wherever an extra hand was needed, so that I got to work with all of them and on all phases of the construction. Working side by side with someone is a pretty good way to get to know them, so we quickly became family. Suzy took charge of the stairway spiraling up the wall, which became one of the most striking features of the "Cell," as we began to call it. She fashioned every vertical support of the banister with a lathe and made each one unique in its design. Freshly stained and varnished, it looked like a wooden stairway to heaven.

The completion of the Cell was marked by two celebrations. The first was for everyone on Timber Ridge Trail and the surrounding community. It was a boisterous affair, with everyone bringing a dish to pass and housewarming gifts that they had made, including a beautiful quilt that the wives of the dirty dozen had made for my bed.

"Now at last I can go beyond camo!" I exclaimed to uproarious laughter. Then Ron stepped in front of the crowd with a wooden object wrapped in a blanket.

"I figured you needed a name for your homestead. Now, it's not up to me to name it, but here is the name that occurred to me. You can just use it as firewood if you don't like it."

He removed the blanket to reveal a plank of wood with the word "ENOUGH" in large letters, carved by a router and stained so that they stood out in sharp relief. Then he stood, awkward and uncertain, to see if I would accept his gift and suggestion for a name. I walked to his side, held the plank in front of me, and leaned it against the railing of the deck.

"It's perfect!" I exclaimed and we fell into an embrace with a cheer from the crowd.

The second celebration was restricted to the dirty dozen, who had built the Cell and would inaugurate the fire pit on the roof. I built the fire in preparation, along with a fire in the wood stove to warm the interior, and met them at about 10pm at the entrance to my property. The plank had been mounted on a tree by the path leading to the Cell. No one said that it would be a solemn affair but it became one as we filed up the trail, with the Cell silhouetted against the night sky, capped with the glow of the fire. We entered on the ground floor and made our way up the stairway to the living area lit by the glow of the wood stove and a few soft LED lights. Up to the sleeping loft. Further up to the office loft. Everything was made by our hands of local wood, freshly stained and varnished. Everything was utilitarian – a mean, lean, living machine – but the structure was also as sacred as a temple. This was felt by all of us without requiring words. We continued to ascend the wooden stairway until we came out onto the roof and sat in a circle around the fire. At that moment, the entire universe consisted of the night sky and this one group that had become united on the basis of what they had built. The bond that we felt was so strong that we would do anything for each other.

After I had spent my first week in the Cell, I sat on a cushion in front of a low table in my office loft and began a letter on a powder blue sheet of paper.

My Darling Eve,

How I wish that you could be with me to share this place that was built not by myself, but by a community. Everything about it is utilitarian but also as sacred as the inside of a church. All who enter feel this way. "Uplifting" is the word they use again and again.

The daily round of my life is much as it was back in Laramie. I arise naturally before dawn, make coffee and a simple breakfast, and get right to work in my office loft or kitchen table, whichever I choose. By late morning I am ready for some physical work and what choices I have! Splitting wood, building a garage on the edge of my property, fishing, or hiking the biological station land. Then, when I am refreshed from physical exercise, it is back to work. No monk is more dedicated to his meditations than I.

For companionship, making the creation of the Cell a community affair has bonded me to the Timber Ridge community even more than if I had been born here. Everyone is my friend and I can drop into their homes, taverns, and church socials whenever I want. Playing pool over beer and country music is a great way to take the world off my shoulders, at least for a few hours. I also invite them up here for potlucks and regularly give tours, since everyone is so proud of what we built together.

Thanks in large part to Ron, the community is also respectful of my privacy. They understand that I am like them and different at the same time. In fact, that combination leads to conversations that would surprise you. Some of them pour their hearts out to me, as if I were a priest, knowing that I will not judge them and that their confessions are safe with me. And sitting around the campfire on the roof at night has a way of turning them into philosophers, no matter how little book learning they have had. As you said about your old boyfriends, everyone is searching for meaning in life, but most people are forced to keep it to themselves so they don't become vulnerable. They crave an opportunity to safely speak their minds even more than their animal desires.

Once a week I travel to Laramie to meet with Howard and Ashley, the executive director of our new Evolution Institute. You've never seen Howard happier or more energized. He has taken a leave of absence from his professorial job and Omar will be teaching his Secret of Life class while he finishes his PhD. Isn't that insane? Howard's salary will be paid from my funds so he can devote full time to catalyzing cultural change, as he puts it. He thinks of it as like a chemical reaction that can be so swift that the future becomes nothing like the past. Let's hope that it doesn't take the form of an explosion! Ashley is an administrative genius. Whenever their work grows so that an additional staff position is needed, the money required is still only a drop in the bucket of my wealth.

What they are planning is a series of meetings that will take place around the world. Instead of standing in front of a bunch of ragtag college students, Howard will be standing in front of the most distinguished experts on topics such as economics, international relations, terrorism, education, and climate change. In each case, our job (yes, I will be present at all of these meetings) will be to convince them that "this view of life" – the evolutionary worldview – can be transformative in how we view these topics and therefore how we act. The first meeting, which we have provisionally titled "Reviving the Body Politic" will be held in Rome in about three months.

That leads me to the most exciting news of all. With the Cell completed and the Evolution Institute in such good hands, I am now in a position to take up the third strand of my life and visit you in Ecuador! Please – when you get this letter, call or email to help me arrange my travel. After waiting this long, I don't want to wait a single unnecessary minute longer. How long has it been? Over a year. Speaking for myself, my love for you has only grown stronger – if that is possible – but now it must have its way. The jungle will be in shambles after I am done with you.

Ferociously yours,

John

p.s. Ron says my life won't be complete until I get a dog. What do you think about that?

🌎

Two weeks later, I was gazing, transfixed, out of an airplane window as it landed at the airport of Quito, Ecuador, a city that was founded in 1556, a half century before the founding of the Jamestown colony of Virginia in 1607. From there I took a bush plane to the remote Remona-Santiago Province in the Amazon basin. Seeing the tropical rainforest from above was mesmerizing, but as we made a rough landing on a crude airstrip by a muddy river, I only had eyes for a small figure standing by the tarmac.

"Eve!" She was wearing shorts, a light khaki shirt with the sleeves rolled up, and sandals. She was thin and muscular and her skin was bronze from all of her time spent outdoors. I approached to envelop her in a hug.

"John! Not here!" Eve's quickly spoken words made it clear that I was not supposed to touch her or display any sign of affection. What the fuck? There was nobody around but one person unloading the plane and another waiting by a dugout canoe with an outboard motor! I had no choice but to obey her command, so I stood helplessly in front of her, ridiculously making small talk as my mind spun worst-case scenarios. Had she found someone else? Had she been waiting to tell me in person?

The Shuar village that Eve used as a home base was an hour up river in the dugout canoe. Eve sat in front, I sat in the middle, and the boatman sat in back steering the canoe with the outboard motor at full throttle. For him it was just another day at work but for me it was all I could do to keep my balance as we roared upstream. The river and banks on each side were a riot of tropical life – parrots, monkeys, iguanas – which Eve pointed out to me as if she was a tour guide and I was a tourist. What on earth was going on?

When we disembarked at the village, Eve made it clear once again that there could be no touching or any sign of affection. Was this some kind of strange custom of the Shuar people? Children flocked around us. Eve was their friend and I was a carnival attraction, towering above the other adults. They had no inhibition about touching, grabbing my legs and climbing me like a tree. Adults looked on with a smile.

"I'll introduce you to my Shuar friends later," Eve said as she showed me where I could drop my backpack. "Now I have a bit of field work to do. You can come with me."

By now I was truly alarmed. What on earth could explain her detached behavior? If the third strand of my life was broken, the other two strands would count for nothing! We headed down a well-worn path along the river and then another path that led upward. Surely, now that we were alone in the forest, we could embrace. But no, she kept walking at a brisk pace, talking about her field work as if I was a colleague. Then, about a mile up this steep trail, she turned around and faced me, her demeanor completely changed.

"OK, tracker! See if you can track me down *this* trail!" She ducked into a small opening in the foliage and disappeared with a laugh that blended with the sounds of the forest.

That vixen! My spirits soared. She had been leading me on the entire time to play some kind of game! I headed after her. The trail was clear enough. The problem was that she had made it just big enough for her, so that my progress was agonizingly slow. At times I had to crawl on my hands and knees. Wasn't it just like her to turn my size against me! I wondered if she was watching me from up in a tree, but for the moment her fresh footprints were still in front of me.

At length the narrow passage led to a clear stream and Eve's wet footprints could be seen on the rocks. Following her up the stream was easier going. After about seventy yards, the stream opened up into a large pool flooded with sunlight from the opening in the forest canopy. A curtain of vegetation enclosed the pool on all sides, with birds and butterflies flitting about like jewels on wings. At the head of the pool was a waterfall and standing underneath the waterfall, the water up to her waist, was Eve, facing me, as naked as the first Eve in her Eden. I tore the clothes from my body and dove into the pool, making my way toward her with mighty strokes of my arms and legs. Our embrace under the waterfall will remain with me forever.

"Oh, John!" Eve said after our first long kiss. "Forgive me for keeping you waiting, but it had to be like this!"

After we had sated ourselves under the waterfall, Eve led me to a campground that she had prepared by the edge of the pool, with a tent and a bed of giant leaves outside for us to lie upon. We lay side by side, face to face, stroking our naked bodies warmed by the sun, and entered into the deep conversation that I craved as much as sex.

"I found this waterfall and pool in the course of my field work and fell in love with it. Waterfalls are sacred to the Shuar, but there are also lots of them, and as soon as my Shuar friends saw my attachment to this one, they dedicated it to me as the waterfall of the monkey woman. No one else is allowed to come here."

"Monkey woman! You wrote that you had been given that name and that it seemed like more than a nickname. Have you learned more?"

"Well, in preparation for coming down here, I read everything that's been written by your Cult of Scholars about the Shuar and neighboring tribes. I also vowed to learn the Shuar language, which was really difficult, since it's completely different from all of the European languages. That, plus the fact that I was out in the jungle with them all the time and that I am not a white person, made them think of me as one of their own more than the Mission priests and sisters, government officials, or other scientists that I work with. When I started to scamper about the jungle canopy, free climbing without the use of any ropes, they started to call me monkey woman and their attitude toward me became reverential."

"Wow! Were they being superstitious?"

"That's what I thought at first and it really bothered me because I didn't want to exploit their superstitions. I felt that I needed to tell them that I was just a person, not any kind of jungle deity. But soon enough I realized that my own way of thinking about it was messed up. Think about my own Christian upbringing. It's chock full of superstitions, but they aren't mindless. Yes, they are a tissue of lies, but they result in a strong and nurturing community. As soon as I started to think about Shuar beliefs that way, they began to command more respect from me. Of course they made little sense from a scientific perspective, but they had organized Shuar life since long before the Judeo-Christian religion existed on the face of the earth."

It was so wonderful lying with Eve and hearing her talk that I interrupted her story with a kiss and nestled closer to her. Then I invited her to continue while gazing lovingly at her face.

"Understanding the logic of Shuar religious beliefs was even more difficult than learning to speak their language. Like devout Christians, traditional Shuar believe that there's a spirit world that's more real than the physical world, but it's not inhabited by anything resembling the Christian God. Instead, it's inhabited by spirits that flow freely from the animate world, such as monkeys, jaguars, and snakes; the inanimate world, such as waterfalls, and people. People acquire soul power by entering the spirit world and can even change their shapes to become other animals. Soul power protects them from danger, especially from human enemies, since killings were so pervasive prior to contact with the Catholic missionaries.

"Now you can see why my arrival, my interest in studying the primates, and my ability to scamper around the forest canopy would cause them to call me a monkey woman and attribute a lot of soul power to me. But it goes deeper than that. Who gets soul power isn't arbitrary. Their spirit world is closely tied to the real world, just as for Christianity. The pastors, deacons, and elders of my church back home who are invested with spiritual power have jobs to do in their community. The same is true with the Shamans and other people invested with soul power down here. The mere fact that I study primates and scamper about in trees would not be sufficient to invest me with soul power. My Shuar friends *need* me for something. That's why they're calling me monkey woman and investing me with soul power."

Eve's eyes had grown wide and her lower lip was trembling. One of her most endearing qualities was to sense what needed to be done and to do it. Now it was being tested to her limits.

"I've come to realize that this is a critical moment in their existence as a people. If we can establish their traditional territory as an ecological reserve under their administrative control, then they can continue as a people without being swallowed up by the mass of modern humanity. It won't be like the old days. In the old days, families remained in one spot until they overhunted their game and their gardens became overgrown with weeds. Then they moved to a new spot. In the old days, 'us' was confined to groups of only a few dozen people, perpetually warring with 'them.' Then the catholic missionaries pacified them, moved them into more stable villages, and helped them transition to cattle ranching, which involved cutting down the forest. Those are the old days.

"Acting as stewards of an ecological reserve, including restoring the deforested areas in addition to preserving the remaining jungle, will be new for them, but they have the will and wherewithal to do it. They've adapted to changing circumstances before, and they can do so again. They see me as the most understanding and trustworthy person to speak for them in all of the meetings that need to take place and agreements that need to be signed. That is why they've invested me with soul power and why I've become far more important in everything taking place down here than my job description as a staff scientist. In order to serve that need, I must exist in both worlds. That's why I have accepted the role of Monkey Woman as understood by the Shuar. Truly assimilating myself to their culture is the most respectful and effective thing I can so. Let me show you something."

Eve hopped to her feet, entered the tent, and came out with an old leather satchel elaborately decorated with bird bones. She carefully withdrew a necklace consisting of woven fiber and a black round object about the size of a child's fist. With a shock I realized that it was a shrunken head, not of a human, but a primate of some sort.

"This was given to me by one of the most powerful Shuar shamans. It's made from the head of a howler monkey, using the same techniques that they used to shrink human heads. This gift from the Shaman is like a Bishop being ordained by the Pope. When I wear this, it commands the respect of the entire Shuar nation."

Sitting cross-legged in front of me, Eve slowly donned the necklace so that the macabre shrunken head was between her naked breasts. Then she seemed to fall into a kind of a trance, as if I wasn't there at all. Suddenly I felt afraid, as if my beloved Eve had been replaced by a powerful sorceress and that my life was in peril. I couldn't shake the fear no matter how hard I tried to cling to my modern sensibilities.

"Eve! EVE!"

Eve snapped out of her trance, which snapped me out of mine. She removed the necklace and placed it back in the leather satchel.

"My role among the Shuar is not what I looked for but it's what needs to be done. Ironic, don't you think? I keep telling you to shrug the world from your shoulders, and now here I am, taking the world upon mine. But let's not think about that now. For the next three days, it can be just you and me in our own personal garden of Eden."

Two weeks after returning home, I wrote a letter to Eve on a sheet of powder blue paper.

My beloved Eve,

After our parting, I became so lonely for companionship that I acted upon Ron's advice. I now "have me a dog," as he would say. Her name is Lizzie and she picked me out at the Laramie dog shelter. She was the only one who wasn't barking. She just looked at me with her big brown eyes, with one ear straight up and the other one bent, and it was love at first sight. She's nine months old and had been in the shelter for three months. Why she wasn't snapped up by someone else is a mystery. Her pedigree is anyone's guess, just like you. She'll be knee high and about 50 pounds when she is full grown, with short tawny fur and all muscle. A real athlete! This will be the perfect life for her. She'll almost never need to be on a leash and we're already sharing the same bed – don't be jealous! I know that you'll love her if you ever make a trip back north. In fact, I will enclose a photo to entice you. Ron says that she can stay with his family when I travel – lucky, as I'll be heading to Rome with Howard and Ashley in a little less than a month. These three strands of my life sure make a crazy braid! In paradise with my Eve in our Eden, in my hermitage up north, and now traveling the world to unite the Ivory Archipelago, as Howard likes to say. If that's not enough for any one person, what would be?

Our time together in Eden will always be with me. J.

Exactly twenty-eight days later, I was taking up the third strand of my braid in an ornate conference room at the Pontifical Gregorian University in Rome, founded more than 450 years ago by the Society of Jesus, commonly known as the Jesuits. Thirty people sat around the large table, ranging in age from their late seventies to their early twenties. Their dress signaled that they came from different islands of the Ivory Archipelago. One, a foremost scholar of the Jesuit order, was himself a Jesuit wearing his long black robes. An economist wore the attire of a business executive. A political scientist wore the tweedy uniform of a university professor. An elderly woman who was an eminent historian of the Enlightenment era added a splash of color with a bright scarf around her neck. Most of the older ones were men but there were actually more women than men among the younger ones. Some of them were sharp-looking in addition to their sharp minds and would keep the older men from dozing. The younger they were, the more casual their dress. Part of my creed of "enough" was not to own clothes for different occasions, so I was dressed in canvas pants and a cotton shirt, as usual, with my notebook strapped to my hip. That made me a sartorial outlier, even for this diverse group.

I sat among them and felt that I knew them already because their scholarly work had been my reading assigned by Howard for the previous six months. Ashley circulated around the room and nipped in and out to keep everything running smoothly. It was Ashley who had identified the University as a good venue for the workshop and made all the arrangements. Howard stood at the front and called the meeting to order, as he would a lecture of his Secret of Life class. He showed no signs of intimidation standing in front of this elite audience. On the contrary, he had the same kind of quiet charisma as a Walter Gold, a self-confidence that was innately attractive because it was not innate – why should anyone care about that? – but acquired, therefore something that could be learned.

"Friends!" Howard began. "It is my great pleasure to inaugurate this workshop on a topic that is both old and new – the concept of society as an organism. First let's have a round of introductions, although hopefully you have read the biographical sketches that were provided as part of your reading packet."

It took about half an hour for everyone to briefly introduce themselves. The group was so diverse that most of them were unknown to each other, even though they were highly respected (for the older ones) or rising stars (for the younger ones) within their own scholarly islands. When it was my turn, I merely said, "Hi, my name is John Galt, and I help to run the Evolution Institute with Howard and Ashley. We'll talk more about the Evolution Institute later."

Howard resumed his introductory remarks. "As all of you know from your respective disciplines, the metaphor of society as like an organism stretches back to the beginning of recorded thought, from Plato's Republic to Hobbes's Leviathan. It is reflected in words such as 'corporation' and phrases such as 'the body politic.' It is central to Christian thought and to many other religions …" Howard nodded to the Jesuit in our midst, who smiled and nodded back. "… and to social scientific thought, such as Emile Durkheim, who was the son of a Rabbi."

Everyone around the table nodded in agreement. Even though they came from different islands of the Ivory Archipelago, this much was common ground for all of them.

"Most of you also know that despite its venerable history, the concept of society as an organism was eclipsed during the last half century by various forms of reductionism and individualism. In the social sciences it is called Methodological Individualism, a commitment to explaining social phenomena in terms of the actions and intentions of individuals. In economics it is called *Homo economicus*, a portrayal of human nature as motivated entirely by self-interest, or 'self-regarding preferences' to be more precise, usually operationalized as the pursuit of money. Even my own field of evolutionary biology took an individualistic turn during the middle of the 20th century, as if everything can and must be explained in terms of maximizing the fitness of individuals and their selfish genes. Against this background, the concept of society as an organism often seemed to disappear entirely. As UK Prime Minister Margaret Thatcher famously said in the 1970s, 'There is no such thing as society – only individuals and their families.'

"In popular culture, some of you will know the names of Ayn Rant and John Galt I and II. In some respects, they were not a part of the intellectual trends that I have just described, which took place before them and would have continued without them. But they added a new dimension by elevating individualism to the status of a moral ideal and spreading it around the world with their creed of Objectivism. As Alan Greenspan, chairman of the US Federal Reserve Board for decades and early disciple of Ayn Rant put it, 'Before Ayn, I thought that the Free Market was good. After Ayn, I thought it was right.' It is thanks in large part to Rant and the first two Galts that the concept of 'Greed is Good' has become the moral standard of our times. And yes, the big guy sitting there is John Galt III, in case you were wondering."

Oh, boy, were they wondering. All eyes turned to me and I could almost hear the wheels turning in their heads. Most of them were sufficiently immersed in their scholarly worlds that they knew none of the juicy details of my family history.

"On behalf of my family I would like to issue an apology to all of you," I joked, and the laughter momentarily dispelled the tension.

"Another thing that can be said about the concept of society as an organism, throughout its long history, is that it was always metaphorical," Howard continued. "No one had the intellectual resources to connect the dots between human societies and actual organisms, such as the birds and the bees, or you and me. One reason that the tradition of functionalism initiated by Durkheim faded, after its day in the sun, was that its assumptions about society as an organism were axiomatic, as if society *must* be like an organism, which ultimately became stultifying."

Nobody around the table could disagree with anything Howard had said so far. It was still common ground for all of them, but that was about to change.

"Now here is what's new. Starting in the 1970s, ideas began to emerge in my field of evolutionary biology that were beyond Darwin's imagination." Howard was putting his theatrical upbringing to good use. The words were arresting enough by themselves, but the tone of his voice and his body language had the little audience at full attention.

"Darwin and everyone else assumed, as a matter of course, that individuals evolve by small mutational steps from other individuals. Then, a cell biologist named Lynn Margulis proposed that nucleated cells – single-celled creatures such as the paramecium and amoeba that you might have viewed through a microscope in a biology class and the cells that make up you and me – evolved not by small mutational steps from bacterial cells but as societies of bacterial cells that became so cooperative that they qualified as higher-level organisms in their own right. In other words, nucleated cells did not evolve from individuals. They evolved from *social groups*. Margulis's symbiotic cell theory was controversial for decades but now it is accepted as fact. What this means is that within my field of evolutionary biology, the concept of an organism as a social group and a social group as an organism became fused. It isn't a metaphor. It is a fact."

Aside from the three members of our group that had been invited as experts in this area, no one else had entertained the slightest notion that a connection might exist between their work and nucleated cells. They had gone from common ground to new territory within a single minute.

"In the 1990s – only about twenty years ago – the concept of social groups evolving into organisms was generalized to include other transitions such as the first cells, multi-cellular organisms, and social insect colonies. The concept might even explain the origin of life itself as groups of cooperating molecular interactions. The social insects provide an especially interesting case because they demonstrate that organisms do not need to be bounded by membranes. That would be a superficial definition. Organisms are defined by the degree of cooperation among their parts. On any given day, the members of a beehive might be dispersed over an area of several square kilometers, but they still qualify as an organism because of the degree to which they coordinate their activities for the common good of the hive. Later this afternoon, Tom Neeley over there will demonstrate how beehives practice a form of democracy, believe it or not." A tall man with long blond hair ringing the bald dome of his head smiled and raised a finger to remind the others who he was.

"Of course," Howard continued, "we humans have been comparing our societies to beehives for as long as we have to organisms, including Bernard Mandeville's *Fable of the Bees*, written in 1714 as an early justification of laissez faire economics. As we shall see, Mandeville got it totally wrong, and reviving the body politic will have profound implications for economic theory and practice." Even in his introductory remarks, Howard was demonstrating his ability to hop from one island of the Ivory Archipelago to another – from biology, to religion, to economics, as if there was no separation.

"But wait! There's more!" The familiar refrain from late night television infomercials made some people around the table smile. "Even more recently, the conversion from groups *of* organisms to groups *as* organisms is making sense of the human evolutionary story, starting with genetic evolution at the scale of small groups and continuing with the cultural evolution of larger societies, leading to the mega-societies of today, as Peter Murchin over there" – a big bearlike man with a thick Russian accent raised a finger and smiled – "will explain tomorrow. Alexis de Tocqueville, the great social theorist who compared French and American society in the 1830s, had this to say about small human groups: 'The village or township is the only association which is so perfectly natural that it seems to constitute itself.' Tocqueville was onto something with his observation about the innateness of human behavior in small groups, along with his insights about France and America as more recent cultural constructions.

"So here is the bottom line. The reason that human societies have been compared to organisms throughout history is because they *are* organisms, at least some of the time. Not axiomatically, but only when special conditions are met. Only now, *for … the … first … time … in … the … history … of … ideas,* can the concept of human society as an organism go beyond metaphor and be placed on a strong scientific foundation. That is what brings us together for this workshop."

A long pause ensued. Howard's delivery had become increasingly intense, with *"for … the … first … time … in … the … history … of … ideas"* delivered like hammer blows. I had seen him like this in front of his Secret of Life class. It wasn't just acting. It was a person trying desperately to impress upon his audience the historic nature of the present moment. Now he seemed to slump from the effort and paused to regain his strength. As for those sitting around the table, they were thinking too hard to speak. In the space of ten minutes, Howard had moved from common ground to terra incognita. Everything he said was simple, free of jargon, and seemed to follow from what came before, but if that were the case, how could such an extravagant claim about its novelty be true? They could see nothing to argue against but they still found it impossible to accept, so they remained silent until Howard resumed in a normal tone of voice.

"Before we break for coffee, John and I would like to say a little more about the Evolution Institute. John, would you like to begin?"

"Sure," I began. "As you have heard, I am part of the Galt dynasty and as such have considerable wealth of my own. A central tenet of Objectivism is that its principles can be justified by science and rationality, as the name suggests. From an early age, I came to the conclusion that the Objectivist movement had become detached from science and rationality and therefore needed to be reformed. Howard became my mentor in college and the concept of society as an organism began to emerge as a robust alternative to the individualism that the Objectivist movement is currently known for. The Evolution Institute is our way of catalyzing scientific research and scholarship in that area."

"Right!" Howard replied, "and don't be misled by John's money and good looks. He also punches above his weight intellectually. This is our very first workshop, to be followed by others at the rate of four per year. For each workshop, we have intentionally included a mix of ages, from senior scientists and scholars to highly promising graduate students. We also have included a mix of academic disciplines. Providing a single theoretical framework that can be 'spoken' across disciplines is one of our major objectives. Finally, each workshop is intended to be the beginning of a long-term inquiry rather than a one-time event. We are in a position to fund the best research ideas that emerge from each workshop. Now let's break for coffee and return in fifteen minutes for our first presentations."

I had used the word "catalyze" in my comments but none of the participants could have guessed how much Howard, Ashley, and I had designed the workshop with chemical catalysis in mind. Just as a chemical catalyst latches onto other molecules and holds them in an orientation that binds them to each other, we had latched onto key people from around the world who otherwise would not have interacted in a million years. Now we were holding them in a way that would bind them to each other by offering an intellectual feast in the most pleasant of settings, where each person could function as both a teacher of their particular discipline and a student of exotic disciplines, all with a focus on finding common ground on a manifestly important topic. Even more enticing, we were offering financial support for continuing the inquiry after the workshop. Most of the people in the room were starving for resources to do their scholarly work. The famine was especially acute in the United States, where attacks on government programs had reduced federal funding for scholarly and scientific activities to an all-time low. How ironic, I thought to myself, that the policies enacted by my father and his kind were making our own efforts at catalysis easier. The people we had brought together had every reason to explore common interests to support their scholarly habit.

Howard's introduction was like sprinkling the catalytic substance into the chemical broth. The conversation started to bubble during the first coffee break and by the time we sat down to dinner on the first night it had become positively frothy. We had heard presentations on topics as diverse as honeybee democracy, hunter-gatherer societies, the Greek democratic experiment, the role of the Freemasons in the cultural evolution of modern democracies, and the rules governing the Jesuit order. The late afternoon had been left free and I had used it to walk among the ancient ruins of Rome, which were intermingled with the modern city. Now we were seated in the outdoor area of a restaurant that had been carefully chosen by Ashley, around a long table with baskets of bread and carafes of red wine within easy reach. The night was balmy and the people sitting at the other tables provided a pleasant backdrop without being too noisy.

I sat with the younger members of the group, who had gravitated to one end of the table. They could scarcely contain their excitement at the intellectual vistas that had opened up before them during the day, which made their own scholarly islands appear provincial by comparison. I had my notebook out and was scribbling the references to books and articles that they were providing me, along with reminders to email my own suggestions for them – more connections that would never have been made otherwise. I was delighted to discover that I could hold up my end of the conversation. They were the rising stars of their respective disciplines and I was merely a year out of college. Nevertheless, Howard had taught me well and the monastic lifestyle that I had been leading since my sophomore year made me far better read than others my age. I had also read their own work in preparation for the workshop and by now had acquired Howard's ability to hop effortlessly from island to island with my single evolutionary toolkit. As I spoke knowledgably to each of them in a way that they could not do to each other, I could see that I had earned their respect and that they were treating me as an equal, even as someone to look up to. Perhaps some of them might even become allies in my assault on my father's evil empire.

Toward the end of the meal I got up to use the bathroom. When I returned I noticed that the conversation at our table had become so animated that we were positively bellowing at each other, oblivious to the people at the other tables who cast furtive looks in our direction. What on earth could we be talking about that commanded such interest?

After the three-day workshop had concluded, Ashley, Howard, and I fell into our airplane seats, exhausted but giddy with excitement. Our cultural catalysis experiment had worked. We had caused a surge of scholarly activity that would never have happened otherwise. Ashley would add staff positions to the Evolution Institute as needed to accommodate the increased activity and the financial expense would still be only a few drops in the bucket of my unimaginable wealth. What's more, we would repeat the experiment four times a year for different topics: Business and economics. Civil wars. Terrorism. Child development and education. As Howard put it, every topic area relevant to improving the human condition requires an evolutionary makeover and the Evolution Institute was going to make it happen. Others might find it hard to grasp, but the three of us understood the historic nature of the present moment and it bonded us firmly to each other.

Thus it was that the three strands of my life came together during my twenty-first year, which I continued to weave into a braid until my twenty-fifth year. For every turn of Earth around the sun, I travelled the world with Howard and Ashley to unite the Ivory Archipelago. By my twenty-fifth year, we had assembled an extensive network of scientists and scholars who spoke the common language of evolutionary theory and were bringing it to bear on the concept of society as an organism and how to stretch its boundaries to envelop the whole Earth. At one point, I calculated that the amount of money I was spending to support their research was a substantial fraction of the money that the entire United States Government spends to support research in the social sciences and humanities – a shameful statistic, similar to the statistic that some individuals had become wealthier than entire nations. Even if the US Government increased its support ten-fold, it would not have had the catalytic effect of the Evolution Institute because we had a deliberate plan for how to bring people together and for what purpose. Along the way, we identified and approached key people who could help us in our plan to combat my father's evil empire, the Death Star of Individualism. At times I felt like my grandfather, John Galt I, approaching doers from the shadows with the offer to join a secret utopian society. In our case, however, we would directly transform the whole world rather than sequestering ourselves in some remote valley and perpetrating a hoax upon the whole world.

For every turn of Earth around the sun, I also visited Eve three times, interspersed between the Evolution Institute workshops. Each time, we began by spending several days together in Eden, as naked and innocent as the original Adam and Eve. Then we would spend several days among the Shuar, where I accompanied her on her field work and got to know her friends and associates. Eve's gift for perceiving what needs to be done, combined with her soul power that was bestowed rather than sought after or taken, had indeed made her a key figure in the negotiations to create an ecological preserve presided over by the Shuar – a source of dismay as much as pride, since so much of what needed to be done seemed beyond her, or anyone else's, control.

Once a year around Christmas time, Eve travelled north to visit her family and stayed with me in my Cell. The first time, I met her at the Laramie airport with Lizzie in my truck. They bonded instantly and we made our way to the Eden ranch, where a big dinner was awaiting. Since I was a frequent dinner guest on my weekly trips back from Laramie, I had become part of the family, completing the quartet of Gospel writers. When we reached the Eden ranch, it was as if Mary and five of Eve's men were welcoming her home.

It was midnight by the time we returned to my homestead. The air was cold and still and the trees were silhouetted against a brilliant night sky, undimmed by earthly lights. We walked past the word "ENOUGH" and made our way up the path, our boots squeaking in the snow. The hexagonal shape of the Cell came into view. We entered, removed our boots and parkas, and ascended the stairs in our stocking feet to the first floor. The interior of varnished wood was illuminated by the last embers of the fire in the wood stove and a few soft lights that I had left on.

"John! It's like a cathedral!"

We fell into an embrace and both started to weep. For me, the experience of two strands of my life coming together in this way was overwhelming. The next three days were every bit as blissful as my visits to our tropical Eden. Making love and waking up together in the sleeping loft. Cooking meals together. Long snowshoe treks on the station property, where it all began. Introducing Eve to my redneck friends to prove that the mystery woman I kept talking about really existed.

"Throw her back! She's too small!" Ron joked at the comical difference in our size. Eve easily fit into Timber Ridge society, which was cut from the same cloth as her own upbringing.

The intensity of our love during the times that we spent together, combined with the support that we gave each other during our absences, honed our relationship into the hardness of a diamond. We never had a chance to grow accustomed to each other. Every time we entered each other's life, whether by a visit or a powder blue letter in the mail, was special. No matter how lonely I became during our absences or how attracted to other women around me, striking up a relationship with anyone else was unthinkable.

My visits with Eve and Evolution Institute workshops collectively occupied about fifty days of the year. The rest of my time was spent alone in my mountaintop hermitage, except for weekly trips to Laramie and tasting the pleasures of redneck society now and then. During the summers, I would also hike over to the Lodge when the biological station was in session to taste the pleasures of that society, sometimes meeting with Howard there instead of in Laramie. The two societies on the mountaintop were like oil and water that never mixed. Yet, I was native to both and understood that they worked well for the same reasons, just like every other village-scale society around the world, from the Shuar in the Amazon basin, to the Eden's church congregation, to the Village School in the Adirondacks. They qualified as organisms and to live within them was to become free from self-imposed suffering. The great challenge was to provide the same ingredients at a planetary scale.

A quote from the Norwegian arctic explorer Fridtjof Nansen captured the way that I felt about my days spent alone in my mountaintop retreat. I liked it so much that I hung a framed copy on the wall of my office loft.

The first great thing is to find yourself and for that you need solitude and contemplation at least sometimes. I can tell you that deliverance will not come from the rushing noisy centers of civilization. It will come from the lonely places.

Nansen was the first person to lead an expedition across the interior of Greenland on cross-country skis in 1888. During a three-year expedition (1893-1896) aboard a stout little ship called the Fram (Norwegian for "forward"), he came closer to the North Pole than anyone else at the time. These exploits captured the attention of the world in the same way that space travel would nearly a century later. As he grew into middle age, Nansen used his celebrity to promote the League of Nations and otherwise advocate for world peace, which earned him the Nobel Peace Prize in 1922. I couldn't help but identify with both sides of Nansen, the side that sought solitude and the side that sought world peace. I even identified my Cell with the Fram. Its interior looked even more like the inside of a ship than the inside of a cathedral. A vehicle for exploration, even if it was rooted on top of a mountain.

Something else that struck me about Nansen's words was that they could have been written by my grandmother. Ayn Rant also elevated the individual to heroic proportions, which is why she appealed so much to idealistic young people like my mother. Could my grandmother have been a kindred soul of Nansen, boldly striking off into the unknown with her ideas? The difference was that Nansen and Rant developed their ideas about individualism in different directions. Rant's vision began and ended with heroic individuals – the doers – who must free themselves from the shackles imposed upon them by society. In Nansen's vision, heroic individuals always operate as members of groups. Nansen didn't traverse the interior of Greenland or get so close to the North Pole by himself. Such a feat would be impossible for any single person. He led expeditions and it was only by a group effort that such feats could be accomplished. This was something that my grandmother could never understand and the proof was the fate of the utopian society that she tried to form with my grandfather. A hand-picked group of doers couldn't survive more than a few years in a Colorado valley, despite being bank-rolled by Midas Mulligan, because they didn't know how to work together to achieve a common goal. The groups assembled by Nansen could survive for years in the harshest conditions on Earth because they did know how to work together to achieve common goals.

It made me think better of my grandmother to imagine her as an intrepid explorer, like Nansen, whose vision just happened to take her on a wrong path. The annals of arctic exploration are filled with expeditions that bravely set forth and never came back. But here the comparison took a disturbing twist. The world was following my grandmother on her wrong path, not Nansen on his right path. My great challenge was to halt the world's journey into oblivion and set it on another path. Not exactly Nansen's path, because his efforts toward world unity were not as successful as his arctic expeditions, but something in that direction based on advances in knowledge that were unavailable to him at the time.

For all the catalysis within the Cult of Scholars that we had accomplished through the Evolution Institute, our impact on the rest of the world was very close to zero. This by itself was proof of how much the decision-makers of the world were ignoring the facts of the world. Even though I introduced every workshop by saying that I was trying to reform the Objectivist movement, this never reached the ears of my father as far as I could tell. That's how much he and his associates operated in a fact-free parallel universe. Neither did our catalytic work make any sort of headline in the popular press. It was only the academic literature that was starting to become frothy. Alas, Howard would comment now and then, even catalytic change is slow in the academic world. Months and years were still required to do the research, write the articles and books, and put them through the peer review process.

While this slow motion foment was happening, the deterioration of the rest of the world was taking place at an accelerating pace. Economies ground to a halt as more and more people became too impoverished to buy the goods that were being produced. Liberal and conservative politicians pummeled each other ineffectually, like punch drunk boxers failing to knock each other out after fifteen rounds. The fact was that neither side had the answers. A member of a village who kept shouting "Me first!" would be quickly ostracized, but a politician who kept shouting "Our nation first!" was likely to get elected. Then national identities started to fall apart as people identified with smaller factions to gain a sense of security. The more people identified with an embattled "us" surrounded by hostile "thems," the more they felt impelled to resort to violent tactics, which only made the problems worse. Saddest of all were the individuals who felt so disrespected that they decided to take their own lives in a blaze of glory, as if to say, "You have reduced me to nothing, so you are nothing to me." I knew from the Cult of Scholars that this form of suicidal protest has taken place around the world and throughout history, but never with so much destructive force as a man with an automatic rifle, a bomb strapped to his chest, or driving a van into a crowd.

Powerful interests were always ready to exploit and even create social chaos for their own short-term gain. The fact that they were destroying the world for their own descendants meant nothing. For them, it was all about being on top at all costs. Power and ranking, where there was no such thing as enough. I could contemplate the destruction from the safety of my mountaintop retreat but Eve was in the direct path of the storm. The relatively enlightened and progressive Ecuadorian government, the kind that might think to create ecological reserves and to respect the rights of its indigenous people, was in danger of being swept away by authoritarian ideologues who would almost certainly serve the interests of the timber, mining, and oil corporations. A violent guerrilla movement across the border in Peru was frightening the voters into supporting a candidate who called for getting tough and expanding the military budget. In Eve's letters, which were growing increasingly despondent, she said that it was not at all beyond the realm of possibility that the guerrilla movement was a set-up supported by the corporate interests in cahoots with the CIA. It wouldn't be the first time that an authoritarian South and Central American government was propped up by US interests.

It was obvious to both Howard and me that cultural catalysis needed to be taken to a new level and that I was the only person who could do it, if such a thing was possible at all. I had many days and nights to reflect upon my plan of attack in my little fortress of solitude and my twenty-sixth lap around the sun seemed like a good time to start. As my twenty-fifth birthday approached, I shared an outline of my plan in a powder blue letter to Eve.

About the time that I started to check my mailbox in hope of a return letter, there was a sharp knock on my door. It was ten o'clock at night and the visitor had approached quietly, so that even Lizzie was surprised by the sound and started to bark defensively. I opened the door and to my astonishment saw Eve standing before me. As if her presence weren't surprising enough, her face was contorted with conflicting emotions. Lizzie was bounding all around us, adding to the confusion.

Without a word, Eve leapt onto me, wrapping her arms around my neck and her legs around my waist. She gave me a fervent kiss and then pressed her head against my neck and shoulder, hugging me as if for dear life. Then, just as quickly, she leapt back off and started to speak.

"John! We can't be together anymore! My path is taking me someplace that you can't go! Forgive me! I can't be there for you on your path! And forgive me for what I might do on mine! *Sometimes it's just necessary to become an outlaw!*"

With those words, Eve disappeared into the night. Before I had time to recover, my cell phone rang. My brain was functioning just enough to guess that the call might have something to do with Eve, so I answered it.

"John, this is Mary. Have you seen Eve?"

"I just saw her in a terrible state. What's happening?"

"We don't know. She showed up out of the blue in a rental car from the airport and spent one night with us. The next day, we got a call from the president of our bank asking if we knew that Eve had withdrawn all her savings and closed her account. It's a tiny bank and he's known Eve since she was a child, so he felt that he had to share his concern. When Eve didn't return, we entered her room and discovered that she had removed everything that could be sold for money. What's happening, John? We're beside ourselves with worry!"

"I don't know, Mary. I think she has decided to take some kind of action down in Ecuador. There's nothing that we can do but trust her resourcefulness. Keep her in your prayers and call me if you hear anything. I'll do the same."

Barely able to walk, I climbed the stairs to the sleeping loft and flung myself on my bed. Lizzie sensed that something was deeply wrong and followed behind me, nuzzling my face before laying down next to me. For four years it seemed that I had been the master of my fate, confidently weaving the three strands of my life into a strong braid and plotting to change the world, safe and secure in my mountain retreat. Now the world had reached out and knocked me flat, using Eve as its agent of destruction. One strand of my life, the most precious for my personal wellbeing, had been severed clean. As for the other two strands, I couldn't even think about them. Concern for Eve had conquered my mind, but for no purpose, because there was nothing that I could do for her. I couldn't rescue her like a knight in shining armor. All I could do was trust her own resourcefulness and continue on my own path without my third strand.

I don't know how long I lay there, immobilized by worry for Eve and a sense of profound fatigue. I had no choice but to proceed, like the character of a tragic play. With a heavy heart, I ascended the stairs to the office loft and began a letter on a white sheet of paper.

"Dear Father ..."

The Trap

My father arranged for his private jet to fly me from the Laramie airport to a small airfield close to his house in the Hamptons on Long Island, one of several estates that he owned around the world. The interior of the jet was richly appointed, with a large plush chair that reclined into a bed and an attractive stewardess to attend to my needs. A martini was placed in my hand as soon as I settled in and a chilled shrimp cocktail was presented after takeoff. Several other courses would follow during the five-hour fight.

The stewardess was flirtatious and it was hard not to respond to her overtures in kind. My love for Eve never diminished my attraction to other women, only trumped it with something stronger. This was a strange new world for me and perhaps being flirtatious was part of her job. For all I knew, she was one of the perks of being ultra-rich, along with the bottomless martini and the gourmet meal. Maybe I could have her during the flight on the reclining seat. Just as I was dismissing this fantasy, she discretely placed a slip of paper with her phone number on my tray table.

"Mandy – right?"

"Yes!" Mandy said brightly, pleased that I had remembered her name. I put the slip of paper in my palm and returned it to her by placing her hand in both of mine. Once we were touching, I didn't want to let her hand go and continued holding it.

"In another life, nothing would please me more."

Mandy smiled at me as we continued holding hands. "I think that's the sweetest way that anyone has ever said 'no' to me. In case you were wondering, that wasn't part of my job. Who *are* you, anyway?"

"I'm the old man's son."

Mandy's mouth fell open and she brought both hands to her face. "I didn't even know he had a son! Please forgive me, Mr. Galt!"

"As I said, in another life ..." For the rest of the trip, she stuck assiduously to her role of stewardess.

A stretch limo was waiting by the airstrip to convey me to my father's house. In the short trip I learned that the driver's name was Eduardo, that he came to America to flee problems in El Salvador, and that his mother also worked for my father as a maid.

"We are grateful to your father," he said.

"That's good to know," I replied.

Based on a little Internet homework, I knew that my father's house had twelve bedrooms, fourteen full and six half baths, a kitchen designed by one of the Iron Chefs, a nine-hole golf course, an expansive patio surrounding an Olympic-sized swimming pool, and a quarter mile of ocean front. Estates in this part of Long Island sold for between 50 and 150 million dollars. Knowing all of this didn't fully prepare me for the real thing, as we rolled down the immaculate white gravel driveway and Eduardo leapt out to open the limo door for me before I had a chance to open it for myself. What a contrast to my thirty-foot diameter Cell with the composting toilet on the ground floor!

"Welcome home!" he grinned.

What is it like for a twenty-five-year old man to meet his father after seventeen years without any contact at all? A father who is a billionaire power broker? Who is responsible for the son's own great wealth? Who is demonized by his mother, adored by half of America and despised by the other half? A father who is causing great harm to the world by the son's own reckoning, whatever else might be said about him as a human being? I was about to find out. The person who answered the door was not my father, however, but Cindi, his wife, a woman in her early forties who still had the perky good looks of a cheerleader. I knew that she had been a reporter starting out at Fox News, with the combination of looks and brains that Fox women are known for, who married my father and now helped to manage his empire. She was dressed in running shoes, form-fitting athletic pants and a soft pink fleece jacket. As we set eyes upon each other for the first time, the first spark was of sexual interest, which we quickly extinguished to assume our roles of stepmother and stepson.

"John! Isn't this amazing! I have a stepson!"

"Hello … um … Mom!" I joked and we lightly embraced. I could tell that we would quickly grow to like each other.

"Is this all you brought?" she asked, pointing to my backpack. "Come in!"

We entered a large entrance space with the kind of stairway leading upstairs that Fred Astaire and Ginger Rogers danced down in their movies.

"Olivia, Mia, Avery! Come meet your half-brother!"

I heard the sound of doors opening and three girls descended the stairs, aged sixteen, fourteen, and ten, in that order. They must have a close relationship to each other, I surmised, because they were descending the stairs in a single clump. All three were slim, blond, and pretty like their mother. As soon as they could see me, the clump stopped in its tracks and stared. Avery, the youngest, broke the silence.

"You're *hot!*"

"*Avery!*" Cindi scolded as the other girls laughed, "He's your *brother!*"

"That's my bad luck – otherwise, I would be happy to be your Prince Charming!"

Avery made a face and Cindi asked the girls to show me to the guest house by the beach where I would be staying. "John is in his recording studio. We air his radio and television shows from right here so he doesn't have to commute. I'll tell him that you're here."

The three girls led me through several palatial rooms to the patio area with tables and a bar, almost like an outdoor restaurant. We passed the gigantic pool with a row of dressing rooms and down a path toward the ocean. The guest house was on the crest of the beach with the wall facing the ocean made entirely of glass. A king-sized bed faced the glass wall with a wide screen TV mounted on one side wall and a mini-bar on the other. The spacious bathroom featured a sink area made out of granite and a shower stall that sprayed you from the top and two sides. A bathrobe was hanging on a hook next to a stack of plush towels and a wicker basket to throw them into when they became dirty.

"I don't know if I'm ready for this," I smiled as I put my backpack on the bed. "I'm just a country boy from Wyoming!"

I changed into a fresh pair of canvas pants and cotton shirt and made my way back to the manor. Cindi said that my father would be right down and departed, sensing that we might want to be alone. I expected him to descend the stairs but instead he entered behind me from one of the other rooms on the ground floor.

"John! Here I am!"

I turned and we faced each other, about six feet apart. Of course I knew what he looked like, since he was all over the media, but seeing him in person was different. He was a head shorter than me and his weight, which was well known to fluctuate between the low and high 200's depending upon the success of his health regimen, was at the low end of this range. His expensive leisurewear made him look fit in his own way and his face was tanned. Evidently he spent a fair amount of time outdoors, perhaps playing golf. He looked unlike me in so many ways and yet I could also see myself in his features. After all, I was his son.

My father had much more to process than I did. Unless he had made a concerted effort to learn about me, he was seeing me for the first time since I was a thin reed of a boy.

"John! My own son! Look at you! You've grown into such a man!" Tears welled up in his eyes as we stood facing each other.

"Father! It's good to see you after all these years!" Tears welled up in my eyes as well. We fell into an embrace, despite the uncertainty about what kind of relationship we were about to form.

"Let's take a walk on the beach. There is so much I want to tell you and so much I want to hear."

My father told me his story as we walked slowly together, side by side, down the path to the ocean. When we reached the beach, we removed our shoes and rolled up our pants so that we could walk where the sand had been made firm by the surf, which rose and fell around our ankles. The surf, a light wind, and the calls of seagulls provided a backdrop to our conversation.

"I hope you don't think poorly of me for failing to reach out to you after your twenty-first birthday. As you know, I was prohibited by the divorce settlement to reach out before then."

"How could I think poorly of you when I could have reached out to you?"

"I loved your mother, you know. I'll never forget the moment that she first walked into Ayn's apartment. It was like the sun rising."

It touched me that my father had feelings for my mother that rivaled my feelings for Eve.

"Working so closely with Ayn to build the Objectivist movement was all consuming. Most of the relationships that we formed were strategic, leaving no room for intimacy. With Elena, I thought I could pour out my soul to her. Imagine my disappointment and shame when she started to reject me before you were even born! For the eight long years that we were married, I felt hideously ugly in her eyes. It was years before I could open up to another woman again. I also experienced a lot of problems with alcohol and drugs, I don't mind telling you. In fact, that began before I met Elena. Ayn put me on just about every boutique medication that was being peddled by the emerging pharmaceutical industry and a lot of them have since been taken off the market. And it's hard to resist booze and recreational drugs when they are all around you, especially when you are unhappy. Thank God for Cindi! I probably wouldn't be here without her. She keeps me on the straight and narrow. I'm totally off drugs and never have more than a glass or two of wine for dinner."

"That's wonderful to hear! I'm a bit of a loner, so I managed to dodge the drug scene among my peers, although I'm happy to have a few rounds of beer."

"You're lucky, believe me. A drug habit is not something that you want. Despite my love for your mother, there was nothing I could do to redeem myself in her eyes. Frankly, she was hopelessly naïve about what it takes to build a movement. It's all about narrative. If you don't have a powerful story, you have nothing. Ayn was a master story-teller and I was learning to become one, too, in my own way. When Elena rejected Objectivism, it was like someone rejecting the Bible for not being literally true. It's not the purpose of the Bible to be literally true!"

"I notice that you don't talk much about Objectivism anymore, on air or in print."

"That's right. Objectivism was Ayn's story. I could see that it played well with a small audience but that another story was required to attract a larger audience. Less highbrow. More down to earth." As he spoke, my father's voice slipped into the Good Old Boy accent that he used on the air. Then he returned to his normal, more cultured tone.

"Your mother's loathing of me poisoned any possibility of forming a relationship with you – my own son! She protected you from me like a mother bear protecting her cub from a predator! How do you think that feels? Then she jerked me around with the help of that high-minded asshole Baryov to remove you from me entirely! By the time they were done working me over, I couldn't take any more. Fine, I thought to myself. Welcome to ten percent of my wealth. Raise our son as you see fit. I just have to put this behind me and get on with repairing my personal life. Then Ayn was diagnosed with lung cancer and passed away within a year. That was an additional burden."

I was only nine years old at my grandmother's death but had since read about it. Evidently, despite a lifetime of chain smoking, she was shocked by the diagnosis. How could someone who had checked all her premises get cancer? My father organized a lavish funeral for her with a six-foot floral display in the shape of a dollar sign. My father helped Ayn Rant live out her objectivist fantasy to the very end. I mentioned none of these thoughts to my father and only replied, "That must have been hard on you."

"Yes, it was." My father's voice trembled as he relived the experience through his words. When he continued, he had collected himself and was back in the present.

"Luckily, I found solace in my work, where I could find a sense of worth, and then eventually Cindi came along. Hopefully, this explains why I never checked up on you, scrupulously honoring your mother's wishes, and treated you as part of a past life when you turned twenty-one. I was amazed when I received your letter and, if you must know, a little frightened."

My father stopped walking and faced me to speak his next words. "If you came here thinking of me in the same way that your mother did, then leave now. I can't take it and won't have it. If you came here to learn about me as I really am, then welcome."

I was stunned by my father's story and ashamed of the caricature that I had been carrying around all these years.

"It's the latter, Father," I stammered. "It's the latter."

Now it was my turn to tell my story as we turned around and headed back toward the manor.

"It's important to begin by distinguishing between you as a person and the Objectivist movement. My mother might have fused the two, but I think I can say that I have kept them separate in my own mind. My memories of you are dim and few, as you might imagine, but they are all acts of kindness that could never be up to the task of forming a proper relationship, like our shopping sprees at FAO Schwarz."

My father's face spread into a broad smile at the memory of these sprees, where he could delight me by buying whatever my heart desired at the world's largest toy store of its day.

"As you know," I went on, "my mother had such a strong sense of principle that she took nothing from the divorce settlement for herself and reserved all of it for me. I inherited the same sense of principle. Who knows how? From her, from you, from your genes, from example. All I know is that I never thought of using my wealth for my own pleasure, only to combat something that my mother regarded as evil. But that thing wasn't you. It was the movement that you formed with my grandmother. And I wasn't sure that it was evil. I didn't take that on faith from my mother. I had to find out for myself. That's what I've been doing ever since, first as a college student and then, after turning twenty-one, by forming a think tank called the Evolution Institute, with the help of one of my college professors named Howard Head."

"Bad word choice!" my father laughed. "I'd call it something else if you want to avoid turning off half of America! What have you decided?" My father's comment confirmed that all of the catalysis taking place within the Cult of Scholars during the last four years had not reached his ears.

"I've tentatively decided that there is a problem with the kind of individualism that became associated with Objectivism. Calling it evil is too simplistic. Regardless of the intentions behind it, the movement has had harmful consequences. So, you could say that I'm trying to rethink the fundamentals of Objectivism to give it a more whole earth focus."

My father became positively ebullient at these words. "That's wonderful, John!" I'm really impressed. There's lots of room for discussion about the fundamentals of Objectivism, as you put it. One of the biggest mistakes that people make about Objectivism is to confuse it for selfishness. Properly understood, Objectivism does have a whole earth focus because the rational pursuit of self-interest, combined with free markets, results in what's best for the whole earth!"

Oh, boy. I was glad that my relationship with my father was off to a good start but strongly suspected that he would never depart from this key tenet of Objectivist faith. This was enough progress for one day.

It seems that I never met a family I didn't like. Whether Eve's or Ron's family, I quickly fit in, without judging them in any way, enjoying the daily round of life that was customary for them but novel and refreshing for me. That was also true for my father's family. Avery helped to break the ice when she plopped herself on my lap as I sat on an oversized couch before dinner on my first day. She was young enough to act more like a little girl than a teenager.

"*Avery!*" Cindi exclaimed. This was evidently a frequently spoken word around the house.

"Mom! He's my *brother!*" Avery shot back. She was a smart-ass little girl and we were to become fast friends during my stay.

In the case of my father's family, there was a lot to fit into – every creature comfort that could be imagined – and I was not immune to their temptations. What's not to like about swimming laps in an Olympic- sized pool or playing pool in the rec room of the basement? Or watching just about any movie of your choice in the screening room? Or sleeping late and having anything you want for breakfast prepared for you when you decide to get up? Or playing video games on the large screen TV with Olivia's and Mia's boyfriends? Or giving everyone a laugh at watching your ineptitude playing tennis or golf? My special passion became windsurfing, which took a little while to master but then became something that I wanted to do every day, the windier the conditions the better. I could see that having this much money and spending it on oneself was a very seductive trap.

My father was devoted to his family and they returned his affection. They saw a lot of each other, since he worked from home. In one of our conversations, he expressed his distaste for the kind of womanizing that was rampant in his world, as Cindi could testify from her experience as a young and attractive reporter at Fox News. But something about having a son who shared a serious interest in his work – even if a skeptical interest – seemed to make him come alive.

"How long can you stay with us?" he asked during my second day.

"I have nothing calling me back to Wyoming," I replied.

"I'd like to throw a party the weekend after next to introduce you to some of our friends and associates, but you can't come dressed like Grizzly Adams! I know that you have your own money, but would you allow me to treat you to some clothing more appropriate for the Hamptons?"

"Will this be 'shopping spree at FAO Schwarz' redux?" I asked with a smile.

"Damn right!" my father responded. He couldn't have been more pleased.

That is how I found myself at a very crowded pool party on a Saturday afternoon, dressed in clothes from a wardrobe that would have consumed about a tenth of my annual income as a ten percenter, complete with a $150 dollar haircut and aviator sunglasses that evidently were essential to complete my look. I had to admit that I did look pretty sharp when I gazed at myself in the full-length mirror in my guest house. Movie star quality, you might even say. On the patio, waiters circulated with trays of drinks and canapés. A photographer was recording the event and seemed to spend a lot of time hovering around me. A DJ spun records to keep the mood lively without drowning out the conversation. The number of women in bikinis, ranging in age from Olivia's and Mia's girlfriends, who had turned out in force to check me out, to elder daughters, mistresses, and trophy wives of some of the powerful men in attendance, made my head spin.

"The key to getting their attention," my father advised me with a wink, "*is to act as if they are not there.*"

My father was eager to introduce me to the other men, including the producers of his radio and television shows and his syndicated column. Our conversation touched on Objectivism but mostly on the challenges of keeping my father's vast audience engaged and motivated.

"Unless you keep them stirred up, all angry and scared, you can lose them real fast." One of them complained.

When the party was in full swing, the DJ caught everyone's attention and handed the microphone to my father.

"Friends, some of the old-timers in this crowd might remember that long ago and far away, before I met Cindi, the love of my life" – the crowd murmured approval as Cindi acknowledged the compliment – "I had a son by a first marriage. That son was taken away from me for reasons that need not concern us. But now, it is with the greatest pleasure that I can say he has come back into my life. Ladies and gentlemen, I would like to introduce you to *John Galt the Third!*"

The DJ had hoopla music ready to play and the crowd burst into applause. This was too much! I had never expected to be introduced to my father's world so soon. I could see that a few comments were required so I made my way over to my father and took the microphone from him.

"Thanks, everyone. My father is right that I have spent a lot of time wandering in the wilderness …"

"Literally!" my father broke in, grabbing the microphone from me. "You should see the clothes that he was wearing when he arrived!"

The crowd laughed as I regained the microphone. "… but I have to tell you that it's really awesome reconnecting to my father. We don't agree on all the details, but we share a passion for the welfare of society. I look forward to sticking around for a while and getting to know some of you better."

There was more applause and the party resumed in high spirits. What better cause for a celebration than the return of a prodigal son? Later on, as the party was winding down, I was cornered by a man who had been introduced to me only by his first name of Steve. Steve didn't go in for fancy clothes and preferred a rumpled unshaven look.

"Look, John Galt III, I'm one of your father's chief strategists and I want to have a man to man with you. Is that OK?"

"Sure. Why not?"

"Do you realize what a gold mine you are?"

"You mean I have money?"

"No, you country bumpkin! Wise up! You're a media gold mine! Your father's act is getting stale. Don't be offended – I'm a realist. With your youth, looks, and your story – prodigal son, heir to the Galt dynasty, and all that – you could be the next star!"

"I'm … I'm not sure that I'm ready for that."

"Well, get ready because it's already starting. This party is going to be in the next issue of *People* magazine and the media is going to explode with interest. You can be certain that your father will be boasting about you every chance he gets. You're going to be in the spotlight whether you want to or not. Is it possible that you're so simple that you didn't know that?"

"I thought that I was just visiting my father!"

"Sweet Jesus Christ! Look, don't make a *move* without me. Do you understand? Not a move. Here's my card. Sweet Jesus Christ! I have the media opportunity of a lifetime and he turns out to be like Jethro on *The Beverly Hillbillies*!"

Sure enough, the party was splashed all over the pages of People magazine and a media frenzy began to ensue. My father indeed started to boast about me on the air and in his syndicated column. Then he invited me into his recording studio for a conversation with a small group of men that included Steve. Cindi was just leaving the recording studio as I entered and gave me a reassuring smile.

"John," my father began, "would you feel comfortable appearing with me on my next live show? I know it's a lot to ask, but the public interest is so high that it represents a golden opportunity for you to present your views to the world. It could be just a few minutes the first time and you could become a regular guest if it works out well."

"Gosh ... that requires some thought ... I never imagined that I might be debating with you on the air ..."

"Don't think of it as a debate. Just a friendly conversation between father and son."

"Well ... if you put it that way ... I guess I could give it a go. What can we lose?"

A cheer arose from the little group and Steve gave me a discreet thumbs up when my father's back was turned.

The live broadcast was three days away. As it approached I had a growing feeling of dread. It got so bad that I found excuses to spend most of my time in the guest house away from the family. My father encouraged me not to overthink my comments. He had a lifetime of experience carrying on a conversation on the air.

When the time arrived, I was seated with my father on a little stage, angled toward each other with a small table between us. My clothes had been selected for me after hours of discussion about how I should be dressed to appeal to the audience that they were aiming for. My hair had been sprayed and my forehead had been dusted to make sure there would be no shine. Two cameramen moved cameras on wheels that filmed us from different angles, and a third person at an electronic console toggled between the camera views for the television audience. Steve sat at the very back to keep an eye on things.

My father began with his usual introduction and then proceeded to introduce me.

"Many of you have heard that I have become reunited with my son, John Galt III, and that he is making a serious study of Objectivism, the movement that was started by my mother, Ayn Rant, and father, John Galt I. My son and I don't see eye to eye on everything, but he represents the fresh views of a new generation of Objectivists, so I have invited him on my show to have a conversation. Welcome, John – my son!"

"Thank you, Father. I have come onto your show to deliver this."

I pulled a manila envelope from my pocket and placed it on the table between us. My father froze. His eyes bugged and his face went ash white. First he stared at the envelope, then at me.

"No! You couldn't ..."

"Open it please, Father."

It was obvious to everyone in the studio that something had gone terribly off script. Steve was motioning frantically to cut the cameras but the cameramen and console operator had their backs turned to him and kept on shooting. Hands trembling, my father opened the envelope and withdrew two pages, the first of which had only three sentences written in large bold letters. He had no choice but to read the words.

You have betrayed the Objectivist cause.
I challenge you to a duel of speeches.
Details attached.

As soon as my father read those words on the air, I was out of my chair, through the door of the studio, and pounding down the hallway. I bounded down the stairs and raced past Cindi and the girls, who had been watching the show on the wide screen monitor and were milling about in confusion.

"John! What have you done?" Cindi called in alarm.

Without answering, I sprinted out the door to the guest house where my backpack was packed except for a pair of canvas pants, a cotton shirt, and my hiking shoes. I tore the new clothes from my body, leaving them with the rest of the wardrobe that my father bought me, and donned my old clothes. Then I raced back up the path toward the patio. To my dismay, my father had joined the girls by the swimming pool. He must have bolted from his chair a moment after I did, leaving an audience of millions wondering what was going on. His face was purple with rage.

"You bastard! You filthy lying bastard! You betrayed my trust! I'm never going to forgive you for this, Nature Boy! I'm going to *crush* you! Blood means nothing to me now! You want a duel of speeches? *You'll get your duel of speeches!*"

I veered off the path and made an arc around the Manor house on the manicured lawn. When I got to the front entrance, Eduardo was polishing the stretch limo.

"Hey, man, what's wrong?"

"I've got to get to an airport"

"Which airport?"

"Any airport."

"Hop in. I'll take you."

"No. My father will fire you if you help me."

"What did he do to you?"

"Nothing. It's what I did to him."

"Go out the entrance, turn left, and keep on going. I know all the drivers around here. I'll get one of them to give you a ride to LaGuardia."

I arrived at LaGuardia clammy with the sweat from my escape. I was lucky to get a flight to Laramie via Denver that left in a few hours. I made my way to the gate and found a spot on the floor as far away from other people as I could get. I sat on my backpack with my back against the wall and withdrew a powder blue sheet of paper from among the leaves of my notebook. Using my notebook for backing, I wrote these words.

My precious Eve,

You were wrong when you said that you couldn't be there for me on my path. You will always be with me in my mind, even if you never read this letter.

I have accomplished my mission but at a terrible, terrible cost to my father and myself. I didn't know exactly how I was going to get on the air with him. I was going to improvise. As it turned out, it was so easy that I couldn't stop them if I wanted to. But in the process, humanity got in the way. We became close and I also became close to his family. I saw his perspective on his marriage to my mother as I never had before. His joy at my return and the prospect of having me become a partner and successor to his empire was boundless. And then I betrayed him. I feel that I have become soiled in a way that can never be washed away.

And yet, I know that it was necessary. My father told me that my mother was hopelessly naïve about how to create a movement, that it is all about narrative, about creating a powerful story. He said that her rejection of Objectivism was like rejecting the Bible for not being literally true. He's right about the necessity of a powerful story – and that's why I had to betray him. He wanted me to become a character in his story, where I would never be able to change his or anyone else's mind. Now he has become a character in my story, whether he wants to or not. The trap has been sprung. We are enacting a drama on my terms and the whole world will be watching from this moment until our duel of speeches. A lot can happen during that period, if Howard's ideas about cultural catalysis are correct.

Still, it makes me sick that I had to betray a flesh and blood human, not to speak of my own father, in order to set the story in motion. Here is what I have learned in my short life: Harm in the world is seldom caused by evil people. It is caused by normal people trying to tell right from wrong by peering through a tissue of lies. That's what you discovered for your Christian faith and what I discovered for Objectivism. My father is not a bad man. He's a good man under the spell of a bad story. The only way to eliminate this kind of harm is to tell a powerful story that does not require peering through a tissue of lies. That story exists. Howard and I are convinced of that. Now the remaining challenge is to tell the story in front of the whole world. That is what I set in motion today. I should be proud, but it still makes me sick that I betrayed my own father.

Eve, I will send this letter to achieve a kind of closure for myself, without knowing if you will ever read it. The only way that I can stop from worrying myself to death over you is by trusting in your resourcefulness. You come from a long line of movers, adventurers and outlaws, so good luck on your path. Even though I am not a Christian, I'm happy to use that idiom, along with your family, to keep you in my prayers and say God bless.

Your John.

Coming east, I had parked my truck at Howard's house and he had given me a ride to the airport. Now I texted him about my abrupt return: *Mission accomplished. Arriving 11:57pm on United Flight 3472.*

Within minutes I had my reply: *Welcome back. Well done. He never knew what hit him. We have a surprise for you. Let the catalysis begin.*

The Catalysis

It was close to midnight – therefore 2 am Eastern time – when my plane landed in Laramie. Howard met me in the baggage claim area of the airport. I would spend the night at his house and we would meet with an expanded staff of the Evolution Institute the next morning. Howard was dressed thoughtlessly in blue jeans, sandals, and a sweatshirt. I felt an upwelling of love for him and his unaffected manner after my month among the super rich. We fell into a hearty embrace.

"Welcome back, Luke Skywalker! You seem to have scored a direct hit on the Death Star. It's all over the media."

"Mission accomplished, I guess, but it was dirty work treating my father as a super villain. I'm still disgusted with myself."

"That's why we love you, John. For your humanity."

I was touched by these words, which I badly needed to hear.

"It seems hard to believe that I have been gone a whole month. How is the Mother Ship?" This was our affectionate name for the Evolution Institute. Running it was a big job, not so different from operating a ship. I was grateful that I did not need to captain the day-to-day operations.

"Great! We're ramping up for phase II while keeping phase I going. Now here is the surprise. We've moved into new headquarters – the second story above the Elbow Room."

"No way!"

The Elbow Room was one of Laramie's most popular cafes and nightspots. Its proprietor was a man named Dennis Embly, who was unabashedly gay. Everyone seemed to love Dennis, regardless of their sexual orientation, because he was so comfortable about being different. I had noticed this with a few other people that I met at Evolution Institute workshops. Perhaps the most remarkable case was a highly regarded economist who not only transgendered from a man to a woman but also spoke with a pronounced stutter. As she addressed our group, her mouth struggling to form the words, it was clear that *we* might be uncomfortable but *she* was not. That meant that *she* had some kind of inner strength that *we* did not. It made me want to get close to her to learn the secret of her inner strength.

That's how Dennis was, which made him the perfect proprietor and the Elbow Room a well-chosen name for his café and night spot. When people came to the Elbow Room, they felt that they had permission to step out of the roles that society had assigned to them, which fit them like a poorly made suit of clothes. It was liberating and made them gay – not in the modern meaning of that word but in the old-fashioned meaning (happy and carefree). This feeling of liberation accounted for the popularity of the Elbow Room as much as the décor, food, drink, and entertainment, which was also among Laramie's best.

The Elbow Room was one of my own favorite spots to hang out with Eve and our friends. Eve had waitressed there during her freshman year and had a standing invitation from Dennis to fill in for other staff members if they became ill or wanted to take a vacation. Howard's news that the Mother Ship was now located directly above it was indeed a delightful surprise.

"Dennis is a big fan of what we are doing and was happy to lease the second floor to us. In fact, we had to talk him into taking money for it. He said that he was only using it for storage and wanted to lease it to us for free. He also wants us to use the Violet Room for a meeting space when it's not being used by other customers."

The Violet Room was located in the back of the restaurant area and was used for private events, mostly in the evenings. It was quiet and would be perfect for daytime meetings with sizable groups of people.

That is where Howard and I were heading the next morning to meet with our expanded staff after a good night's sleep.

More than twenty people were awaiting us when we entered the Violet Room – Dennis, Ashley, our first staff members who I knew well, some key people that we had met through our workshops who had joined us, and a few more new staff members who I would be meeting for the first time. To my surprise, my image was on a flat screen TV monitor mounted on the wall. CNN was reporting the juicy story of John Galt III challenging John Galt II to a duel of speeches. At our entrance, the group turned away from my screen image and broke into applause. There were hugs from the old-timers and introductions and handshakes with the new recruits. Dennis made a little speech before leaving us to our business.

"Friends, I've known Howard for many years as a patron of the Elbow Room and I've known the Big Guy since he was a college freshman showing up with Eve, who used to waitress here. I never thought that such an odd assortment of people might have an impact on the world. Yet, there is the Big Guy on CNN, challenging his father and all that he represents. I just want you to know that I'm proud to play a small role in your effort by making the second story of this building available to you, and this room when it's not being reserved by other customers."

Dennis's voice quaked as he spoke these words and the little crowd broke into a second round of applause. Ashley spoke next.

"Before we begin our meeting, we want to show you the upstairs."

It was indeed the entire group, and not just Ashley, that wanted to show me the upstairs. Evidently, they had spent the entire month that I was gone cleaning it up and furnishing it. The whole building was old and ramshackle and had been built in stages, so the upstairs was a warren of rooms connected by corridors. In keeping with our philosophy of "enough," the staff were organized into teams and each team was assigned a room to furnish exclusively from garage sales and Goodwill stores. There ensued a hilarious competition as each team tried to outdo the others for kitsch. The overall effect was so fascinating that you could almost charge admission to see it. It was like a museum of Laramie folk culture, a collection of objects taken from the homes of everyday people as they shed their old stuff to make room for their new stuff. Some of the rooms had been outfitted as offices, with desktop computers on mismatched desks and tables. Other rooms were for meeting and relaxing and had the feel of somebody's living room. Two rooms were outfitted as bedrooms where I, or visitors from out of town, could spend the night without the expense of a hotel. The room that they saved for last to show me had a big ornate pool table.

"Incredible! Our own pool room!"

"We thought you'd approve," Howard smiled. "It's so big and heavy that the owner begged us to haul it away for free. By the time we got it up here, we were beginning to think that he overcharged us!"

After our tour of the new Mother Ship, we reassembled in the Violet Room, seated around a number of tables. CNN had stopped covering me and was now reporting on the dissolution of the European Union. We turned off the monitor. It was time to get to work. I was the leader of the Phase II operation, not Howard. I stood up to speak, moving slowly around the room rather than staying in one place.

"It's hard for me to fully express my joy at being with you," I began. "Some of you have been with us from the beginning, while others are new. Since we are entering a new phase of our operation, I think it will be useful for all of us to take stock of what we are trying to accomplish.

"The mission of the Evolution Institute is to accomplish transformative cultural change in a short period of time. The future that we are working toward will treat the welfare of the whole Earth as sacred and will use science as the form of worship. 99.999% of humanity would be mystified by what I just said, but we know that words such as 'sacred' and 'worship' are fully compatible with a purely scientific worldview.

"The idea that we can quickly cause the rest of humanity to share this worldview might seem unrealistic to the extreme, but not if you understand the concept of catalysis and the very real possibility that cultural change can be catalyzed in the same way as chemical change. That was one of Howard's critical insights ..."

I paused to look at Howard, my friend and mentor, and he returned my gaze with a smile. In my eight years as his apprentice, I had grown stronger and he had grown more frail. He still had plenty of fire in him, but he was also proud to see me take center stage with the energy of a young man fully confident in my own abilities. What a difference from the shy little boy who struggled to speak!

"… that we have put into practice during the last four years with our workshops and research projects. Thanks to these efforts, it is not an exaggeration to say that we have catalyzed change within the academic world, or the Cult of Scholars, as I like to put it. We have brought people together around the concept of society as an organism in ways that never would have happened otherwise. As a result, all of the relevant bodies of knowledge that developed in isolation are becoming unified. By now, the arguments we can make and the network of experts that we can draw upon are unparalleled. Nobody can beat us on the playing field of science."

I paused to let this sink in before continuing. It was heartening to think that we were operating from such a position of strength on the scientific playing field, especially since we were such underdogs in every other respect.

"That's the good news. The bad news is that our catalytic success within the Cult of Scholars has had virtually no impact on the world at large. That is the degree to which the events taking place all around us have become detached from factual knowledge. It follows that for the Evolution Institute to succeed at its mission, we need to make a different kind of catalytic effort in addition to what we are already doing, which will continue. The new effort must capture the attention of the entire world and change minds by offering a new story. Of course, our story must be firmly anchored in factual reality to remain true to our sacred principles, which will distinguish our story – our grand narrative – from all others in circulation today.

"This is what we call our Phase II operation, which began with my visit to my father during the past month. I am uniquely positioned to capture the attention of the whole world, as you can see from this morning's news. Let me briefly take you back to the beginning, with apologies for those who already know the story well. My grandfather and grandmother, Ayn Rant, crafted a grand narrative that provided moral justification for the unbridled pursuit of self-interest. Then they captured the attention of the world with a hoax – a speech that was broadcast on radio as if my grandfather had taken over the airwaves.

Shortly afterwards my grandfather disappeared. To this day no one knows what happened to him, although my grandmother pretended that he was in hiding and in communication with her. She capitalized on The Speech to build her own movement, which she called Objectivism, as if its principles could be justified by rationality and science. This, too, was a fiction. Everything about Objectivism was a fiction, disconnected from factual reality, but it did make a damn good story, especially for those who stood to gain by indulging in pure greed, which they could now do with a clear conscience and brushing aside efforts at social control. Then my father got involved and adapted the story to an even larger audience with his down-home style and his media empire. It is not an exaggeration to say that my family is contributing to the destruction of the world with their grand narrative, as my mother perceived when the movement was in its infancy.

"Our challenge and opportunity is to turn this grand narrative against itself in the construction of our own story. The good son who rebels against his powerful and corrupt father is a staple of myths throughout history, most recently in the *Star Wars* franchise. Hence, you'll hear Howard calling me Luke Skywalker and my father's media empire the Death Star."

The group laughed as one of the newcomers sang the first few bars of the *Star Wars* theme song and pantomimed fighting with a light saber from his chair.

"So, we're going to play that theme to the hilt, culminating in the duel of speeches that will take place in front of the whole world. That was the trap that I set for my father, and he walked right into it."

"One of your father's minions named Steve called me yesterday to accept the challenge," Ashley reported. "He sounds like a very crude man."

"He'll tell you that he's a realist!" I laughed. "What my father and his team might not realize is that we expect the cultural catalysis to take place right away and to be largely complete by the time the duel of speeches takes place, which will be in October – four months from now – in Philadelphia if they accept our terms. If we succeed, then the world will become very different than it is today."

The room was completely still as everyone absorbed the import of these words. We were to be the agents of historic change.

"To succeed," I went on, "we must be able to toggle easily from story mode to science mode in our own minds. Scientifically, all human societies are coordinated by norms, which define what's right, and therefore worthy of reward, and wrong, therefore worthy of punishment. Norms are relatively easy to form, enforce, and change to adapt to new circumstances at the scale of small groups. Everything becomes more difficult at larger scales, but it still happens. In fact, examples of changing norms are all around us when we know how to look for them. Consider Dennis. He could never have openly practiced his lifestyle in Laramie fifty or even twenty years ago, but now he can based on norms that make it wrong to be intolerant of sexual orientation.

"Or consider norms governing the sexual conduct of powerful men. Fifty years ago, it was taken for granted that powerful men would have their way with women under their control – lords with their domestic servants, movie moguls with their secretaries and aspiring starlets. It wasn't approved, but it was regarded as an aspect of human nature that one could do nothing about. Now, remarkably quickly, it is becoming wrong and shameful. Women are coming forward with their stories and the men are being roundly condemned. Their reputations plummet. They lose their jobs. They plead that they are addicted and go into rehab.

"This new norm is new only in the scale of its implementation. It has always existed at smaller scales in at least some societies. Up on Timber Ridge where I live, there aren't big differences in power in the first place – that's something else governed by norms, by the way. If someone tried to have his way with a woman against her will, she'd fight like a bobcat and her boyfriend, husband, or father would kill him in a hunting accident. Given these consequences, it doesn't happen very often. Men find ways to control their impulses for their own good. In the not so distant future, we can look forward to a world where women won't have to worry so much about being harassed by powerful men. This isn't inevitable – in fact a lot of work is required. But it's the kind of work that we do all time as we morally police each other. We are natural born moral policemen.

"Our challenge and opportunity is to accomplish a norm shift for truth-telling. The situation is comparable to sexual bullying in every way. Norms that enforce truth-telling are strongly established within the Cult of Scholars, in courtroom procedures, in responsible journalism, and other social settings. Up on Timber Ridge, if you gain a reputation as a liar, you won't get very far. But those norms have fallen into disrepair for much of modern life, including politics and journalism, where lying is regarded as just something that comes with the territory, however much we might wish otherwise. Well, lying is no more inevitable than sexual bullying and I am in a unique position to re-assert the norm of truth-telling where it has fallen into disrepair. Why? Because Objectivism rests upon the claim that its principles can be justified by science and rationality. That was just a stage prop for my grandmother, which has been largely tossed aside by my father, but when I hold their movement accountable for its own presumptions and announce myself as the true objectivist, my father will be forced to defend himself in a fight that he can't win."

I was so immersed in my analysis that I had become unaware of the others in the room. When I snapped out of my trance, I realized what a strange spectacle I must appear to them: a giant of a man, stalking the room like a wrestler about to throw his opponent to the mat. Like Howard, I couldn't repress my convictions, which put me in danger of acting a bit unhinged. If anyone could understand my convictions, however, it was this group, so I allowed myself to continue without apology.

"Once we have re-established the norm of truth-telling in politics and journalism, the rest of our job will be made easy. All of a sudden, the Cult of Scholars, which has been almost entirely ignored, will assume a position of central importance. In other words, *they will be consulted to govern the affairs of the world* much more than in the present. Our work of the last four years, which has seemed to have zero impact on public discourse, will become decisive. My father's team will scramble to find experts to support their position, but whoever they find will be outgunned for the simple reason that their position is scientifically untenable and we have already assembled the expertise to show this. It is simply not the case that self-interest, combined with free markets, constitutes a viable moral system or economy.

"Of course, it's not enough to destroy one moral system without replacing it with another. We have to assert that all current political grand narratives have failed, not just my father's, and that our narrative – a scientific account of society as an organism – is new in the history of ideas, as Howard likes to put it at the beginning of our workshops. Since that account is itself in its infancy, we can't pretend that we have all the answers. All we can confidently assert is that we have found the right path. Our challenge and opportunity is to set the world on the right path during the one year that we have its attention."

Having poured my soul into my unrehearsed speech, I sat down with a feeling of profound fatigue that I had often seen in Howard after his lectures. Now Howard rose to continue where I left off.

"We'll take a break in a few minutes, but first I want to say just a bit more about the idea of catalysis. A chemical catalyst is a substance that can increase the rate of a reaction, sometimes by orders of magnitude, even when added in tiny amounts. If the rate becomes too fast, an explosion occurs. A bomb is an example of chemical catalysis that is designed to explode.

"Our strategy is predicated on the idea that cultural change can be catalyzed in the same way as chemical change. When John issued his challenge to his father in front of an audience of millions, that was the sprinkling of the catalytic substance into the broth of world culture. Now the catalytic reaction is already starting to take place, in a single day. Compare that to the months and years required for catalysis to take place within the Cult of Scholars! During the coming days, there will be a tsunami of media attention. We caused it. It's what we want. And we'll do our best to channel it to our desired outcomes. But there is always the possibility that it will get out of control and blow up in our faces. That's why we have enlarged our staff and brought in some of the best and brightest minds on cultural change in the Internet Age that we have encountered during our workshops. I want to thank everyone in this room for being present at a critical moment in world history. After our break, we'll get down to the mechanics of how to channel the cultural reaction that we have set in motion."

I took part in the strategy sessions until mid-afternoon, when I excused myself to head back home to Timber Ridge. As I was leaving the Elbow Room, I texted Ron: "Coming up to pick up Lizzie around 6pm. How is it up there?" By the time I got to my truck, I had my answer: "Lizzie and ribs waiting for you. Crazy up here, just like you said. But the Sheriff of Timber Ridge has it under control."

As I headed toward the mountains, my mood was a mixture of elation and dread. Everything was going according to plan, but that tsunami of media attention that Howard mentioned would be channeled primarily through me. Two strands of my life had been reduced to the thinnest of threads. Eve existed only as an avatar in my mind and the press would be swarming around my mountain hermitage. How long could I sustain myself on the one strand of changing the world? It was going to be literally dehumanizing. Just as I had dehumanized my father, turning him into a cardboard super villain, I would be dehumanizing myself, striking poses to become the hero of the story that we were constructing for the world. And that was the best that I could hope for. The only alternative was to lose control of the narrative and become the villain or fool of someone else's story. No wonder that Eve worried about me! I could become unrecognizable to her, even if I succeeded at my quest! Yet, there was nothing to do but stay the course. I had set the cultural winds in motion and must ride out the storm.

On my way to Timber Ridge, I stopped by the Eden Ranch to say hello and see if they had any news about Eve.

"John! It's so good to see you! It's sweet of you to drop by. No, we've heard nothing from Eve and it worries us sick. We did get a phone call today from someone asking about you, though."

"What?! Incredible. So soon ..." If they had called Eve's parents, they must be snooping around every corner of my life.

"He was trying to get us to say that you weren't a Christian. Joe took the call and said that you acted more like a Christian than most Christians and a lot more than the person he was talking to. Then he hung up. I was proud of him for saying that."

"You'll never hear us talking trash about you," Joseph added. "Why are they nosing around trying to dig up dirt?"

"Let's just say that I'm going to be a public figure for a while. Thanks for sticking up for me and letting actions speak more loudly than words."

"We know better than to fix what's not broke. You're a good man and wonderful to Eve. We'll have you as our son anytime."

These words caused me to burst into tears. The idea of marrying Eve and living anything like a normal life with her seemed impossibly remote. Mary offered herself for an embrace as Joseph stood by, awkwardly patting me on the back.

When I arrived at Ron's house at about 6pm, Lizzie greeted me with the insane delight that only a dog separated from her human for a month can express. She leapt into my arms and licked my face all over as I hugged her. Then she raced in circles around me before flopping on her back so I could rub her belly. Ron and his family gathered around the wild reunion. They were bubbling over with news of how the press had descended upon Timber Ridge.

"They came steaming up the road to your place but I had the entrance blocked with my pickup. I told 'em to come back tomorrow and suggested the Three Bear Motel as a place to stay in Timber Ridge. Then they started to interview me! I told 'em that I was your deputy and had been authorized by you to keep 'em off your land. They asked me what I thought about you and I said that you were the truest redneck that ever was. That got me on television!

"It seems that there isn't a single person on Timber Ridge that hasn't been asked about you," Sarah added. "They're all saying that you're one of us."

"That means a lot to me. Are we ready to host them tomorrow?"

"Yep!" Ron and Sarah replied in unison. "You don't have to worry about a thing. Have some ribs and get a good night's sleep."

It was past eight when Lizzie and I left Ron's house and made our way to the end of Timber Ridge trail. Entering the Cell was like taking a huge weight off my shoulders. Tonight, at least, I would be alone in this wonderful space, built not by myself but by a community. Little did I know at the time that this community would become a key character in the story that I was now trying to create for the world.

The next morning, all twelve of the dirty dozen and their families, including their children and older folk, were on hand to help me greet the press. We were lucky to have a sparkling day with cottony clouds against a brilliant blue sky. Each family brought dishes to share, potluck style, which were placed on tables set up on the wrap around deck. To the reporters and their crews that arrived in their vans, it was as if they had dropped in on a community picnic. They were told to make themselves comfortable and take a tour of the cell, led by the people who had helped to build it, prior to the press conference that would take place at 11am. I circulated among the crowd, chatting with the families that I had grown to know well along with the visiting press. Lizzie also circulated among the crowd, charming everyone and accepting pats and scraps. A swarm of photographers hovered around me, asking me to pose next to my neighbors, next to the cell, next to Lizzie, next to the ENOUGH sign.

The press conference was held outdoors facing the reporters and cameras with the families standing on either side and the cell standing behind me. Even the children seemed to sense that something important was taking place and were on their best behavior. I made my own introduction.

"I wanted to welcome you to my first press conference, not by myself, but as a member of the community up here on Timber Ridge. Even though I am a newcomer, we became close in the construction of the beautiful structure standing behind me, which we call the Cell. That word has many meanings – a jail cell, a terrorist cell – but the meaning that I have in mind is a biological cell, the building block of all living organisms. Not only is this structure like a living cell, but so is this community up here on Timber Ridge. People like to think of rednecks as rugged individuals, and they are. But they are also there for each other when needed and they don't take lying, cheating, and bullying lightly. Being a redneck is about individualism *and* community. Both are needed, and that's why life up here on Timber Ridge is so great."

The families standing on each side stood proudly as the cameras beamed their images around the world.

"Another reason that I wanted to introduce you to my community is because it represents the essence of Objectivism, properly understood, in contrast to the corrupt form promulgated by my father. His form of objectivism is about individualism only, without community. It is destroying communities like this one in America and all over the world. To repair the damage, we need to restore the balance between individualism and community. That is what I have stepped forward to do – to offer the world a clear choice between right and wrong, True Objectivism and its corrupt form, my Speech in contrast to my father's.

"Before I take questions, I want to establish the relationship that I intend to have with the press. I'm a believer in the importance of a free press for holding government accountable – the so-called Fourth Estate. I therefore plan to make myself available to you as much as you want, perhaps even more than you want …"

There was a murmur of appreciation. Earlier public figures such as Teddy and Franklin D. Roosevelt cultivated this kind of relationship with the press, but that was long ago. Lately, my father and his kind had vilified the press that was not under their control.

"… But for this open relationship to work, the press must hold up its side of the bargain – to tell the truth. Liars don't get very far up here on Timber Ridge and neither will you if you create and spread so-called fake news. When I'm not up here in my Cell, I'm traveling the world in the company of scientists and scholars. They know how to hold each other accountable for telling the truth. That's what I expect from you and what you can demand from me. I am only asking you to uphold the norms of your own profession, which used to be strongly enforced but now go largely unpunished. One of the most shameful things about my father is his wanton disregard of the facts. What is it about the word 'Objective' that he doesn't understand?"

True to Howard's theatrical style and my own strong feelings, the last words were delivered like thunder. I paused to let them have their full impact and resumed in my normal voice.

"I will be happy to take questions now."

All of the reporters began speaking at once.

"Is it true that you hadn't spoken to your father from the time you were a young boy to only a month ago?"

"Yes. My mother saw the Objectivist movement for what it was and removed me from its influence when I was eight. I did not resume contact with my father until a month ago."

"Is it true that you own exactly ten percent of your father's fortune?"

"Correct. These were the terms of the divorce settlement that my mother forced upon my father."

"How could your mother dictate such terms?"

"Because even back then she had compelling evidence of the Objectivist Movement's fraudulent nature."

"Is it true that you've capped your personal income to the upper tenth percentile of the American income distribution?"

"Yes. The lower edge of the upper ten percent. If that's not enough, I need my head examined, not more money."

"Your father says that you betrayed his trust."

"I suppose I did and it's not something I'm proud of. I had to meet him and get to know him as a person. He wanted to groom me to take over his media empire but I knew that change from within would be impossible. I had to offer a clear contrast, hence my challenge to a duel of speeches. I want to make it clear that I am not battling my father as a person. I mean him no malice. I'm battling for what he stands for in the eyes of the world."

"Isn't it outrageous to say that you have all the answers?"

That question got my blood up.

"I don't have all the answers but I do have a path to the answers. Let me tell you what's really outrageous – the degree to which my father and other self-styled Masters of the Universe ignore the facts of the world. For four years, I've used my share of my father's wealth to organize a community of scientists and scholars to address the problems of our age. They are the ones in a position to provide the answers, not me. For four years, I've been transparent about wanting to rethink Objectivism, but do you think that ever reached my father's ears? No! That's the degree to which he and his kind lives within a hermetically sealed fact-free universe!

"But here's something else for you. The path to the right answers doesn't reside in the details. It is so elementary, once you see it from the right perspective, that I can convince anyone who cares to learn on the basis of their own knowledge, which I look forward to doing in future conversations. Let's call an end to this one."

There I was again, acting like a wrestler throwing his opponent to the mat, this time in front of the whole world.

The next day's edition of the *New York Times* featured a front-page article with the headline "Who is John Galt?" and a photograph of the earlier edition that asked the same question for my grandfather so many years ago. Who my grandfather was, how he became famous through The Speech, how Ayn Rant parlayed The Speech into her own cult under the banner of Objectivism, and how my father parlayed that into his media empire. It was the perfect background for the story that Howard and I were now trying to construct.

The next edition of *Time* magazine featured me on its cover with the single word ENOUGH as the headline. The image showed me standing next to the ENOUGH sign on my property, looking directly into the camera with my arms crossed and legs apart, as if barring the path of the reader. The article highlighted three meanings of the word. First, the remarkable fact that I had declared being a ten percenter enough when I could have been a 0.1 percenter. Second, enough is enough when it comes to the world falling apart. Third, we have enough knowledge to make it better. All three meanings resonated with the worldwide public and the demand to learn more about me as a harbinger of a new order became insatiable. The idea that cultural catalysis could take place within a year began to appear as more than wishful thinking. So far it was going according to plan.

I was amused how various aspects of my persona, which I had never intended as display, assumed iconic status. My outdoor work clothes turned me into a man of the people. The notebook strapped to my hip became a symbol of the power of ideas over brute force. Yet, the National Rifle Association couldn't demonize me because I was a hunter who acknowledged the right to bear arms, at least within limits. My hermitage on top of a mountain gave me a monk-like status. Yet, I also had the manly stature and good looks of a movie star. None of this was posturing on my part – at least I didn't think it was – but it provided all the elements needed to become the hero of the story that I was constructing for the world.

This was not lost on my father and his team, as I learned during one of my weekly trips to the Mother Ship above the Elbow Room. I arrived with a latte that I had purchased downstairs.

"It looks like we have a mole helping us out," Ashley commented as I entered her office. Howard was already present.

"What?"

"A mole. A spy. We received this flash drive in the mail with an audio recording of one of your father's strategy sessions. Listen to this."

Ashley played the file through a pair of desktop speakers. The mole must have been sitting next to the speaker, who sounded like he was right there with us in the room.

"Listen carefully, children. I've been helping to keep this ship afloat for a long time and sometimes you don't take my advice as seriously as you should."

The derogatory tone of the voice was unmistakably Steve's.

"Do you remember the story of David and Goliath? Do you remember how it turned out? Well, we're Goliath, John's son is David, and there is a river stone hurling toward our forehead as I speak. Don't for a second think that we have an advantage in this fight.

"To begin, John Galt III is a total unknown, and that's an *asset*. To be unknown is to be a blank movie screen that anything can be projected upon, and they have their hands on the projector.

"To make matters worse, John Galt III has enormous physical appeal, in part because he's enormous. Seventy-five percent of elections are won by the taller person. Don't be offended, John, you know that I'm a realist. When you stand on that stage next to your son, he'll have a decisive advantage before either one of you opens your mouth.

"To make matters still worse, the guy is a fucking chameleon! The rednecks think he's a redneck. The tree huggers think he's a tree hugger. The eggheads think he's an egghead. We can't even get the religious right to come out strongly against him!

"But wait. There's more! Usually when we're faced with an opponent with lots of appeal, we can dig up some dirt on him. A mistress. Dodging the draft. Financial ties to special interests. But this fucker is as clean as a whistle! Do you realize that he's had only one girlfriend in his entire life? Do you know her name? You can't make this up. It's *Eve Eden*. Does she come from a devout Christian family? *Of course* she does! Does her family love him? *Of course* they do! Do they care that he talks about evolution? *Of course* they don't! He's even turned that into a glamour word!

"Then there's the cherry on top of this banana sundae of wholesomeness, Lizzie the wonder dog! Did you see the footage of the press losing their minds over that dog at that fucking church social that he organized? The guy's a fucking marketing genius! He even had me fooled with that Jethro act of his. John! Pay attention!"

"What? Oh. Sorry." My father's voice was barely audible. He must have been dozing at the far end of the room. Then someone else spoke up in mild protest.

"Steve, why is this such a big deal? It will blow over. You're treating it like the presidential election!"

An ominous pause ensued before Steve replied.

"It's that kind of dumbass question that makes me want to leave this sinking ship. Let me remind you that we survive only thanks to the unlikeliest of coalitions – fat cats like us, the religious right, and rednecks. The only reason that this coalition hangs together is because everyone but the fat cats is desperate for change and the liberal opposition is so worn out that no one can stand to look at them anymore, like a fifty-year-old whore."

All of us winced at this comparison. "I wouldn't want to spend a single minute in a room with this man!" Ashley shuddered. The voice from the speaker continued.

"If there is a bright new alternative for people hungry for change, then we're done. Our coalition will fall apart and it will be the fat cats against the world. We'll lose every presidential election for the rest of our lives. Does that answer your question?"

No one in the room offered any more resistance to Steve's analysis.

"As a realist, I see only two ways to save our sorry asses. First, get some experts to oppose their experts. Right now, they've got us by the balls over this Objectivism label. Who would have thought that we'd ever be held accountable for that? Second, we'll need to play the fear card – again and again and again. What I'd give for another 9/11 right now!"

That was the end of the audio recording. Howard was the first to speak.

"Fascinating! Our friend Steve might be a slime ball, but he has a pretty good grasp of the situation. That river stone is indeed hurling toward their foreheads."

"I wonder who our mole is?" Ashley added.

"My father's team is pretty large," I replied. I'm guessing that one of the younger members is sick of being bullied by Steve and wants to jump ship. Maybe we'll be hearing from him or her soon."

"Are there women on his team? I can't imagine how they could tolerate such a toxic environment."

"That's mostly Steve. My dad's a family man, believe it or not, and devoted to my stepmom, who helps him run his empire. She acts as a counterweight to Al and has brought in a few women. Al can't bully her and get away with it."

"As much fun as that was to listen to, it doesn't alter our own next steps," Howard concluded. "Full speed ahead."

As the press swarmed over my story, the Mother Ship launched a full-scale attack on the Death Star. Unlike the Death Star of *Star Wars*, which was immune to attack except for one vulnerable point, my father had left himself wide open to the accusation of living in a fact-free universe. Of course, this accusation was nothing new. My father was accused daily of lying, but he accused his critics in return and his loyal following didn't seem to care. The whole world had become numb to fake news. Our goal was nothing less than re-sensitizing the world to the virtue of truth-telling. We forced my father to acknowledge the roots of his own movement. Was it not called Objectivism? Did that not mean that it could be justified on the basis of rationality and science? Had he ever revoked this claim? If so, then he needed to stand by it.

Then the Evolution Institute contracted with three separate think tanks to serve as fact checkers and issue report cards on both my father and myself on a weekly basis. One of the think tanks was progressive, another was conservative, and the third was libertarian. All were chosen on the basis of their integrity and if they differed in their report cards, then they were charged with resolving the discrepancy among themselves. My father was encouraged to contract his own fact checkers if he liked, although we pointed out that no one had ever operated in that capacity in his organization up to this point. My father refused, calling the whole thing a hoax, but the public was impressed by the impartiality of the arrangement and week after week he received D's to my A's.

From the second floor of the Elbow Room, the crew of the Mother Ship watched breathlessly to see if a tipping point would be reached. We knew it had happened for sexual bullying. Men who acted with impunity were suddenly held accountable and lost everything. What previously had been an open secret that everyone had become numb to became shocking and so reprehensible that there was no possible excuse for it. After being bombarded with verifiable accusations of falsehoods for four weeks, my father caved. His new defense was that his Greed is Good philosophy could be justified by science and rationality and he was prepared to come up with experts of his own.

A cheer went up among the crew of the Mother Ship at these words and we went downstairs to the Elbow Room to celebrate. The battle had shifted onto the playing field of science, where we had the advantage. We had been preparing for this moment for over four years. The catalysis that had been taking place among the Cult of Scholars would now contribute decisively to the worldwide catalysis.

We knew his next move. He would engage the orthodox economic establishment, which had been justifying the Greed is Good worldview in its own way for over a half century. Ever since the Intro economics course that I flunked as a freshman, I knew that my father's empire and the orthodox economics establishment occupied parallel universes with only a few points of connection. My father and grandmother were never mentioned in economics textbooks and they couldn't begin to fathom the mathematical equations that seemed to give orthodox economics such authority. Yet, the parallel universes worked in concert to reinforce the same Greed is Good worldview.

Based on everything I had learned since my freshman year, I also knew that orthodox economic theory was as fictitious as Objectivism. It pretended that an economic system could be modeled with the same kind of mathematical precision as the solar system. Maintaining this conceit required making assumptions about human nature and economic transactions that were manifestly false. The whole charade was constructed to justify Adam Smith's metaphor of the invisible hand, whereby the pursuit of self-interest benefits the common good. Never mind that Adam Smith invoked the metaphor only three times and the entire corpus of his work provided a much richer conception of economics that could never be precisely modeled by a set of equations. The whole idea that a complex system of any sort could be modeled with precision by a set of equations had proven to be a folly in mathematics, physics, chemistry and biology, but that did not prevent the economic establishment from using their mathematical edifice as a kind of a fortress to protect their Greed is Good worldview.

Just as my father had been daily accused of lying, but to no effect until now, smart people had been pointing out the unreality of orthodox economics for decades to no avail. One economist named Maurice Allais, who was so smart that he became a Nobel laureate, complained that the orthodoxy exerted "a dogmatic and intolerant, powerful and tyrannical domination over the academic world." That was in 1987 and it still maintained an iron grip up to the present.

Now that my father had been forced to appeal to the authority of orthodox economics, we had to achieve the same kind of tipping point to bring about its downfall. Like a naval vessel delivering a broadside, we unleashed the ammunition that we had been accumulating over a period of four years. Then, the experts that we had convened swarmed over the experts that my father had engaged to beat them at their own game.

One piece of ammunition that proved exceptionally effective in this battle was a study of income inequality. For decades, critics of the Greed is Good worldview argued that income inequality is toxic for social welfare, while defenders argued that empowering the super-rich trickles down to benefit everyone else. The study that we commissioned used census statistics to measure income inequality in every county of the United States during the 2000 and 2010 censuses. Then the *change* in inequality during this ten-year period was related to changes in social welfare, such as bankruptcies, divorces, and home foreclosures. The result was inescapable. The greater the change in inequality, the greater the decline in welfare. The social fabric of America was rotting before our very eyes, once you knew what to look for. Not only was this study published in one of the most elite academic journals, but it was made available on the Internet in plain language accompanied by interactive maps that enabled everyone to view the statistics for their own county. Trickle-down economics could be seen for what it was – a fiction.

Once again, we watched breathlessly to see if a tipping point would be reached for the economic orthodoxy, where the open secret of its unreality would suddenly become shocking and unacceptable. As we were waiting, we did something that took everyone by surprise. We unleashed a broadside against the progressive political and economic establishment for *their* ineffectiveness at running the ship of state whenever they had the chance. We pointed out that there was a baby in the bathwater of conservative and libertarian critiques of big government. Laissez faire and centralized planning, the two main modes of governing, were *both* doomed to failure. A new path needed to be blazed that didn't fall into any current political or economic camp. The beacon to follow was the concept of society as an organism and the way to get there was through a managed process of cultural evolution.

Firing at all sides, yet also acknowledging a degree of truth on all sides, created havoc. No one knew what to think anymore, or rather they were being forced to think in new ways for the first time in a long time, rather than relying upon the separate narratives that they had constructed for themselves. We knew that it would take a while for the smoke to clear – certainly more than the year that we had allowed ourselves for the worldwide catalysis to take place – but in a world starving for change, we had established ourselves as the bright new alternative, with a fresh way of looking at the world and a straight-A average for telling the truth. Everything else appeared old and tattered by comparison. That was good enough for our purposes.

Most of this was taking place under the command of Howard and Ashley on the second floor of the Elbow Room. Apart from my once-a-week visit and a conference call every morning, I remained remarkably to myself in my hermitage and available to meet with the press. They were brought in groups of eight for all-day sessions. Expenses were paid by the Evolution Institute, although some news organizations footed the bill to avoid the appearance of conflicts of interest. The journalists for each group were chosen to be diverse with respect to age, sex, ethnicity, and politics. All of them were screened for their integrity. Even though truth-telling norms had eroded, there were still plenty of journalists who maintained high standards for themselves and deplored what was happening to their profession. Those who had succumbed to the temptations of fake news simply weren't invited.

The most senior member of the first group was the legendary journalist and public intellectual from National Public Radio, Bill Noyers, in his mid-eighties and mostly retired but still, we hoped, approachable. It was a thrill when he accepted our invitation, signaling that our catalytic efforts were indeed working. Next in seniority was George Mill, arguably the most distinguished conservative and libertarian commentator with degrees from both Oxford and Harvard, feared by progressive thinkers everywhere for his biting sarcasm and command of the subject matter. Then there was Natalie Alters, one of the best known science journalists for the *New York Times*; Jake White, a young black independent journalist who had distinguished himself covering the Black Lives Matter movement; Noah Coan, the libertarian economist whose blog reached an audience of over half a million; Ed Wang, *Wired*'s technology editor; Sami Desai, who covered health & wellbeing for the *Los Angeles Times*, and Angelina Garcia, who covered politics for *La Opinión*, America's largest Hispanic newspaper.

The Mother Ship made the airline reservations and Ron managed the ground transportation, first from the Laramie airport to the Three Bears Motel on the night before, and then to my hermitage the next morning for breakfast. When they arrived in the small convoy of cars and pickups arranged by Ron, they appeared a bit shell-shocked. Each had found the personal invitation to meet with John Galt, the most talked-about person of the moment, unexpected and irresistible – a bit like John Galt I emerging from the shadows to invite a Doer to join a secret society. They knew that they would be part of a group but were unprepared for its diversity, much less the redneck limo service and rustic accommodations of the Three Bears Motel. Whatever confidence they owed to being highly successful in their respective worlds was shaken a bit, now that they were out of their element and mingling with people from other worlds. On the other hand, they couldn't help but respond to the sparkling morning and mountain scenery. Ron led them past the ENOUGH sign to the Cell. I greeted them from the deck with Lizzie jumping against the gate to meet her new friends.

"Hello! Welcome! This is Lizzie – she hasn't bitten anyone yet. Thanks for coming. Thanks, Ron! I'll let you know the pickup time. Come on up!"

They walked up the external stairs to the deck and entered the Cell to deposit their jackets, briefcases, and other belongings. The interior of the Cell never failed to instill a sense of awe and reverence, and this group was no exception. I invited them to look around and climb the spiral staircase to the roof while I completed breakfast preparations. Sami, Angelina, and Jake offered to help. Jake revealed that he was a foodie, inspired by his Jamaican grandmother, whose vegetable garden was famous in the Philadelphia neighborhood where he grew up.

I had learned enough from Eve to rustle up an impressive rancher's breakfast of eggs, sausage, home-made bread, with butter and jam, juice, fruit and lots of coffee or tea, which we carried out to the picnic table on the deck. Natalie was on the deck. She had removed her jacket and over-shirt so that her bare arms could be exposed to the sun and was standing, trance-like, with her hands on the rail, gazing into the forest. She snapped out of it when we started to set the table and apologized for not helping.

"John, you're so lucky to be living here!" she exclaimed.

"Indeed I am," I smiled in reply.

Bill Noyers descended from the staircase. "John, the workmanship of your Cell is incredible! How much of it is yours?"

"I thought I was going to build my own homestead but Ron talked me out of it. We designed it together and he rounded up a group of locals to build it. They poured their hearts into it as a matter of pride. Isn't it something?"

"It certainly is. I envy you for your office loft."

"Thanks. Not to rub it in, but it's only one of several places where I might decide to work on any particular day."

Ed emerged from the ground floor, eager to talk about my solar panels and battery storage system. George and Noah had decided to walk the paths around my three acres and joined us when they heard our chatter and clink of utensils. The fact that I was serving them breakfast, coupled with the delightful surroundings, created a celebratory mood. Most of them were relaxing more than they had in a long time.

After the breakfast dishes had been cleared and coffee and tea cups refilled, we sat around the big table inside the Cell to begin the day's conversation.

"We have the whole day to talk, so I'd like to begin by having you introduce yourselves to me and each other. I've done my own homework, so I already know about and admire your work, but tell us how you got to where you are today. Where were you born? How did you grow up? Why did you become a journalist?"

Eyebrows rose in surprise. They were supposed to be asking me the questions. Nevertheless, the relaxing atmosphere and the day stretching before us made it easy for each to spend a few minutes telling their life stories. Perceived differences melted away as they saw each other as fellow human beings with common hopes, fears, and aspirations, starting from childhood. Lizzie added to the contentment by offering herself to anyone who wished to caress her.

"That was great!" I said after everyone had taken their turn. "I needn't tell you my story because you're probably sick of it by now." The group laughed appreciatively. Everything that I said and did was designed to put me on an equal footing, not to place myself above them, and they could see that it was genuine. That won them over more than anything else I could have done.

"You're welcome to ask me more about myself, but I'm more interested to discuss the new view that I and my colleagues are trying to introduce to the world, using the duel of speeches with my father to emphasize the contrast."

Everyone looked to Bill Noyers to ask the first question and he was happy to oblige. "What I want to know, John, is how you can be so self-assured. Here you are, a mere pup of twenty-five years – the youngest person in this room, if I am not mistaken – and you convey yourself with utter confidence. I'm eighty-six years old and still don't have your confidence. Where do you get it?"

The rest of the group murmured their approval. They were wondering just the same thing. I paused for a few seconds to gather my thoughts, the fingers of my two hands touching each other to form a cage in front of my face, much as Howard had done during our weekly meetings. Then I began.

"Actually, that question gets to the heart of the new worldview. I promise you that my confidence is not something I was born with. I was painfully shy as a child and ever since I learned of the course that my mother set me upon, I was wracked with anxiety that some kind of greatness was expected of me, with no way to deliver. That anxiety reached its peak during my freshman year of college, when I flunked my Econ 101 class and only barely passed my other courses."

Everyone smiled and looked toward George and Noah, the two members of the group most knowledgeable about economics, to see how they would respond. Noah was smiling with the others but George had the look of a prize fighter sizing up his opponent.

"Then I was saved during the second half of my freshman year by Professor Howard Head, who you will meet during the afternoon. My confidence can be attributed entirely to what Howard taught me and others can learn. It is not innate. It is what I have come to see as Objectivism, properly understood, and what I will compare to my father's fraudulent form of Objectivism in our duel of speeches."

"Do we have to wait?" asked Sami.

"No! I'm wanting to tell you! I'm wishing to tell you! I'm *waiting* to tell you!" Several members of the group smiled with recognition at this quote from the old Broadway play *My Fair Lady*, where Eliza Doolittle's father is trying to get a word in edgewise with Professor Harold Higgins. Even George couldn't suppress a smile.

"It's not only teachable but *easy* to teach, as Howard has proven many times. Let me begin by telling you some things that you already know. First, nobody can learn random collections of facts and retain them for long. That's why I struggled so hard during my first semester at college. Facts have to be related to each other in some way to be remembered and put into action. Is that something that you already knew?"

Their expressions confirmed that it was and that I should continue.

"So, every one of us has some sort of system inside our heads for relating facts and beliefs to each other. You might call it a worldview or a meaning system. I like the term 'meaning system' because it emphasizes that the facts and beliefs that we carry around play a role in how we act. If something inside our head has no influence on how we act, then we should get rid of it and make room for something else that does. Have I said anything new yet?"

"Well, yes and no," replied Ed. "I can't disagree with it, but I haven't exactly been brooding upon it on my own!" The others nodded their agreement, except for George, who continued his predatory stare.

"Right! Point well taken." As I warmed to my subject, I was displaying the very confidence that they wondered about, more typical of a full professor than a twenty-five-year-old pup.

"Here is more that you already know, even if it didn't occur to you. Meaning systems vary in their comprehensiveness. Most are good enough to get by on, but they leave so much unexplained. There is a good analogy to be had with our basic perceptual abilities. We see only a narrow slice of the light spectrum and hear only a narrow slice of the sound spectrum. Our sense of smell is terrible compared to a dog like Lizzie. And some physical forces, such as magnetism and mild electrical currents, we can't sense at all, even though some other species can. Evolution has been frugal in giving us the ability to sense only what contributes to our survival and reproduction. Our culturally constructed meaning systems are like that, too. Think of your own meaning systems as like a flashlight that illuminates a little space around you but leaves everything else in darkness."

I paused a moment to give them time to reflect upon this image. I could see from their expressions that it struck a chord. There was so much that they – that nearly every person – didn't know and had no way of knowing. Only George seemed unmoved.

"Here is another point that you already know. Meaning systems include more than just facts. They also include unproven beliefs and downright falsehoods which nevertheless play a useful role in terms of what they cause us to do. That's the only criterion for the retention of an element of a meaning system, as far as evolution is concerned. So we can begin to understand the human penchant for inventing, remembering and defending blatant falsehoods. Fake news isn't new and isn't even necessarily bad, although the current epidemic of fake news in modern life is deeply destructive."

"Can you give us an example of fake news that isn't bad?" This question came from Jake.

"Sure. How about the fact that most people regard themselves as above average?"

There was a laugh of recognition. Of course! This was an example of a useful fiction that was in front of their faces. No elaboration was needed. George smiled and raised one eyebrow, conceding the point.

"Or imagine that you're in a conflict situation. Is it more motivating to think of your enemies as human beings, much like yourself, or as inhuman monsters?"

"OK, I get it."

"This is an example of a falsehood that is both good and bad. It's good from the narrow perspective of the individual trying to win the fight, but bad from the broader perspective of achieving a peaceful resolution, and so on. I think you can see it as obvious, upon just a little reflection, that our minds are designed in part to help us survive and reproduce from the more narrow perspective, making distortions of reality useful in a thousand different ways, even if they also create problems for others and even the perpetrators of the fake news in the long run.

"It's not as if factual reality counts for nothing. Sometimes the best way to survive and reproduce is to perceive the world as it really is, even from a narrow perspective. If I'm a hunter, I need to know the exact location of my game to bring home dinner. And even when the facts interfere with our narrow self-interests, they are useful for everyone's long term benefit. Like Dr. Jekyll and Mr. Hyde, we have the capacity to both honor the truth and ride roughshod over the truth, wrestling for control."

My reply was hitting its full stride and no one wished to slow me down. This was the kind of big picture philosophizing that they yearned for as intellectuals, but often found sadly lacking even in their elite profession.

"In this day and age, the need to respect the truth for our long-term welfare is greater than ever. This is something else that you already know. *We will never be able to manage our affairs on a planetary scale without seeing the world as it really is.* This requires a commitment to scientific knowledge, since our evolved capacity to perceive the truth is far too limited without the tools of science and the norms that bind scientists to tell the truth."

Yes, I had allowed myself to get carried away again. I sounded like Moses delivering the Ten Commandments to his people. All eight of them stared at me with wide eyes, but not entirely as if I was a freak. After all, these values were also their values, which they knew to be endangered in the age of fake news. To have them stated like a call to battle was heartening and rousing in its own way, even if a bit awkward for the occasion. Also, it helped that I wasn't putting on an act. They could see that it was emanating from strong feelings and that I was struggling to get myself back under control. The expression on Bill Noyers's face was especially bemused. He had been around a long time and had never seen anything like this. And George's face had softened a bit. He was famous for getting his facts right and skewering his opponents when they didn't. We were allies at least in this regard. I resumed in a more normal tone of voice.

"This commitment to truth-telling was my first breakthrough, at least in my own mind, and my first step toward the self-confidence that you see today. Until then, I had no real way of knowing whether my father's empire was as evil as my mother thought it was. But once I grasped the importance of truth-telling and could see how wantonly my grandmother and father had gone over to the dark side of bending and disregarding the truth whenever it suited their purposes, then I knew that I was on a righteous path. It might seem funny to employ that kind of religious imagery to describe a commitment to science and objective knowledge, but there is nothing intrinsically religious about a phrase such as "righteous path" or indeed most of the other words associated with religion, such as "sacred," "spiritual," "worship," or even "God." That's a conversation that I am happy to have with you, but let me continue describing how I acquired my self-confidence."

The others were also eager to continue, so they remained wordless. An hour had passed as if it were a few minutes.

"A commitment to truth-telling, which requires a commitment to scholarship and science, was only the first step. The second step was evolutionary theory, which is what I learned from Howard. I have no idea what each of you knows or thinks about evolution – other than

Natalie, who writes about it beautifully – but here is what you need to know. It has an unparalleled ability to relate facts to each other, like the pieces of a giant jigsaw puzzle, into a coherent system of meaning. That's what Howard was able to relate on the very first day of his class, which he immodestly calls 'The Secret of Life.' Imagine my amazement and relief, after trying and failing to learn disconnected facts during my first semester, to witness Howard assemble facts in a way that was almost effortless to remember and endowed with meaning! It is not an exaggeration to say that I felt saved by Howard, despite its humorous juxtaposition with the more common phrase, 'Saved by Jesus.'"

Laughter all around, George included.

"The best kept secret about evolutionary theory, outside of evolutionary biology, is its ability to unify knowledge. If everyone knew that, they would be rushing to learn it. Imagine that flashlight that I was talking about, that meaning system you have, which enables you to see just enough to get by but otherwise envelops you in darkness, suddenly becoming a floodlight and then the sun, illuminating everything that you might want to know about. That is the potential of evolutionary theory, although it is only in the process of being realized."

Natalie was visibly nodding her head. She had been relatively impassive up to now, but now that the conversation had entered her area of expertise, she was happy to agree.

"That's something else that I learned from Howard, although it was a more gradual process than the first revelation. It's hard to see yourself and your time as history in the making, but that's precisely what we need to do. Bill, what was the Enlightenment?"

The whole group was startled at my question, Bill most of all. They had grown accustomed to listening to my torrent of words and were not expecting a give and take, much less me calling upon the revered Bill Noyers as if he was a student.

"It was the dawn of Reason and Science, starting in the 1600s," he replied.

"Correct," I answered with a smile, acknowledging the humor of the young pup lecturing the wise old master. "Is it safe to say that the Enlightenment was also a new culture that sanctified Reason and Science, that gave it an authority rivaling the authority of Religion, impelling us to capitalize the words, similar to the way that we feel impelled to capitalize the word God?"

"Yes," replied Bill with a smile. "I couldn't put it better myself. That's why it was contested by religious authorities."

"Right! But reason and science are just procedures that generate knowledge, and that process takes time. Mathematics, physics, and chemistry came first in the 17th and 18th centuries. Darwin's theory didn't arrive until the second half of the 19th century. The application of Darwin's theory to the biological world took place during the 20th century. And the application of Darwin's theory to understand the human condition is only now taking place and is still largely in the future. That's what it means to see this moment as history in the making."

Once again, the whole group stared at me in silence. What do you tell someone who is asking you to help make history?

"Bill, George, Natalie – help me make this point to the others. You are among the great public intellectuals of our time and you cover dozens of topics."

All three gave a little jolt. My compliment was unexpected and struck them like a dart. They couldn't help feeling a bit flattered by the supremely self-confident pup. Even George was disarmed.

"When you cover topics that are about nature and the environment, does evolution ever get mentioned?"

"Of course. All the time." Natalie was best qualified to answer this question, but Bill and George nodded in agreement.

"And when you cover human topics, such as education, the environment, economics, politics, international relations, does evolution ever get mentioned?"

Bill: "Hardly ever."

"Is that because the experts were Creationists?"

George: "Not in most cases."

"If you had asked them whether they accepted Darwin's theory of evolution, what do you think they would say?"

Natalie: "Well, first they would be surprised by the question, and then they would probably say, 'Of course.'"

"Yet, they didn't see fit to mention evolution while holding forth as experts, the way that I did repeatedly during the start of our conversation this morning?"

Bill: "No. Nothing like what you did."

Bill, George, and Natalie had made a silent decision that they agreed with me and would help to make my point to the others. It was as if we had momentarily become a quartet.

"That's what I mean!" I replied triumphantly. "They're not closed-minded about evolution! It's just that the theory hasn't yet arrived for them! The Enlightenment is still a work in progress!"

Ed had remained silent but now raised a finger to indicate his desire to speak. His voice mimicked a timid student asking to clarify his homework assignment.

"So you asked us up here to help you complete the Enlightenment?"

The group burst into laughter and I joined in, releasing the tension.

"If you can't hand it in tomorrow, I'll give you an extension until Tuesday. Let me wrap up my answer to Bill's question so we can take a break and move on to other topics. All of this came together for me in rapid succession during the summer after my freshman year. I asked Howard to become my mentor and he agreed. Given the path that my mother had set me upon, I had a far greater incentive to learn than other students, which I did with a monk-like devotion. Then, when I turned twenty-one, Howard and I used my wealth to create the Evolution Institute. For the last four years, we have been catalyzing the Enlightenment, so to speak, meeting with hundreds of scientists and scholars to formulate and fund their research. Given the unparalleled ability of evolutionary theory to unify knowledge, we can cross disciplinary boundaries in a way that seems miraculous to others, as if we are able to walk through walls. This means that in your capacity as journalists, we can put you in touch with experts for any topic that you might want to cover, but I have been sufficiently engaged to give you a pretty good account on my own. Howard and some Evolution Institute staff members will be joining us during the afternoon and you can try us out. To conclude: Have I answered your first question concerning how I acquired my self-confidence?"

"Please, Bill, say yes!" shouted George in mock desperation, and the group again erupted into laughter. The first conversation of the day had been intense and it was time for a break.

"Friends, Howard and some members of the Evolution Institute will be joining us for the afternoon. I suggest that we take a walk to clear our heads. I have access to the University of Wyoming's biological station land, which adjoins my property and includes one of the prettiest mountain lakes that you'll ever see. The hike is a little more than a mile. You are welcome to come or stay here and chill."

George and Noah elected to stay and the rest of us set off with Lizzie, who was overjoyed to be on the move. Her infectious enthusiasm, coupled with the philosophizing and the gorgeous surroundings, put everyone in a giddy mood. The air was infused with the smell of pine and the sun fell in shafts through their branches. A light breeze caressed our skin and a brook next to trail added music. We set our pace to be comfortable for Bill, who found a walking stick to help him down some of the steeper pitches.

"This place was part of my education," I said as we ambled along. "I was already an avid outdoorsman, but it was a revelation to learn that every species, from the mightiest tree to the smallest insect, is a master of survival and reproduction in an unbroken chain stretching back to the origin of life. Yet, as exalting as that might sound, and as tranquil as this forest might seem to us at this moment, we are in fact surrounded by suffering. Evolution doesn't make everything nice! Isn't that right, Natalie?"

Natalie, who had covered many stories from the annals of nature, was pleased to share some that illustrated the dark side of evolution – ants that enslave other ants, spiders that are paralyzed by wasps and eaten alive by the wasp larvae, bark beetles capable of destroying entire forests.

"Here's an example right in front of us." I added, calling them over to the brook. "Natalie, didn't you cover the research by Omar Eldabar on the sexual strategies of water striders?"

"Yes!" exclaimed Natalie. "Was that research done here?"

"Some of it. He's a good example of someone else who was saved by Howard. He came to UW on a track scholarship and nobody expected him to excel academically, but then he came under Howard's wing and now he's a kickass professor at the University of Florida. I assisted him when he was a graduate student."

Jake perked up his ears. Jocks almost never become professors. What sort of alchemy had Howard Head performed on this person named Omar? Natalie and I entertained the others with Omar's research, complete with my lurid description of the anatomy of the water strider penis, which made the eyes of Sami and Angelina bug out in amazement and disgust.

Everyone fell silent with awe when we reached the lake. The image of the peak on the lake's surface was fractured by the light breeze, the same breeze that caressed our skin and set the leaves of the aspens shimmering along the shore.

After we paid our respect with our silence, I pointed out the biological station on the far shore and privately gazed at the spot where I first saw the lake on my mad dash to the lodge on snowshoes to make love with Eve. A crow calling in the distance brought Eve even more vividly to my mind. Tears welled up in my eyes and I turned away to conceal them, but not before Angelina had noticed. When I regained my composure and faced the group, she was looking at me, her face wreathed in sympathy. Our eyes locked and I began to become undone again. Now everyone noticed and an awkward silence ensued. The young pup who had taken on the world with such supreme confidence was overcome with sorrow for unknown reasons. A silent consensus formed that the best thing to do was to let it pass, as if it had not happened at all.

Bill returned us to normalcy by saying that he was the stone-skipping champion of his hometown as a boy. That led to a search for skipping stones and a contest among ourselves. Natalie, Samee, and Angelina declared that this must be a man thing and sat down by the shore to watch. Bill, Ed, and I were evenly matched, as we released the stones with a sidearm throw, counting the number of times that they touched the surface and became airborne again. This was a new sport for Jake, but he proved to be a quick study. It turned out that playing baseball was good preparation and he ended up beating us all.

We returned a little later than planned to find that Howard, Ashley, and most other members of the Mother Ship had already arrived. No one wanted to miss the opportunity to meet Bill Noyers – and to a lesser extent George Mill – in person. They brought food and drinks, potluck style, which was already laid out on the deck. The beat-up cooler with beer bottle necks sticking out of cracked ice made me smile with memories of the weekly potlucks back then. How far we had come! Howard was already engaged in animated conversation with George and Noah, beer bottles in hand.

"Friends!" I called in a loud voice to get everyone's attention. "I know that there is a strong temptation to focus on individuals, such as my father or myself, and we have been smart enough to capitalize on that weakness of the human mind to get the world's attention. But the essence of Objectivism, properly understood, is that all of us are part of something larger than ourselves. Just as it took a community to build this beautiful physical structure, it takes a community to build an edifice of knowledge. I am therefore proud to introduce you to some of my brethren at the Evolution Institute, starting with Howard Head. If you prefer to think in mythic terms, then you can regard Howard as Obi-wan Kenobi, or maybe even Yoda, to my Luke Skywalker."

"Very wise, I am!" Howard mimed the silly syntax of Yoda to everyone's amusement.

"We invited you here, not only because of your fine reputations as journalists, but also for the topics that you cover, such as health and wellness, technology, and race and prejudice. We have also covered each of these topics in our workshops and research programs, and we're eager to share our perspective and findings with you. In the process, we hope to demonstrate the main point that I made this morning – the unifying power of evolutionary theory."

What a relief it was to no longer be the center of attention, to drift from conversation to conversation and even to play the role of host, clearing away dirty dishes, restocking the cooler with beer bottles, and positioning logs for the fire on the roof of the cell that would bring the day to a close. It was on the roof that Angelina caught me alone. Her face had the look of someone summoning all of her courage to speak.

"John, please don't take this the wrong way. What happened by the lake made my heart go out to you. I don't know what swept over you. I know hardly anything about you. All that stuff about your father and speeches isn't part of my world. I was mystified to receive your invitation to come here. You seemed so strong this morning, holding your own with great men such as Bill and George. But then at the lake I realized that maybe you weren't that strong. That you might just be a person like myself, and if so, how incredibly brave you must be. It made me want to comfort you, to offer you any support that I could. Isn't that ridiculous? I've never thrown myself at anyone before, much less a total stranger until today, and one who must have all manner of people throwing themselves at you. I don't even know what I am asking! All I know is that what the others are trying to decide with their heads, I have already decided with my heart. I'm ready to dedicate my life to the purpose that you have brought me here for."

Angelina's words went straight to my own heart. Our eyes locked and we entered that place beyond words. I began to notice her face and body as I had not before. Her face was terror-stricken. She had confessed her deepest wants and placed her entire future in my hands. She looked as I must have looked to Eve after our first kiss. I was also terror-stricken. Angelina was right that my supreme self-confidence required an enormous effort of will that I could sustain only by periods of time alone and my love for Eve. I couldn't possibly abandon my love for Eve, not for my own sake and especially when she was facing unknown dangers on her own path. Yet, my yearning for warm human touch was almost more than I could bear. This was not necessarily what Angelina was even offering, but it would require yet more strength to resist falling into her orbit. It was a long time before I could speak.

"Angelina, when I fell apart, it was in memory of someone named Eve, which is bound up with my memories of the lake and biological station. We are soul mates but she is on her own path and possibly in great danger. Between my longing for Eve and worrying about her, I am sometimes overcome with grief. "

Angelina's face registered equal measures of compassion and disappointment as I continued.

"Now that you understand what happened by the lake, your sympathy and the way that you have responded with your heart, as you say, means more to me than you might guess."

Angelina's face brightened.

"I would be honored for you to become part of what I am trying to accomplish. I don't need more experts, that's for sure. I do need someone who can sustain me emotionally. This is so awkward – to declare my undying love for one person and reach out emotionally to another. You should know that I am really quite inexperienced at love and old-fashioned about matters such as faithfulness. But if you could help me in this strange way, it would mean so much."

With this understanding, we fell into an embrace, against the background of the chatter of the company on the deck below.

As twilight fell, the crew of the Mother Ship packed up for their two-hour drive back to Laramie, leaving me alone again with my eight new friends.

"Ron and his entourage will be picking you up at ten. If you will, please follow me onto the roof for our final session."

Already tired from such a long day, we ascended the spiral staircase, illuminated by soft white battery-powered LED lights. As I had observed so many times before, the procession took on a ritual significance. The small talk stopped, the pace slowed, and the steps were taken in unison. I had lit the fire earlier and it was blazing underneath the screen dome that contained the sparks. As we came onto the roof, most of them murmured in appreciation, as if a forgotten desire had unexpectedly been filled. I removed the screen dome and we spaced ourselves evenly around the fire, sitting on the logs arranged around the perimeter, and they leaned forward, warming their hands and gazing pensively into its center or the illuminated faces around them. The stars were beginning to appear in the darkening sky. There would be trillions of them by the time we were done, a sight that almost no one gets to see any more in a world polluted by artificial light.

"I like to bring people up here because it is how our ancestors spent their evenings since time immemorial. I have nothing to add to our already full day and mean this time as an opportunity to reflect."

Bill knew that everyone expected him to speak first. Nevertheless, he waited almost a minute to gather his words. Words are chosen carefully in an atmosphere such as this.

"John, in all my years I have never seen anything like you and the movement that you are trying to create. You are like the Buddha, renouncing your great wealth, although not obsessively, and offering a path to end suffering. The value that you place on knowledge and the welfare of the whole Earth is as laudable and idealistic as can be. It would be easy to dismiss you as just another New Age Guru, but your scientific literacy is amazing – far enough above my own that I am not qualified to judge it. And when you come to the end of your own knowledge, you have a community of experts to refer us to. These experts are not converts and most of them don't even think about what they do in spiritual terms. The fact that you can rely upon them makes your claims sound even more plausible. Something else that amazes me is how close I feel to all of you. It's as if we have become family within a single day!"

The others, except for George, nodded their assent. They might have been afraid to admit it on their own, but for a revered father figure such as Bill to say it relaxed their inhibitions.

"It's in part because I feel such affection for you that I worry for you," Bill went on. "I worry that despite your brilliance, self-confidence, and preparation, you have a weakness that can be attributed to both your youth and the pretentions of our age. Not only do you want Enlightenment, but you want Enlightenment *now*."

Ouch! In a single stoke, Bill had switched the story so that he was the wise master and I was the naïve lad who needed to learn from him.

"I worry that the Nirvana you seek can't be had in a year, a decade, or even a lifetime. I'm old enough to know that most people won't abandon their ways no matter how destructive their practices or how much you reason with them. I agree with you that the Enlightenment is still a work in progress. God knows, lately it seems that we have been going backward, not forward. But can you really believe that there is some kind of fast forward button that can be pressed to accomplish in years what otherwise might require centuries? For your sake and the credibility of your movement, you and your friend Howard need to learn more patience!"

The others nodded their assent to this, and George was the next to speak.

"John, I'm known as a champion of conservatism, who eats old lefties like Bill here for breakfast."

Everyone laughed, including Bill. It was clear that Bill and George had fondness and respect for each other, despite their political differences.

"You didn't invite me up here to pat you on the back or offer a rubber stamp endorsement. In the material that you have been releasing to the press, you say that Objectivism, properly understood, is a fresh new alternative that does not fall into any current political camp. I disagree. It seems to me that your Objectivism affirms the core conservative values of character, integrity, freedom of individual choice, and limited government."

These words made me smile and recollect Steve's complaint that I was such a chameleon. The rednecks thought I was a redneck, the tree huggers thought I was a tree hugger, and now one of the most prominent voices for conservatism in America had concluded that I'm a conservative. I could not hope for a better outcome, because one of the biggest dangers that Howard and I were trying to avoid was to become classified as old-fashioned lefties. George continued.

"Your main complaint, as far as I can tell, is against free market capitalism. Welcome to the club. That said, it's refreshing for you to also speak out against big government and centralized planning. When you call for a middle path between these extremes, that intrigues me, although I think you might overstate the novelty of your approach. Have you considered that practitioners, as opposed to ideologues, already travel your middle path?

"But let me end on some positive notes. First, I commend you on your scholarship and strong moral stance toward truth-telling. In political discourse, figures such as Adam Smith and Friedrich Hayek have been reduced to memes. Despite your rocky beginning flunking Econ 101, I can see that you have a scholar's knowledge of the history of economics, and I know from my conversations with Noah on the deck that he agrees. When you say that Hayek was a pioneer who needs to be updated, I want to learn more. And you have introduced me to experts who were unknown to me before, which is very helpful. The fact that you can offer the same service to everyone else for their respective topic areas is impressive. You do have an ability to walk through academic walls, as you put it.

"I also want to acknowledge to all of you here around this campfire, as I do in my writing, that something has gone terribly wrong with the conservative movement in America. It has abandoned its own values and now appears to be nothing more than the deliberate creation of chaos to grab power. It frightens me and I don't know what to do about it. Against this grim background, John, your optimism and return to core conservative values, as I deem them, is a breath of fresh air. And finally, even if I don't ooze warmth the way that Bill does, I have enjoyed our day together and getting to know all of you as people."

We all felt an upwelling of affection for George, knowing how difficult it must have been for such a proud person to open up to that degree. Then the others followed suit, praising my optimism, praising my moral stance on truth-telling, praising the network of scientists that I had assembled, praising the closeness that we felt toward each other – but nevertheless refusing to believe that rapid transformational change might be possible.

Angelina was the last to speak. She had become emboldened by our earlier conversation on the roof.

"I feel so humble to be among such greatness. Who am I? A mere Latina girl trying to make a go of it as a journalist. John, what amazed me most about today was how you put me at my ease. You acted as an equal, rather than a superior. You served us food that you prepared yourself and even cleared the dishes. You attributed your self-confidence to your mentor, not yourself. Despite placing yourself on center stage in your battle with your father, your real message is the need for all of us to become part of something larger than ourselves. I have no way to pass judgment on all of the high ideas about economics, the enlightenment, and technology, but when I just listen to what you say, it makes perfect sense. It makes me wonder if my empty head might be an asset!"

This elicited a burst of laughter and appreciation, not only because it was funny but because it had such a large grain of truth. For all of the others, their full heads were the main impediment to adding anything new.

"I'm also a believer in following my heart in addition to my head. By heart, I don't mean romantic love, but something that pulls you for reasons that you don't pretend to understand. One nice thing about following your heart is that you don't put a probability on success. You just go for it, no matter what the odds. That's what my heart pulls me to do, after only a single day. It's like falling in love at first sight, not for a person – sorry, John! – but for some ideas. You can be sure that I'll be questioning my own judgment, just as someone who falls in love with a person at first sight does, but at this moment, all I can say is that I am smitten."

Everyone looked at Angelina with amazement. She had spoken more eloquently than all of the others, even Bill. I was especially impressed by how she could declare love for the ideas while deftly side-stepping the question of a romantic attachment with me – something that I could not help but question in my own mind, no matter how strong my devotion to Eve.

Now it was up to me to bring the day to a close.

"First, let me say what an honor it has been to spend this day with you. I'm gratified that we could talk so constructively with each other and agree upon so much, if not everything. I'm not surprised that you find the possibility of rapid worldwide transformation difficult to accept. Yet, all of you have remarked upon how special this day has been and how it has made us feel like family. In other words, *we* have experienced a transformation of sorts in a single day. Allow me to reflect upon the ingredients of this miniature transformation.

"First, we were surrounded by nature. This day would not have been so special in a city office building – except, perhaps, if it had been beautified to emulate nature.

"Second, we are a small group and we grew to know each other as fellow human beings, therefore to regard each other as equals.

"Third, we were discussing matters of importance. Our work had *meaning* for us.

"Fourth, our discussion was oriented toward action – what we can *do* together to improve our common good.

"Fifth, we shared a feeling of dependency, which in our case was more subjectively experienced than real, especially now around this campfire. Imagine what that feeling must have been like for our ancestors, where members of small groups depended upon each other for nearly everything!

"As human beings, we are primed to think and act 'as family' when these ingredients are provided. The miniature transformation can – and *did* – happen for us in a single day. It didn't matter that we come from different races, cultures, and professions, and were strangers to each other for the most part until this morning. In other words, what happened today for our group is a proof of concept for rapid transformation. Of course, there is the non-trivial matter of scaling up. I could be wrong, but I think that you might be in for a pleasant surprise."

Buoyed by Angelina's emotional support, the supremely self-confident pup had returned.

1 2

The Trek

My Darling Avatar Eve,

It is late at night and I just finished meeting with the last of five groups of journalists over the past five weeks. It's hard to believe that only three months have passed since I saw you. A month with my father and two months of hurricane-force media attention. I wonder if any of it has reached you down there. It's hard to find much news about Ecuador up here and if I tried too hard it would tear me up speculating about your safety. All I can do is have faith that my mover and adventuress knows what she is doing.

Astonishingly — for those who don't know the underlying logic — our efforts at cultural catalysis are working. We have gone a long way toward re-establishing the norm of truth-telling in public life. The three think tanks that grade my father and me are now doing a brisk business providing the same service to other individuals and organizations who want to stake their reputations on telling the truth. A number of advertisers have stopped airing their commercials on my father's shows until he improves his grades! After trying to bluster his way out of the mess, he did the only thing he could — appeal to the economic establishment for authority — causing the next domino to fall. Our own economists are beginning to occupy center stage more than they ever did before!

Through all of this, one of my greatest personal fears has been allayed. I worried that I would rob both my father and myself of our humanity by turning us into characters of the story that Howard and I are creating for the world. But the very opposite has taken place in the meetings with the journalists that just concluded. In every case, we came to recognize our common humanity and even to feel like family in the space of a single day. Most can't bring themselves to believe in the possibility of transformative change for the whole world, but they all admire the effort and our commitment to telling the truth. And they all become connected to our network of scientists and scholars, who therefore have access to the press more than they ever did before. In this way, our catalytic efforts over the last four years are bearing fruit and spreading outside the confines of the Ivory Tower.

Compared to all the activity on our end, my father has been strangely passive. A spy within their organization has been sending us audio files of their strategy sessions at regular intervals. They are all run by an operative name Steve with my father scarcely saying anything. After attention shifted from his populist rantings to serious economics, it was as if he had been sidelined, which is exactly what we intended. He is merely a gateway for discussing the serious issues, about which he has nothing to say.

All of this in two months, and now we move into Phase III, which will take everyone by surprise. Howard often seems cool and collected, planning his strategy of worldwide cultural catalysis like a wizard sure of his magic spells, but now that the broth of world culture is truly starting to bubble, he is beside himself with excitement and anticipation!

I have already told you about Angelina, the journalist who was so moved by her visit that she quit her job and now works for us. She realizes that for many people, the main barrier to accepting the obvious is everything that has been stuffed into their heads beforehand. The way around that is to get them to follow their hearts, as she puts it, and she's especially good at writing about it. It doesn't work for the experts, who are trained to ignore their hearts, but it sure works for the average person! We talk often and I must confess that we have become close. So much of what I am trying to accomplish is headwork that leaves my heart longing for companionship. She could never replace you and we stay away from sex. I know what you would tell me – stop being such a puritan and have fun – but it would violate something sacred so I don't go there. And she seems to have her own reasons for not going there that I don't question. Without talking about it, we both think that it's right to keep it platonic. Besides, when you're trying to change the world and have a solid shot at it, it puts your own personal needs into perspective.

I yearn to hear from you. Now onto Stage III.

On July 15, exactly 100 days before my duel with my father, I placed my letter to Eve in the mailbox, whistled up Lizzie, and headed down Timber Ridge Trail on foot. The weather was cool and unsettled, dark low clouds racing against a background of higher light gray clouds and patches of blue sky. That suited me fine, as I would be generating my own heat. All of my clothes were new, right down to socks and underwear, but in my usual style, including canvas pants and a cotton shirt that could stand up to a good day's work. My notebook was in its belt holder. My windbreaker was in a new style – green on top and white on the bottom, with an insignia on the chest and down each arm consisting of four symbols arranged in a vertical column: a dot, placed below a circle, placed below an American flag, placed below an image of the planet Earth. My daypack carried a light sweater, a dog leash, a water bottle, and a bag of trail mix. My iPhone was in my shirt pocket and a Bluetooth receiver was inserted into my ear.

"Dial Ashley … Good morning, Ashley! I'm on my way. Is everything set on your end? Great. Go ahead and send out the press release."

Within fifteen minutes I arrived at Ron's house. Lizzie was in high spirits at this break in her routine and bounded around Zeus, who, being an old dog, responded to the best of his ability. The door opened and Tyler emerged, followed by the rest of the family. Tyler was dressed exactly like me, even down to his own notebook in a belt holster, and the same style of windbreaker.

"Good morning, Tyler. You're looking sharp! Are you ready for a little walk?"

"Sure, why not!" he replied with a smile. Tyler didn't talk much but he was an acute observer and there was a lot going on under his hood. I handed him the dog leash and he placed it in his daypack, which was not new for the occasion.

"You are now the official keeper of Lizzie." Turning to Ron and Sarah, I added, "Thanks for loaning me your son. Did you have a problem getting him excused from school?"

"Naw!" replied Ron. "The Principal said that he would get a much better civics education this way and can catch up on the rest of his studies when he returns."

Ron, Sarah, and I spent a few seconds gazing into each other's eyes. We had been through a lot together and were more than family. By now, they knew as well as I did that we were playing a role in history. The next time they saw their son, the whole world might have turned a corner.

"Keep an eye on the Cell and have some ribs waiting for us when we return!"

With a round of hugs, I resumed my journey with Tyler and Lizzie at my side. As we walked toward the town of Timber Ridge, the morning talk shows were reporting the breaking news that John Galt III was walking to Philadelphia to keep his appointment with John Galt II and inviting others to join him. For more information, visit Change.world. Residents of Timber Ridge who heard the news called and texted their friends. By the time we arrived, a crowd had gathered to greet us. I had grown close to these folks during the construction of the Cell. They had rallied around me during the last two months and even came to enjoy the glare of media attention, not to speak of the economic boon of having so many journalists and their crews pass through the town. Ron had helped them to see that I was "the truest redneck that ever was" and they were proud to assert their values of rugged independence *and* community to the world. I hadn't planned it, but their support, beamed around the world by the media, was a major blow to the good old boy image cultivated by my father, as Steve knew only too well. Now they treated Tyler and me, with our matching outfits, as heroes going off to war.

"Give 'em hell, John! You always keep 'em guessing!"

"Looks like you're going to work off some of that belly fat, Tyler!"

"Walk with us a while and visit Change.world to see what comes next!" I laughed. Some of them indeed fell in and we made our way through town with the festivity of a parade. As we passed the Three Bear Motel, we were joined by a young woman on a bicycle wearing an outfit just like ours and long blond hair in a braid emerging from the back of a helmet with the same four symbols arranged in a column. A dot, a circle, the American flag, and Earth.

"Good morning, Sigrid. This is Tyler – keeper of the dog."

"Hi there, Tyler!" Sigrid replied, flashing a brilliant smile and reaching her hand down to pet Lizzie. Tyler was shy around girls and could barely mumble a reply. I turned to the others to explain.

"Sigrid is part of a team of bicyclists who will be helping to manage our trek. We don't know how big our following will become, but we have it figured out so that we can redirect traffic, distribute food and water, and respond to minor emergencies. If you register on the website, you'll be able to follow our progress and assist our trek in a number of ways. Are we ready, Sigrid?"

Sigrid spoke into a microphone embedded in her helmet and listened to a reply.

"Ready!" she replied and pedaled ahead of us, her long braid swinging back and forth against her back. Gradually our parade dwindled as the Timber Ridgers returned to town, until it was just Lizzie, Tyler, and me. We had the road to ourselves because bicyclists were stationed at all the intersecting roads to direct traffic around us. As soon as we passed, bicyclists in the rear were instructed to pedal ahead to new locations. All of this was orchestrated by Evolution Institute personnel at the Mother Ship following our progress on a large screen monitor.

It was exhilarating to be striding along with Tyler and Lizzie, combining the euphoria of vigorous outdoor exercise with anticipation of what was taking place around the world. Several hours into our Trek, the forest was starting to yield to prairie. I dialed Ashley for a progress report.

"Greetings, Ashley! Do we have the problem of too few or too many?"

"Too many, John! We're barely able to keep up with the traffic!"

"Good!" I smiled. "That's the best problem to have."

There is something inherently unpredictable about the size and strength of a social movement. Whether a desperate street vendor's self-immolation will lead to an Arab Spring. Whether the gathering resentment against the one percent will result in occupying Wall Street. Whether an oddball socialist such as Bernie Sanders will give the Democratic establishment a run for its money. When a social movement does occur, its outcome is more predictable. Most of the time, the burst of energy is short-lived, like a flash of lightning and clap of thunder, and the movement falls far short of its aspirations.

Our movement would be different. The tsunami of media attention had built up a tremendous reservoir of energy in the general public, which now wanted to *act* upon its mounting frustration and desperation about the state of the world. My 100-day trek to Philadelphia was an attempt to channel that energy, in the same way that water from an actual reservoir is used to generate electricity. By visiting Change.world, people could now *do* something. They could register as a True Objectivist. They could join the trek or converge upon Philadelphia for the duel of speeches. They could donate money, following my example of restricting my wealth to the ten percent. If they lay along our route, they could help to feed and lodge us. Above all, no matter where they lived, they could organize into groups, or cells, to accomplish more together than they ever could alone.

Joining the True Objectivist movement required signing an Oath:

I SWEAR BY MY LIFE AND LOVE OF IT THAT I WILL UPHOLD THE TRUTH AND THE SANCTITY OF THE EARTH, UPON WHICH ALL OF OUR WELFARE DEPENDS.

This oath was true to the meaning of the word "Objective" and flew in the face of the oath that members of my grandfather's ill-fated community were required to recite. By downloading an app, they also gave permission to become part of a communication system that included having their geographical location monitored. The personal information that they provided would be protected by the same high standards of scientific research on human subjects, including a code name that they could adopt if they wished to withhold their real name.

There would be no commercial or political use of their information whatsoever.

That was the plan, but how big was the reservoir and how much of it would flow through Change.world? That's what I meant when I asked Ashley if we had the problem of too few or too many.

"Check out the map on the website," Ashley told me through my earphone. I fetched my iPhone from my pocket and clicked on the app.

"Tyler, look at this."

I set the phone on speaker mode so that Tyler could be included in the conversation. The app displayed a map of the United States colored in light brown. Already, it was illuminated by points of green light representing people who had joined the movement. The points looked like plants growing in what was previously a barren desert. There was a counter at the bottom of the screen that looked like a car odometer. The numbers on the right end were whirling so fast that you couldn't see them. The numbers at the left end indicated that over 20,000 people had already joined the New Objectivist Movement. The United States was greening before our eyes.

This was what we were hoping for and I had been involved in all phases of the creation of the website, but to see the True Objectivist movement growing in the palm of my hand left both me and Tyler speechless.

"Zoom in on Wyoming," Ashley instructed. A few swipes brought the state into view. There was a concentration of points along the route that we were traveling through the state. The system was tracking our location, which was represented on the map by a pulsating red circle. Zooming in on our location, we could see that the nearest green point was about three miles down the road.

"That person says that you are welcome to use their bathroom," Ashley reported.

"What the fuck???" was all that Tyler could say in his amazement. Everyone burst out laughing.

"Howard, is that you?" Ashley had set her phone on speaker mode and I heard his unmistakable laughter.

"It sure is! This is what we planned, but isn't it amazing to see it materialize before our eyes? Over twenty thousand have signed up and we're only a few hours in. Zoom out to see the rest of the world."

A few swipes revealed an image of the globe, slowly rotating in space. The app was beautifully designed so that you could easily zoom in on any particular region. Already, the movement had spread beyond the United States of America. Europe had a faint green blush and there was even a smattering of points in Asia, Africa, and Central and South America.

"You truly are a catalytic wizard, Howard! The greatest alchemist in the history of the world!"

"Hold your praise until later. This reaction can still fall flat or blow up in our faces."

"How are the financial donations?"

"Terrific," Ashley reported. "Already we're generating a surplus. Unless I'm mistaken, we won't have to draw upon your personal wealth at all for the whole operation."

"Incredible. Well, we had better get going to reach our destination for the night."

Never had I been so giddy with excitement. I pranced about, leaping from foot to foot and flinging my arms in the air, laughing maniacally, while Lizzie followed suit and Tyler looked on in amusement. Never had my surroundings appeared more beautiful – the turbulent sky, the tall pines, and the ranchland that began to appear as we descended in elevation. We did stop at the house of the person who had invited us to use the bathroom. He was a retired school teacher who had a lot of time to listen to the news and joined the movement the minute he heard about it earlier in the day. Tyler took a picture of us with the gentleman's cell phone and he said that he would treasure it for the rest of his life.

An hour further down the road, Sigrid appeared with a bag lunch for each of us and dog food for Lizzie, reminding us that we were surrounded at all times by a circle of people on bicycles, shielding us from traffic. She stayed with us while we ate our lunch by the side of the road. Hunger being the best sauce, we ate ravenously.

"How many motorists do you encounter and how do they respond to being re-directed?"

"Not too many yet, because the traffic is light and we're routing you through secondary roads where the detours are easy to construct.

We have written permission from the State Police to redirect traffic. They realize that when your numbers grow, they'll need our help with traffic control and we'll need their help if anything gets out of hand. We're in regular communication with them.

"Do we have our campsite set up?"

"Yes, 'we' do," Sigrid replied with a smile and a voice drenched in friendly sarcasm, letting it be known that an entire team of other people was making life easy for us. "The Eden family was happy to have us camp on their land and say that they are excited to see you."

The Eden ranch was thirty-six miles from my Cell on Timber Ridge, a bit less than an hour's drive, as I knew from the many times that I had stopped to visit on my way to and from Laramie. A bit more than ten hours was required to arrive by foot, providing a vivid demonstration of how modern transportation had shrunk distances. Electronic communication had overcome distance altogether, making it possible for me to converse with Ashley and Howard in Laramie at the very same moment as with Tyler by my side.

The campsite that we approached on the edge of the Eden Ranch at about 5pm revealed the scope of our operation on its first day. Three white domed tents stood in a row, each about twenty feet in diameter. They were manufactured by a company that made tents for emergency relief efforts, such as hurricanes and refugee camps, but to our specifications, including our four symbols arranged in a column down the right side of the entrance: a dot, a circle, the American flag, and the earth. The support structure for the tents consisted of black flexible rods that cleverly reinforced each other without needing to be inserted into the ground and carved the domes into visually pleasing crescents. On top of each dome was a colored triangular flag with a number, giving the appearance of a Renaissance fair. Each one could be erected or taken down in about thirty minutes.

A kitchen crew was preparing dinner on a propane grill and portable tables. A truck, two trailers, and a few cars were parked behind the tents. The bicyclists were converging on the campsite, their day's work completed, and parking their bikes in a row next to one of the tents. Luke Eden was standing next to a man who appeared to be in his sixties, very fit, with a crew cut and erect posture. Luke was the youngest Eden brother, closest to my own age, and the most closely attached to Eve. We had developed a warm brotherly relationship and I enjoyed watching him and Eve kid each other. Now we shared a hearty handshake and pulled each other into an embrace with our free arms.

"It's great to see you! Thanks for letting us camp on your land."

"Of course! This is an amazing operation. Nelson here tells me that he oversaw the construction and operation of refugee camps in the army and then was a chief field officer for FEMA after Hurricane Katrina."

A tiny smile crept over Nelson's face at this acknowledgment of his accomplishments, as he continued to survey the operation to make sure that everything was proceeding smoothly.

"That's right," I replied to Luke while shaking hands with Nelson. "We're lucky to lure him out of retirement to oversee our campsites on the trek."

"This is like a Sunday picnic," Nelson commented, "but I admire the way that your bicycle team shielded you from the traffic. That was clever logistics."

"Thanks! I'll be interested to see if the campsites test your mettle when our numbers grow. It's great to have you with us."

Tyler fell in with the bicyclists, who crowded around Lizzie. In her doggy exuberance, she had travelled an even longer distance than Tyler and me, although her movements became more economical toward the end of the day. Now she was dog tired and lying in a shady spot with her hind legs extended backward and front legs extended forward to maximize her exposure to the relatively cool ground. Tyler placed a bowl of water between her front legs so she could drink it without moving. Then she responded to pats and hugs from the bicyclists by turning on her back so they could rub her belly and all four legs simultaneously, with her mouth open and tongue hanging out in a crazy ecstatic look, to everyone's delight. Tyler also had a smile on his face. As Keeper of the Dog, he was automatically welcomed into the society of the bicyclists.

Nelson accompanied me into one of the tents, where eight cots were arranged in a neat circle. One of them was extra long and had a cloth bag resting on it with a towel and change of clothes. Then we exited the tent and entered one of the trailers, which was outfitted as a mobile bathroom, complete with toilets and a row of shower stalls fed by water from one storage tank that drained into another storage tank.

"Amazing!" I marveled.

"These are used for everything from disaster relief to music festivals," Nelson observed. "It has been honed to a pretty fine art. The other trailer is a mobile laundry facility. Every night, we'll be collecting the dirty clothes and issuing clean clothes, based on size information that each person provides when they register on the website."

Refreshed by a shower, shave, and clean clothes, I informed Nelson and Tyler that I would be having dinner with the Edens and climbed into the passenger seat of Luke's pickup. It was impossible to drive down the road to the ranch and enter the house to be greeted by Joseph and Mary without being flooded with memories of Eve. There was nothing to say, however, because we knew that if anyone had news about her, they would instantly share it. Instead, there was a new topic for conversation. The same image of the planet that I viewed from my iPhone earlier in the day was rotating on their living room monitor, which was connected to Luke's laptop by a cable. Our website development team had spared no effort on the graphics, which could be seen to its full advantage on the large screen. There was much more topography than needed, except to give the impression of realism. It was like a movie in which the planet Earth is being viewed from a spaceship, except that all of the continents have become barren brown deserts. Against this background, the appearance of brilliant green points of light, blending into a hue when they became sufficiently dense, could not help but give a sense of hope and rejuvenation. You *wanted* Earth to become green, and you could do your part by joining the True Objectivist movement. The counter on the bottom of the screen proved that you were not alone. Over a million people had joined the movement on the first day alone. Such was the distance-dissolving power of modern communication that the entire world had been swept into the drama that we had set in motion. As the continent of South America rotated into view, I noticed a few points emanating from the nation of Ecuador and my heart leapt to think that somehow, some way, the worldwide catalysis that was now in motion might provide assistance to Eve on her mysterious path.

For the Edens, the image on the screen and the events leading up to it changed their demeanor toward me entirely. Before, I fit into their world without requiring many adjustments on their part. I was good to their daughter, enjoyed working side by side with the men, and relished being treated as a member of the family. They had long stopped questioning Eve's religious beliefs and extended that courtesy to me, especially since both of us enjoyed partaking in the community aspects of church life.

From the moment that I sprang the trap on my father, they were forced to think about me in a new way. Suddenly, I was all over the news and strangers were calling them trying to dig up dirt on me. At first they found it easy to be protective, but they couldn't help but wonder what all of this was about and how it related to their own faith. The values that I embraced were broadly Christian, at least in its most expansive form of peace on Earth and good will toward all humans, but I never mentioned God or Christ. Now, after two months of incessant news coverage and commentary, including some members of the religious right doing their best to demonize me, an historic event appeared to be unfolding in the space of a single day on their wide screen monitor. Around the world, people were converting to a new something that wasn't a religion. By becoming True Objectivists, they were transcending all current religious and national identities. And the whole thing was centered around me. What did that make me – some kind of modern Jesus? What were the symbols on the front of my windbreaker, which I was wearing like a uniform? What were the dot and the circle supposed to mean? Why was the American flag placed below Earth? *Where was the Cross?*

Joseph and Mary were not agile with words, so all of this just hung in the air for me to infer. How could I tell them that the greening of Earth and the whirling odometer on their screen *was* like the origin and spread of Christianity; that it was based on a new cosmology more in tune with our age; that it was taking place several thousand times faster thanks to electronic communication; that they should be rejoicing because it was in the same spirit as Christian love? As for me being comparable to Jesus,

I was merely a conduit that cultural change was rushing through, and perhaps he was, too. By now I had lost any sense of ego. I saw myself as a node in a social process and only hoped that I could be strong and wise enough to fulfill my role. In my weaker moments I wished that it could have happened to someone else. All of this also just hung in the air as Mary invited us to sit around the dinner table.

Joseph had been drinking a beer when I arrived and popped another can for dinner. Mary's worried glances told me that this was not his second. He sat sullen and silent during the meal until I asked about the congregation over dessert.

"It's not the same anymore!" he blurted out. "The young people are staying away!" Then he lapsed back into silence.

Luke remarked that my day's trek must be catching up with me and offered to return me to the camp. As soon as we were alone in his pickup, he began to speak.

"Please forgive my father. He isn't reacting well to something I told him earlier today."

"What's that?"

"That I'm coming with you."

I was stunned. "Luke! I don't know what to say ..."

Luke became more agitated than I had ever seen him.

"You *do* know what to say and I've been reading every word of it! I get it. You've figured out a way to tell right from wrong without peering through a tissue of lies."

Now I was doubly stunned. Those were the words that Eve spoke to me after making love for the first time at the Lodge. They were so apt that we often repeated them to each other, but I had not spoken them to another soul. To hear them uttered by Luke was as if Eve herself had been channeled through him. At first I leapt to the conclusion that he was in contact with her. Then the greater likelihood dawned upon me: that Eve shared her most intimate doubts about her religion with her favorite brother in addition to me. She must have told him quite a bit about me and our relationship as well. As if reading my thoughts, Luke continued to speak.

"Eve and I have always been close. I was the one person in the family with whom she could share her doubts about religion. Then I started to read some of the books that she told me about, especially after meeting you. Soon enough I became hooked and I have been following your work with the Evolution Institute ever since."

This was a revelation to me. All these years, I thought I knew Luke as an unquestioningly devout rancher without an intellectual side to him at all.

"Luke! Why didn't you talk with me about these matters?"

"Why didn't you bring them up?"

I had to laugh at the irony of how life can become so partitioned and Luke joined me.

"OK, you have me there. I guess I found it easiest to fit in and didn't want to cause any discomfort. But now it means the world to me, first that you have absorbed so much and second that you will be joining the trek."

"I figure that you'll need someone to translate True Objectivism into a Christian idiom."

At first I marveled at Luke's eloquence and self-confidence that he could rise to such a challenge. Then I remembered that Jesus was a carpenter and his disciples came from other humble walks of life.

"We leave at 9am tomorrow morning."

"I know."

After Luke dropped me off, I clicked on the app on my iPhone and began zooming in – the world, America, Wyoming, Albany County, and my immediate location. Sure enough, one of the points on the map was the Eden Ranch. Luke had joined the True Objectivist movement earlier in the day and had the same information as everyone else.

Despite the long day, it was still only 9:30. I found Tyler sitting with Lizzie around a campfire with the bicyclists outside their tent. They were talking to each other as if they were family. I had never seen Tyler with a more open expression of joy.

At first, the most newsworthy fact about my trek was that I would be walking a little over 1,000 miles in 100 days. That seemed like a superhuman feat to most people, but only in an age of pathological sloth. According to the Cult of Scholars, our hunter-gatherer ancestors walked an average of about twenty miles a day and could easily go longer, especially when tracking wounded game. Armies throughout history have covered long distances on foot, carrying a lot more gear than I would be lugging. Long distance walking even became a craze called Pedestrianism in the 19th century. People aspired to walk 100 miles in twenty-four hours or even 1,000 miles in 1,000 hours, or 41.6 days, which made my trek tame by comparison. There was a risk that I might physically break down, which would be embarrassing, but on the morning of my second day I experienced only minor soreness and Lizzie was bounding among her many friends and admirers, accepting hugs and breakfast scraps, as good as new.

The really newsworthy fact about my trek, as the world would soon come to realize, was social. Huge numbers of people would be moving with me or cheering us on as we passed by. They would need to be transported to select locations, fed and kept hydrated, and provided with bathroom facilities along the way. Those who stayed at our campsites would additionally need shower facilities and a change of clothes. Along the way, they would be learning about the meaning of True Objectivism and how to put it to use in their own lives. Our challenge – far greater than my own challenge of walking 1,000 miles – was to coordinate such a massive effort. Our social movement was literally to be a social *movement*.

Cars started to arrive around 7am the next morning, disgorging passengers who bid the drivers goodbye as if they were the best of friends. Those joining the trek for more than one day were instructed to wear old clothes that they were willing to donate to charity and directed to one of the trailers to exchange them for their new clothes and windbreakers. Then they emerged, all wearing the same uniform, to introduce themselves to each other. About sixty had accumulated by the time we set off at 9am, leaving Nelson and his crew to pack up camp. Young and old. Men and women. All colors. Rich and poor. Not bad, considering that it was only day two and we were in rural Wyoming. I made a short speech before we began.

"Friends! Thanks so much for joining us on this Trek. I'm glad that our system for conveying you here by others who have joined the movement has worked smoothly. More will be joining our trek during the day or assembling to cheer us on. Our destination is Laramie, forty-six miles away. If any of you tire or experience injuries, you can arrange to be picked up on the app.

"You'll notice two people with red windbreakers instead of green. They are part of our communication team, along with the bicyclists who will be protecting us from traffic, and can help you with any questions that you might have. There is also someone with a blue windbreaker who has training in First Aid. As our numbers grow, these specialists will always exist in a ratio of about 1:50 for the communication team and 1:100 for the medics, so one will always be close at hand. If you would like to be trained to join them, indicate your desire on the Change.world app. Are there any questions? Then let's head to Laramie!"

Off we went with a cheer, with Tyler, Luke, and me in the lead and Lizzie circulating among the crowd, heedless of how tired she would be by the end of the day. Another unsettled day with scudding clouds would help to keep us cool.

"How did you get everyone here so smoothly?" Luke asked.

"I need to go back to the beginning of the Objectivist movement to do justice to that question," I replied. "My grandmother was a master at communicating to a highbrow audience, which is why she portrayed Objectivism as a philosophy. Then my father became a master at communicating to mass audiences through radio, television, and the Internet, which is why he cultivated his Good Old Boy persona. But my father and his handlers failed to grasp the true import of the Internet – the capacity to create an entirely new society within the current society. A metamorphosis, like a butterfly emerging from a caterpillar."

I smiled at the puzzled expression on each of their faces and continued.

"Have you noticed that when you joined the True Objectivist movement you received an electronic wallet?"

"Yes," Luke replied, "With 1,000 True Dollars. But I haven't had time to learn more about it."

"Well, the True Objectivist movement has its own currency that can only be spent among members. When you join the movement, there are opportunities for employment, including driving other members where they need to go. No doubt you have heard about Uber and Lyft, where anyone can become a taxi driver, or AirBNB, where anyone can become a hotelier. It's called a gig economy and it's already spreading in regular society, although the wages tend to be low and there are no benefits. We offer a good wage and benefits."

"Benefits?"

"Yes, like medical insurance. I told you! We are creating a whole new society, complete with health care, social services, a justice system, even a United Nations."

"Wait. You've got to be kidding!" Luke protested.

"I'm not kidding! Our Mother Ship has been busy during the last four years setting this up! If we attract millions of members to our movement, then we have the means to create our own society without making or breaking a single law, and as of this moment," I concluded, glancing at my iPhone, "we're up to 1.3 million members."

I flashed Luke and Tyler a huge grin as they tried to wrap their heads around the scope of the True Objectivist movement.

"So, you pay people to join the movement, rather than asking them to give you money?" Tyler asked dubiously. "Isn't that like bribery?"

"Think of it as like an airline giving you free miles for joining their frequent flyer program," I replied. "For those who want to donate, the money goes to the True Central Bank that underpins the currency. You can also convert your US dollars to True Dollars for your own bank account. Every US dollar is worth 1.15 True Dollars. And you can convert True Dollars back to US dollars, but the exchange rate goes the other way. One True Dollar is worth 0.85 US dollars. That creates an incentive to keep your money in True Dollars."

"Where can you spend your True Dollars?" Luke asked.

"Well, members can pay each other for their services, such as transport, as we saw this morning. There is an automatic line of credit with zero interest, up to a point, so your account can dip into the negative zone without consequence. We also have an online store similar to Amazon.com. Not as extensive, of course, but with plenty of basic items, including food. And any merchant can become part of the economy by joining the movement and accepting True Dollars. For example, if your local hardware store accepts True Dollars, you can buy whatever you like and pay the US dollar price on your app, like paying with a credit card. This is like receiving a 15% discount. If the hardware store is close to your home, you get an additional 5% discount, which encourages local buying. One more thing – negative interest rate. If you don't spend your True Dollars, then they decline at a rate of five percent per year. This encourages everyone to keep their True Dollars circulating."

"Negative interest rates? I never heard of such a thing!" Luke exclaimed.

"Neither did I until the Evolution Institute held a workshop on the concept of money several years ago," I replied. "I admit that it took me a long time to wrap my head around it. We take money for granted so much that we don't see it for what it really is – a symbolic system for helping people cooperate with each other, but one that is deeply flawed in regular society. When money is lent by people or institutions whose main interest is to enrich themselves, then it tends to accumulate into the hands of a few people and leave everyone else impoverished. But you can design a currency to work for the common good and such currencies have even arisen here and there in human history, usually at a small scale.

"One of my favorite examples took place in a town in Germany during the depression that preceded World War II. The national currency was worthless and everyone was out of work, so the town created its own currency and affixed stamps on them that decreased their value if they weren't spent. Like magic, everyone started working again, using the local currency to provide services for each other and improving the infrastructure of the town. The currency even started to be accepted in neighboring towns! It worked so well that the Nazi government shut it down.

"Then there was a bank strike in Ireland during the 1940s where nobody could withdraw their savings for a period of months. People started writing checks to purchase their supplies, and if they were respected in their community, then their checks were used as a form of money. In other words, Joe buys ten dollars worth of goods from Mike and pays with a check, and Mike buys ten dollars of goods from Sam and pays with Joe's check. Pretty soon the employers began to pay their employees with checks in small denominations, so an entire currency sprang up spontaneously, with the pubs serving as the banks. Isn't that amazing?"

"I can hardly believe it!" Luke marveled. Tyler was all ears but didn't feel qualified to speak.

"These cooperative currencies tend to be short lived," I continued, "because they threaten the national currencies and also because they are cumbersome to maintain – like printing the money, avoiding counterfeiting and so on. Also, the range of what you can buy and sell is limited to the local community. All of that changes with the Internet Age and a worldwide movement that is now up to … 1.32 million members."

I gave them another huge grin.

At last Tyler ventured a comment. "You make it sound as if you can create money out of thin air!"

"Almost, but not quite. Trust is paramount. If people trust the currency, then it can indeed be created out of thin air, but there must be something that backs up the trust. In the old days, it was a store of something that was regarded as precious, like silver and gold, although even this is a social convention. In modern times, you can't trade your money for gold, but if you keep your money in a bank, you expect to be able to withdraw it whenever you want. The banks have invested the deposits in loans and only keep a certain amount in reserve. If too many depositors demand their money, then the bank fails and there is a panic. In our case, when people convert their US dollars to True Dollars, we hold their US dollars in reserve and invest some of it, much like a bank. We don't do this ourselves, but by cooperating with some Credit Unions that have become part of the movement. This means that if someone wants to convert their True Dollars into US dollars, we can do this at the exchange rate of 0.85. But if people are happy with their True Dollars, this won't happen very often. Suffice it to say that as long as the True Objectivist movement earns the trust of its members, then its currency will remain strong, almost as if created out of thin air."

Now it was Luke's turn. "If you are too successful, won't the US government come after you the same way that the Nazi government did?"

"That's possible, even though we're not breaking any laws and have a cadre of top lawyers waiting to fend off litigation. After all, there are a bunch of alternative currencies already out there, such as Bitcoin, although they're not designed for the common good. Even if the Feds come after us it will be a slow process, whereas we are planning to accomplish our objectives in 100 – or rather ninety-nine – days.

I flashed them another huge grin. Now Tyler was becoming more comfortable taking part in the conversation.

"It sounds like you've fixed things so that people will join the movement just because they need work, not because they're interested in the movement."

"That's right!" I exclaimed in reply. "Have you ever wondered why so-called terrorist organizations often have the support of the people? It's because they provide basic services that the governments have become too corrupt and ineffective to provide. Those movements aren't strong because of their ideologies, but because they help people get by on a daily basis. That's what we're doing, although of course we're committed to peaceful action as part of the covenant for joining the movement. Violence immediately results in exclusion. In any case, I'm proud to offer basic services and for these to be the primary incentive for some people joining. It will save the movement from becoming dominated by affluent white folks who have the luxury of being motivated primarily by their ideals. We can even see the diversity in the people who have joined us today. Let's get to know some of them!"

Seeing that we were immersed in conversation, the rest of our caravan kept a respectful distance and talked among themselves. Now, by the simple expedient of slowing down, we entered their ranks and began to engage with them. The weather was clearing up a little, with shafts of sun piercing the clouds and illuminating the rangeland in swiftly moving patches of light. The bicyclists were routing us along secondary roads dotted with farmhouses. A large fraction of their residents had joined the movement and sported signs on their lawns, similar to the signs that politicians use during election season, with the four vertical symbols: A dot, a circle, the American flag, and Earth. The signs had been delivered by members of the bicycle team, along with a windbreaker for every member of the family. More often than not, the homeowners were by the roadside next to their signs, wearing their jackets, cheering us on, welcoming us to use their bathrooms, and offering drinks and sandwiches that they had prepared.

The other trekkers were delighted to be joined by the three of us. They assumed that Luke and Tyler must have some special status within the movement; why else would we have started out in such deep conversation? Luke found it easy to rise to the occasion. Engaging the trekkers in friendly conversation was little different than the meet-and-greets that took place every Sunday at his church. They quickly opened up to him and, if they had a Christian upbringing, Luke lost no time explaining how True Objectivism was in the true spirit of Jesus.

For Tyler, being treated as a leader of the movement took more getting used to. He started out on the trek thinking of himself as mere keeper of the dog. But something was happening to Tyler in the space of only two days. Despite all that took place on Timber Ridge during the past months, he still regarded himself as his father's son, destined to take up the same lifestyle. High school would be the end of his education. He'd become a builder like his dad, getting a part time job at someplace like Advance Auto Parts until he became established. He would fish, hunt, and tear around on his ATV. Maybe he'd take up NASCAR racing. He already had a girlfriend and his dad jokingly warned him that he didn't want to be a grandfather before the age of fifty. But what would be the point of waiting?

Now Tyler had been thrust into an entirely new society, one that he didn't understand, but in which he had mysteriously been granted a high status; first by becoming the center of attention along with Lizzie, and now through his association with Luke and me on the trek. He could have stepped away from the role, but he didn't. Something inside him reasoned that if he could fake it for a while, he might actually be able to step into a leadership role, and that this was something he might want to do. His dad said over and over that I was the truest redneck that ever was, so that became his compliment to Luke's missionary work among the Christians.

As for myself, I delighted in the story of each and every person who had joined us on our trek. A few were hardcore athletes and outdoor addicts, like myself, who relished the challenge of a 1,000-mile trek in addition to what it represented. Others knew that they might only walk part of the way but still wanted to be part of history. A few were highly educated and could understand the arcane tongues of the Cult of Scholars. Most were following their hearts rather than their heads, as Angelina would put it – Angelina, who I would be seeing at day's end in Laramie. Mostly what they knew was that something was broken, for society as a whole and in many cases their own lives, and that the True Objectivist movement offered hope. They had decided to listen to their heart and now they were walking by the side of the human embodiment of the movement, the center of the world's attention, asking to hear about *their* story. For them, it was the greatest honor that anyone could bestow upon them. For me, it was the greatest responsibility.

The closer we drew to Laramie, the longer our caravan became and the larger the crowds lining the road cheering us on our way. Anyone who wanted to become involved first had to join the movement online. Once they became electronically connected, they could indicate their desire to join the trek or become a spectator on the app. Our algorithms calculated their geographical locations and arranged for pickup by other members of the movement in the vicinity who had become drivers. Those who were planning to join the trek for more than a single day were asked to wear old clothes that could be donated to charity after being exchanged for our standard issue. The main purpose for standard issue clothing was practical, so that we could collect soiled clothing and issue clean clothing for large numbers of people. Coincidentally, it became the uniform for the movement, which quickly became known as Galt's army.

Spectators were conveyed by drivers to collection points where they were issued windbreakers. Then they were taken by bus to points on our route in advance of our arrival. They were asked to bring something for the trekkers to drink or eat. Some also offered keepsakes that were often quite heart-rending, such as a photograph of a son or daughter who had died by suicide, an opioid addiction, or an overseas conflict – as if the True Objectivism movement could heal past wounds. These were to become so numerous on our trek that we had to create a special detail to collect and find a way to display them, such as a local church or library on our route. We also had a detail to clean the litter as soon as our caravan passed, so that by the end of the day it was as if nothing had happened before. Everyone who worked was paid in True Dollars. The public and press marveled at our efficiency. Why couldn't the rest of society work this well?

The last mile through the streets of Laramie was like we were returning war heroes or a local sports team that had won the championship. We couldn't restrict the crowds to members of the movement, but hundreds were sporting the green windbreakers with a sprinkling of red and blue, held in a proportion of 1:50 and 1:100 respectively, to accommodate a potential increased demand for their services. A wedge of bicyclists cleared the path in front of us and others redirected the cross-street traffic. The police were out in force but standing idle, trusting our red jackets to notify them if they were needed. In our strategy sessions leading up to the trek, we discussed the possibility of attacks incited by my father, or more likely by Steve as my father's handler. In that event, green jackets closest to the attack would immediately signal the red jackets on their apps, who would surround the attackers and offer non-violent resistance as the police were being called in. The red jackets would also videotape the attackers from all sides. Our contingency plan did not need to be put into action, however. If any would-be attackers lurked in the crowds, they were subdued by the festive exuberance of everyone else. How could such a seemingly benign movement be worth attacking?

The day's trek ended at the doorstep of the Elbow Room, with Dennis, Howard, Ashley, Angelina, Nelson, and the crew of the Mother Ship, now numbering over fifty, waiting outside to greet us. A small platform with a microphone had been erected for me to speak to the crowd. My speech was very short.

"Friends! Thanks for accompanying me on day two of my trek to Philadelphia. This is not the time for a speech, but neither do I plan to wait for my duel of speeches with my father to explain what is unfolding before our eyes. I will say more in three days at a campground that can accommodate 10,000 people. Please visit the Change.world website to see how you can be a part of it. Until then, get a good night's sleep and we'll be leaving at eight sharp tomorrow morning!

A cheer went up from the crowd. Then, as if guided by an invisible hand, all of the green, red, and blue jackets who didn't live close by made their way to locations designated on their apps, where they climbed into cars and buses and were conveyed by jacketed drivers to be welcomed by jacketed home and apartment owners for a meal and night's lodging. Most of the drivers and hoteliers would have volunteered their services for the movement they had joined, but they didn't need to. All who offered their services were well paid in True Dollars.

As my army was disbanding for the night, except for Luke, Tyler, and Lizzie, I exchanged a round of hugs with the leaders and crew of the Mother Ship. Angelina, who moved to Laramie to be our press secretary, had become part of the family in only two weeks. We made our hug as heartfelt as we could without attracting notice. Nelson was a relatively new member of the team and his military bearing wasn't very huggable, but he did offer a firm handshake and high praise for the logistics of the day, which had scarcely required his services at all.

"You'll have your chance at the camp meeting in three days," I replied.

This trek had been years in the making and our final planning session was only a week ago. Yet, the events of the last two days had been so momentous that it seemed as if we had been transported to another time and place.

"There's someone inside waiting for you," Ashley said.

My heart leapt. Eve! Eve! Could it be Eve?

It wasn't Eve, but it was the next best thing.

OMAR!!! There he was, in all his magnificence, radiating charm and self-confidence. I hadn't seen him since he received his PhD and became an assistant professor at the University of Florida, where he received tenure in only four years. He had acquired a slightly professorial look but must be working out with the sports teams because he still had the body of an elite athlete. We ran at each other and playfully tried to throw each other to the ground before standing back, hands on each other's shoulders to gaze at each other.

"This is ..."

"... in*sane!*" I completed Omar's signature sentence for him and we fell into another hug as the others stood around smiling, Howard most of all. Two souls that had been saved by Howard.

"How long can you stay with us?"

"All the way to Philly. I need the exercise!"

"Awesome! How can you take that much time away from your classes?"

"I found ways to cover my classes and they'll never fire their most popular professor."

"I see you haven't lost your modesty. God, it's good to see you!"

"I thought you didn't believe in him."

"I'll make an exception for you!"

A buffet was waiting for us in the Violet Room and the food and drink never tasted so good after covering forty-six miles on foot. A big cushion had been thoughtfully provided for Lizzie, who lay regally as her loyal subjects brought her food and a dish of water. Tyler and Sigrid, the bicyclist who he met on the first day of our trek, were moving through the line together. She was the only bicyclist present and must be there as his guest. Tyler blushed and smiled as our eyes met. The Violet Room was now dedicated entirely to the Mother Ship for its strategy sessions and a floor-to-ceiling multi-paneled monitor had been installed on one of the walls. The rotating planet Earth filled the monitor. The larger the image, the more gorgeous it looked in its details, as if we really were in a spaceship hovering above it. The greening of the planet had continued, most advanced in the USA, with a discernable thread that outlined our route to Philadelphia. Then Europe, with the rest of the world further behind but still developing its own blush. I entertained the hope – was it really so absurd? – that the points of light beginning to appear in Ecuador might help Eve on her own mysterious path. The whirling odometer at the bottom of the screen had surpassed two million.

The dishes cleared and beverages of our choice in hand, Howard stood by the monitor to address the crew of the Mother Ship. The expression on his face was as if he was about to tell a good joke.

"What better way to summarize the events of the last two days than from the mouth of our favorite observer of the True Objectivist movement ?"

The room burst into laughter as Ashley prepared to play the latest recording of Steve, my father's operative, now emailed to us nearly every week by a mole whose identity we could only guess at. Steve's comments on the progress of our movement were both perceptive and comical when viewed from his debauched – he called it realist – perspective. Amazingly, his spot-on analyses seldom called for altering what we were already planning to do. It was as if our first attack on the Death Star had permanently disabled it, so that all they could do was watch helplessly as our own plan unfolded. As Steve had pointed out the first time we met, my father's act was already getting stale and the only way to keep his fan base was by constantly riling them up with fake news. Since the original Objectivist movement and his own empire were based on a tissue of lies, our first achievement – restoring the norm of truth-telling in public life – was indeed like exploding the power source of the Death Star. Then the battle shifted to the economic establishment, about which my father had nothing to say. No matter how much he huffed and puffed on his radio and television shows, my trek ensured that we would control the news cycle right up to our duel of speeches.

"Listen up, children, our situation has never been more critical." Steve's condescending voice filled the room as if he were with us. "How many of you have joined the True Objectivist movement by registering on their website?"

Evidently, Steve didn't like the silent response to his question.

"Well, what the fuck have you been doing – jerking off? How do you expect to fight an enemy if you don't infiltrate its ranks? This trek is more than a publicity stunt. In fact, I can scarcely believe what it is. Nothing less than a new world order, inserting itself without asking anyone's permission. No national elections. No international treaties. Just people joining on their own volition and making it their primary identity, putting it above their nations and religions! They have their own money! Their own courts! Their own fucking United Nations!"

A stunned silence ensued before my father spoke, barely audible on the recording. He must have been sitting in the back of the room.

"How could such a thing be possible?"

"You're right to be dumbstruck. I'm only beginning to comprehend it myself. The new world order couldn't exist without the existing world order. The currency is tied to the US dollar. The court system has no legal authority and must resort to the real court system for anything that it can't resolve by mutual consent. The United Nations is a group of scholars from every nation that meets to formulate policy without having any authority to implement it, but nevertheless can shift the weight of public opinion. As the website puts it, the True United Nations does what the current United Nations should be doing. This isn't something that they just threw together. They've been preparing it for years, under our very noses!

"A new currency isn't new – Bitcoin and all that. But there is something new about the way that this one is managed. They give it away and it rots if you don't spend it! It's called negative interest rate. Can you imagine such a thing? True Dollars – they put the fucking word 'True' in front of everything – is a total game changer. Before, joining the True Objectivist movement would cost you money and time, restricting it mostly to white progressives. Now you can *make* money by joining the movement. Almost a million joined up on the first day! At that rate, a sizeable fraction of the country might have joined by the time he gets to Philadelphia! John, your duel of speeches isn't going to be the main event. It's going to be the postscript and your epitaph!"

This dire prediction occasioned only silence from my father.

"What can we do?" someone else in the room asked in a frightened voice.

"One problem is that we can't get the President or any of our allies in Congress to take the threat seriously. Because John Galt III isn't running for any office, they don't feel threatened. They think that it's just a media circus surrounding John Galt II. They don't understand that every one of them will be swept from office if the True Objectivist movement grows as fast as it might. Mark my words, unless we do something within the next ninety-nine days, John Galt III could be the next president of the United States."

Another stunned silence ensued except for one soft "Shit!" issued from someone in the room.

"Our only hope is to make the True Objectivist movement seem like a revolution by communists, socialists and globalists. We must rally people to the banner of freedom, liberty, and putting America first. Our improbable coalition of fat cats, rednecks, and the religious right might be breaking up, but we still have some allies that can help us take control of the story and put a stop to the trek."

"No violence, Steve. Remember that we agreed on no violence." The voice was my father's and his concern for my safety brought a lump to my throat.

"Of course, John. Violence never crossed my mind."

Something about the tone of Steve's voice was not reassuring.

That was the end of the recording and everyone in the room turned their attention back to Howard, standing by the monitor with the rotating globe. Talk of stopping the trek and the possibility of violence had dampened the collective mood and Howard was eager to restore it.

"As usual, our friend Steve has an excellent grasp of the situation, but not in a way that alters our own strategy. We have known all along that violent confrontations are a possibility and have already taken steps to avoid them. By taking the concept of society as an organism seriously, we have endowed our body politic with a strong immune system. Any disturbance can be quickly relayed to command headquarters and people in the immediate vicinity. Our red jackets and blue jackets know that part of their responsibility is to rush to the scene. They are trained to surround and record the disturbance so that anonymity of the perpetrator is impossible. Our commitment to nonviolence is absolute – a single violation results in exclusion – so we will never be tempted to retaliate in kind. Best of all, we are working with local law enforcement officers wherever we go. The moment a disturbance occurs, they will be called in and our people will get out of the way. All of the local jurisdictions that we have passed through know that they couldn't have managed crowd control as well as we can and are grateful to be cooperating with us. We have put them in touch with the local jurisdictions in front of us to help make similar arrangements. Other than an aerial attack or something truly horrendous such as a van plowing into us, we have minimized the possibility of violent confrontation. We don't want anyone to be harmed, but if something did happen we would be the clear victim and public opinion would turn even more in our favor. That's why nonviolent social movements almost always tend to be more successful than violent movements, as our cult of scholars has shown."

Howard had indeed succeeded in restoring our confidence and morale.

"So, we proceed according to plan. John and his growing caravan will march rapidly to the town of Sidney, Nebraska, approximately 150 miles away. We chose this town as the one most receptive to working with us after a review of over twenty towns that lie along feasible routes. It is the county seat of Cheyenne County and they have authorized us to use their fairground for our first major gathering, which we are limiting to 10,000 people. This is where Nelson will prove his worth, based on his extensive experience organizing encampments for refugees and victims of disaster. Nelson, we are so grateful to have you with us."

Once again, Nelson allowed only the slightest of smiles to escape from his craggy face. Then, unexpectedly, he revealed a sense of humor.

"I'm only in it for the True money."

The room erupted in laughter as Nelson's smile widened into a broad grin.

"Our people are already in Sidney for meetings with the Mayor, City Council, and other stakeholders to prepare for John's arrival," Howard said. "That is where John will make his next major statement to the movement and the media. Angelina, would you like to say a word about how the media has responded so far?"

Angelina rose from her chair and joined Howard in front of the monitor.

"First, I'd like to thank everyone here for welcoming me to the True Objectivist movement. I have never felt part of a family more quickly than I have with you. News of John's trek has spread around the world and we are besieged with requests for interviews, especially since John has so freely made himself available to the press up until now. I am fending them off, saying that his next major statement will take place in three days in Sidney. This is only making curiosity more intense. We can be sure that John's speech will be heard around the world, long before his duel of speeches with his father. In the meantime, I will be joining John on the trek to start writing human interest stories of some of those who have joined the movement – at least for as long as I can last! As you know, anyone who needs to drop out can join the work crews or well-wishers on the sidelines and rejoin the caravan when they are able. I will also be holding regular press conferences, so all news that we want to relate and inquiries from the press should be funneled through me and my staff."

Angelina made her way back to her seat to applause while Howard resumed his moderator role.

"I know that John and the other trekkers need to get to bed early, but we all want to know how the website is performing. Ashley, can you provide a brief report?"

Now Ashley made her way to Howard's side.

"First, let's have a big round of applause for our IT staff, now numbering over thirty!"

Thunderous applause, accompanied by shouts and whistles, erupted even before Ashley completed her sentence. Almost everyone knew who they were, so there was no need for them to stand. Instead they just acknowledged the praise washing over them from their seats, clearly moved by its intensity.

"A society can't be an organism unless it has a brain and nervous system, and that's what these folks have provided. The idea of visualizing our movement as the greening of Earth is brilliant and their attention to graphic detail speaks for itself. On the back end, the traffic that we've experienced so far is within the range of what we're designed to handle. The user experience for registration has been smooth and we're learning from the few people who have problems. All of us staff the help service, in part to learn first-hand from the people who are using our system and in part to provide a human face to the movement. Most people who call in are stunned to get a real live friendly person right away, as opposed to a chatbot. As the volume grows, we'll keep pace by training members of the movement to staff a help service, paying them with True Dollars, of course."

I glanced at Omar, Luke, and Tyler, who were encountering our operation for the first time. They looked highly impressed.

"Our currency is starting out really strong. Members are only beginning to learn about it, but far more US dollars are coming into our central bank to support the currency than True Dollars being converted to US dollars, and we expect this imbalance to continue. Our first priority for constructing our gig economy was transportation and housing. Enough people in our vicinity registered as drivers and hoteliers to accommodate the size of the caravan so far and we expect supply to meet demand at least over the next few days. You can see from the map that people living along our route are especially likely to join up to feed, house, and transport those who are on the move. Our job board for diversifying our gig economy will be online within a few days. All in all, our biggest danger is for website registration traffic to exceed the high end of what we have designed. It's lucky that we were optimistic about how fast Howard's cultural catalysis might proceed, because we are definitely operating on the high end of our projections!"

After Ashley stopped speaking, I stood to address the crowded room from my table.

"Howard, you will go down in history as a true genius who could envision a future that was beyond the imagination of the rest of humanity. Ashley, I want to personally thank you for all you have done for the movement since day one, when you were the only staff member of the Evolution Institute. Your ability to get things done is amazing. We truly could not have arrived at this point without you."

Now it was Howard's and Ashley's turn to receive a tsunami of applause, hoots, and hollers from the throng. Howard responded with a theatrical bow and Ashley, taking his cue, gave a dainty curtsy and returned to her seat. I continued, standing by my table.

"It's been a memorable two days and my job has been the easiest – an eighty-eight mile stroll. I plan to cover the next 156 miles to Sidney in three and a half days, arriving in plenty of time on the fourth day for the caravan to settle in. A crew is already there to prepare for my speech and festivities at the county fairground. Now I am indeed looking forward to a good night's sleep upstairs in one of the guest rooms. Thanks again to everyone for their respective roles. We are truly making history together."

With that, the room broke into noisy conversation. Most of the others did not need to retire early, so I took my leave. Arrangements had been made for Omar, Luke, Tyler, Sigrid, and Lizzie.

"Good night, John," Angelina said as I prepared to leave.

"Good night, Angelina." Our eyes locked for only a second so as not to attract attention. There would be no touching or intimate conversation tonight. I had become a conduit for cultural change and nothing else mattered. Tending to my personal needs at this moment of history would be an act of supreme selfishness.

Our departure from Laramie on the third day of our trek was featured on the cover of *Time* magazine, which became an icon for the True Objectivist movement. Angelina, Omar, myself, Luke, and Tyler stood in a row with Lizzie the wonder dog in front of us and a throng of green jackets and sprinkling of red and blue jackets standing behind. A Latina, an African American, an evangelical cattle rancher, and a redneck kid signified that this movement was for everyone. Traffic control was flawless as a wedge of bicyclists led the way and other bicyclists diverted traffic at the crossroads. The streets were lined with well-wishers, about a third sporting True Objectivist jackets. There were no signs of protesters yet. Police officers were out in force but had nothing to do but watch. Members of the movement had been told about the vital role that the police were playing, first by letting us organize our own affairs and second by their readiness to spring into action if necessary. The police were therefore showered with praise, which couldn't help but put them into a festive mood along with the others.

News helicopters and drones captured our progress toward Sidney from the air. From that vantage, we looked like an army ant column or blood corpuscles streaming down an artery – not surprising to us, since we took our inspiration from nature. The world became mesmerized by the sheer efficiency of our operation when seen from the air. A fleet of bicyclists deflecting traffic, with those at the back racing up to the front as soon as our caravan had passed their station. A fleet of cars disgorging people at select points to join the trek or cheer us on and provision us with food and drink, then whisking them away again after we had passed. Members of the caravan peeling off to use the bathrooms of houses along the route or portable restrooms that we placed at regular intervals along remote stretches. A cleanup crew making sure that not a single item of trash was left behind and bagging the roadside trash that was already there for good measure. Then, at the end of each day, the entire caravan magically dispersed into surrounding homes, only to reappear the next morning. Everyone being paid a good wage for their work. Why couldn't the rest of society work this well?

The town of Sidney, Nebraska, might seem to be the last place on Earth to experience a cultural renaissance. Originally a military outpost to protect the railroads from the Indians, its current economic base was cattle, wheat, and the traffic that flowed along Route 80. Its citizens numbered only about 6,000 in a county that numbered only about 10,000. Almost all of the residents were white except for a growing number of Hispanic immigrants working the low wage jobs. Politically, it was a red town in a red state.

But that didn't mean that the citizens of Sidney were resistant to change. When you're a little town in big sky country, you know that sometimes you have to change to stay alive. The business community was always on the lookout for new economic development and had installed some new parks, bike paths, and a farmer's market to attract new residents. The wheat farmers and cattle ranchers looked at every new year as if it might be their last, with their costs spiraling and their returns at the mercy of global markets no more under their control than the weather. The wheat farmers had become totally dependent upon agro-business, forced to buy the combination of genetically modified wheat and herbicides and pesticides that were supposed to kill everything else. Nature was not so easily defeated and produced resistant varieties of weeds and insect pests, requiring new and ever more toxic formulations of chemical controls.

One farmer's young son came down with a rare form of cancer – who ever heard of a child getting cancer? – but there was no way to prove that Sidney was a cancer hot spot with such a small population. Some of the daughters of the cattle ranchers started to develop their breasts before they even entered their teens. It was shocking to see it and hormone supplements in the cattle feed were thought to be the cause, but there was no way to hold the giant Ag corporations responsible and the University cooperative extension service staff were no help. They were the ones who peddled the herbicides, pesticides, and hormone-laced cattle feed in the first place.

Children grew overweight, disappeared into their smart phones, and then disappeared altogether after graduating from high school. Hardly any of them wanted to become farmers or ranchers and what else was there to keep them here? Sidney was not immune from the opioid epidemic and rising suicide rates that were discussed ad nauseam on the television and radio. When it happened in Sidney, however, it was likely to be someone you knew, or at least knew of, your whole life. It was as if an invisible killer was at large who could strike anyone at any time. The churches, whose steeples dotted the town skyline, seemed powerless to offer any comfort or protection. More and more, people drifted away from their congregations. Life during the week seemed so hard that Sundays were needed to recuperate at home. The movie theater had gone out of business long ago. The diners and taverns were the only places where people got together anymore.

Against this bleak background, when I sprung the trap on my father only a few months ago, the citizens of Sidney, Nebraska, took notice. When I couldn't be pigeonholed as a lefty Democrat, they took even more notice. Before long, they reached the same tipping point as the rest of the nation. Why didn't my father just shut up with all the garbage that he was shoveling into their ears? A tiny fraction of my father's precipitous rating drop was thanks to the citizens of Sidney, Nebraska.

When the Mayor's office was contacted by someone claiming to represent John Galt III himself, the Mayor was all ears. First, he was sworn to secrecy. Then he was informed of my trek and told that Sidney was one of twenty towns being considered for a gathering of 10,000 people. The economic stimulus of this event was alone worth competing for, but there was more.

John Galt III wanted to invest a million dollars in the town that would be chosen. The money was to be used to create a development plan for the town and could be followed by more money. There was a specific process for creating the development plan that required the participation of every constituency of the town. The twenty towns were being compared on their ability to assemble such a congress, as it was termed. For towns that did not win the competition, all was not lost. They could continue to develop their plans for later consideration.

The mayor and his staff sprang into action and were proud to win the competition. Next, the town was visited by a contingent of the True Objectivist movement under conditions of top secrecy. In truth, everyone in the county knew that something was going on but collectively kept the secret, as people who gossip so successfully do. John Galt III's emissaries did not seem like outsiders. Their leader was an Ag economist who knew the business of cattle ranching and wheat farming through and through, but was not in the pocket of the Ag corporations. When he spoke of their trials and tribulations, it was as if he was reading their minds. He also had solutions that were beyond their imagination and his confidence that the solutions would work was contagious. The million dollars would be in a new currency called True Dollars, which could be converted to US dollars at a discount but would have more buying power left alone. For their full power to be realized, local merchants would need to accept True Dollars in their stores. Financial transactions would take place electronically in a way that was easier than using cash or a credit card. Once again, True Dollars could be converted into US dollars at any time, but anyone with business sense should want to keep their money in True Dollars and even convert their US dollars into True Dollars to increase their purchasing power.

There was more – much more – and the citizens of Sidney had twenty-seven days to work feverishly with members of the Mother Ship to prepare for the arrival of my caravan, precisely three and a half days after leaving Laramie. Far more than ten thousand nationwide applied to be part of history by attending the first gathering. Ten thousand were chosen by lottery and instructed to join the caravan before we entered the town. They streamed in during the three-and-a-half day period and we paused on the morning of the fourth day to complete our numbers.

The caravan had started to acquire discipline during this period. Those with military or marching band experience taught the others how to march in step, which was more efficient than everyone walking at their own pace. It was also more pleasurable; in fact, those without such experience were surprised to discover how moving their bodies in synchrony with others created a feeling of unity all by itself, quite apart from what they might be marching for. Chanting increased the effect. Groups formed spontaneously with one person in the lead shouting out a military cadence, which his or her followers repeated with gusto. These groups marched smartly past the less organized trekkers and experienced less fatigue. In fact, it was amazing how energizing it was to march and chant in unison. And if some trekkers wanted to march at a slower pace and to their own drummer, that was OK, too. Wherever they ended up at day's end, a car would appear to take them to their lodging for the night.

Our entrance into the town of Sidney was therefore quite a sight, beamed around the world by circling drones and the press awaiting our arrival. No resident of the town or county would dream of missing the historic day and over half were sporting green windbreakers, signifying that they had joined the movement. Every store sported a sign on its door that read, "WE ACCEPT TRUE DOLLARS." When we reached the Town Hall, the mayor gave an effusive speech and the high school band led us to the county fairground surrounded by over a thousand white domed tents attractively carved into crescent shapes by their flexible black support rods. Nelson had done his job well with the help of a crew from the Mother Ship and town residents paid in True Dollars.

The True Objectivist app directed each trekker to his or her appointed tent, topped with a colorful numbered triangular flag that gave the tent city the look of a Renaissance fair. Every restaurant in the county and every organization that had ever held a pancake breakfast or chicken barbeque was using the fairground facilities to feed the crowd, with Nelson on hand to make sure that supply met demand. There were even games, crafts on sale, and local bands setting up to entertain the crowd leading up to my speech. It was as if the Cheyenne County Fair, the high point of Sidney's annual calendar, had been brought back for an encore.

The blossoming of Sidney, Nebraska became the talk of the nation and eclipsed every other event on the news. If this wasn't like a magician accomplishing a transformation with a wave of his wand, what would be? And if a red town in a red state had been won over so completely, politics would indeed become a whole new ballgame, as Steve had surmised.

The mayor and his wife had requested that I be their honored guest for the two nights of our stay before the caravan moved on. They had two extra bedrooms, their grown son's and daughter's rooms, which were used as guest rooms when they weren't back to visit. Sensing an opportunity to be alone with Angelina, I suggested that she be their second guest so that we could discuss the press releases that would follow my speech that would take place at 8pm at the fairground. In fact there was little to discuss and Angelina left their home in the mid-afternoon to take part in the preparations, leaving me to rest and gather my thoughts.

It was soothing to be in the house of the mayor and his wife. I never met a family that I didn't like, and this one still radiated warmth even though the children had fledged the nest. I entertained myself by viewing the photographs in the hallway and memorabilia in their son's room. A ragged teddy bear propped against the pillow. A frame containing boy scout merit badges. The antlers of his first deer. His high school pennant and photograph of him in his football uniform, in a frame that also contained a photograph of the whole team. A poster of a sexy girl standing next to an oversize pickup truck with all the trimmings. A photo of a girl who would not be called pretty but had a beautiful smile, with a cluster of little hearts drawn in the corner. A sense of longing for a normal placid life swept over me. I gently moved the teddy bear to the top of the bureau and lay down on the bed to review the words I would be saying to the ten thousand people who had come to this place to change the world.

By the time I arrived on the stage of the county fairground, the crowd was already like the audience of a rock concert waiting for the star event. Their march, the media attention, and standing in a mass that swayed to the loud music from local bands that had been playing for the last hour had given them a sense of invincibility. The stage, sound system, and area in front was large enough to accommodate the major performers that were featured during the annual county fair, but ten thousand people completely filled the space and extended backward into the lanes and alleys of the fairground. A crew from the Mother Ship had erected a giant screen behind me and powerful light projectors in front, along with the cameras of the major media outlets. I joined the mayor, Angelina, and a member of our crew behind the stage, where he outfitted the mayor and me with remote mics and did a sound check. He was a veteran of stage shows but the rest of us were tense with anticipation.

"Mayor, you go first to introduce John. Keep it short, please."

The crowd erupted at his approach, at first thinking that it was me, and then died down to a polite round of applause that quickly subsided so that they could hear what he had to say.

"Oh … my … golly!" he began to a titter of laughter. "I have never seen anything like this! As mayor of the town of Sidney – welcome to *John Galt's army!*"

A huge roar arose, like heavy surf crashing against a rocky shore, that took a full minute to subside enough for him to continue.

"This is much more than a single event for Sidney. I have learned that when John Galt III visits a town, he doesn't just pass through. He offers help. Help unlike anything I have seen before. The help that our politicians and governments are supposed to provide but somehow never do. Help that isn't just a handout. The kind of help that enables us to help ourselves. But you don't want to hear about it from me when you can hear about it from him. Please help me welcome John Galt III, *the True Objectivist!*"

There was pandemonium as I strode onto the stage. Without having rehearsed anything, we shared a strong handshake, pulled each other into a hug with our free arms, and then stood facing the crowd with our joined hands raised above our heads, like a presidential candidate and his running mate. The crowd roared its approval for another full minute. For all the talking that I had done since springing the trap on my father, I had never faced a sea of people like this, each face looking up at me with an expression of hope and longing. It electrified me in a way that I had never experienced before. My voice became saturated with emotion. Instinctively, I spoke in a slow cadence so that my words would have time to drift to the far reaches of the audience to have their effect.

"I want to thank everyone in this town and this crowd for being here to help make history. By now I think it has become clear to the world that this trek is not just a single person walking a thousand miles to battle his father for the soul of the Objectivist movement. And it's not just a crowd of supporters coming with him. *It ... is ... a ... demonstration ... of ... how ... a ... society ... can... function ... with ... the ... precision ... of ... a ... single ... organism."*

These words were spoken especially slowly and forcefully, like hammer blows, in the same way that Howard spoke the words *for ... the ... first ... time ... in ... the ... history ... of ... human ... thought* at our first workshop in Rome. Those words were received in awkward silence by a tiny group of scholars and he was referring to the mere concept of society as an organism being placed on a scientific foundation. Now, only four years later, we had built one and it was crawling across the United States of America like a caterpillar! My hammer blows elicited another round of pandemonium from the crowd. Instinctively, I lowered my arms with my hands open and palms facing downward and the crowd quieted. I was like the conductor of an orchestra.

"Our society has a peculiar purpose – to move a large number of people to Philadelphia in 100 days. If you're impressed with it now, wait until it grows ten and 100 times larger and still functions well!"

Sensing my connection to the crowd, I started to conduct them more actively. Like Howard, I had learned to be theatrical even in front of a small group of people. Usually I kept myself under control but this crowd caused me to lose my inhibitions. My boast was spoken in a crescendo and upward sweep of my arms. A mighty crescendo also rose from the crowd. A wave of euphoria swept over me. We could do anything together! We were invincible! A downward sweep of my arm brought quiet again.

"The town of Sidney is also a society that happens to stay in one place, but it can also function with the precision of an organism. That's what your mayor meant when he said that we were offering help to the town of Sidney. The same principles of True Objectivism that enable our caravan to move can help Sidney thrive and prosper where it has taken root on the banks of Lodgepole Creek – *or my name isn't John Galt III!*

That boast came out of my mouth unscripted, so powerful did I feel, and another collective roar emerged from the sea of delirious faces.

"And if Sidney can function with the precision of an organism, then so can Chappell, and Ogallala, and North Platte, and Lincoln, and every town, city, and state in America, and every nation in the world!"

It didn't seem possible that the crowd could roar any louder, but they could and did. I had spoken those words with violent jabs of my arms into the air, as if every punch brought order into the world. My movements caused the sea of bodies to heave as if roiled by a great wind. I paced the stage like a victorious gladiator to let them continue at full throttle before quieting them down again. My heart was thumping against my chest and my brain felt that it had been taken over by a part of me that I never even knew existed. In my pacing I caught sight of Angelina standing in the wings of the stage. Her eyes were like saucers and her hands were to her mouth. A tiny voice within me warned that I was out of control and I struggled to heed it. When I resumed I was more subdued.

"The time has come to explain the symbols that True Objectivists literally wear on their sleeves – a point, a circle, the American flag, and the world."

I turned my arm to the crowd to display the symbols that they all wore.

"The world, of course, stands for the planet Earth, our home, the only home we will ever have."

Until then the giant screen behind me had been blank but now the projectors were switched on and the image of the greening planet and whirling odometer appeared, sending a jolt through the crowd at the appearance of a visual element to my speech. The left end of the odometer revealed that our numbers had exceeded five million. The whirling right end revealed that 10,000 more would be added to the movement during the course of my speech. The bright green points of light, blending into a green hue when they became sufficiently dense, gave a sense of hope, like the return of spring. In addition, there was something new on the globe: a very few red points of light, as if some of the plants had burst into flower. I continued.

"The reason that Earth is at the top of our column of symbols is because it represents the highest good. It is our God, our Gaia, of the True Objectivist movement. Everything we do must be oriented toward her welfare. *True ... Objectivists ... believe ... that ... harming ... Earth ... is ... a ... sin.*"

A series of images of environmental devastation flashed upon the screen in rapid succession. Degraded farmland. A clear cut forest. A polluted river. A melting glacier. An oil spill.

"This is what True Objectivists work toward."

A pristine tropical rain forest. An undamaged coral reef. An organic farming operation. An urban space integrated with nature. The crowd had momentarily grown silent, more like attending a church service than a political rally at this invocation of the profane and sacred. The image of the rotating planet reappeared on the screen as I concluded my explanation of the four symbols.

"The point, at the bottom of the column, stands for the individual person – in other words, you."

Images of the trekkers now appeared on the screen, which they had taken of each other during the trek and posted on a section of the True Objectivist website. The selection that had been chosen radiated a feeling of bliss at becoming part of something larger than themselves. The fact that the images represented all ages, ethnicities, and walks of life added to the feeling of oneness. The crowd remained reverent as they gazed at this portrayal of themselves.

"The fact that the point is small and located at the bottom of the column does not mean that you, a single person, are unimportant or dispensable. On the contrary, the whole column rests upon you and your welfare is paramount. *True ... Objectivists ... believe ... in ... the ... sanctity ... of ... the ... whole ... Earth ... AND ... the ... individual.* Not only is Earth sacred, but *you* are sacred. Not only can we change the world together, but *you* can change as an individual. You are even capable of *transformational* change, and your journey begins with the notebooks that each and every one of you wears on your hip."

My hand went for my notebook and thrust it toward the crowd. Ten thousand hands went toward their notebooks and thrust them toward me. Ten thousand voices spontaneously chanted in unison.

"*Change! Change! Change! Change! ...*"

With a shock, an image of old newsreels leapt into my head with vast crowds of German citizens thrusting their arms toward Hitler and shouting "*Heil! Heil! Heil! Heil!*" and Hitler acting in the same electrified way that I was. I struggled to break the spell on myself and the crowd, quieting them down with my arms.

"The two symbols in the middle of the column, the circle and the American flag, are just as important as Earth and the single person. The circle stands for the small group – people working together to get things done. Your family. Your friends. Your neighborhood. Your school. Your team. Your church. Your business. Your fire department. One of the great falsehoods preached by my father is that society is constructed out of individuals who only care about themselves. This lie has become so pervasive that people working in small groups to accomplish meaningful goals have nearly disappeared from American life, in Sidney and every other town and city in America."

"Amen!" someone shouted, followed by a ripple of approval by the rest of the crowd.

"The truth is that we evolved to function as members of small cooperative groups, which are necessary for both our personal welfare and efficacious action at a larger scale. That is a core insight of the True Objectivist movement. Society needs to be constructed out of *groups* of individuals, just as our bodies are composed of cells. And the groups must be healthy for the larger society to be healthy. For this reason, a core objective of the True Objectivist movement is to form its members into groups, and for every group that forms, a red point will appear on the globe."

Now the crowd understood the meaning of the red points that were beginning to appear, like flowers among the fields of green.

"And that is the kind of help that the True Objectivist movement is offering to the town of Sidney, Nebraska, which your mayor alluded to in his introduction."

The planet started to enlarge, as if viewed from a spaceship that was descending to land on the surface. Within a few seconds the imaginary spaceship was hovering over the town of Sidney, Nebraska, and a dense cluster of red points.

"Working with the mayor and his team during the last few weeks, we have already organized the town into action groups to collectively evolve their future. These groups are open to every citizen of the town. No one is excluded. Just as you are in charge of evolving your own personal future, the town of Sidney is in charge of evolving its collective future, but not in a way that causes harm to others. That would violate the sanctity of Earth. And when the town comes up with its plan, the True Objectivist movement will help to realize it with an infusion of True Dollars. We will also help to monitor progress, suggest best practices, and assist in mid-course corrections. This is the kind of assistance that we are in a position to offer every town and city in America and ultimately the world, with Sidney, Nebraska leading the way!"

Once again the crowd roared at full throttle, led by the citizens of Sidney, filled with pride for their little town. I glanced behind me at the mayor to see him beside himself with joy.

"There is one more symbol in our column to explain – the American flag. It stands not just for America, but for any institution that currently exists to organize human affairs. As the True Objectivist movement spreads around the world, this position will be occupied by the flags of the other nations. It could also be occupied by religious symbols – the Cross, the Crescent, the Star of David. This level of organization, above the single group but below the whole Earth, is vital for human societies to function. Our goal is not to replace them but to improve them so that they do a better job of doing what they are already supposed to do – offer a high quality of life for their citizens or adherents, but never in a way that causes harm to others. That is why the symbol for our current institutions is placed below the symbol of the whole Earth. Our nations and creeds must treat the whole earth as sacred, no less than our groups and individuals. To do otherwise is immoral. Sinful. It is for this reason that we can be patriots of our nations, believers in our faiths, and citizens of the world at the same time."

Yet another roar erupted as the crowd expressed its collective relief that they could join this new movement without necessarily abandoning their previous attachments. Once again I had become electrified by my own rhetoric and sea of bodies in front of me. My own final words were delivered with my hand formed into a fist and thrust high into the air.

"We are not revolutionaries. We are *evolutionaries! Let ... the ... evolution ... begin!*"

A final roar crashed against my ears and subsided as the emotionally spent crowd began to disperse and make their way to their tents. I, too, felt limp, as if an animating current had been turned off. It seemed that everyone around me – the mayor, our crew member, Angelina – were also struggling to reclaim their private minds. We walked in silence back to the mayor's house, through crowds that parted as we approached, like the Red Sea parting before Moses. At the mayor's house, we quickly said our goodnights and prepared for bed.

After the house became quiet, I exited my room and tapped lightly on Angelina's door. I heard soft footsteps and Angelina stood framed in the doorway. She was wearing a light nightgown that lay against the contours of her breasts. Her hair was loose and fell in abundance around her shoulders. Her brown eyes, always large, seemed even larger. We embraced and she led me inside her room.

We embraced again and lay down on the bed facing each other. I grasped her head in both hands and brought it toward me so I could kiss her forehead and smell her aroma. The feel of her along the length of my body made me alive with joy. Then I spoke.

"Angelina. What happened back there?"

Angelina remained silent for several seconds before replying.

"I don't know, John. It was inspiring and terrifying at the same time. One moment I was a part of it and the next moment I was standing outside of it and fearing that it might kill me. It was holy and bestial at the same time!"

"That's how I felt, too, but maybe even stronger because it was running through me. There was a moment when I felt like I was Hitler and that I could order the crowd to do anything, no matter how depraved!"

We clung to each other in silence before I resumed speaking.

"How do you think the media is going to respond to what happened?"

"I don't know, John. I don't know."

"No sex. I just want to be held."

"Wake up, America! Is this what you want for your future? Here is your True Objectivist, showing his true colors!"

That was how my father opened his morning television show, followed by footage of me strutting around on the stage and the crowd thrusting its notebooks toward me. In the chair next to my father to help with the commentary was Steve, looking triumphant. At last I had made a blunder that he could exploit.

"Look at him, John! I haven't seen a display of fanaticism like that since Hitler and Mussolini!"

Angelina and I were watching on the mayor's wide screen monitor in his living room. The mayor and his wife had no inkling that we had spent the night together. Coffee was brewing and a breakfast table was awaiting us when we came downstairs. Then the mayor and his wife departed to begin their day, leaving us alone with my father and Steve on the screen and a sinking sensation in my heart.

Angelina's cell phone rang.

"It's Howard. He wants to consult with us on Zoom."

In a few keystrokes of Angelina's laptop, Howard and Ashley had joined Angelina, my father, Steve and me in the mayor's living room. We turned the sound off the television monitor for our conversation with Howard and Ashley.

"Good morning, John. Who did you think you were on that stage – Mick Jagger?"

Howard was smiling and trying to make light, but I could see that it was an effort and Ashley's somber expression conveyed the truth of the matter. My performance last night could be a major setback for the movement. I sank down into my chair to make myself as small as possible.

"I'm sorry! I never faced a crowd like that before and I don't know what came over me!"

Howard's face softened. "Don't beat yourself up too much over it. What's done is done. I've said all along that this can blow up in our faces. So far, we've had the advantage of coming out of left field. Those with real power haven't felt threatened. They think it's a media circus that will blow over, as so many have in the past. At some point, they're going to come to the same realization as Steve – that their power hangs in the balance. That's when all hell can break loose. There will be no logic to it, just whatever it takes to preserve the existing order. Our strategy has been for the catalysis to take place quickly enough so that it is over before the elites have time to react. That's what Steve has been warning your father and everyone else about from the moment you sprang the trap. Fortunately for us, he hasn't been taken seriously. Now he has your performance to get their attention. Our risk factor for a cultural explosion has been increased."

No words could express my shame, so I just sat in abject silence. It was Angelina who spoke next.

"What can we do to salvage the situation?"

"The situation is not hopeless. On the bright side, John's performance helped to galvanize our rapidly growing base. The people in that crowd will march to the end of the world with you, John. They will even die for you. That's the way it has been with mass movements since human history began, for better *and* for worse."

Howard's analysis nailed it for me. That's why I could suddenly feel like Hitler, and why Angelina described the crowd as holy and bestial at the same time.

"John's performance just turned up the temperature on the whole process," Howard went on. "The best we can do is carry on and try to bring down the temperature as best we can. That's why Ashley and I think that you should lay low for a while, John. No public statements. Angelina is our press secretary and the movement needs to speak through her."

Now it was Angelina's turn to remain silent as the awesome responsibility left her without words. Ashley spoke next.

"All the major news and talk shows want you to appear, Angelina. The local television station has made its studio available. Your first interview is with Sean Hennesee at Fox News. He's a bully, especially with women. Don't let him bully you."

This day was set aside as a day of rest, bonding and training for how to form a strong group before resuming our trek the next day. The eight occupants of each tent were the groups for training purposes. During the morning over breakfast, they told their stories to each other, much as I did with the groups of journalists who visited me at the Cell. During the day, they attended seminars on the system that the True Objectivist movement had created to facilitate the formation of groups – the circles in the vertical column of symbols – anywhere in the world, resulting in the creation of a red dot on the globe. During the evening, they sat around campfires at the entrances to their tents to discuss their plans for creating groups after the trek was over. They had only just joined the movement and already they were being groomed to function as leaders of the cells that would make up the new world order. The ten thousand hands who thrust their notebooks toward me last night were now madly scribbling in those notebooks, evolving their respective futures.

All of this had been organized by the Mother Ship without requiring my attention, leaving me free to walk around the tent city and fairground buildings where the seminars were being held. Howard was right. My performance last night might have provided ammunition to the enemies of the movement, but it also increased the resolve of the movement itself. Everywhere I went on my meandering path, people crowded around me to express gratitude for the future that had opened up for them. They would never go back, no matter what the cost. Their support helped to revive my own confidence.

My iPhone rang. It was Omar.

"Dude, log onto Fox News to see the Hennesee Report. Angelina *owned* Hennesee!

A few swipes brought up a video of Hennesee's split screen interview with Angelina. If she felt nervous, she didn't look it.

"Angelina ..."

"Ms. Garcia to you ..."

"Ms. Garcia, how do you respond to the accusation that John Galt III is a fanatic?"

"He is a fanatic."

"What?" Hennesee was not expecting such an easy victory.

"Here is what he is fanatic about: The Truth. Equity. Non-violence ..."

"Ms. Garcia ..."

"A good living for the average person. Peace on Earth. Living in balance with the planet ..."

"*Ms. Garcia!*"

"What are you fanatic about, Sean?"

"Mr. Hennesee to you!"

"What are you fanatic about, Mr. Hennesee?"

"I'm not a fanatic!"

"What are your convictions then? What will you walk a thousand miles to uphold?"

"This interview isn't about me!"

"This interview is about the values that John Galt III represents and is putting into action as we speak. Do you have anything against those values?"

"I sure do! He's a socialist! A communist! A globalist! He's everything that America doesn't stand for!"

"You're forgetting something, Mr. Hennesee."

"What? What am I forgetting?"

"The socialism, communism, and globalism that you're talking about didn't work well. The True Objectivism movement works well as it moves to Philadelphia, for all the world to see. And every town and city that works with the True Objectivist movement will also work well. Is it part of your hope for America that it doesn't work well?"

"Of course not, but …"

"And is there a problem with every nation on Earth working well?"

"That's a fantasy!"

"Do you mean that it's beyond your imagination?"

"Yes! … No!"

"YES!" I shouted, throwing my iPhone high into the air and catching it again. "Angelina! You're an angel!"

So it went. Angelina's shutdown of Hennesee and her other interviews went a long way toward turning down the temperature of the cultural catalysis, as Howard put it. Over a thousand campfires burned brightly that night as the training groups became like family in a single day, just like the groups of journalists brought to the Cell. The harder the masters of the old order tried to oppose us, the more it became the wind at our backs as we moved toward Philadelphia. The green fields of the rotating planet burst into flower as individuals formed into groups. Towns in every state of the union lined up to become the next Sidney. One hundred thousand people attended our second camp meeting in Greenwhich, Ohio. Our third and final camp meeting near Gettysburg, Pennsylvania, was bigger than Woodstock and featured top performers representing every musical genre.

By the time we approached Philadelphia, a day ahead of schedule, over a third of the American voting population had joined the True Objectivist movement , with the European nations close behind and the other nations of the world greening at a slower pace. Only the most authoritarian regimes remained barren. Every elected politician who stared at the rotating globe and whirling odometer was faced with a stark new reality. Either come to terms with the True Objectivist movement or be voted out of office.

Steve had been exactly right, but he wasn't around to gloat anymore. In the final audio file sent by our mysterious mole, he announced that he was leaving my father's sinking ship.

"I'm no fool. I've stashed my money in the Bahamas, where they know how to treat people like me right. If you want me, you'll find me on my yacht."

"We'll miss you, Steve!" someone shouted after the recording was played to members of the Mother Ship, with me taking part remotely, to uproarious laughter from our crew.

My father was left to face me on his own.

The Speech

My darling avatar Eve,

There is never a day when you aren't in my thoughts, even though I haven't written in quite a while. There was little privacy on the trek, but we have arrived in Philadelphia a day ahead of schedule, giving me this time to be with you at last.

Howard's cultural catalysis has gone according to plan, but only by making a mid-course correction. I was becoming too much of a lightning rod, so for most of the trek other people have spoken for the movement. Angelina is the one who does regular briefings and I pity the fool who tries to confront her! Omar and Luke are also much sought after. You'd laugh if you heard how the True Objectivist movement gets rendered by Omar, and your brother has almost single-handedly blunted attacks from the religious right. Even Tyler has become a spokesperson and was featured in an interview in Nascar! Magazine. He's also become an item with Sigrid, a member of the bicycle team, and they are awfully cute together. He's lost all his belly fat and I'm as lean as a beanpole and as brown as a migrant farmer. Lizzie is holding up well and if anything has gained weight from all the scraps she gets from the trekkers and the crowds cheering us on.

Just as eloquent as the main spokespeople are the members of the movement who come from all walks of life. You could pick one at random from the caravan and get an articulate response. The fact that each one is on a personal journey, chronicled in their notebooks and nurtured by the small groups that they have formed, give them an authenticity that cannot be denied. Add to that the sheer economic incentives for joining the movement – a good wage for an honest day's work – and all the assistance that we can give to towns and cities to thrive as communities, and we're unstoppable.

Another reason for me to keep silent is to build up anticipation for my duel with my father, now only two days away. I've had 100 days to mull over my speech and have it memorized by heart. It's hard to know what my father could do to alter the course of history at this point. The cleverest part of our trap is that while he has been preparing for the event, we have achieved all of our major objectives before the event. Only Steve saw through our plan and he was unable to get anyone to listen. By the time the masters of the old order came to their senses, it was too late and I was protected by a shield of people speaking for me.

The trek has changed me, maybe forever. It has certainly changed me in the eyes of others. They don't see me as a person. They see the future of humanity and their own salvation. I see them as people but I know that my role is to help them on their path. That is my fate. It is what I have worked toward my whole life and have been lucky enough to achieve. But how I long for the days when we lay together, flesh to flesh, and poured out our hearts to each other. That was when I felt most whole and what I cling to in my mind, no matter where you are, if you never return to me, or even if you have ceased to exist in bodily form.

Forever yours,

John

Philadelphia, the city of brotherly love. Thanks to the Cult of Scholars, I knew a thing or two about the Quaker religion that emerged in England in the mid-1600s, migrated to the New World to escape persecution by the Anglican Church, and then migrated west from New England to escape persecution by the Puritans. Viewed in hindsight, the Quaker movement was a step in the journey that the

True Objectivist movement was completing. By replacing the concept of original sin with the concept of an inner light, Quakerism sanctified the individual in addition to the community of believers. Quakerism also offered a good economic deal to its members. Everyone shopped at the stores of Quaker merchants because they knew that they would not be cheated. The Quakers did well by doing good, just like the economy of the True Objectivists.

Philadelphia, the cradle of the American democratic experiment – another step in the journey that the True Objectivist movement was completing. Inspired by a heady mix of Enlightenment values and religious values shorn of intolerance to other religions (at least to a degree), the fledgling nation also sanctified both the individual and the community, starting with each colony and painfully, awkwardly, expanding to a federation of colonies.

Philadelphia, 140 miles from Gettysburg, where Abraham Lincoln delivered his immortal address. Thanks to the Cult of Scholars, I knew a thing or two about the Gettysburg Address. Despite its brevity, it was regarded as a new founding document for the nation that went beyond the American Constitution in its commitment to the proposition that all men are created equal. After all, many of the founding fathers were slave owners and their insistence on preserving that form of inequality was tearing the nation apart. Like the Quaker religion and the American Constitution, the Gettysburg address sanctified both the individual and something larger than the individual, something so noble that it was even worth dying for. It also described America as an experiment that, if successful, could serve as a model for the rest of the world. If Abe Lincoln were alive today, he would be a True Objectivist.

Philadelphia, home of the Kimmel Center for the Performing Arts, where the duel of speeches with my father would take place in front of an audience of 2,500 people and broadcast around the world to an audience of over a billion. The terms of the agreement specified that each of us was responsible for inviting half of the audience, which would be seated on different sides of the center aisle, so we would be evenly matched as far as audience support inside the building was concerned.

Not so outside the building. Over a third of the voting population joining our movement was the national average. Some regions were much higher, especially along the route of our trek, which could be seen as a green and red thread on our rotating planet. In Philadelphia, the trek's destination, over half of the voting population had joined the movement. That included the city's progressive mayor, who was no friend of my father and his kind and happy to become one of the first major politicians to come over to our side. We were already in conversation with his administration to work in the Philadelphia neighborhoods in the same way as we had in the towns of the heartland, such as Sidney.

In addition to the majority of the residents sporting green windbreakers, I was arriving with a caravan of over 20,000 trekkers and others were streaming in from all compass directions. Our estimates, by far the most accurate, were that the population of Philadelphia would swell more for the duel of speeches than for the Democratic National Convention in 2016. Large screen monitors were being placed on the streets surrounding the Kimmel Center, and car traffic was to be blocked off to accommodate an outdoor crowd that would be larger than the New Year's celebration in New York City's Times Square. The Philadelphia police department gratefully accepted our offer to coordinate with them to handle the logistics, knowing the chaos that might result if they tried to do it on their own.

Our invitations to attend the event inside the Kimmel Center were by lottery except for the crew of the Mother Ship and a few that were allotted to me, which I extended to the most important people in my life who had brought me to this point: My mother and her family. Walter and Leonora Gold. Abraham Baryov. Eve's family. Omar, Tyler, and Sigrid. All of them accepted, with the exception of Joseph and Mary, who apologized on behalf of her husband.

"Please forgive him, he's a little bit stuck in his ways."

Oddly, Howard opted to stay at home.

"Howard!" I asked by phone. "Why aren't you coming to the culmination of what you caused to happen?"

"As strange as it might seem, I have never felt comfortable around crowds. Nancy and I will be watching on the television and I look forward to talking with you when you return."

I sensed that there might be more behind Howard's decision, but didn't try to talk him out of it.

Everyone on my invitation list was invited to be the guest of Andrew Cope, a descendent of one of Philadelphia's prominent Quaker families during the colonial era, in his spacious historic home. Andrew had greatly enlarged the family fortune as an investment banker, but one with a strong sense of civic responsibility, in keeping with the Quaker tradition that he upheld. Such people were rare but not entirely absent in the banking world, which made him a kindred spirit of Abraham Baryov in the accounting profession. Andrew was one of the first to start investing in the True Objectivist currency system, which was now backed by over twelve billion US dollars, far more than my father's personal wealth. Nearly every commercial establishment in Philadelphia sported "WE ACCEPT TRUE DOLLARS" signs.

I was the last person to arrive at the Cope mansion for the reception that preceded dinner on the night before the duel of speeches. What a strange experience, after walking the length of the continent, to walk into a room that took me back in time to the American revolution, filled with the most important people from all stages of my own life! Stranger still was the fact that our common culture had taken a quantum leap during the last 100 days, which everyone was still struggling to comprehend. Tears filled my eyes as I embraced each of them in turn. There was so much to discuss. Where to begin?

On the day of the duel, I arrived at the Kimmel Center in plenty of time to rest and collect my thoughts. My clothes were the same as I always wore: cotton shirt, canvas pants, and my notebook by my side. I entered the front door and was led through the lobby and down the front aisle of the concert hall, with three tiers of balconies curving around the crescent-shaped stage where the duel would take place. Then backstage, past a warren of rooms to my dressing room, which included a long couch, a makeup table facing a large mirror, and a table of drinks and snacks.

I had scarcely glanced at myself during my 100-day trek and when I did it was to hurriedly shave in front of a small bathroom mirror. The large mirror in the small dressing room made my image look like another occupant. I sat down and looked at this person with a strange kind of detachment, as someone else might look at me. My weathered face, tall gaunt frame, and somber expression of my eyes were more Abe-like than ever.

With more time to spare, I started to explore the backstage area.
Turning a corner, I came abruptly upon my father and stepmother.
They were inside his dressing room and had failed to close the door.
My father was wearing a white sleeveless undershirt, white boxer shorts,
and black socks held up with garters. His weight had ballooned since I
saw him last and his skin had a ghastly pallor. Cindi was helping him
put his arms through what appeared to be a giant corset. She looked as
if she had aged years since I last saw her. With a shock I realized that
it was indeed a giant corset, meant to gather up the great folds of his
flesh into a more compact mass.

As Cindi struggled to tighten the corset, my father caught sight of me.

"Shut the door! Shut the door!" he cried to Cindi in panic. Now
Cindi caught sight of me and rushed to the door, gave me a look of
loathing, and slammed it shut.

I returned to my room, shaken. The poor man should be in a hospital,
not appearing on stage in front of over a billion people worldwide! I
made my way to the stage. The lecterns had been set up and people
were filing into their seats. Everyone on the right side was wearing
their green windbreaker, as requested on their apps, in stark contrast
to those on the left, whose clothing was not coordinated in any way at
all. I retreated back to the bowels of the backstage, found an exit, and
opened it to face a sea of people in green windbreakers filling the open
area around the Kimmel Center and the streets and alleys as far as I
could see, with the exception of one street that was clear to allow cars
escorted by the police to reach the center. There was no turning back.
The duel of speeches would begin in one hour.

The time had come. An attendant fitted me with a microphone and
led me to a side entrance to the stage. At a signal, she instructed me to
walk to my lectern. My father entered and walked to his lectern from
the opposite side. I could see Cindi waiting in the wings. The packed
audience, a solid block of green and white on the right and formless
patchwork of colors on the left, burst into applause.

My father was dressed in a blue suit of the highest quality, the
kind of quality that masters of the universe use to rank each other.

Tiny details that spell the difference between ten thousand dollars and five thousand dollars. The corset had worked its deception. His body seemed firm underneath the fine clothes. He looked fit and imposing, not obese. His face also radiated good health. Only I, and not the audience, could see that he was wearing thick makeup, with beads of sweat beginning to trickle down the back of his neck. The rings on his fingers and his gold watch glinted from the stage lights. There could not be a stronger contrast between a man of wealth at one lectern and a man of the Earth at the other.

The moderator of the event strode onto the stage to another round of applause, louder from the left side than the right side. The choice of moderator was part of the negotiation that took place to organize the event. My father's side began with Sean Hennesee from Fox News, clearly a partisan choice, in the same way that a bargainer begins with an unrealistic offer to strike an acceptable final deal. They were surprised when we accepted their choice. For them it was an early victory that they attributed to our naivety. Didn't we know that we had given them an advantage? For us, it was a detail so small that it wasn't worth bothering about. If our attempt at cultural catalysis was successful, the choice of moderator would be irrelevant.

We were more insistent about the seating arrangement, another detail that was part of the negotiation. We agreed about dividing the auditorium in half, but my father's team wanted their audience to be on the right side and we insisted that they take the left side. They argued long and hard before giving up in exasperation. Every time that they talked about their audience being on the left, they could barely get the words out of their mouth, and that was precisely why we insisted upon the arrangement! Our goal was to do away with the entire concept of left and right in politics. True Objectivists were not limited to the political left, as conventionally defined. There were plenty of independents, libertarians, and Republicans – especially old school Republicans who had been displaced by the cancerous creed of my father and grandmother. If the word "right" was to be used at all, it should refer to the right way of doing things to achieve agreed-upon goals, as opposed to the wrong way. "Left" should mean left behind because it doesn't work. That was why we fought so hard for the right side of the auditorium. It was part of our effort to reclaim the words "right" and "left."

"Ladies and gentlemen," Hennesee began, in a voice already familiar to millions. "Welcome to the event that the whole world has been waiting for, the duel of speeches between John Galt II and John Galt III for the soul of the Objectivist movement. Two shots that will be heard around the world!"

More raucous applause, more from the left side than the right side, which Hennesee made little effort to suppress. We had requested through our app that our audience behave in a civil manner. The other side, no doubt feeling threatened by the solidarity on our side and the massive crowds outside, wanted to assert their strength as best they could, which they could only do by hooting and hollering at the top of their lungs as individuals.

After about fifteen seconds of applause, the people on the right side were signaled by our app to stop clapping and look at the people on the other side of the aisle. It took only a moment for them to notice the sudden diminution of sound and collective gaze, as if to say, "Don't you know the *rules*?" Most stopped clapping immediately with expressions of shame and confusion on their faces. Others defied the new convention signaled by the collective gaze, but not for long. The smaller their numbers became, the more pathetic their protest appeared until they too lapsed into silence.

The silence lingered for longer than it should have. There was something terrifying about what had just taken place for Hennesee, my father, the audience on the left, and everyone else in the world who was watching and had not yet joined the True Objectivist movement. The audience on the right had been nothing but polite, but their collective behavior suggested that they could turn aggressive at any time they chose and there would be little that the audience on the left could do to defend themselves. It was like being placed inside a cage with a tiger and being told that it was a *friendly* tiger. Finally, Hennesee regained his voice and continued with his prepared remarks.

"Very few people need reminding that the original speech was by the first John Galt and was also heard around the world, changing the course of history …"

Very few people needed reminding now, but that was thanks only to the attention that I had brought to it by springing the trap on my father. Before then, it had been forgotten even by him, a construction of a father that he never knew, built upon by his mother, but then left behind as my father expanded the empire in his own populist way. I knew that my father would need to go back to the original speech to remind himself of what his father had set in motion. What we would find was thirty pages in length, which required over an hour to recite on the air. It was written in dense philosophical prose and was militantly atheistic, something that would need to be hidden from my father's following, which ironically included the religious right. It was so elitist and scornful of the great mass of humanity that one commentator at the time summarized it with the words, "Get ye to the gas chamber." According to the original speech, society had already collapsed based on the doers going on strike. In the mind of John Galt I, his radio audience was the enemy that had already been defeated and must accept the rule of the new masters. Never mind that John Galt's own little society was on the verge of collapse and that he was about to disappear without a trace. This was the founding text of Objectivism that John Galt II must consult to craft his own speech. I did not envy him his task.

Yet, I also knew that there was continuity between this founding text, made almost incomprehensible by the passage of time, and my father's populist empire. The core idea, which could be called the soul of the original Objectivist movement, was *each individual as his own God*. This was the allure when stated in the dense philosophical prose of the first speech. With a bit of repackaging, it could be equally alluring to the redneck who didn't want anyone telling him what to do, to the young idealist chaffing against conventional society, or to elites eager to be told that their wealth is a sign of their moral worth, no matter what their religious persuasion. In fact, there was a clear family resemblance between the atheistic speech of John Galt I and the "Gospel of Wealth" that made the robber barons of the 19th century feel morally superior. The core idea of *each individual as his own God* was equally comfortable wearing atheistic, religious, or populist clothes. That was why my father found it so easy to discard his father's speech when it went out of fashion.

I had consulted the original speech many times in my own formulation of True Objectivism and even acquired a kind of admiration for it. Yes, it was a tissue of lies, but when considered as a work of mosaic art it had a kind of majesty. Ayn Rant claimed again and again that her brand of Objectivism was not a license for some to gain at the expense of others, and in a superficial sense she was right. According to the founding text, there were no conflicts of interest among rational men. The Objectivist might have rejected the conventional virtues preached by both religions and socialist doctrines, but still made a distinction between good and bad forms of selfishness that gave back just about everything that it seemed to take away.

The great error of the founding document, from my perspective, was the weight that it placed on rational thought as the one and only guide to behavior. As if each person, merely by thinking rigorously about the nature of reality and avoiding false premises, would converge upon the same course of action. Only then would there be no conflicts of interest among rational men. Always men. Even Ayn Rant spoke in a masculine voice and never used female pronouns.

In reality, it was absurd to expect that such an outcome would ever take place. Instead, each individual acting as their own God would invariably come to different conclusions about what was right and good that privileged their own welfare. And given each person's reliance upon their own thoughts and intolerance of the claims of others, conflicts among Objectivists and against society as a whole would invariably result. That is exactly what happened and led to the collapse of the Galtian's utopian society after only a few years. It is also what was happening for society at large. The only difference was that a few more decades were required in the latter case.

Had my grandfather, grandmother, and father intended this result? Were they evil geniuses plotting to destroy the world for their own gain? Or were their intentions pure but merely mistaken? The most important conclusion that I came to on this question was that *it didn't matter*. Either way, it was a cultural mutation that spread like a cancer and was now destroying the body politic.

Given what I knew about organisms as societies and societies as organisms, thinking of the original Objectivism as the morality of a cancer cell was more than metaphorical. An actual cancer begins with a mutant cell that ignores the regulatory imperatives of the whole body and proliferates more than its neighboring cells. A cancer cell can boast of a certain kind of success. By pretending that there is no such thing as a whole body, it can present itself as a model for other cells to emulate. This is precisely what the original speech did – pretend that there was no such thing as society, other than what self-interested individuals do to each other. As long as the comparison is between cancer cells and normal cells within the same body, then the cancer cells can boast of their superiority right up to the end.

In contrast, Lincoln's Gettysburg address, building upon the Declaration of Independence and US Constitution, was the morality of a whole body, envisioned as a government of the people, for the people, and by the people. Individual people were not ignored; it was their happiness that government was designed to ensure. But this required individuals to coordinate with others in pursuit of their collective happiness and at times to make the ultimate sacrifice of their own lives so that whole can endure. Such a sacrifice was only required when the survival of the whole body was at stake. Under normal conditions, the prosperity of the whole body was shared by each and every cell. My challenge, in crafting my speech, was to replace the morality of the cancer cell with the morality of the whole Earth.

The preliminaries over, Hennesee seated himself on a chair on the left corner of the stage and the attention of over a billion people around the world became focused on my father. He had remained motionless during the introductions, staring straight ahead, as if in a trance. He had no written notes in front of him; nor did I. Despite the makeup, the sweat pouring down his neck, and the deception of the corset that I knew lay beneath his fine clothes, he conveyed a sense of dignity, as if he was at peace with himself, no matter what the verdict of the rest of the world.

As he began to speak, I quickly realized that he was not going to base his speech closely on the original speech and that he was wise not to do so. Instead, he was going to stick to his own rendering of each individual as his own God, which was already so familiar to his base. The left side of the concert hall didn't want to hear anything new. They wanted their old habits of thought to be affirmed. Hennesee had instructed the audience not to interrupt the speeches with applause, cheers, or boos. The audience on the right remained respectfully silent but the audience on the left found it impossible to comply. With each comforting phrase that emerged from my father's mouth, they felt impelled to communicate their approval.

Hennesee was secretly pleased but also had his responsibility as moderator to uphold. He looked at me to gauge my reaction and was surprised when I signaled to let the left side of the audience have its way. Left unchallenged, the waves of approval grew in strength and each one seemed to invigorate my father. Soon he had left his trance-like state and was back in his old form, his voice booming, his chest thrust out, and his arms stabbing the air. America was founded on the values of individual liberty and rescued from socialism by his father's speech. Now American values were being threatened once again, by his own son, of all people. If I had my way, America as we know it would cease to exist. Everyone would be forced to become mindless drones; forced to dress alike and think alike. The audience on the right was living proof. Was its solidarity something to be admired? Didn't the *Nazis* and the *Communists* have that kind of solidarity?

Over an hour passed in this fashion, beyond the time that had been allotted. Hennesee kept looking at me to see if I expected him to apply the rules and I kept signaling to let my father's speech take its course, which it finally did with a tidal wave of affirmation by the left side of the great hall and polite applause from the right side. I knew what had just taken place. It was the same thing that happened to me on the stage of the county fair in Sidney, Nebraska, in front of ten thousand of my ardent supporters. It was amazing that our cultural catalysis had succeeded as well as it had, but there would not be a clean sweep. There would always be a contingent of true believers on my father's side, ready to follow him to the end of the Earth, permanently seduced by the morality of the cancer cell.

When at last these true believers had spent their energy, the time had arrived for my speech. I began by remaining silent for what might have seemed an unreasonably long time. I couldn't help but reflect that my whole life had been devoted to making this moment possible. During the period of my own silence, the audience of the great hall also became utterly silent in expectation. Indeed, profound silence reigned on the streets of Philadelphia and everywhere else on Earth where crowds had gathered to hear the duel of speeches. Finally I began.

"Four score and seven million years ago ..."

If I was going to be compared to Abe Lincoln. I might as well go all the way. I paused again to let it sink in around the world that my speech was going to be based, not on my grandfather's speech, but on that *other* speech.

Four score and seven million years ago, evolution had already brought forth a rich tapestry of life, with every life form a symphony of coordination among its parts.

But many of these life forms were engaged in a great war against each other, so that life on Earth was a battlefield of suffering.

Then, something happened to one primate species that would alter the fate of life on Earth. The members of their groups ceased to make war on each other and behaved as if they were a single organism. They ended self-imposed suffering within their own groups.

At first this achievement had little impact on the larger battlefield of suffering and even fanned its flames as groups made war against other groups. But the circles of cooperation kept expanding until millions of people were living in harmony with each other, at least in comparison with their pasts.

Now we are met on the last great battlefield of this expansion. All of humanity and the rest of life on Earth is at a crossroad. Either we take the final step and become a planetary organism, or continue to impose suffering on each other and other life forms with more destructive force than ever before.

The final step is not a deviation from religion and the concept of government of the people, by the people, for the people. Those were intermediate steps. The final step merely recognizes that "the people" are all of the people and that their welfare requires becoming wise stewards of all other living forms. Only when we achieve the final step will self-imposed suffering perish from Earth.

Two hundred and seventy-one words, just like the Gettysburg address. If I had my way, my speech would go down in history as a new founding document built upon the Gettysburg address, just as the Gettysburg address was viewed as a founding document built upon the US Constitution and Declaration of Independence.

As with Lincoln's address, my speech was over almost as soon as it began and the preceding speech seemed bloated and forgettable by comparison. The audience on the right forgot their discipline and leapt to their feet with a roar of affirmation that made the previous ruckus on the left seem tame by comparison. Then, out of the continuous roar of voices, a chant emerged.

"*Change!* ... *Change!* ... *Change!* ... *Change!* ... *Change* ... *Change!* ..."

This was the original plan and it rapidly took hold on the right side of the great hall, while the left side remained in stunned silence. The pace of the chant was slow, with a full second separating each repetition. The app was acting as a pacemaker. There was something strange about the blast of sound that came with each repetition, something so low in the bass register that it was more felt than heard. Abruptly the right side of the great hall stopped chanting and the source of the bass register was revealed. It was the people *outside* in the streets continuing the chant. Their combined voices, hurled toward the building from all sides, beat upon it like a drum. From the inside, it sounded like the heartbeat of a giant organism.

The event was over and accomplished everything that we had planned for it. It wasn't a complete victory. As with the Gettysburg address, my speech was delivered at the turning point of the war, not its conclusion. There was still a determined enemy that would fight to the end. My father looked lost and disoriented in the confusion and the thud, thud, thud of voices beating against the building. My heart went out to him. I left my lectern and took a step in his direction. My movement attracted his attention and he looked startled. Then something happened that I didn't expect and could not comprehend as it unfolded. His heavily made-up face contorted into a tragic mask of grief. He took a step toward me, then another, and literally ran into me, wrapping his arms around my waist, the great bulk of his body leaning against me for support, his head buried against my chest, sobbing uncontrollably.

The entire audience, left and right, and a sizable fraction of the entire world, gasped in disbelief as I wrapped one arm around his back and the other around his head, comforting him like a father consoling his child. Cindi ran in from the side entrance and also wrapped her arms around him. Together, we walked him off the stage.

The sight of my father collapsing into my arms, beamed around the world, was a deathblow to his movement that I could never have accomplished by myself. Thanks to this event that I could not fathom, the morality of the cancer cell was in permanent remission.

Cindi and I guided my father back to his dressing room surrounded by a knot of attendants. She instructed them to call an ambulance. I returned to my dressing room, not knowing what else to do. I didn't want to see anyone and I couldn't sit still, so I just paced back and forth. Celebrating my victory was out of the question until I could process what had just happened out there on the stage. I don't know how much time elapsed before there was a sharp knock on my door and Cindi entered without asking my permission. She closed the door behind her and slumped into one of the chairs, threw her head back with a look of utter exhaustion, and began to speak.

"Your father is on the way to the hospital and I will join him soon. He has cancer."

"*What?*"

"An aggressive form of brain cancer. The doctors are trying to cure it with drugs but it isn't working and the drugs make him foggy and lethargic. They'll probably need to operate and no one knows what his mental capacity will be after they remove the tumor."

I was speechless. Cindi looked at me and a cruel smile crept upon her worn face.

"Do you know when he first received the diagnosis?"

"When?"

"A week before he received your letter asking to visit him."

"My God …" was all I could say as I frantically tried to reprocess my memories of the visit and its aftermath. His joy at seeing me. His pain at my betrayal. His lackluster participation in the strategy sessions led by Steve. Cindi continued to smile at the pain that she had inflicted upon me.

"You'll never know the hell that you put him through. Him and his whole family. *We welcomed you into our home.*"

Cindi stabbed me with her words and seeing me suffer only made her want to stab harder until she abruptly burst into tears and buried her head into her hands. I wanted to comfort her but knew that it would be utterly inappropriate. All I could do was sit on the couch in abject misery until the storm of her tears passed.

At length I couldn't stand the cessation of our conversation anymore and said the only thing that came into my head.

"Did you know that someone from my father's team was sending us recordings of their strategy sessions?"

"Of course I do. It was me."

"*What?*"

Cindi erupted into another burst of fury.

"You don't understand anything! I love the man, not the god-damned movement! When I joined Fox News as a cub reporter and met your father, he was drinking himself into oblivion! He was nice to me when everyone else was trying to get me into bed! He was destroyed by his frigid mother and your mother's contempt for him! Our hearts went out to each other and that's how it's been ever since! I'm a small-town girl from Kansas! I don't need all that stuff! I admired you for saying that being a ten percenter was enough! I hated Steve and his kind! I wanted you to succeed, but did you have to do it that way? *Couldn't you have done it without destroying the man I love?*"

Again I was left to my own misery as a new round of tears broke upon her. I tried to imagine another course of action. What if I had stayed to become the heir of my father's empire, as he and Steve wanted me to do? Could I have reformed the Objectivist movement from within? Try as I might, I did not see how this would have been possible. Changing the world had required inflicting pain on my father and his family. This was something that I would live with for the rest of my life.

I couldn't bear the sight of Cindi's misery anymore and reached out to touch her shoulder, but she slapped my hand away.

"Don't touch me. I need time to heal. But your father still loves you. Give us time and I'll let you know when you can visit us again."

1 4

The Recluse

My darling avatar Eve,

This is my third day at home, my beloved Cell on top of Timber Ridge. Never have I felt so much joy in the small things of life. Waking up and lingering in bed while my mind wanders. Peeling an orange as the sun streams in the windows. Training my entire mind, not on changing the world, but on hitting the center of a log with my splitting maul.

I also feel a profound need to be alone, except for you, who is always with me in my mind. Angelina returned a day earlier than me and it was she who met me at the airport to drive me home. When I got out of her car, I was surprised that she did, too, and walked with me to the entrance of the Cell. Only then did I realize that she had arranged the whole thing and wanted to come in with me. Well, you know how thick I am when it comes to the intentions of women! I embraced her. Her aroma and the touch of her hair against my face flooded my senses, but I whispered into her ear, "Angelina, please forgive me, but I need time."

I need so much time to think about what happens next. Howard asked me to meet with him at the Lodge today. When I do, your ghost will be everywhere.

Forever yours,
John

The parking lot of the Lodge was empty except for Howard's car. The biological station had been prepared for winter, although this day was warm for late October. I walked around the side of the Lodge and saw Howard sitting on the great patio in a light jacket. He had moved a small table and two chairs, perhaps the very ones that we used the first time we met together up here, so that they were facing the lake and majestic peak. He was sitting in one of the chairs, motionless, as I approached from behind. The same sun that illuminated the peak and shimmering surface of the lake lit up his hair like a halo.

"Howard."

The sound of his name brought him out of his trance. He stood up and gazed at me before speaking. The last time that we had set eyes on each other was at the beginning of my trek.

"The big guy!"

Tears sprung to my eyes and we fell into a hug. The master and his apprentice had succeeded in changing the world. We sat down, both facing the lake. The same heightened joy that I felt toward the small things in life made the scene before me appear almost unbearably beautiful. The cottony clouds against the brilliant blue sky. The shadows of the fissures of the great peak, always changing with the angle of the sun. The evergreen firs and aspens shedding their leaves along the rim of the lake. The diamond points of light dancing on its ruffled surface. The small waves lapping the stony shore in a lullaby. The breeze caressing us in a last breath of warmth before winter. Harold must have felt the same way because he too remained silent for a period of time that we did not care to measure. Finally he spoke.

"Forgive me for not being present at the climactic moment. To be honest, as soon as I became convinced that our mission was going to succeed, I felt an almost overpowering urge to be alone. It was as if I had been carrying some crushing weight that I wasn't even aware of until I could shed it."

"Exactly!" I laughed in response. "That's just how I feel right now. And does everything seem beautiful to you?"

"Precisely. I go around beaming like an idiot. But if I knew that you were going to pull off something as historic as updating the Gettysburg address, I might have made more of an effort to be there.

And who could have predicted your father collapsing into your arms? I feel sorry for him."

"They operated on him a day after the speech. They had to cut quite a bit out and he can only speak with difficulty, but in other respects he seems to be his old self. Cindi says that he is looking forward to giving up all his shows and spending time with his family. I wonder if he has the same feeling of shedding a great weight that we do."

"I'll bet that he does. I know that you feel guilty for using him as a pawn in our chess game."

"I do, but he and Cindi seem willing to forgive me. I'm planning to spend the Christmas holidays with them and also dropping in on my mother."

"Excellent! And what about Eve?"

Howard was one of the few people who I confided in about Eve.

"Still no word. That's the remaining great dark cloud in my life. I can't go down there as if I'm rescuing a damsel in distress. That would be ridiculous and could upset whatever she is trying to accomplish. When she said that we can't be together, I am honor bound to obey. That's how we express our love toward each other. Yet, I can't do nothing, either, and I can't contemplate another love as long as there is a chance that she is alive."

"I feel so sorry for both of you."

"How about you? What's next, after changing the world?"

"I've thought a lot about it, as I imagine that you have. There is still much to be done, of course, but I have come to the conclusion that I am not required to do it. If I were to be hit by the proverbial bus, then everything that I would have done would be done by someone else – maybe even faster and better, given all the talent that has been attracted to the Mother Ship and the movement as a whole. I want to stay a part of it, of course, but others can do the heavy lifting. Do you remember when we stood in front of this lake at the beginning of our journey and I told you to take a long look, that where we were going wouldn't be as much fun, although it was necessary? Well, I just might start showing up here during the summers again. There are still some questions about personality in trout that I've been meaning to answer."

"Can I be your assistant?" I replied merrily. I had opened the True Objectivist app while Howard was talking. The rotating planet was continuing to green and blossom and the odometer was continuing to whirl without any help from us whatsoever.

"How about you?" Howard asked in return. "They're already saying that you could become the next president of the United States."

"That's the last thing I want!" I laughed in protest. "What you just said for yourself also goes for me. That one blunder on my trek convinced me that what we have accomplished needn't have a figurehead, much less my personal involvement. What we have done is like changing the course of a river. Once accomplished, the river flows on its own. Like you, I will always be involved, but I don't want to do what others can do and I can't be just a figurehead. I also must be a human being. Right now, I only want to revel in the moment."

So it went for the next few days. The cell was never such a sanctuary. Lizzie was never such a charming companion. Ron's ribs never tasted so good. Tyler returned a changed man. He announced his intention to attend college next fall and offered to help the town of Timber Ridge join the True Objectivist movement up until then. Who needed me when Tyler wanted to step up to the plate?

Then my solitude was interrupted during the night by a sharp rap on the door. Whoever it was had approached quietly and caught Lizzie unaware. Remembering that the last rap like that was Eve, it seemed as if I reached the door in a single leap. But the person standing on the other side wasn't Eve. It was an old, old, man.

"Hello, John. I am your grandfather."

I stared at him, speechless. Was this possible? John Galt I was born in the 1920s, which would put him in his nineties now. The man in front of me seemed ageless, but it was possible that he could be my grandfather. Still, the thought crossed my mind that he might also be an imposter trying to scam me.

"May I come in?"

Still speechless, I stepped aside and he entered. Lizzie was barking and the fur along the top of her back was raised, but the old man knelt down and petted her with such assurance that she calmed down immediately. He removed his coat and placed it on one of the wooden pegs. We ascended the stairs to the first floor and he examined the Cell's interior.

"Nice. Real nice!"

I asked if he would like a beverage and he chose a beer, which he took with a thin, sinewy arm. With her love of modernity, Ayn Rant described John Galt I in metallic terms. Skin with the luster of iron freshly poured from the foundry. Hair like copper strands. The old man in front of me looked more like driftwood. Still, in his lean frame, facial features, and still clear blue eyes, I could see myself even more than I could in my father. I positioned two chairs in front of the wood stove and invited him to sit down. Lizzie lay in front of our feet.

"This is quite a surprise."

"It took me a while to find my courage, but I decided that I had to meet you and tell you my story."

His voice was strong and clear for such an old man. I began to relax about his identity. If he was going to tell me his story, then I would have ample opportunity to check for details that no con man could possibly know.

"Please. Take as long as you like."

"How old are you?

"Twenty-six."

"Then I will start when I was twenty-six and certain that I would change the world."

It was my grandfather. No doubt about it.

"I was the kind of person who thought that a man could do anything if he put his mind to it. No goal too large or far-fetched. If you could put a man on the moon, you could build a space colony on Mars or turn static electricity into an inexhaustible source of energy. When others said it couldn't be done, that just made me work harder and push the doubters out of the way.

"You can go far with that attitude. At least I did. I made lots of enemies but that didn't matter because I also made a few powerful friends who believed in my abilities and claims. I raced through engineering school and in no time had my own laboratory and financial backing to build my static electricity machine.

"There was only one problem. Reality. It turns out that the real world doesn't always yield to a man's mind. My critics were right. You can't make a machine powered by static electricity. Only I was too proud to admit it, or at least to admit that I couldn't do other great things, even if I had failed in that one case.

"That's when I went underground. The news reported that I took the plans for the static electricity machine with me but there were no plans. I had abandoned that project but couldn't let others know. Before that, I was guilty of arrogance but not of being a bald-faced liar. Now I was living with a bald-faced lie and it ate away at me like a cancer.

"The next great goal that I fastened upon was to show the world what a society of doers could do. It was easy to convince Midas Mulligan to bankroll the venture, although I had to maintain my lie about the static electricity engine. Other doers that I approached were easy to convince as well. They were so puffed up with their own sense of importance and scorn for anyone who stood in their way that it never crossed their minds that their success might be due to anything other than their own abilities.

"But boy, oh boy, if you want to disabuse yourself of that notion, just put a bunch of self-styled doers in a remote Colorado valley and let them try to form an ideal society! You never saw such a mess as all of them tried to get their way and push against each other! This was the second time that my mind pushed against reality and reality won. Have you ever felt like a total fraud?"

"Yes, actually, but nothing like this."

"Well, I was near rock bottom when Ayn joined the group and she pumped me up again. Until Ayn, all my relationships with women were short because the only ones who could stand being around me were so needy that I couldn't stand being around them. Ayn was my intellectual equal and I found it easy to get sucked back into my doer philosophy, even as I was thoroughly disproving it with my utopian experiment. We wrote the speech together, most of it naked after making love, at the same time that we were conceiving our son."

My grandfather paused and I could see from the faraway look on his face that he was reliving that time of his life. I fetched another two beers and we brought them together with a clink to acknowledge our newly forming bond. Then he continued his story.

"That seemed like the best time of my life, to be in love and off on a great crusade again. But when the hoax of the speech succeeded beyond our wildest dreams, I had a crisis of faith. I realized that my life was becoming enveloped by a tissue of lies. It was a lie that I could harness static electricity. It was a lie that the world was run by a class of doers. It was a lie that I had taken over the airwaves to deliver my speech. It was thanks only to lies that our great crusade could move forward.

"Ayn didn't have a problem with that. It was hard to admit, but when I peered through my love for her I was frightened by what I saw. She was a lie-monger who didn't live any of the values that she preached to others. Lying was so habitual for her that she didn't know any other way.

"I saw that I only had two choices. I could step into a world constructed entirely of lies or I could disappear. There was nothing noble about the decision I made. I had no pride or dignity left. I had become so weak that the only way I could make the decision was by impulse, by climbing onto my motorcycle in the dead of night and racing away with nothing but the clothes on my back.

"The faster I went, the more liberated I felt. Away! Away! But what toward? Maybe toward death. Death seemed like a pretty good option and I almost got my wish as I failed to make a hairpin turn on the mountain road and went hurling on my motorcycle through the air into the forest below.

"The next thing I knew, I was lying on the forest floor and a woman was kneeling over me. She had been driving the other way, saw my accident, parked her car, and rushed down to help me. I had separated from my motorcycle and hit the canopy of a big pine tree. Miraculously, I had bounced down the branches onto the forest floor and felt badly bruised but otherwise unhurt.

"'Thank God you're alive! Don't try to move,' she said. To my surprise, she started to feel my ankle with her hands and worked her way up my leg.

"'You're lucky that I'm a nurse. Tell me if anything hurts. It will be a miracle if you haven't broken any bones.' She checked my limbs, ribs, neck, and rolled me carefully over to check my back.

"'Unbelievable. Still, I think it's best for me to call an ambulance so they take you out of here on a stretcher. There's a gas station with a telephone booth a few miles down the road. Then I'll come back. Will you be OK by yourself?'

"'No!' My hand shot out and grabbed her wrist before she could stand to leave. Her face froze in fear.

"'Please!' I pleaded with her. 'You have nothing to fear! I would never hurt you! I have done nothing wrong! But I need to hide from something! Won't you please help me?'

"The woman looked in astonishment at my pleading face as I continued to grip her wrist.

"'Please don't call an ambulance! Take me to your car and drive me to someplace where I can hide! We can leave the motorcycle here! No one will find it! I will never harm you! I can explain later but I'm leaving something and can't be returned to it!'

"The woman's face softened a little and took on a puzzled look. There was an intelligence behind her eyes that wasn't frightened and was trying to figure me out. To my shame, I found myself noticing that she wasn't pretty and wore cheap clothes. How could I be noticing such things when I was pleading for her help?

"'If you're not going to hurt me, then take your hand off me.'

"Slowly, reluctantly, I released my grip. Now she could race off if she wanted to and call the police. But she didn't. She just backed away a little and continued staring into my eyes, as if that might be a better source of information than my words. Finally she spoke.

"'OK. I know what it means to hide. But watch your step. I also know how to take care of myself.'

"She helped me to my feet and up the steep forested slope to the road. My motorcycle was completely hidden and indeed might never be found. Who descends into the forest at the elbow of a hairpin turn? Even though no bones were broken, every muscle felt bruised and I moved like an old man. I move more easily now than I did on that night.

"'You're doubly lucky,' the woman said as she helped me into her car. 'Not only am I a nurse, but I live alone in a trailer in the woods. No one will find you there.'

"That's how I was able to make a clean break from my past. Her name was Beth. She was a country nurse, which meant that she visited people in their homes. She kept long hours, which is why she was on the road when I had my accident. When we got to her trailer, she said that my muscles and soft tissue would require time to heal and gave me her bed. She would sleep on the couch in the living room, she said, because I needed to lie flat and she could easily curl up. She seemed to think of my needs as a matter of course, as easily as she thought of her own needs."

I felt a lump in my throat. That's what I loved about Eve.

"Beth was right about needing to recover. Imagine the worst bruise you ever had and then imagine your whole body like that. I was the ugliest thing that you ever saw! For three days, I could barely hobble around the tiny trailer and spent most of my time in her bed, staring at her ceiling, with her cat, Whiskers, by my side, while she made the rounds of her patients. I never had a pet and scorned the idea of them, but I had to admit that Whiskers was a comfort. Stroking her fur and hearing her purr gave both of us pleasure.

"I was a staunch atheist and my miraculous escape from death was not going to change my mind on that score. Nevertheless, I was presented with the opportunity to be born again, and if there was no god, then it was up to me to create a new man out of myself. Since the word 'give' had been banned from the vocabulary of the Objectivists, I decided that the best way to begin my rebirth was to do the opposite; to restore the word 'give' and ban the word 'take.'

"Beth provided a role model. She would return from her long day tending her patients to take care of another dependent within her own home, which she did without complaint or a word about payment. It made me ashamed that the Galtians never did a single thing for each other without an exchange of coinage. Her phone was ringing constantly. As far as I could tell, most of the people on the other end of the line were her patients, who wanted even more of her attention than she was being paid to give during her visits. She was always kind to them, even when I could see that she was utterly exhausted. How could she give so much, and why was she getting so little in return?

"As soon as I could move around the tiny trailer, I started to give back, feeling like a toddler learning to walk on wobbly legs. The first thing I did was clean the house, which was pretty dirty given her long hours. It was a tiny trailer but it is amazing how fractal housecleaning can be, especially when you have time on your hands. I'd start to clean the stove top, and then I'd see that the knobs needed cleaning. Then I'd see that the grooves around the knobs needed cleaning, and when you removed the knobs to clean the grooves, the area behind the knobs needed cleaning. When she came home that evening, the trailer was gleaming and a simple soup was waiting for her. She was stunned and burst into tears. Why was she so surprised and grateful when I had done so little, compared to what she had done for me? The calculus of giving was completely different than the calculus of monetary exchange. I didn't pretend to understand it but I found it pretty simple to practice. All you did was give unsparingly.

"In such a tiny trailer, Beth was the exclusive object of my attention. When we ate together over the meals that I made, I asked her to tell me her story. This was the greatest gift that I gave to her and it took a while for her to accept it, like a squirrel learning to feed from someone's open hand. I learned that she had an abusive father and ran away when she was sixteen. She put herself through nursing school. The men in her life were nothing but trouble and one threatened to kill her if she left him. That's why she had to run away again and ended up in this trailer in the woods, hundreds of miles away. That must be what she meant when she said that she knew what it was like to hide.

"'Are you worried that he will find you?' I asked.

"'Not too much. In the first place, he's too stupid. In the second place, he's too lazy. In the third place, he's too much of a coward. In the fourth place, I have a gun and know how to use it.'

"Beth's look of confidence mixed with humor as she spoke these words made me laugh out loud. What strength! The more I talked with her, the more I grew to know a person who could be distinguished from her bodily form. That person was neither male nor female. The word 'soul' came to mind but stripped of any supernatural connotations. Beth's soul had feelings, values, and thoughts. It was shaped by its experiences and in turn shaped its experiences with its own actions.

Beth's soul was strong and giving but also capable of defending itself. Somehow it found a way to keep on giving, day after day, even though it received precious little in return. That made her soul beautiful to me.

"I felt impelled to use the word 'it' when thinking about Beth's soul because giving it a gender seemed like a distraction. My bodily form was male but I also had a soul – everyone does – that didn't have a gender. My soul had collapsed – my entire way of thinking, feeling, and behaving – and now I was trying to reconstruct it. I would give anything to have Beth's strong soul and perhaps I could by giving unstintingly. Being male or female had nothing to do with it.

"Then, to my surprise, I discovered that my admiration for Beth's soul was changing the way I viewed her bodily form. It was becoming more beautiful to me, to match my estimation of her soul. At first I was flustered by these thoughts. Who was I to make sexual advances, when I had nothing to give and men had been nothing but trouble in her life? Besides, she was opening up her soul to me while I remained a closed book to her. I had no right to seek closeness until I bared my soul, but the thought terrified me. We had been living together for three weeks before I found the courage. The house was immaculately clean, every possible repair had been made, every weed in her garden had been pulled and every vegetable plant staked, and I had started to cook fancy meals for her.

"'I ... am John Galt.'

"'John who?'

"She had never heard of me, my static electricity machine, my dramatic disappearance, or the speech. Whatever hot air that remained in my previous soul escaped with farting noises in my mind. I would have to tell her everything from scratch, and when I did it sounded ridiculous. Finally I gave up and cut to the bottom line.

"'Beth, the long and short of it is that I've been a taker all my life and I want to become a giver. Please help me learn to become a giver.'

"With those words, sexual attraction overcame both of us. We rushed into each other's arms and danced a tango to her bedroom, tearing each other's clothes from our bodies. I never knew what sex was before that night. Before it was always a conquest and performance, even with Ayn. This was a merging of our bodies into a dual organism."

An hour had passed as if in a minute. My grandfather broke the spell by saying that he needed to pee. So did Lizzie and I, so the three of us went outside to relieve ourselves underneath the starry sky and the brisk early November air. Then I gave him a tour of the Cell and told the story of its construction as also an act of giving. Returning to our seats, I placed a few more logs in the wood stove and he resumed his story.

"I'll keep it brief so you can get some sleep. Beth and I got married and had four wonderful kids. We moved to a village a few valleys over so we wouldn't be so isolated. There's always work for a country nurse and I made money fixing cars. Country folk are accustomed to paying cash under the table, so I didn't pay taxes or anything else that required me to have an identity. I grew a beard and long hair in a ponytail that gave me a different appearance, not that anyone around there would have recognized me. John Galt and his speech might be notorious in some circles, but not among just plain folk, and that suited me just fine.

"I did perform one final dishonest act. After doing some research, I discovered that it's not so difficult to forge a new identity, complete with a birth certificate and social security number, so that's what I did. Do you know what I changed my name to?"

"What?"

"John Wiser."

I laughed at the joke and reached my hand over to grasp his thin shoulder.

"Beth and I spent our lives in that little town until she passed at the age of eighty-seven. That would be eight years ago. Our kids are fine and I'm losing count of our grandkids. One of them brought me here. He's passing time down in Timber Ridge and will fetch me when I call him."

My grandfather called his other grandson on his cell phone.

"He says that he's been playing pool at the tavern and they're talking about you. They think you're real down to earth."

"That's the highest compliment I could ask for."

"There's one more thing that I came here to say."

"What's that, Grampa?"

"Even though I found the right way and had a good life, I never quite lost my ambition to change the world. In retrospect it was so simple. You can't power an engine from static electricity, but you can power an engine from giving if it is channeled in the right way. I finally succeeded in knowing how to fuel an engine with a potentially inexhaustible source of clean energy, but I didn't know how to scale it up. All I could do was foster it in my own family and community, while the rest of the world was being overrun by taking, thanks in large part to the soul-destroying creed that bears my name!

"That's what you, my own grandson, have accomplished. You've made giving the engine for the whole world. I can't claim any credit for it and please don't say a word about me to your father. I couldn't bear for him to know that I've been alive all these years without reaching out to him. He is part of my past life and all I could do was live a better new life. But I do keep a little pride that however convoluted, my path led to his path, which led to your path, which led to a better world. I'm proud of you."

The headlights down the hill signaled that one of my grandfather's other grandsons had arrived. I leaned down and enveloped him in a hug, being careful not to break the fragile bodily form that contained such a beautiful soul, which disappeared back into the night.

The Homecoming

My Darling Avatar Eve,

Winter has finally descended upon Timber Ridge with its first major snowfall. Lizzie is thrilled to be catching snowballs again and I am thrilled to be back on snowshoes, bringing back memories of our race and start of our love. A month has now passed since returning from Philadelphia. I expected the savoring of every moment that Howard and I experienced to wane, but it seems to have become our permanent state of mind. I wonder if this is what the Buddhists describe as Nirvana.

One reason for such contentment is to have turned the tide of human history in a way that doesn't require our further effort. Politics has become transformed, for example. Candidates of all parties are rushing to embrace the principles of True Objectivism, especially the idea that the rightful place for the American flag, and all national flags, is below Earth in our vertical column of symbols, not at the top. The very concept of left vs. right is changing, as we hoped it would. Individuals are joining the movement and forming into groups — the greening and blooming of the planet Earth on our website — at a record pace, thanks in part to camp meetings that are now taking place around the world, even in Ecuador!

The fact that I have become capable of savoring every moment does not mean that I lack sadness or that I will become some kind of celibate monk who forsakes all the pleasures of life. On the contrary, it is the pleasures of daily life that I savor and continue to want to savor with you, more strongly than ever before!

Angelina visits me often and we talk about our dilemma openly now. She pleads with me to make love but I tell her that only your death or certain knowledge that our paths will never merge again can release me. My ability to withstand her advances is another sign that I have achieved Nirvana. The Buddha is reputed to have said if a second urge as strong as the sex urge existed, even he couldn't have done it!

But I can't put Angelina off forever. I know that our paths could joyfully merge. If these letters are finding you, then please answer to release me. A single sentence will do. If there is no answer, then I must travel to Ecuador to confirm what I fear most – your passing from the Earth.

Forever yours,

John

The frigid air felt great against my skin as I walked from the Cell to my mailbox on the edge of my property to mail my most recent letter to Eve. The wind picked up the fallen snow and whirled it into the air before redepositing it in drifts. A pale sun peeked through an angry sky announcing that more snow would be on the way soon. Lizzie bounded around me, in her own doggy Nirvana, encouraging me to throw snowballs for her to catch.

Fresh tire tracks, not yet covered by the blowing snow, revealed that the mailman had already come. My avatar Eve would need to wait an extra day to read my newest letter. The lid of the mailbox was cold against my fingers as I opened it, with a prick of hope at seeing a powder blue envelope that never died. Once again I was disappointed and retrieved the wad of mail, which included an unusual looking thick manila envelope. With a shock I recognized Eve's handwriting, even her name written with the return address on the top left corner, as normal as could be. She was alive! Eve was alive!

Turning, I churned passed the ENOUGH sign back up the hill with Lizzie bounding around me. I entered the utility area on the ground floor, threw off my outdoor clothes and raced up the stairs to the kitchen area in my sock feet. I opened the manila envelope and shook out its contents. Out came a flurry of powder blue envelopes that lay on the table like big flower petals. Each envelope was numbered on the bottom left corner to indicate the order in which I should read them. With trembling hands, I inserted the small blade of my pocketknife along the edge of the first to open it, carefully, as if it was a priceless object, which indeed it was.

John,

It is with a trembling hand that I write you, not knowing what to think or do. I don't even know how to address you. With the terms of endearment that I feel — dear, darling, precious — or as someone I left and whose intimacy I no longer have any claim upon? All I can do is tell you my story and let you judge for yourself.

Well you know my joy at coming down here, now over five years ago, to help turn this region into an ecological reserve for the rain forest and a cultural reserve for the Shuar. At first it was everything that I dreamt it would be. Wild child that I am, I felt more at home spending my days in the jungle than in the modern world. But soon enough I realized that the modern world hadn't gone away. It was always hovering around the world that I was trying to conserve, like an unseen malevolent force.

My Shuar friends knew about that malevolent force and had been dealing with it for five centuries. It's not that they were "noble savages" or even conservationists on their own. Their deep history was to live in tiny groups that warred with each other unless united by a common enemy. And their economy was for the tiny groups to exploit their immediate environment and then move on to a new location.

Nevertheless, amazingly for such a fragmented people, they found ways to band together to repel first the Inca and then the Spanish, maintaining their sovereignty up to the present. That's not to say that they isolated themselves. They craved the axes, machetes, and guns that were so superior to their tools and weapons, but they found ways to trade for them on their own terms, often paying with the shrunken heads of their enemies that earned them such a reputation as a fierce people.

Even more amazing, they found allies in the Catholic mission-aries, who helped to put an end to their incessant internal strife and form into a federation of villages. They sent representatives to the national government in Quito and served proudly in the military, while still maintaining a strong tribal identity. Now, an enlightened administration had decided that the Shuar territory was more valuable as an ecological reserve administered by the Shuar than exploiting its resources. The Shuar might not have been conservationists in the past, but they were capable of assuming a new role, especially with their incredible knowledge of all of the plants and animals in the rainforest. That's what I was to become a part of to help bring about.

But it was so fragile! The more I learned about South American politics, the more menacing and chaotic it seemed. Americans don't know how good they have it. Between authoritarian regimes on the right and Marxist regimes on the left, the average citizen is left destitute and unprotected. Ecuador had risen above that and was beginning to function as a democracy capable of making enlightened decisions such as the formation of an ecological reserve, but it could become dragged back into chaos at any time. The timber and oil interests weren't about to take no for an answer and had plenty of right wing politicians on hand to press their case. The ruination of all of my efforts always seemed like just an election away. And this time it wouldn't be just another cycle of corruption and exploitation. It would be the permanent destruction of an ecosystem that had existed for millions upon millions of years — including our precious Eden — never to return again on the face of the Earth. Realizing this was like a heavy weight on my shoulders that I could not put down.

Then, the hovering menace became all too real in a single day. A splinter group of the Shining Path, the Peruvian Marxist move-ment, crossed the border and massacred one of the Shuar villages — men, women, children, and priests — without any provocation whatsoever. The Shuar nation was as angry as a hornet's nest and ready to charge into Peru to retaliate, which could precipitate a war. The massacre made no sense, unless its purpose was to provoke just such a response.

It was all that government representatives and I could do to hold them back. As you know, I have a special status among the Shuar as a monkey woman with potent soul power. I strongly suspected that this splinter group was in league with powerful Ecuadorian and maybe even international interests who wanted to upset the fragile democracy. Ideology had nothing to do with it. The Shining Path splinter groups were fighting against each other and it wouldn't surprise me in the least if one of them teamed up with powerful interests of any sort to get the upper hand. Ideology counts for nothing when your survival is at stake. But how could I prove my theory? The only way was to infiltrate the splinter group and gather the evidence that I needed.

That was the plan that I got the Shuar federation and government representatives to agree upon. I flew back home to gather up all the money I could and to say goodbye to you. John, if only you knew how much it broke my heart to see the delight on your face when you opened the door, only to break your heart with the news that our paths must diverge, just when you needed me the most. It was the hardest thing I ever did and left an indelible scar on me. That scar would not be the last.

Rebel groups are said to hide out in the jungle but they can never hide from the locals. It's just a matter of whether the locals decide to tell the authorities. And since the authorities are often as brutal and corrupt as the rebels, the locals often remain silent. After all, it is the rebels who are there and the authorities are not. The locals might even support the rebels if they are seen as the lesser of two evils. Also, the locals have their own social network that preceded national boundaries by centuries. Even enemy tribes traded goods and information across long distances when it was in their interests. Word spread fast that a powerful monkey woman was going to confront the splinter group and it captured everyone's imagination. It was like the revenge of indigenous cultures against modern life. I traveled fast across jungle paths guided by the locals, and when we came to the edge of their territory, there was another group of locals waiting to continue me on my journey. I stayed in their humble households as their honored guest. In return, they asked me to share my soul power to cure their illnesses and bless their children, which I did by laying hands upon them and muttering incantations in English, for them a foreign tongue. This did not seem strange to me, because it was little different than the laying on of hands that I had witnessed so many times in my own Christian church.

Crossing the border into Peru was easy. There are no check points in the jungle. By the time I arrived in the neighborhood of the splinter group's camp, I had learned that its leader was a man named Carlos Cortez. He was described as a "nobody" before the massacre, but now he was acting like a big man. Somebody had given him a lot of arms and supplies for what he had done, but who?

In the hours before dawn, I was guided by the locals to their camp. They were asleep and felt no need to post sentries. Still, I did not want to approach too closely on foot, so I climbed a tree about 100 meters away and entered the canopy. As you know, in the rainforest the canopy is a dense web of the branches of adjacent trees connected by vines. That's how the monkeys move about, and that's how the monkey woman did also, until I found a perch directly above their camp. It's funny how terrestrial animals never think to look up. That's why deer hunters hunt in tree stands and I could eavesdrop on their conversation in plain sight.

As dawn broke, they emerged from their tents and began their day. There were only about a dozen of them and it was easy to identify the person at the center of attention. He wasn't particularly handsome and no larger than the others. He didn't speak in a commanding voice but still had something about him that commanded the respect of the others – leadership given rather than taken. I couldn't guess his ethnicity. Maybe he was a mongrel, like me.

Since their conversation was unguarded, it didn't take long for me to confirm my suspicions. They had carried out the massacre on behalf of some powerful patrons. Names were mentioned that I didn't recognize. The main topic of conversation was why the massacre had not provoked the intended response and whether another one might be called for. There was also talk of what they would do with all of the money that they would be receiving. There was no talk of the people's struggle or Marxist ideology. It was exactly as I surmised. Carlos Cortez was out for himself, or maybe himself and his tiny group of buddies. Big ideas had nothing to do with it and were only slapped on for appearances.

Carlos and two of his buddies prepared to go into town for Carlos to make some transactions. They entered one of the tents and came out with automatic weapons. No local could resist that kind of force, especially since it had been used upon them in the past, by government forces and other Shining Path factions if not this one. As soon as they left the camp, I left my perch as quietly as a monkey (when a monkey wants to!) and made my way through the canopy to a place where I could descend to Earth without being noticed. I ran back to the compound of the locals who had guided me to the camp, and they guided me to the neighboring town. I used some of my money to buy some fresh clothes and a suitcase. I checked into a hotel, cleaned myself up, and left transformed from monkey woman to modern society woman.

It wasn't hard to find Carlos and his two companions in that dusty little town. They were in one of the only cafes that had Internet service. They were sitting around a table with Carlos on his laptop and the other two looking bored. Their weapons were carelessly strewn about, since the government had no presence in this region of Peru and no other Shining Path factions were contesting it either. They were the law and they knew it. Taking a deep breath, I strode directly to their table.

"Carlos Cortez."

All three of them nearly fell out of their chairs in a mad scramble for their weapons, which they trained upon me. I was one finger twitch away from death.

"How do you know my name?" Carlos asked menacingly.

"I come bearing greetings from Presidente Gonzolo."

All three of their jaws dropped open. Presidente Gonzolo was the Shining Path's title for Abimael Guzman, the founder of the movement. He had been captured years ago and was languishing in jail, but he still commanded utmost respect. It was not unthinkable that he continued to wield power behind bars. To be contacted by

Presidente Gonzolo was the highest honor that could possibly be bestowed upon a member of the Shining Path movement. That's why he was my ticket for infiltrating their group. I continued.

"Presidente Gonzolo admires your bold action carrying the movement into Ecuador and wants to help you"

A long silence ensued as they tried to absorb this information, while their weapons continued to point in my direction. Could this possibly be true? Presidente Gonzolo was only a mythical figure to them. So was the entire Shining Path movement, for that matter, which had deteriorated into its warring factions. The idea that there might still be a movement, that it continued to be directed by its founder, and that they were at its vanguard seemed too good to be true. At length, Carlos spoke.

"How can we know that you come from the Presidente?"

"You can't. But how else could I know your name, where you are, and what you have so bravely done?"

Indeed, they could think of no other explanation, so slowly their guns came down. I accompanied them back to their camp. The others were shocked to see me. Leaving me under the guard of one of them, the others rushed off to discuss me. I could hear them chattering away, although I couldn't hear their words. When they returned, they evidently had decided that I must be who I said I was, which placed them in a dilemma. They never talked Marxist ideology among themselves and now they needed to recite the catechism to no less than an emissary from the grand master. They also had to conceal the identity of their powerful patrons, who were the very imperial and capitalist enemies that the Shining Path had declared war against!

I wish I could say that I had devised this plan from the beginning, but it was pure improvisation. Luckily, I knew enough about the Shining Path movement to take advantage of it. I knew that they conducted long sessions examining each other's doctrinal purity, which was really a form of competition for power, a bit like the way you described the way your grandmother and father made everyone check their premises. I wasn't just a woman walking into their camp. I was a grand inquisitor, and if I knew their whereabouts, then who else did? They were terrified of me! I must admit that I made the most of the comical situation, forcing them to rack their brains about Presidente Gonzolo's peculiar rendering of Marx and Mao and pile lie upon lie about where their support came from. It was almost too easy!

John, it is difficult for me to tell you about what came next. Please remember that the only way that I could proceed on my path was to make a clean break with you and to think that it would be forever. I told my Shuar friend who was collecting my mail to destroy any letters that were powder blue. I couldn't bear to do what I needed to do if you were still lingering in my mind.

The next part of my plan was to come on to Carlos Cortez. Men have the power of force over women and women have the power of sex over men. As a mover and adventuress, I wasn't afraid to use it. Seducing Carlos Cortez was absurdly easy. During my second day in camp, I slipped into the jungle and made a bed of giant leaves. Then, when everyone had retired, I woke him gently with a finger on my lips to remain quiet and led him to the place. He couldn't believe his good luck. First he was the anointed successor of Presidente Gonzolo and now his grand inquisitor was about to become his lover! He made love to me like an animal. Afterward, we lay naked, side by side on the bed of giant leaves, looking up at the sky through the canopy of trees, and began to talk.

John, now I come to the part that is most difficult to confess to you. I would conceal it from anyone else, but you — or at least the avatar of you in my mind — insist upon knowing the truth so I must give it to you.

Do you remember when I told you about the bad boys that I used to date and how they opened up after having sex? How they shared their sad lives, their vulnerabilities and their doubts? How they craved a sympathetic ear even more than sex? How they fell in love in a single night, even though they thought it was going to be a one-night stand? Well, with Carlos you could multiply that by ten. No American boy could possibly fathom the hardships he endured growing up in the slums of Lima or his resilience and resourcefulness in making something of himself, starting with nothing. And something like that is never done alone. He succeeded with a tiny group of friends who would die for each other. The fact that they were running drugs and that they would also kill for each other was taken for granted. It was the only game in town, the game of us versus them, that has been played for eternity in one way or another. Carlos and his tiny group of friends played it well and he became their acknowledged leader for his street smarts, courage, and generosity. All of this came pouring out of him as we lay naked on our bed of leaves, staring at the night sky through the canopy of trees.

When I tried to put together the suffering inflicted upon Carlos with the suffering he was inflicting upon others, all I could think of were the last words of Jesus upon the Cross: "Father, forgive them, for they know not what they do."

Oh, John, please forgive me! Now that you are coming back into my mind, if not my life, through this letter, it kills me to tell you this, but those words caused me to fall in love with Carlos on that night. You were part of a past life and he was the living embodiment of my own ancestors! He was my half-breed great-great-grandfather, whose only choice in life was to be an outlaw and who did it well!

He was no different from my Shuar friends, who until a blink of time ago killed and shrunk the heads of their enemies as a matter of course! He was no different from the Spanish conquistadors who gave him his surname or the powerful patrons funding him to massacre innocent people — patrons who were merely playing the eternal game of us vs. them at a larger scale and paying others to do their dirty work for them! Carlos Cortez was my people, all people!

Do you think that the others in camp became jealous of my affair with Carlos? Hardly! As his lover, how could I go hard on them for their doctrinal purity? They all breathed a collective sigh of relief and began treating me as one of them. They even began to drop their guard about the source of their arms and supplies after I indicated that winning the good fight sometimes required consorting with one's enemies. We were men (and one woman) of action, not armchair theorists.

The fact that I had fallen in love with Carlos did not alter what needed to be done. I learned that a second massacre was indeed in the planning and would take place in a couple of weeks. I found it easy to slip away to the compound of the locals who originally showed me the camp and send word to my Shuar men who were waiting to hear from me. A week before the planned incursion into Ecuador, I once again roused Carlos from his sleep with my finger to my lips and led him to my bed of leaves, lighting our way with a little battery-powered lantern. As we removed our clothes, I placed the lantern close by and left it on.

"I want to see you when we make love," I said.

We had been making love every few nights and Carlos had learned to become gentle. I pulled him on top and we gazed into each other's eyes as we began to make love. There was the soft sound of a night bird. I gripped his hair with my hands and pulled his head against the nape of my neck so he wouldn't see me crying. Lovers and soul mates, who happened to fall on either side of the us-them divide. There was a second call of the night bird and a sharp puff of wind that nobody would have heard if they hadn't been expecting it. Five poison darts entered Carlos's back in a tight cluster. The Shuar can hit a bird the size of a sparrow with their blowguns and they hadn't missed.

Carlos leaped up with a cry, as if he had been stung by bees, while I scrambled onto my own feet and threw my clothes back on. He plucked out one of the darts and stared at it uncomprehendingly. He shifted his gaze to me and then past me as five figures climbed down from the trees and stepped into the lantern's light, my Shuar men who I had summoned with my message. Then a sixth man, much older than the others, stepped from the shadows and joined them – the Shaman who had given me the monkey necklace.

They were dressed not in western clothes but in the old way, with body markings and feathered headdresses that I had never seen, except in the photographs of books written by the first westerners to live among the Shuar. Each held a blowgun in his hand. The old Shaman was more highly ornamented than the others, with a shrunken human head around his neck. These had become illegal but that didn't prevent the Shuar from keeping them in secret and bringing one out for this occasion.

I, too, had placed my shrunken head around my neck and took my place in a ring that we formed around Carlos, who had sunk down, naked, on his hands and knees. I will never, ever, forget the expression on his face, like a tragic mask, as my deception and his impending death dawned upon him. The poison was already starting to work its way through his system.

The old Shaman spoke in a high unearthly voice that sent chills down my spine. It was as if he was not speaking but that a spirit was speaking through him.

"Why did you visit death upon the Shuar?"

"Forgive me!"

"God only forgives those who confess their sins!"

This invocation of the Christian God through the medium of the Shuar spirit world, a world that preceded Christianity by many thousands of years, sent another round of chills down my spine. At a signal from the old Shaman, one of the men placed a gourd with a stopper in front of Carlos. Another placed a smart phone next to it and turned on a voice recorder. Another weird juxtaposition of the modern and ancient. The old Shaman continued in his high unearthly voice.

"This drink can save you but first you must confess your sins. Who caused you to do this great evil?"

"Please! I can't feel my hands or feet!"

"Then speak!"

Carlos spoke into the smart phone. His words came gushing out. Everything that I had heard in camp and much that I had not heard. Toward the end his speech started to slur. The poison was spreading to his chest and larynx.

"Please! I have told you everything! I can't breathe!"

One of the men retrieved the smart phone and turned off the audio recorder. Then the old Shaman stepped forward and picked up the gourd. Slowly, ceremoniously, he removed the stopper and turned the gourd upside down. Nothing came out.

"There is no cure for the poison within you. The most we can do is hasten your death."

One by one, the men withdrew a little dart from a satchel around their neck, fitted it into their blowguns, and blew it into Carlos's body. When they finished, the old man withdrew a second dart from his satchel and held it toward me. I knew what was demanded of the monkey woman. I must validate the execution by taking part in it. I took the dart by its feathered end and plunged it into his back. The poison had spread to his face and frozen it into a tragic mask that could not register his response to the final act of his lover.

When Carlos Cortez died, something inside me died with him. I was in a state of shock and barely able to follow the commands of the old Shaman. They took images of him with the smart phone.

"You cannot see what happens next," one of the men said as he led me away. Soon enough we were joined by the others and I knew what had happened next. The old man was carrying something bulky in a bloodstained pouch. It was Carlos's head.

Our trek back to Shuar territory was a prolonged celebration. Word of what we had done raced ahead of us through the social network of the locals. Each contingent that escorted us through their territory treated us as heroes. My soul power became so great that I was treated as a goddess. The five young men who took part in the execution were especially ecstatic. They had been told stories of the glory days of the Shuar but now they had lived it. During the evenings, they would leave me with our hosts and slip away with the old man. I knew from the old anthropological accounts that they were processing the head; peeling the skin from the skull, rubbing it with charcoal to preserve it, holding it over a fire to shrink it.

I should have been satisfied as well. I had accomplished every-thing that I set out to do. The Shuar had their revenge against the first massacre without precipitating a war. A second massacre had been averted. Best of all, Carlos had revealed all of his patrons, who indeed extended nationally and internationally to those who wished to disrupt Ecuador's fragile democracy. But I couldn't rejoice because I couldn't feel anything. My soul felt as empty and hollow as that gourd that was placed in front of Carlos.

After we returned to my home village, I made a trip to Quito with the ghastly images of Carlos, naked on his hands and knees, his face a frozen tragic mask, darts sticking out of his body like a pin cushion. I made copies and mailed them to every person that Carlos had implicated, along with a sheet of paper with two words in big block letters: BACK OFF. I did take a grim pleasure imagining each villain opening the envelope, the shock of seeing the image, and the flurry of phone calls confirming that everyone else associated with the conspiracy had received the same warning. Back off they did. The most right-wing candidate for the presidential election even dropped out, citing poor health.

My work on the ecological reserve could resume but my passion for it had been extinguished. Life itself had lost its purpose for me. I had achieved a victory, but I had not won the war of us against them. That war would take place endlessly and at ever larger scales until life on Earth became destitute. Our Eden and everything surrounding it would be obliterated, if not now, then ten years from now. If not ten years, then twenty or thirty. There was no stopping it, so what was the use of trying?

I don't know how many weeks passed in this state, going through the motions without any joy of any kind. Then, while taking a bus to Quito, I saw the strangest sight. It was a field of white domed tents, with triangular flags on top like a Renaissance fair. Curious, I exited the bus and walked back to the field. It was late afternoon and people were beginning to light campfires at the entrance to each tent. They were wearing green and white windbreakers with curious symbols down each arm: a dot, a circle, the Ecuadorian flag, and the planet Earth. Although everyone was wearing the same jacket, I could see from their faces and other clothes that they came from all walks of life. You would never see such a collection of people anywhere else. And their faces were beaming with contentment.

"What is this?" I asked one of them.

"Haven't you heard? It is the campfire movement of John Galt!"

"John Galt!" I cried, and tears burst from my eyes. It was the first time in weeks that I had felt anything. I registered for the event and spent two days there in the company of you on the screen and

the rotating planet, greening and blooming in front of my eyes. My God, I thought. He's done it. He's actually done it.

When I returned to my village, I couldn't help talking about my experience to my friends, including the one who had been keeping my mail during my own trek.

"John Galt? You mean your John Galt?" she asked.

"Yes," I answered, "but he isn't mine anymore."

"Are you sure? Let me show you something."

My friend disappeared into another room and returned with a stack of powder blue envelopes held together by a rubber band.

"You told me to destroy these, but I couldn't bring myself to do it. I knew that the time might come when you would want to see them."

A fresh burst of tears sprang from my eyes as I rushed to embrace her. I knew where I had to read them – in Eden. I was there within an hour. One by one I read your letters where we used to lie together by the waterfall, chronicling your own amazing path. Every time you began with "My darling avatar Eve," more tears sprang to my eyes. To think that you actually created a mental clone of me to remain with you on your own journey. I'm so proud that I could be with you in spirit while my body was on its separate journey.

John, the real Eve is no longer the same as your darling avatar Eve. My soul has been wounded and I don't know if it can recover. I have no right to make a claim upon you. Angelina deserves you. She is strong and you can be happy together. But John, I am too weak to let you go like that. If you will have me, I want to heal and become once again the Eve that you have preserved in your mind. I want to be with you in Eden and feel joy that it will forever be safe from destruction. I want to have dinner with you and my family at the Ranch. I want to wake up with you and Lizzie in your Cell. I want to have children with you. I want to have a normal life with you. A glorious, normal life!

The Science Behind *Atlas Hugged*

Atlas Hugged is first and foremost an academic critique of the ideas of Ayn Rand and their impact on the world. Since Rand developed and disseminated her ideas in both fictional and nonfictional form, I, too, have transcended that boundary, but every major theme in *Atlas Hugged* can be supported by contemporary science – something that cannot be said for her philosophy of Objectivism.

In this epilogue, I will briefly cross over from fiction to non-fiction to explore the science behind the major themes of *Atlas Hugged*, along with resources for you to learn more.

On the Concept of a Stylized Universe

Nathaniel Branden was a disciple of Ayn Rand who also became her lover and later wrote an expose of her movement titled *Judgment Day: My Years with Ayn Rand*. Like my fictional character of Elena Lane, Branden was captivated by Rand as a teenager because it appealed to his sense of possibility at the dawn of his adult life. It was Branden who described Rand's cosmology as a "stylized universe," a phrase that delighted her, and described being part of her movement as like flying in the air over the real world, which appeared unendurably dull by comparison.

What does it mean for a worldview to be a "stylized universe" and to be "better than real," as I put it in *Atlas Hugged*? Let's begin with our genetically evolved ability to see the world through our eyes. We do not see the world as it really is. Our eyes are sensitive to only a narrow slice of the light spectrum, which we process in a way that turns them into discrete colors rather than the continuum that actually exists. These "falsehoods" evolved because they are superior to more accurate perceptions of the world in helping us to survive and reproduce. When it comes to survival and reproduction, our distorted ability to see is quite literally better than real. The same can be said for all our other senses (sound, smell, taste, touch), along with forces in the real world (such as mild electrical currents) that we can't sense at all because they are irrelevant to our fitness, but other species (such as electric eels) can because it *is* relevant to *their* fitness.

It is sobering to reflect that our culturally evolved worldviews are no different than our genetically evolved perceptual abilities in this regard. Why do most of us regard ourselves as above average? Why do we demonize our enemies? Why do we invent invisible gods and glorious pasts for our ancestors that any historian can easily debunk? Because these "adaptive fictions" help us to survive and reproduce in the real world better than more accurate perceptions of reality. They are better than real.

It's not as if an accurate perception of reality counts for nothing. Sometimes it is crucial, as when a hunter needs to know the exact location of his prey to capture it. Anthropologists have documented that people around the world have the ability to toggle back and forth between a factual reasoning mode and an "adaptive fiction" mode, depending upon the context. This is also exactly what we should expect from an evolutionary perspective.

As a familiar example, imagine that you are about to testify in court, which requires placing your hand upon the bible and reciting, "I vow to tell the truth, the whole truth, and nothing but the truth, so help me God." What just happened? In the first place, you have committed to sticking to the facts of the matter in your testimony, because this is a context where knowing what actually happened is important. In the second place, you invoked a religious belief system that subordinates people to their gods and leaves you no excuse whatsoever if you get caught lying. Factual realism mode and adaptive fiction mode have been artfully blended together to determine the facts of the matter, which is the main point of a court proceeding.

It is very important to avoid confusing adaptive fiction mode with religion. Religions richly indulge in adaptive fictions with their gods, but they also operate in factual reasoning mode in certain contexts, as we just saw with court proceedings. Secular worldviews don't invoke any gods (by definition) but most of them richly indulge in adaptive fictions in other ways. A great book on this topic is *The Invention of Tradition*, a collection of scholarly essays edited by the historians Eric Hobsbawm and Terence Ranger. How a culture imagines its past is at least as consequential for motivating and structuring action as how it imagines its gods. Hence, nearly every culture fabricates its traditions and attributes much more antiquity to them than the facts warrant, as any competent historian can show.

Against this background, my description of Ayn Rant in *Atlas Hugged* describes a propensity in all of us as individuals and whole cultures as accumulations of individual biases:

> *She was like a mosaic artist using truth as her tiles. If a particular fact fit, she would use it intact. Otherwise she would clip it until its shape was just right. Remaining gaps were filled with wholesale fictions presented as fact. The completed work of art acted like a magic spell to convince people of the reasonableness of the Objectivist creed.*

To the extent that Ayn Rand's philosophy of Objectivism indulges in adaptive fictions, it is little different than a religion such as Christianity. But there is one big difference. Religions rely upon their imagined gods for their authority. As an atheist, Rand was forced to invoke the authority of science and rational thought – the very thing she was departing from with her adaptive fictions! Hence, what John Galt III observed about Ayn Rant also goes for Ayn Rand:

> *The biggest deception of all was to call the movement Objectivism, as if it could be fully validated by rationality and science!*

Did Ayn Rand intend her deceptions and their consequences? As John Galt III realized, the most important answer to this question is *it doesn't matter*. My most recent nonfiction book, *This View of Life: Completing the Darwinian Revolution*, begins with this quote from the philosopher Albert Camus' novel *The Plague*:

> *The evil in the world comes almost always from ignorance, and goodwill can cause as much damage as ill-will if it is not enlightened … There is no true goodness or fine love without the greatest possible degree of clear-sightedness.*

This passage perfectly describes Alan Greenspan, another Ayn Rand disciple, who had an enormous impact on US economic policy over a period of decades. By all accounts he was a decent man who thought he was doing the right thing for his country and the world. He was dumbfounded by the economic collapse of 2008, which finally convinced him of the errors of his free market views. Hence, it is important to avoid getting too distracted over the intentions of people and concentrate on the consequences of their ideas. This is why John Galt III ended up feeling compassion for Ayn Rant as an intrepid explorer who just happened to take a wrong path, which can be extended to Ayn Rand as well.

Is it possible to actually prove that Rand's creed of Objectivism is little different than a religion such as Christianity in its reliance on adaptive fictions? A hallmark of adaptive fictions is that they portray a world without messy tradeoffs, as if the only choice is between a path to glory and a path to ruin. Back in 1995 I wrote an article titled "Language as a Community of Interacting Belief Systems: A Case Study Involving Conduct Toward Self and Others," which was published in the academic journal *Biology and Philosophy*[1]. It was one of my first explorations of the idea that human worldviews can be like life forms that interact with each other in cultural ecosystems, similar to the interactions among species in biological ecosystems. If so, then each "species of thought" (the title of one of my other articles published five

---

1 Wilson, D. S. (1995). Language as a community of interacting belief systems: a case study involving conduct toward self and others. *Biology and Philosophy, 10*, 77–97.

years earlier[2]) would necessarily use key words such as "altruism" and "selfishness" in different ways. The usages would be largely consistent within each worldview but discordant between worldviews, in the same way that genetic interactions are largely harmonious within each biological species but become discordant when different species mate with each other.

To test my hypothesis, I chose a number of texts representing different worldviews and scored every word and phrase that referred to conduct toward self and others. For any given usage, the effect on self might be positive or negative and the effect on others might be positive or negative, leading to four combinations (+/+, +/-, -/+, -/-). In the real world, one expects to find all four combinations. In other words, if you and I were to interact with each other, a given behavior might benefit both of us (+/+), me but not you (+/-), you but not me (-/+), or might harm both of us (-/-). But in some of the texts that I examined, only the win-win and lose-lose situations were represented, as if there are never any messy tradeoffs. That might be a good way to motivate behavior, but it's a lousy description of the real world. In other words, it's a sure sign of an adaptive fiction.

Here is one example from a 17th century Christian text. Words such as "brotherli-ness," "faithfulness," and even "sacrifice" and "surrender" are portrayed as good for both self and others. Words such as "arrogance," "individu-ality," and "selfishness" are portrayed as bad for both self and others. There was not a single word or phrase

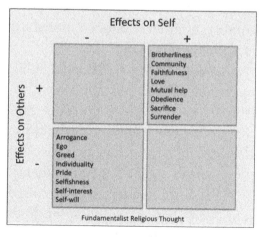

acknowledging behaviors in the (+/- or -/+) quadrants! This is clearly a departure from factual reality that makes life easy and motivating for

2 Wilson, D. S. (1990). Species of thought: a comment on evolutionary epistemology. *Biol and Phil*, 5, 37–62.

the believer. Simply express the behaviors in the (+,+) quadrant and avoid the behaviors in the (-,-) quadrant and everything will be OK.

Here is an analysis of a collection of essays published by Ayn Rand and Nathaniel Branden titled *The Virtue of Selfishness*, published in 1961. Note that this is Ayn Rand in nonfiction mode, not fiction mode. As with the Christian text, only two quadrants are occupied, but the words and phrases in them have been turned upside down. Now

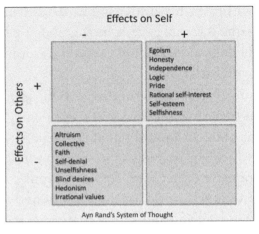

it is the virtues of individualism that benefit everyone and a mix of the conventional virtues and stupid forms of selfishness that harm everyone. Hence, Ayn Rand's worldview is very different from the Christian worldview in the behaviors that they motivate, but they are just alike in how they do it – by portraying an imaginary world without tradeoffs. Ayn Rand even claimed outright that "there are no conflicts of interest among rational men" (p 50), words that I also put in the mouth of Ayn Rant.

At the very least, Ayn Rand's philosophy of Objectivism does count as a moral system. It is not correct to say that she licensed selfishness without regard to the welfare of others. She preached a form of selfishness that, in her own mind, was best for society as a whole. As John Galt III put it, "the true Objectivist [in Ayn Rant's mind] was a paragon of moral virtue, even if the new morality differed from the old."

This is the academic background for my fictional portrayal of John Galt III and Eve Eden, both searching for "a way to tell right from wrong without peering through a tissue of lies." Eve's tissue was Christianity, John's tissue was Objectivism, and their quest was to seek a worldview that operates entirely in factual reasoning mode, scrupulously avoiding adaptive fictions but nevertheless providing a compelling guide to action. John's first breakthrough was his commitment to operate in factual reasoning mode by joining the "Cult of

Scholars." But he quickly realizes that this isn't good enough, because the fortress of scholarly books that he stacks around him doesn't tell him how to act. That requires his second breakthrough: The key to ending self-imposed suffering, which can be justified entirely by science, is the construction of a planetary superorganism.

Would the World Be Much Different if Ayn Rand Never Existed?

When John Galt III goes to college and takes Economics 101, he is dismayed by what he encounters:

> *These ideas filled me with confusion and anxiety. My economics professor was saying that society works best when people are allowed to make as much money as possible for themselves, unfettered by rules and regulations. That was the creed of my grandmother and father, but they weren't mentioned by my professor or my economics textbook. The ideal Objectivist portrayed by Ayn Rant was nothing like a flesh and blood person. Neither was Homo economicus, but the two fictions were also different from each other! My grandmother and father claimed that Objectivist principles were fully supported by science, but they never used a single equation or graph. Economists seemed to use nothing but equations and graphs and their first fundamental theorem made it sound as if "laissez faire leads to the common good" had the same certainty as Newton's Laws of Motion. How on earth could I stand up to such certainty, when I couldn't even understand the graphs and equations that were filling the blackboard during the first week of Econ 101?*

The disconnect between Ayn Rand's philosophy of Objectivism and economic theory, other than providing separate justifications for the pursuit of self-interest, is a fact that I imported into my fiction. Truth be told, even within economic theory there are two major justifications for the pursuit of self-interest, one based on the work of Friedrich Hayek and another based on the work of Milton Friedman, which are difficult to reconcile with each other. And all of these fall within a still broader intellectual tradition called Individualism that is the true target of my critique in *Atlas Hugged*. While Ayn Rand gave expression to individualism, if she never existed the tradition would probably have been just as strong and influential.

Individualism is the claim that the individual person is the fundamental unit of analysis and that everything social can be understood in terms of the motives and actions of individuals. It has deep historical roots but didn't become dominant until the second half of the 20th century. Up until then, the dominant intellectual tradition envisioned society as something that cannot be reduced to individual psychology or even biology. Here are two quotes that I often use in my academic writing to illustrate the watershed change that took place.

Social commentators once found it very useful to analyze the behavior of groups by the same expedient used in analyzing the behavior of individuals. The group, like the person, was assumed to be sentient, to have a form of mental activity that guides action. Rousseau (1767) and Hegel (1807) were the early architects of this form of analysis, and it became so widely used in the 19th and early 20th centuries that almost every early social theorist we now recognize as a contributor to modern social psychology held a similar view.[3]

Methodological individualism dominates our neighboring field of economics, much of sociology, and all of psychology's excursions into organizational theory. This is the dogma that all human social group processes are to be explained by laws of individual behavior – that groups and social organizations have no ontological reality – and that where used, references to organizations, etc. are but convenient summaries of individual behavior.[4]

---

3 Wegner, D. M. (1986). Transactive memory: A contemporary analysis of the group mind. In B. Mullen & G. R. Goethals (Eds.), *Theories of group behavior*. New York: Springer-Verlag.

4 Campbell, D. T. (1994). How individual and face-to-face-group selection undermine firm selection in organizational evolution. In J. A. C. Baum & J. V Singh (Eds.), *Evolutionary dynamics of organizations* (pp. 23–38). New York: Oxford University Press.

The first passage illustrates that viewing a human society as a kind of organism is not new. The problem with its earlier formulation is that it was axiomatic – as if all societies must be like organisms, without a strong theory explaining how they got that way or the role of individual agency in their functioning. In its axiomatic form, functionalism (as it was called) deserved to be rejected.

Individualism had the allure of scientific reductionism. If everything social is carried out by individuals, then what is there that can't be reduced? To appreciate the fallacy of this reasoning, consider that everything about an individual is carried out by its cells, genes, and ultimately molecular reactions. Does this mean that we can study individuals entirely in terms of their molecules? No, because individuals are the units of natural selection. Evolutionary scientists distinguish two forms of causation, called proximate and ultimate[5]. Proximate causation involves the physical basis of living processes and can indeed be reduced to the molecular level (although this does not mean that higher levels of analysis become obsolete[6]). Ultimate causation refers to the molding action of natural selection. Howard Head makes this point in his first lecture with his examples of camouflage and infanticide. His students could predict the three major environmental contexts for infanticide without knowing anything about the physical makeup of organisms, thanks to heritable variation as a kind of malleable clay.

The fallacy of reductionism is that it applies only to proximate causation. Ultimate causation justifies the holistic statement, "The parts permit but do not cause the properties of the whole." And if the properties of individual organisms can be irreducible in this way, so can the properties of whole societies – to the degree that they are units of selection.

In the end, the tradition of Individualism fails for the same reason as the tradition of functionalism that it replaced. Both treat a given unit (groups in the case of functionalism, individuals in the case of

5 Wilson, D. S. (1988). Holism and reductionism in evolutionary biology. *Oikos*, *53*, 269–273.
6 Sober, E. (1999). The Multiple realizability argument against reductionism. *Philosophy of Science*, *66*, 542–564.

individualism) as axiomatically the center of analysis. We need a theory that can identify the unit of functional organization, and therefore the center of analysis, on a case by case basis.

The Dot, The Circle, The American Flag, and the Planet

Atlas Hugged is not only a negative critique of Ayn Rand's thought and the intellectual tradition of Individualism, but a positive vision of what can replace them. That vision is based on a theory called Multilevel Selection (MLS), which is concisely explained (150pp) in my book *Does Altruism Exist? Culture, Genes, and the Welfare of Others*. MLS thinking pervades *Atlas Hugged*, although never by name.

For example, cancer is a theme that I have woven throughout *Atlas Hugged*. Objectivism is described as the morality of the cancer cell. Elena's second husband is an oncologist who "cures cancer rather than being one." Ayn Rant succumbs to lung cancer (a fact for Ayn Rand) and John Galt II is stricken down by cancer at the end of the book. I am not merely hurling insults at Objectivism by calling it cancerous. Cancer is literally a process of natural selection taking place among the cells of our bodies. Cancer illustrates that evolution has no foresight. Mutant cells that proliferate at the expense of neighboring cells will simply take over, even if they eventually result in their own demise. Only natural selection taking place at a higher level – between individual organisms – can result in the evolution of mechanisms that protect against cancer. A great book on this topic is *The Cheating Cell: How Evolution Helps Us Understand and Treat Cancer*, by Athena Aktipis.

The fact that cancer biologists use words such as "cheating," drawn from the lexicon of human social interactions, is not an accident. Cheating behaviors are just like cancers. They benefit the cheater at the expense of cooperators within the same social group and even at the expense at the group as a whole, including the cheaters. Only a process of selection at the group level – groups well-protected against cheaters outcompeting groups vulnerable to cheaters – can oppose disruptive selection within groups. To call social cheaters cancerous is as apt as calling cancer cells cheaters.

This multi-level logic repeats itself at every rung of a multi-level social hierarchy. What's good for me can be bad for my family. What's good for my family can be bad for my clan. What's good for my clan can be bad for my nation. What's good for my nation or corporation can be bad for Earth.

Against this background, small groups emerge as a fundamental unit of human social life and a major theme of *Atlas Hugged*. When small groups are appropriately structured (and this is a big when!), they come as close as we will ever get to a utopia. Hence, the Village School, the Eden family's church community, the Lodge Biological Station, and the redneck community of Timber Ridge are all described as utopias by virtue of their small size and social controls that protect against disruption from within. The great challenge, as John Galt III explains to his redneck friend Ron, is how to scale up the kind of governance that makes villages work so well.

"So that's exactly how much money I'm made out of. The rest of it is for making the rest of the world more like Timber Ridge Trail."

"Well, shit!" Ron concluded, "That makes you the truest redneck there ever was!"

The most profound implication of MLS theory is represented by the stack of symbols that comes to represent True Objectivism: the dot, below a circle, below the American Flag, below the Planet Earth. The only way to prevent the cancerous effects of lower-level selection is to organize everything we do with the welfare of the whole Earth in mind. That makes the Earth sacred, which can be rendered in either religious or non-religious terms. The whole earth focus does not diminish the importance of the lower-level units. They remain essential but must be oriented toward the global common good to become part of the solution rather than part of the problem. It is essential for individuals (the dot) to form into groups (the circle) for their own wellbeing and for efficacious action at a larger scale. And our existing institutions – our governments, religions, and corporations – can become part of the solution as soon as they imagine themselves as solid citizens of Earth.

On Cultural Catalysis

Another major theme of *Atlas Hugged* is that the rate of cultural evolution can be vastly accelerated, similar to chemical catalysis.

> *"Even though the concept of catalysis is easy to understand, it is almost miraculous in what it can do. Imagine a chemical reaction taking place slowly or not at all, and then – poof! – just a sprinkling of the catalytic substance is transformative. If that's not magic, what would be?"*

> *"Right!" I laughed. "As magical as any spell."*

> *"Now let's think about catalysis in the context of cultural change."*

> *Poof! No one could do metaphorical transfer better than Howard. First he rehearsed the familiar, in this case chemical catalysis, and then moved it over to a new context, in this case rates of cultural change. I began to get the connections immediately but let him continue.*

The possibility of cultural catalysis is fact, not fiction, even if it might not take place in 100 days. We already know that worldwide cultural change can be rapid – look at technological innovations such as smart phones, social media platforms such as Facebook and Twitter, or the advent of the gig economy. The problem with these examples of rapid cultural evolution is that they were not managed with the welfare of the whole Earth in mind. A single change in orientation represented by the stack of symbols can make all the difference in the rapid evolution of a global superorganism.

I hope that my excursion into the world of fiction has given this sense of possibility to readers of *Atlas Hugged*. I now invite you to cross over to the world of nonfiction to make the vision of *Atlas Hugged* a reality.

Acknowledgments

Writing *Atlas Hugged* has been an extraordinary journey for me, spanning over seven years. In many respects it has been a private journey, a project so close to my heart that I couldn't even share it with my loved ones without feeling vulnerable. Nevertheless, in mosaic art fashion, I drew upon many people from my life as tiles to be shaped and fitted together to create my own stylized universe. They'll know who they are because I didn't work very hard to change their names, any more than I did for public figures such as Ayn Rand, Sean Hannity, Bill Moyers, and George Will. I hope that my loved ones, friends, colleagues, and students enjoy their fictional avatars, realizing that they have been freely altered to suit the purposes of the story!

The first person I dared show a copy was my friend and colleague, Nina Witoszek, who has written both fiction and nonfiction. It was an experience in tough love but the story is much better for it, especially at key junctures where the sympathy of the reader for the characters might otherwise have been lost.

As someone who has published numerous nonfiction books with conventional academic and trade presses, I must say that I have enjoyed the process of independently publishing and marketing *Atlas Hugged* in a way that is true to the spirit of the book. The team that came together, including Caroline Levine, Liz Dubelman, Paul Slansky, and

Sage Gibbons, has been great fun to work with and has given me faith that *Atlas Hugged* passes muster as both a good story and an effective vehicle for conveying the same ideas that I study as a scientist and write about in my nonfiction books.

My final thanks go to my wife and colleague of forty-five years, Anne B. Clark. Superficially, she appears in *Atlas Hugged* as Professor Anne McDougall, but she is also the inspiration for many aspects of Eve and especially the relationship between Eve and John, which is based on honoring each other's work. It is thanks to Anne that I had the freedom to disappear inside myself to write *Atlas Hugged*.

Non-fiction books by
David Sloan Wilson

Unto Others: The Evolution and Psychology of
Unselfish Behavior (with Elliott Sober)

•

Darwin's Cathedral: Evolution, Religion, and the Nature of Society

•

Evolution for Everyone: How Darwin's Theory Can
Change the Way We Think about Our Lives

•

The Neighborhood Project: Using Evolution to
Improve My City, One Block at a Time

•

Does Altruism Exist? Culture, Genes, and the Welfare of Others

•

This View of Life: Completing the Darwinian Revolution

•

Prosocial: Using Evolutionary Science to Build
Productive, Equitable, and Collaborative Groups
(with Paul Atkins and Steven C. Hayes)